Connect

SECOND EDITION

Jack C. Richards
Carlos Barbisan
with Chuck Sandy

Teacher's Edition

CAMBRIDGE
UNIVERSITY PRESS

CAMBRIDGE UNIVERSITY PRESS
Cambridge, New York, Melbourne, Madrid, Cape Town, Singapore,
São Paulo, Delhi, Dubai, Tokyo

Cambridge University Press
32 Avenue of the Americas, New York, NY 10013-2473, USA

www.cambridge.org
Information on this title: www.cambridge.org/9780521737272

© Cambridge University Press 2010

First published 2004
Second Edition 2010

Printed in Hong Kong, China, by Golden Cup Printing Company Limited

A catalog record for this publication is available from the British Library.

ISBN 978-0-521-73721-0 Student's Book 4 (English)
ISBN 978-0-521-73722-7 Student's Book 4 (Portuguese)
ISBN 978-0-521-73725-8 Workbook 4 (English)
ISBN 978-0-521-73726-5 Workbook 4 (Portuguese)
ISBN 978-0-521-73727-2 Teacher's Edition 4 (English)
ISBN 978-0-521-73728-9 Teacher's Edition 4 (Portuguese)
ISBN 978-0-521-73724-1 Class Audio CDs

Art direction, photo research, and layout services: A+ comunicação
Audio production: Full House, NYC
Book design: Adventure House, NYC

Table of Contents

Syllabus

Connect Student's Book 4

Unit 1 — My Life

Lesson	Function	Grammar	Vocabulary
Lesson 1 Last summer	Describing what you did last summer	Simple past and past continuous	Summer activities
Lesson 2 A new school year	Talking about plans for the new school year	*be going to, would like to, want to,* and *have to*	Classes, hobbies, and sports
Lesson 3 Life events	Describing life events and special accomplishments	*when* clauses of time + simple past	Life events
Lesson 4 Then and now	Describing past situations that have changed	*used to* and *not anymore*	Activities and physical descriptions
Get Connected	Reading • Listening • Writing		
Theme Project	Make a group booklet about people who make a difference.		

Unit 2 — The Future

Lesson	Function	Grammar	Vocabulary
Lesson 5 Predictions	Making predictions about the future	Future with *will* and *won't*	Future situations and actions
Lesson 6 When I'm older	Making guesses / predictions about the future	Future probability with *will probably / probably won't*	Life events
Lesson 7 Teen Center	Talking about activities at a Teen Center	Future possibility with *might / might not*	Activities offered at a Teen Center
Lesson 8 After high school	Talking about future plans	Definite plans with *will* and *be going to* / Probable plans with *will probably* / Possible plans with *might*	Life events
Get Connected	Reading • Listening • Writing		
Theme Project	Make a bookmark about your future.		

Unit 3 — Plans

Lesson	Function	Grammar	Vocabulary
Lesson 9 Weekend plans	Talking about weekend plans	*Would you like to . . . ?* for invitations	Weekend activities
Lesson 10 Evening plans	Asking permission and making requests	*Can / Could* for permission and requests	Evening activities
Lesson 11 Making plans	Talking about future plans	*if* with *will / will probably / won't / might*	Free-time activities
Lesson 12 Vacation plans	Talking about vacation plans	Clauses of time with *before / while / after*	Travel activities
Get Connected	Reading • Listening • Writing		
Theme Project	Make fact cards about an environmental issue.		

Unit 4 — People

Lesson	Function	Grammar	Vocabulary
Lesson 13 Teens online	Talking about activities teens enjoy	Gerunds as subjects Gerunds as objects	Popular teen activities
Lesson 14 Personality types	Describing people's personalities	*too* *either*	Personality descriptions
Lesson 15 Unusual people	Describing people's talents, habits, or collections	*who* clauses	Talents, habits, and collections
Lesson 16 Who's that girl?	Asking questions to confirm beliefs	Tag questions and answers with *be* / Tag questions and answers with the simple present	Describing people
Get Connected	Reading • Listening • Writing		
Theme Project	Make a group personality profile booklet.		

Unit 5 Entertainment	Lesson	Function	Grammar	Vocabulary
	Lesson 17 For fun	Describing activities done during the week	Present perfect with *I* and *We*	Everyday activities
	Lesson 18 Young entertainers	Describing someone's achievements	Present perfect with *he, she,* and *they*	Activities of famous people
	Lesson 19 Are you a fan?	Asking about past activities	Present perfect Yes / No questions with *ever*	Experiences
	Lesson 20 Pop culture trivia	Asking trivia questions about pop culture	*How long has / How long have . . . ?; since* and *for*	Pop culture
	Get Connected	Reading • Listening • Writing		
	Theme Project	Make a cross-cultural experiences poster.		

Unit 6 Experiences	Lesson	Function	Grammar	Vocabulary
	Lesson 21 Taking risks	Talking about new or risky activities	Present perfect with *never*	New or risky activities
	Lesson 22 What we've done	Talking about activities done in the past year	Simple past Present perfect	Interesting activities
	Lesson 23 Amazing teens	Talking about life events	*has already / hasn't . . . yet*	Life events
	Lesson 24 In the spotlight	Asking questions to confirm beliefs	Tag questions with the simple past and present perfect	Life events
	Get Connected	Reading • Listening • Writing		
	Theme Project	Make a booklet about amazing people.		

Unit 7 Teen Time	Lesson	Function	Grammar	Vocabulary
	Lesson 25 Teen opinions	Expressing opinions	*good / better / the best bad / worse / the worst*	Adjectives
	Lesson 26 Unforgettable moments	Talking about unforgettable moments	Superlative + *. . . have ever . . .*	Superlative adjectives
	Lesson 27 Are we alike?	Comparing people and their abilities	Formal and informal comparisons: *as . . . as / not as . . . as*	Adjectives to describe personality and abilities
	Lesson 28 I'd rather . . .	Talking about preferences	*would . . . rather* for preferences	Life preferences
	Get Connected	Reading • Listening • Writing		
	Theme Project	Make a poster about group preferences.		

Unit 8 Dreams and Reality	Lesson	Function	Grammar	Vocabulary
	Lesson 29 Our dreams	Talking about dreams and aspirations	*If* clauses with *could . . . would*	Dreams and aspirations
	Lesson 30 What would you do?	Talking about behavior in imagined situations	Unreal conditional with *if* clauses	Bad behavior
	Lesson 31 What I'm going to be	Talking about different professions	Infinitives to give a reason	Professions
	Lesson 32 The past year	Asking about life experiences	Indefinite pronouns	Interesting experiences
	Get Connected	Reading • Listening • Writing		
	Theme Project	Make a group booklet showing how you could help others with $5,000.		

Course description

Connect, Second Edition is an updated and revised edition of the popular *Connect, First Edition*. It is a fun, multi-skill course, written and designed especially for adolescents who are studying English for the first time. It develops speaking, listening, reading, and writing skills while simultaneously connecting students with one another, their community, and the world outside the classroom. Theme Projects provide a local perspective, encouraging students to find out more about the world in which we live. High-interest topics provide a global perspective and present relevant, up-to-date information, motivating students to learn.

Course principles

Connect, Second Edition is based on the notion that generating and maintaining motivation is essential for successful learning. This is incorporated into the series in the following ways:

Motivational strategies	Features
Generate and maintain interest	• Units are built around contemporary, high-interest topics. • Students can relate all tasks to their own interests and experience.
Promote success	• Students are provided with adequate preparation and support for tasks throughout the learning process. • Tests and quizzes assess only language that students know and do not assume that students know more.
Promote fun in learning	• The tasks are varied. • A multitude of games and game-like activities make learning fun.
Provide opportunities for students to speak about themselves	• The personalization activities provide opportunities for students to use target language to speak about themselves.

Components

Each level of *Connect, Second Edition* consists of a Student's Book with Self-study Audio CD, Class Audio CDs, a Workbook, and a Teacher's Edition. Web-based material includes *Connect* Arcade (online activities for students) and the Teacher Support Site.

Student's Book with Self-study Audio CD

Each Student's Book contains eight units divided into two-page lessons. Two lessons of each unit are review lessons. All lesson themes and content are pertinent to adolescent learners. At the back of each Student's Book, there is a Game and a Theme Project section. The Games provide enjoyable practice of the grammar and / or vocabulary of each unit. The Theme Projects foster cooperation and strong relationships within the classroom. Additionally, they help students connect their English to the world outside the classroom.

The Student's Book Self-study Audio CD is intended for student use and includes recordings for specific sections of each lesson. The recordings are in natural, conversational American English. Students can use the CD for practice at home or in a language lab.

Class Audio CDs

The Class Audio CDs are intended for class use. They are in natural, conversational American English.

A unique feature of the audio program is the recordings for the "Listen and check your answers" tasks in many of the Language Focus practice activities. This feature reduces teacher-talking time and encourages greater student autonomy in the process of checking answers. Track numbers appear in the Teacher's Edition and make it easy to locate specific recordings on the CDs.

Workbook

The Workbook is a natural extension of the Student's Book. Each Workbook provides reading and writing reinforcement of the vocabulary and grammar in the Student's Book lesson. No new language is presented in the Workbook. The wide variety of exercise types keeps students motivated, and photographs and illustrations provide context and support for many of the activities. There is one Workbook page for each Student's Book lesson.

A unique feature of the Workbook is the Check Yourself section at the end of each unit. These pages provide students with the opportunity to assess their performance and ascertain where they need further practice. This section prepares students to do the worksheet activities and quizzes that are provided in the Teacher's Edition.

The Workbook activities can be done at home or in class. They can be assigned individually after each lesson is completed or all at once at the end of each unit. The Answer key for the Workbook is provided in the Teacher's Edition.

Teacher's Edition

The comprehensive, interleaved Teacher's Edition provides step-by-step instructions to present, practice, and review the language in each lesson of the Student's Book. The Teacher's Edition offers a wide variety of communicative, interactive classroom activities. It also features suggestions for optional activities and linguistic, methodological, and cultural notes where appropriate. The Answer key to the Student's Book is printed in red on the reproduced Student's Book pages for ease of use.

There is a rich source of support materials in the back of each Teacher's Edition. These materials include audio scripts for all recorded material, photocopiable worksheets for each unit, one quiz per unit, and answer keys for all photocopiable materials as well as for the Workbook. There is also a special Games and Activities section for practicing vocabulary, grammar, listening, pronunciation, and speaking skills.

Teacher Support Site

The Teacher Support Site contains a wealth of downloadable support material, including Extra Grammar worksheets, Extra Reading worksheets, Placement Tests, Unit Tests, Oral Quizzes, and Learning Logs.

All Extra Grammar and Extra Reading worksheets are provided in two forms (Form A and Form B) to offer variety for both teachers and students. They can be assigned to all students or to individual students who need additional practice.

Unit Tests are also provided in Form A and Form B for greater flexibility in giving tests to different classes.

All answer keys are available upon request. Many of the materials are password-protected to prevent student access, and it is easy for teachers to create their own passwords once on the Teacher Support Site. See **www.cambridge.org/connect2e/teacher**

The following material is found on the Teacher Support Site:

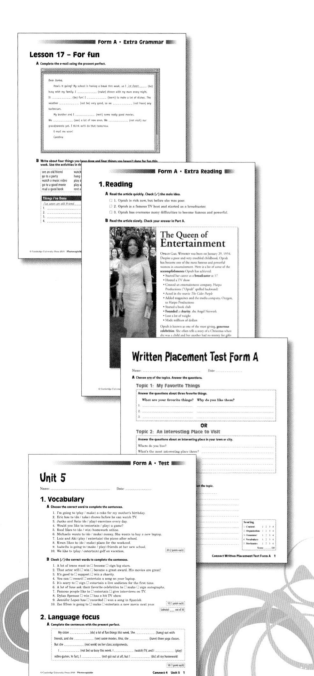

Extra Grammar worksheets

The Extra Grammar worksheets provide students with additional grammar practice and are similar in style to the activities in the Student's Book and Workbook.

Extra Reading worksheets

The Extra Reading worksheets provide students with additional reading and writing practice and are similar in style to the Get Connected lessons in the Student's Book. The Extra Reading worksheets can be assigned after the Get Connected lessons.

Placement Tests

The Placement Tests are to be done by students before they begin *Connect* to help determine the level of *Connect* best suited to them. They are extremely comprehensive and test all four skills (listening, speaking, reading, and writing). They include Objective Tests with an audio program, Written Tests, an Oral Test, Answer keys, and student answer sheets.

Unit Tests

Each Unit Test is designed to assess students' progress in Vocabulary, Language Focus (grammar), Reading, and Writing. The Unit Tests can be given after each unit.

Oral Quizzes

There is one Oral Quiz for each unit. Each Oral Quiz consists of questions and sample answers that teachers can use, along with a rating guide to evaluate students' speaking ability. The Oral Quizzes can be given after the Unit Test or at the teacher's discretion.

Learning Logs

The Learning Logs provide students with the opportunity to reflect on their progress as they complete each unit of the Student's Book. They can also help teachers determine which students might need extra practice. There is one Learning Log for each unit. They can be assigned after each unit and can be done at home or in class.

Web-Based Student Arcade Activities

The Arcade is a free student support Web site with a wealth of interactive, self-study activities for each unit of the Student's Book. These activities provide engaging vocabulary, grammar, and pronunciation practice. They feature animation, audio, and illustrations that make English practice come to life. Students can do these activities at home or in a language lab.

The following task types are included in each level of Arcade: Choose the right word, Crossword, Drag and drop, Fill in the blank, Guess the word, Matching, Multiple choice, Put the sentences in order, What do you hear?, and What do you see?

See **www.cambridge.org/connectarcade**

Student's Book Unit Structure

- Two language lessons →

- Followed by a mini-review —

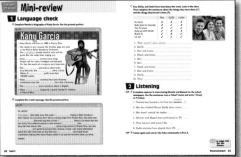

- Two more language lessons —

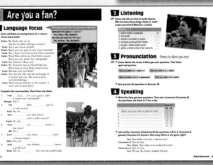

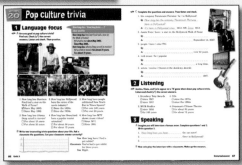

- Followed by Get Connected and a unit review

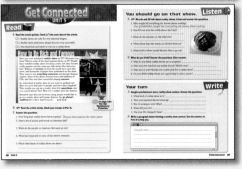

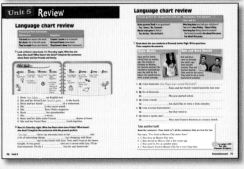

At the back of the book

- Game

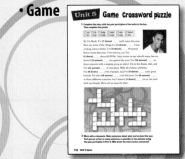

- Get Connected Vocabulary Practice

- Theme Project

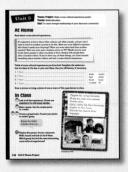

Student's Book Unit Features

Language lessons

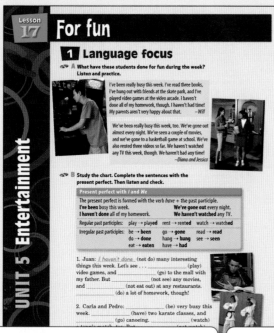

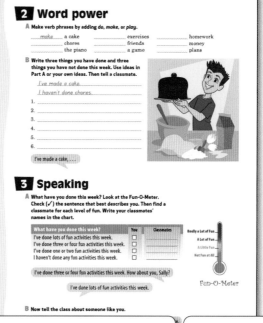

Language focus Presents and practices the target grammar, beginning with either a conversation or a text to help students understand how the new grammar is used. A language chart highlights the form of the new structures. Additional exercises provide controlled practice of the new grammar.

Word power Presents and practices the words and phrases students need to talk about the topic of the unit. Part A introduces the target words and illustrates their meanings. Part B provides additional practice of the words and phrases.

Speaking Provides an opportunity for students to practice the new grammar in a natural context. Most of the tasks are interactive and allow students to personalize the grammar.

Listening Helps to develop receptive skills such as identifying the purpose of conversations and listening for specific information.

Pronunciation Highlights a pronunciation point that students often find challenging. The exercise allows students to listen to and practice the pronunciation point.

Mini-review

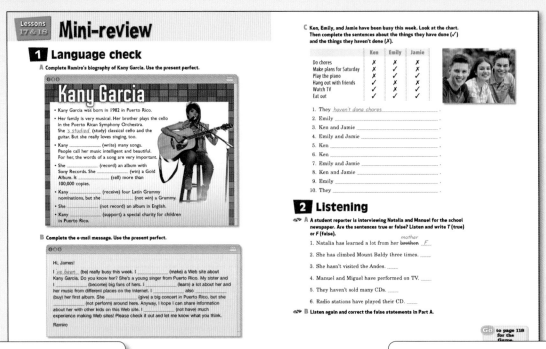

Language check Provides further review and practice of the grammar and vocabulary presented in the first two lessons of each unit.

Listening Offers further listening practice to reinforce grammar and vocabulary presented in the first two lessons of each unit.

Get Connected

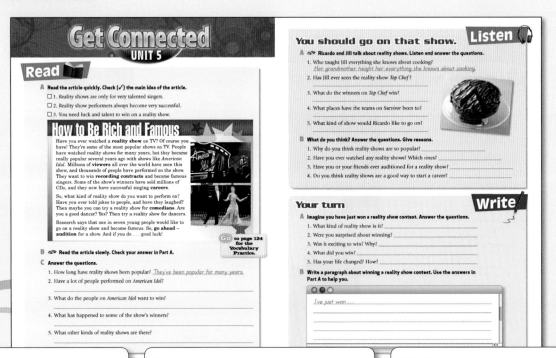

Read Provides tasks to develop reading skills such as skimming and scanning, and answering comprehension questions. A recorded version of the reading is provided.

Listen Part A helps students to improve receptive skills such as listening for specific information.
Part B encourages students to think critically about the theme of the Get Connected lesson.

Write Provides writing tasks that are natural extensions of the readings. Part A helps students organize their ideas for the writing task in Part B.

Review

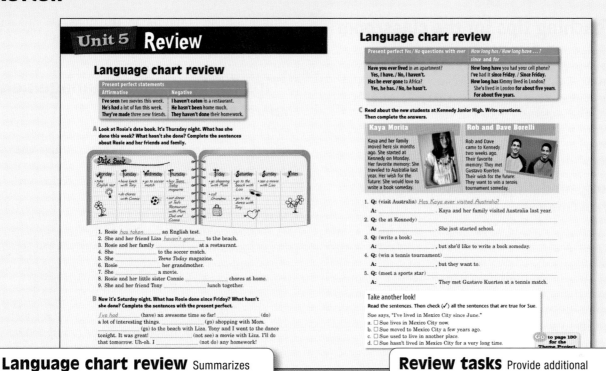

Language chart review Summarizes and provides further review and practice of the grammar introduced in the unit.

Review tasks Provide additional practice of the unit grammar and vocabulary.

At the back of the book

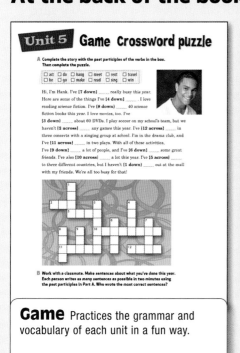

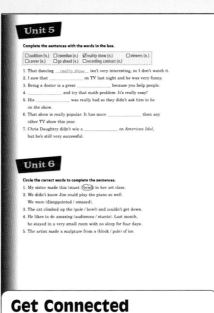

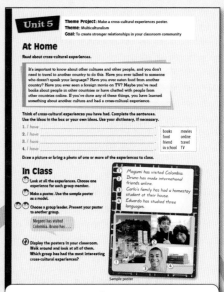

Game Practices the grammar and vocabulary of each unit in a fun way.

Get Connected Vocabulary Practice Provides additional practice for new words (in bold) in the Get Connected readings.

Theme project Connects students' English to the world outside the classroom. The At Home section helps students organize their ideas for the In Class activity.

Teaching Tips

A Teaching tips for the classroom

The following are some suggestions for teachers when using *Connect, Second Edition*. Each teaching situation is different and there are many teaching philosophies. For this reason, it may be necessary to modify the suggestions to suit individual needs. For an expanded version of these suggestions, please see the Teacher Support Site at:
www.cambridge.org/connect2e/teacher

Giving, modeling, and checking task instructions

- At the beginning of a course, give oral instructions for each activity as the task will be new to students. After a few units, students can read the instructions on their own. The Student's Book instructions are simple and consistent so students should understand them.

- After students understand the instructions, model the activity or invite volunteers to model it. Students need to understand how to do the activity in order to complete it successfully.

- To be sure they understand, follow up instructions and / or modeling by asking students *Yes / No* questions.

- Once students begin an activity, monitor their progress. Walk around the class and check that students are doing the activity correctly. Offer help and correct students when necessary.

Error correction

- Correction is an integral and crucial part of the learning process. Once students become aware of mistakes they are making, they are able to focus their attention on further study of the language item in question.

- For vocabulary, grammar, and pronunciation activities, it is important to correct mistakes since these types of activities are accuracy focused. It is advisable to correct mistakes as they occur. Speaking activities are fluency focused, so it is better to correct mistakes after students finish the activity, so as not to interrupt "real" communication.

Use of native language

- In a monolingual class, judicious use of the students' native language can be beneficial. Use of the native language can not only convey the meaning of target or incidental vocabulary and grammar but also can help students understand information in listening and reading texts.

- In a monolingual class, it may be beneficial to use the students' native language to check that students understand the instructions. Do this only when using English would be too difficult or too time consuming.

B Tips for large class management
General tips

- Tell students where to sit so that friends are separated, as friends tend to chat. Change the seating arrangement from time to time to give students a chance to interact and practice with different classmates.

- Establish class rules at the beginning of the course and enforce them in a consistent way. It can be helpful to have students make a list of rules with you at the beginning of the year as students will be more likely to follow them.

- Always try to have more activities than necessary for class. Make use of all the suggested activities in the Teacher's Edition and prepare any extra worksheets for that lesson. This will fill time if and when the lesson runs short.

- Vary the way activities are done to avoid being predictable. Vary between whole class work, individual work, group work, and pair work to allow for a more interesting class.

Tips for pair and group work

- For successful completion of a task, make sure that the majority of students are familiar with the language to be practiced before having them work in pairs or groups.

- Confirm that pairs know exactly what to do in order to complete an activity. Model the activity first before having pairs or groups do it.

- Match pairs and groups according to ability and personality. In many cases, pairing stronger students with weaker ones can be beneficial. Pair or group shy students with more extroverted students, as well as disruptive students with well-behaved ones. This way the burden of class management is shared with students.

- If pair work is not possible for your entire class, you can have a few pairs or small groups do the activity in front of the class. The rest of the class listens and offers help as necessary.

C Tips for multilevel class management

Every class is a multilevel class to some degree. Try to understand what the differences are among students in a class. These can be differences in learning styles and speed, ability to focus, and students' experiences and attitudes toward learning.

- Identify the *who*, *what*, and *why* of a difficult situation so that you can then decide how best to proceed. One way to do this is to observe students when they are working in pairs or groups, and keep a list of names of students who need help.
- Determine why some students are sufficiently challenged and others are over- or under-challenged. Take steps to remedy the situation in the following ways:
  - If a student has not had much exposure to English, it may be necessary to provide extra help or supplementary materials at the student's level.
  - If a student finds the materials too easy, group him or her with other students at a similar level to increase the challenge.
  - For under-challenged students, increase the quantity and / or difficulty of the work given. The photocopiable worksheets are useful for this.
  - Call on the more-advanced students in the class to participate first. This will allow the advanced students to be challenged, and at the same time, give the less-advanced students a chance to absorb the new material before they have to participate.
- Include many interesting and varied activities in lessons. The more-advanced students will have a good time just joining in and using what they know, and the less-advanced students will be motivated to improve because the activities are interesting and fun. The more varied the class, the more students will be inspired to participate.
- Avoid having rigid expectations for students, as this will only lead to frustration on your part and theirs.
- Remember to encourage the less-advanced students frequently, but do not forget to encourage the more-advanced students. Encouragement is a great motivator.
- Alert parents to any difficulties that students are experiencing and ask for their support in making sure students study and complete homework.

D Tips for establishing and maintaining discipline

Teacher's role
- Communicate your expectations for students' behavior, tell students what consequences they can expect for breaking the rules, and be consistent in carrying them out.

- Plan lessons carefully and always have more material than necessary, in order to keep students engaged at all times. This will increase students' motivation and decrease opportunities for misbehavior.
- Give clear instructions when explaining how to do an activity to ensure that all students understand what they are to do.
- Establish a method to get students to stop what they are doing and focus their attention on you when needed – for example, by turning off the lights or ringing a bell.

Tips for resolving discipline problems
- To stop disruptive talking, you can simply ask the student to stop in a friendly, yet authoritative, way. If this does not work, have the student sit in the back of the room away from his or her friends for a few minutes. If the talking persists, meet with the student after class and try to find out why he or she is not paying attention.
- Students who come late to class disrupt the flow of a lesson. Keep vacant desks near the door so late students can sit there and not interrupt the class. Discourage lateness and absenteeism by establishing a policy at the beginning of the year whereby points are deducted from the student's final grade if he or she is often late or disruptive.
- If students consistently do not do their homework, meet with them one-on-one to find out why. Encourage completion of homework by correcting the assignments in class the next day and giving points for completed homework.
- To deter cheating on tests, place students' desks with enough space between them to make it impossible to look at another student's work without being noticed. If a particular student has been known to cheat in the past, move his or her desk away from other classmates.
- If a student is unwilling to speak English in class, meet with that student to find out why. Low self-esteem and a fear of appearing foolish are two common reasons for not speaking in class.
- Remember not to take any students' misbehavior personally. Deal with problems quietly and individually after class. Be sure to treat all students with dignity, even when reprimanding them.

Last summer

1 What did you do last summer?

A Read about the students at Wells International School.
What did they do last summer? Listen and practice.

Hi. I'm Jessica Chen. I'm from the U.S. I stayed at my grandparents' house near the beach last summer. One day, I met a girl from Colombia. We became great friends! We e-mail each other every day now.

My name is Will Martins. I'm from New Zealand. I went camping with my friends. One day, when we were hiking, we got lost. We were afraid. Luckily, we had a compass, and we found our way back to the campground.

Hi. My name is Juan Ramirez. I'm from Puerto Rico. I traveled all over Canada with my family. My favorite city was Toronto, but I liked Ottawa and Vancouver, too. When we were visiting the CN Tower, we saw a movie crew filming a movie. It was very exciting!

Hello. I'm Carla Russo. I'm from Brazil. I went back to São Paulo – my hometown – for the summer. I hung out with my best friend a lot. We had a good time together. We went to some good movies. I was sad to leave São Paulo.

B Who did these things? Complete each sentence with *Jessica,*
Carla, Will, or *Juan.*

1. __Juan__ took a family trip.
2. __Jessica__ visited grandparents.
3. __Carla__ spent time with a best friend.
4. __Will__ got lost.
5. __Jessica__ made a new friend.
6. __Juan__ went to a few different cities.

Lesson 1 Last summer

This lesson reviews the simple past and the past continuous and vocabulary to talk about summer activities.

1 What did you do last summer?

This exercise reviews and practices vocabulary and expressions for introducing oneself and for talking about past experiences.

A CD1, Track 2

- Have students look quickly through their Student's Book. Explain that, as in Student's Books 1, 2, and 3, there are 8 units and that each unit contains 4 lessons. There is a mini-review in the middle of each unit, a "Get Connected" lesson (reading, listening, and writing practice), and a review at the end. Tell students that there are six new characters in this level. Encourage students to ask any questions they may have about *Connect*.

- Have students read the directions and look at the photos. Ask: *Who are the people in the photos?* (Students at Wells International School.)

- Tell students that in this exercise, they will read about four of the characters.

- Have students read the captions.

Note: Students can read the text silently or out loud as a group. There are benefits to both. The benefit of having students read silently is that they can read at their own pace and not be distracted by other students' voices. The benefit of having students read aloud as a group is that weaker students will be prompted by the stronger students as they read, and that the whole class will finish the reading at the same time.

- **Optional** Play the recording. Students listen and read along.

> **Audio script**
> Same as the captions in the Student's Book.

- Ask: *Who's from the U.S.?* (Jessica.) *What's Jessica's last name?* (Chen.) *Where did she go in the summer?* (To her grandparents' house.) Ask similar questions about the other three captions.

Note: If you think that students will understand the questions in English, ask them exactly as they appear in the Teacher's Edition. If you do not think students will understand them, either explain the questions or rephrase them in simpler language.

- Invite volunteers to ask their classmates similar questions about the characters.

- Play the recording or model the captions. Students listen and repeat.

Note: Whenever students listen to the recording, be sure to pause the recording after individual items. This gives students time to repeat or complete the task.

B

- Have students read the directions and the example. Ask: *What's missing from the sentences?* (The names of the characters.)

- Have students read the captions again and complete the exercise.

- Check answers with the class. Invite volunteers to read aloud one of the sentences they completed.

> **Culture Note** About 73 percent of all American teens ages 12 to 17 (about 17 million teens) use the Internet to write e-mail messages, to IM (instant message) friends and family members, and to research information for school projects.

This unit reviews and introduces language to talk about past experiences and habits, to express wishes, and to talk about the future.

2 Language focus review

This exercise reviews and practices statements and questions in the simple past and the past continuous.

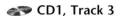 **CD1, Track 3**

- **Language Chart** Have students study the examples in the left-hand side of the language chart. Ask: *What form is used in these sentences?* (Simple past.) *Which statement is affirmative?* (I went camping.) *Which word indicates the negative in the negative statement?* (Didn't.) *What's the main verb?* (Do.) *Which is a Yes / No question?* (Did he go to the beach?) *Where does the question word go in the information question, at the beginning or in the middle?* (At the beginning.)

- Focus students' attention on the right-hand side of the chart. Ask: *What form is used in these sentences?* (Past continuous.) *What's different about the main verbs in the sentences on this side of the chart?* (They end in *-ing*.) *Which statement is affirmative?* (I was eating popcorn when the basketball hit me.) *Which word indicates the negative in the negative statement?* (Wasn't.) *Which is an information question?* (What was she studying?)

- Ask: *You want to show that something happened over a period of time. Which form do you use?* (Past continuous.) *You talk about one complete action that happened in the past. Which form do you use?* (Simple past.)

- **Optional** Model the examples, pausing for students to repeat.

- **Optional** Invite volunteers to tell the class about one thing they did and one thing did not do last summer.

- Focus students' attention on the text in number 1 and the conversation in number 2. Have them read the first few lines of each. Ask: *What's Pedro talking about?* (His summer.) *Who are Sue and Brian talking about?* (Diana Martinez.) Explain that Pedro and Diana are also main characters in Student's Book 4.

- Give students several minutes to read the text and the conversation.

- Have students work individually to complete the sentences with the correct forms of the verbs in parentheses.

- Play the recording. Students listen and verify their answers.

Audio script

Same as the text and the conversation in the Student's Book.

- Check answers with the class. Invite volunteers to read aloud one of the sentences they completed.

3 Speaking

This exercise practices talking about past experiences.

- Have students read the directions. Ask: *What do you do first?* (Write your answers to the questions.) *Then what do you do?* (Ask a classmate the questions.)

- Have students work individually to answer the questions.

- Demonstrate the activity. Tell the class what you did last summer. Then ask a random student what he or she did last summer.

- Have students ask a classmate the questions.

- Invite volunteers to tell the class what they found out about their classmates' summer.

Teaching Tip It is important that students know exactly how to do the speaking activities. Tasks often fail because students do not know what they have to do. If students know what to do, they can concentrate on producing the correct language, and thus gain maximum benefit from the activity. One way is to ask students clarification questions to make sure they understand the directions.

- **Optional** As students report on their classmates' activities, have the class write down the names of two or three classmates who did interesting things last summer and their activities. Invite volunteers to read aloud the names they wrote down and what those students did.

Teaching Tip Provide simple tasks for the class to do while they listen to individual students reporting. This will help keep students focused on the task for a longer period of time.

Workbook

Note: Explain that the Workbook provides extra practice of the language studied in the Student's Book. All Workbook exercises can be done either in class or for homework.

- Assign the exercises on Workbook page 2. (Workbook answers begin on page T-192.)

Extra Grammar

Note: The Extra Grammar activities can be downloaded from the Teacher Support Site at: www.cambridge.org/connect2e/teacher

The activities are intended to be done as homework. The site also has information about how teachers can obtain an answer key.

- Assign the grammar exercises for the Extra Grammar, Lesson 1.

2 Language focus review

Study the chart. Then complete the sentences about the other students, Pedro and Diana. Use the correct forms of the verbs. Then listen and check.

Simple past	Past continuous
Statements	**Statements**
I **went** camping. She **didn't do** anything else.	I **was eating** popcorn when the basketball hit me. She **wasn't studying** math.
Questions	**Questions**

What **did** you **do** last summer?
  I **went** to the beach.
Did he **go** to the beach?
  Yes, he **did**. / No, he **didn't**.
	What **was** she **studying**?
	  She **was making** her Web site. She **wasn't studying** English.
	Were they **having** fun?
	  Yes, they **were**. / No, they **weren't**.

1. Hi. I'm Pedro Domingo. I'm from Spain. My summer was OK. I ___took___ (take) tennis lessons, and I ___played___ (play) basketball. One day, I ___went___ (go) to watch a basketball game. I _was eating_ (eat) popcorn when the basketball ___hit___ (hit) me on the arm. It ___broke___ (break) my arm! I _didn't play_ (not / play) tennis or basketball for the rest of the summer.

2. **Sue** This is Diana Martinez. She's from Ecuador. She has a twin brother. Last summer, she went to summer school.
   Brian What was she _studying_ (study)? ___Was___ she _studying_ (study) English?
   Sue No, she ___wasn't___ (not / be). She _was making_ (make) her own Web site. Diana ___worked___ (work) on her Web site every day. She _didn't do_ (not / do) anything else. One day, when she _was putting_ (put) pictures of Ecuador on her Web site, she ___got___ (get) an instant message from a boy in Italy. He ___wanted___ (want) to know about Ecuador.
   Brian Wow! How exciting.

3 Speaking

What did you do last summer? Answer the questions for yourself. Then ask a classmate the questions. (Answers will vary.)

1. What did you do last summer? _____

2. Did anything interesting happen? _____

A new school year

1 Language focus review

A Will and Carla talk about their plans for the new
school year. Listen and practice.

Will So, do you have any special plans
for this year?

Carla Yes. I'm going to join the drama club.

Will Really?

Carla Yeah. I'd like to act in the school play.
How about you? Are you going to do
anything special this year?

Will Well, I really want to learn to play the
guitar, so I'm going to take music lessons.
I'd love to play in a band someday.

Carla Wow, that's great.

Will And I'm going to study a lot this year.
I have to get good grades.

Carla That's what *I* say every year!

B Study the chart. Complete the conversations with *(be) going to*,
(would) like to, *want to*, or *have to*. Then listen and check.

be going to, would like to, want to, and *have to*		
Definite plans	**Hopes and wishes**	**Obligations**
I**'m going to** join the drama club.	I**'d like to** act in the school play. I **want to** learn to play the guitar.	I **have to** get good grades.

1. **Jessica** Hi, Juan. Are you _going to_ join the
photography club this year?

   Juan I'd _like to_ join, but I can't. I
have to work at my uncle's restaurant
after school. It's so boring.

   Jessica Oh, that's too bad. I'm _going to_ be a
photographer for the school newspaper.

2. **Pedro** Hey, Diana. You're _going to_ take
Mr. Bentley's science class, right?

   Diana Yes. I'd rather take a computer class, but
I _have to_ take two science classes
this year.

   Pedro I'd _like to_ take a computer class
this year, too. I _want to_ design
a computer game.

A new school year

This lesson reviews language for talking about plans, wishes, and obligations, and introduces and practices verb phrases related to hobbies or school.

Review of Lesson 1

- Have students look at page 2 in their Student's Book.
- Say incorrect statements about activities the characters did last summer. Have the class correct your statements in two different ways:

  You: *Jessica went camping.*

  Classmate 1: *Jessica didn't go camping. She stayed at her grandparents' house.* (The mistake is corrected by saying what the person did do.)

  Classmate 2: *Will went camping.* (The mistake is corrected by saying who actually did that activity.)

- Give students several minutes to try to remember as much as possible about what their classmates did last summer. (Lesson 1, Exercise 3)
- Play a memory game. Divide the class into two teams, A and B. Students take turns asking about what their classmates did last summer.

  Classmate 1 (Team A): *Where did Paul go last summer?*

  Classmate 2 (Team B): *He went to Orlando.*

  Paul: *That's right.*

- When students answer correctly, their team scores a point.

1 Language focus review

This exercise reviews *(be) going to, (would) like to, want to,* and *have to.*

A 💿 CD1, Track 4

- Have students read the directions and look at the photo. Ask: *What are Will and Carla talking about?* (Their plans for the new school year.)
- Have students read the conversation.
- **Optional** Play the recording. Students listen and read along.

> ### Audio script
> Same as the conversation in the Student's Book.

- Ask: *Who's going to join the drama club?* (Carla.) *Why?* (Because she'd like to act in the school play.) *What does Will want to learn?* (He wants to learn to play the guitar.) *What's he going to do?* (He's going to take music lessons.) *Who's going to study a lot?* (Will.) *Why?* (Because he has to get good grades.)
- Play the recording or model the conversation. Students listen and repeat.
- **Optional** Have students practice in pairs.

B 💿 CD1, Track 5

- **Language Chart** Have students study the examples in the language chart. Ask: *What expression do we use for a definite plan?* ([Be] going to.) *What do we use* (would) *like to and* want to *for?* (Expressing a hope and wish.) *What expression do we use for an obligation?* (Have to.)
- **Optional** Model the examples, pausing for students to repeat.
- Focus students' attention on the exercise. Explain that they are to write *going to, like to, want to,* or *have to* in the blanks.
- Have students work individually to complete the conversations.
- Play the recording. Students listen and verify their answers.

> ### Audio script
> Same as the conversations in the Student's Book.

- Check answers with the class. Invite volunteers to read aloud one of the sentences they completed.
- **Optional** Have students practice the conversations in pairs.

2 Listening

In this exercise, students listen for the speakers of different topics.

💿 CD1, Track 6

- Have students read the directions.
- Ask: *What do Jessica and Pedro talk about?* (The new school year.) *What do you have to do?* (Check the correct boxes of the speakers who talk about the items in the chart.)

Note: Remind students that in the Listening section of a lesson you will usually play the recording three times: first for them to listen *only*, a second time for them to do the task, and a third time for them to verify their answers.

- Play the recording. Students only listen.

Audio script
See page T-204.

- Play the recording again. Students listen and check the correct boxes.
- Play the recording once again. Students listen and verify their answers.
- Check answers with the class. Ask the questions in the chart and invite volunteers to answer them.
- **Optional** Ask students whether they have any plans similar to Jessica's or Pedro's.

3 Word power

This exercise introduces and practices verb phrases related to classes, hobbies, and sports.

A

- Ask students to read the directions, the verb phrases in the box, and the column heads in the chart. Have students call out any verb phrases they do not understand. Explain them by using them in sentences or by miming them.
- Explain to students that some of the verb phrases can be placed under more than one column. For example, *do karate* can be a hobby or a sport. Accept any answers from students as long as they can defend their rationale for their choices.
- Ask: *What do you have to do once you have classified all the verb phrases in the box?* (Write two more verb phrases in each column.)
- Have students work individually to complete the chart.
- Have students check their answers in pairs.
- Check answers with the class. Invite three volunteers to read aloud one of the lists they wrote. Then invite other volunteers to say one of the extra verb phrases they added.

B

- Have students read the directions.
- Have students work individually to complete the sentences with the verb phrases in Part A or their own ideas.
- Ask random students to read aloud one of the sentences they wrote.

Teaching Tip
Before students carry out a vocabulary task, check which words they already know and which ones they do not know. Also, make sure that students know what to do by going over one or two additional examples from the exercise.

Culture Note
When kids were surveyed for a *USA Weekend Magazine* poll about what would make them feel better about themselves, 49 percent said getting better grades, 38 percent said toning up their muscles, 38 percent said losing weight, 36 percent said doing better in sports, and 30 percent said having a better relationship with their parents.

4 Speaking

This exercise practices talking about plans for the future.

- Have students read the directions. Demonstrate the activity by reading the example conversation with a volunteer.
- Invite two other volunteers to come to the front to demonstrate the activity for the class.
- Have students work in groups of four and talk about their plans for the new school year.
- **Optional** Have a few volunteers tell the class their plans for the new school year.

Workbook
Assign the exercises on Workbook page 3. (Workbook answers begin on page T-192.)

Extra Grammar
Assign the exercises for the Extra Grammar, Lesson 2.

2 Listening

Jessica and Pedro talk about the new school year. Who talks about these things? Listen and check (✓) the correct boxes.

Who talks about ... ?	Jessica	Pedro
studying French	☐	✓
playing on a sports team	☐	✓
joining a club	✓	☐
meeting new students	✓	☐
getting good grades	☐	✓
having free time	✓	☐

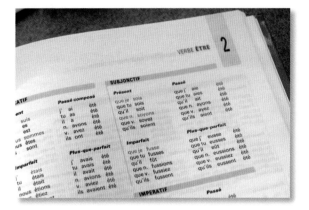

3 Word power

A Write these verb phrases in the correct columns. Then write two more verb phrases in each column. (The order of the answers may vary.)

☐ do gymnastics   ☐ join a fan club   ☐ study Web design
☐ do karate   ☐ play volleyball   ☐ take a computer course
✓ get good grades   ☐ start a comic-book collection   ☐ visit museums

Classes	Hobbies	Sports
get good grades	join a fan club	do gymnastics
study Web design	start a comic book collection	do karate
take a computer course	visit museums	play volleyball
(Answers will vary.)	(Answers will vary.)	(Answers will vary.)
(Answers will vary.)	(Answers will vary.)	(Answers will vary.)

B What are your plans for the year? Complete the sentences with the verb phrases in Part A or your own ideas. (Answers will vary.)

1. I'm going to _____ this year.

2. I'd like to _____ this year.

3. I have to _____ this year.

4 Speaking

What are your classmates' plans for the new school year? Ask four classmates.

You   What are your plans for the new school year, Jane?
Jane   Well, I'm going to join the chess club. What are your plans?

Mini-review

1 Language check

A Jake and Tania are very busy at school this year. Complete the questions and write short answers.

1. **A** ___Did___ Jake and Tania join the chess club?
   B _Yes, they did._ They both love to play chess.

2. **A** ___Did___ Jake join the volleyball team?
   B _No, he didn't._ Tania joined the volleyball team.

3. **A** ___Did___ Jake have French club after school last Tuesday?
   B _Yes, he did._ He always studies French on Tuesday.

4. **A** ___Was___ Tania practicing volleyball at 3:00 p.m. yesterday?
   B _Yes, she was._ We were all watching her.

5. **A** ___Were___ Jake and Tania studying for the math test yesterday?
   B _No, they weren't._ He was practicing the guitar, and she was practicing the piano.

6. **A** ___Did___ they pass the math test?
   B _No, they didn't._ They have too many extra activities. They have to study more.

B Check (✓) the correct words to complete the sentences.

1. **A** Are you taking Ms. Larson's geography class this year?
   B No. I'd like to take her class, but _____ to take Mr. Todd's history class this year.
   ☑ I have to   ☐ I'd like to

2. **A** Are you going to take the computer course?
   B _____ take the course, but I don't have time.
   ☐ I'm going to   ☑ I'd like to

3. **A** _____ do gymnastics this year. I love gymnastics.
   B Really? I don't like it at all. Gymnastics is too difficult for me.
   ☑ I want to   ☐ I have to

4. **A** _____ start a stamp collection in my free time. I think stamps are cool.
   B That sounds like a good idea. Good luck!
   ☑ I'm going to   ☐ I have to

Mini-review

This lesson reviews the language presented and practiced in Lessons 1 and 2.

1 Language check

This exercise reviews the structures presented so far in this unit.

A

- Focus students' attention on the picture on page 6. Ask: *What is Jake carrying?* (A chess board, a French book, and a guitar.) *What does Tania have?* (A chess book, a piano book, and a volleyball.)
- Have students read the directions.
- Invite two volunteers to read the example question and answer aloud.
- Have students work individually to complete the exercise.
- Have students check answers in pairs by reading the questions and answers aloud.
- Check answers with the class. Invite pairs to read the conversations aloud.

B

- Have students read the directions and the example.
- Have students work individually to check the correct words to complete the sentences.
- Check answers with the class. Invite several pairs of volunteers to read the conversations aloud.

C

- Have students look at the text and the photos. Ask: *Do you think this is a regular newspaper or a school newspaper edited by students?* (A school newspaper.)

- Tell students the article is about fun things students did last summer. Give students several minutes to read the text.

- Explain the meaning of *bumper cars* (point to the picture) and *reflection*.

- Say the following sentences. Students say the number of the text the sentence is about.

  This person spent 14 days in the open air and slept one night in an uncomfortable place. (2.)

  This person met a friend from home in a fun place. (1.)

  This person found a place where you can eat in a weird location. (4.)

  This person ate interesting things and saw something awesome. (3.)

- Have students read the directions.

- Focus students' attention on the examples. Ask: *Why do we use* went *in the first example?* (Because this sentence talks about a completed action that happened in the past.) *Why do we use* were waiting *in the second example?* (Because this sentence talks about an action that happened over a period of time in the past.)

- Have students work individually to complete the texts with the correct forms of the verbs in parentheses, using the simple past or the past continuous.

- Check answers with the class. Invite volunteers to read aloud one of the sentences they completed. Sentences should be read aloud in the order in which they appear in the texts.

Teaching Tip

Give students further practice by having them create their own practice exercises. Then they exchange papers with a classmate and do the exercises. For example, in this lesson, have students write short texts in their notebooks, like the ones in the article, about their own summer vacations. They then copy the text onto a separate piece of paper, leaving blanks whenever the simple past or past continuous occurs and writing the simple form of the verbs in parentheses. Students can write these for homework and then exchange papers the following day.

2 Listening

In this exercise, students listen for past and future plans.

CD1, Track 7

- Tell students they will listen to teenagers talking to friends about plans they had in the past and plans they have for the future. Each teenager asks his or her friend one or two questions. Students should choose the correct response for each question.

- Play the recording. Students only listen.

Audio script
See page T-204.

- Play the recording again. Students listen and check the correct responses.

- Play the recording once again. Students listen and verify their answers.

- Check answers with the class. Invite volunteers to read aloud one answer each.

Workbook
Assign the exercises on Workbook page 4. (Workbook answers begin on page T-192.)

Game
Assign the game on Student's Book page T-114.

C Read the newspaper article about fun things these students did last summer. Complete the sentences with the correct forms of the verbs. Use the simple past or the past continuous.

What did you do last summer?

1 My family and I ___went___ (go) to Disneyland on vacation. We _were waiting_ (wait) in line for a ride when I ___saw___ (see) someone I knew in front of me. Guess who? Tina! She and her family _were visiting_ (visit) Disneyland, too. So we ___spent___ (spend) the day together there.

2 I ___went___ (go) camping for two weeks. We ___drove___ (drive) to a campsite in the woods and _put up_ (put up) our tents. One night, we _were sleeping_ (sleep) when a big storm ___started___ (start). We ___were___ (be) scared, and so we ___slept___ (sleep) in the car that night. It was so uncomfortable that I _woke up_ (wake up) with a sore back.

3 I ___had___ (have) a lot of fun at the city summer fair with my friends. We ___rode___ (ride) on bumper cars, and we ___tried___ (try) a lot of interesting foods. When the fireworks ___started___ (start), we _were eating_ (eat) at a picnic table near the lake. The reflection of the fireworks on the water ___was___ (be) awesome!

4 My family and I ___took___ (take) a car trip. One day, we _were driving_ (drive) down the highway when we ___saw___ (see) a huge brown and white building in the shape of a cow. It ___was___ (be) a restaurant! We ___stopped___ (stop) and ___had___ (have) – what else? – ice cream. It was great!

2 Listening

What's next? Listen and check (✓) the correct responses.

1. ☑ I stayed home.
   ☐ I was watching TV.

2. ☐ Yes, I do. I like Spanish.
   ☑ Yes. I'm going to learn Spanish and French.

3. ☑ I'd like to join, but I have to take guitar lessons on Thursday.
   ☐ I was learning chess last year.

4. ☑ I was studying for the math test.
   ☐ I studied for the math test.

5. ☐ Yes, I do. I want to study a lot.
   ☑ Yes, I do. I want to join the photography club.

6. ☐ Yes, I was. I was traveling with my family.
   ☑ Yes, I did. I went on a trip with my family.

 Go to page 114 for the Game.

1 Language focus

when clauses of time + simple past

I joined a soccer team **when I was eight**.
When I was eight, I joined a soccer team.
I saw his concert **when he performed here**.
When he performed here, I saw his concert.

A Read about people Carla, Pedro, and Will admire. Complete the sentences. Use *when* and the correct form of the verbs. Listen and check. Then practice.

Mia Hamm

Ryan Sheckler

1. I love everything about soccer. When I was eight, I joined a soccer team. I'd love to be like Mia Hamm someday. She won a World Cup championship when she was only 19. –Carla

Lang Lang

2. Lang Lang is amazing. He _learned_ (learn) to play the piano _when_ he _was_ (be) only three years old. _When_ he _was_ (be) 13, he _played_ (play) with an orchestra in Moscow. I love to play the piano, too. I _saw_ (see) Lang Lang's concert _when_ he _performed_ (perform) in my town. It was incredible. –Pedro

3. _When_ I first _saw_ (see) Ryan Sheckler in a competition, I _wanted_ (want) to be a champion skateboarder like him. He's the best in the world. Ryan _was_ (be) only 18 months old _when_ he _found_ (find) his father's old skateboard and started to push it around. He became a professional at the age of 14. –Will

B Look at Carla's notes about soccer superstar Mia Hamm and complete the sentences. Then listen and check.

When Mia Hamm . . .		
was a young girl	was a teenager	was on the U.S. National Team
* moved a lot with her family	* joined the U.S. National Team	* helped the team win Olympic gold medals
* her parents gave her the nickname Mia	* played in her first World Cup match	* became famous

1. (young girl) When _Mia Hamm was a young girl, she moved a lot with her family_ .
2. (young girl) _Her parents gave her the nickname Mia_ when _she was a young girl_ .
3. (teenager) When _she was a teenager_ , _she joined the U.S. National Team_ .
4. (teenager) _She played in her first World Cup match_ when _she was a teenager_ .
5. (on the U.S. National Team) _She was on the U.S. National Team_ when _she helped the team win Olympic gold medals_ .
6. (famous) When _she became famous_ , _she was on the U.S. National Team_ .

Lesson 3 Life events

This lesson presents and practices verb phrases related to life events and when *clauses of time + simple past.*

Review of Lesson 2

• Write on the board:

Definite plans:
Hopes and wishes:
Obligations:

• Have the class suggest expressions that are used for each of the purposes on the board. Write them next to the purposes. (Definite plans: *[be] going to.* Hopes and wishes: *[would] like to, want to.* Obligations: *have to.*)

• Give students several minutes to think about their next few days and write three sentences about a plan, a hope or a wish, and an obligation for those days.

• Invite volunteers to tell the class one of the sentences they wrote.

1 Language focus

This exercise presents and practices *when* clauses of time + simple past.

A ⊚ CD1, Track 8

• Focus students' attention on the photos. Ask them to share with the class anything they may know, or can tell from the photos, about the people in them.

• Have students read Carla's text about Mia Hamm. Ask: *How old was Carla when she joined a soccer team?* (She was eight.) *How old was Mia Hamm when she won a World Cup championship?* (She was 19.)

• **Language Chart** Have students study the examples in the language chart. Focus students' attention on the first two sentences. Ask: *Which of the two sentences occurs in Carla's text?* (The second one.) *What are the differences between these two sentences?* (The order of the clauses. The position of *when.*) Explain that, as with *when* clauses in the simple present, the *when* time clause in the simple past can occur in either the beginning clause or the ending clause of a sentence. Usually, the part that is most important to the speaker or the writer comes at the beginning of the sentence. Draw students' attention to the comma after the *when* clause in the second sentence. Do the same with the other two sentences in the chart.

• **Optional** Model the examples, pausing for students to repeat.

• Have students read the directions. Make sure students notice that for blanks that are not followed by a verb in parentheses they have to supply the missing word.

• Have students work individually to complete the texts.

• **Optional** Have students read the other two texts. Focus students' attention on Pedro's text about Lang Lang. Ask: *How old was Lang Lang when he learned to play the piano?* (He was three.) *How old was he when he played with an orchestra?* (He was 13.) Follow the same procedure with Will's text about Ryan Sheckler.

• Play the recording. Students listen and verify their answers.

Audio script

Same as the texts in the Student's Book.

• Check answers with the class. Invite volunteers to read aloud one of the sentences they completed.

• Play the recording again or model the sentences. Students listen and practice.

B ⊚ CD1, Track 9

• Give students several minutes to read the directions and the information in the chart. Ask: *Was there anything that you didn't know about Mia Hamm?*

• Have students work individually to complete the sentences. Point out that each sentence indicates where the *when* clause should go.

• Play the recording. Students listen and verify their answers.

Audio script

Same as the sentences in the Student's Book.

• Check answers with the class. Say the sentences yourself, one at a time, but give incorrect information. For example: *Mia Hamm was a teenager when her parents gave her the nickname Mia.* Ask random students to say the correct sentences.

2 Listening

In this exercise, students listen for the time when events happened.

CD1, Track 10

- Have students read the directions and the information in items 1–6. Ask: *What events does Juan talk about?* (Learning to ride a horse, breaking his leg, getting a dog, a visit from his cousin, joining a basketball team, and moving.) *What should you listen for?* (Whether he was a young boy or a teenager when these events happened.)

- Play the recording. Students only listen.

Audio script
See page T-204.

- Play the recording again. Students listen and complete the exercise.

- Play the recording once again. Students listen and verify their answers.

- Check answers with the class. Read each item. Students respond with *young boy* or *teenager.*

- **Optional** Ask students to share with their classmates any additional information they may have learned from the recording. For example: *Juan's cousin lives in New York.*

Teaching Tip An alternative way of checking answers is to play the recording again and ask students to call out *Stop!* when they hear the answer to a question. Every time they do so, ask them to repeat the words that are pertinent to the answer. For example, in this exercise, the words for the first answer are *when I was a small boy.*

3 Word power

This exercise introduces and practices verb phrases related to life events.

A

- Have students read the directions, the words and phrases in the box, and the list of verbs. Ask: *What should you do?* (Complete the verb phrases with the words and phrases in the box, and then check the events that you have done or experienced.)

- Focus students' attention on the box. Have students call out any words or phrases they do not understand. Explain them by using them in sentences or by miming them.

- Have students work individually to complete the list of events.

- Check answers with the class. Copy the list of verbs on the board. Invite volunteers to come to the front and write their answers.

B

- Have students read the directions and the example.

- Have students work individually to write sentences about events in their life, using events from Part A or their own ideas.

- Invite volunteers to read their sentences to the class.

4 Speaking

This exercise practices *when* clauses of time + simple past.

- Have students read the directions and the examples. Invite a volunteer to come to the front to demonstrate the activity with you.

- **Optional** Invite two volunteers to demonstrate the example conversations once again.

- Invite volunteers to tell the class about the events they wrote about in Exercise 3B. Have the class ask for more information, as in the example.

Note: For large classes, have students do this activity in groups of three or four.

Workbook
Assign the exercises on Workbook page 5. (Workbook answers begin on page T-192.)

Extra Grammar
Assign the exercises for the Extra Grammar, Lesson 3.

2 Listening

Juan talks about events in his life. He is 15 years old now.
When did these events happen? Was he a young boy or a teenager?
Listen and check (✓) the correct boxes.

	Young boy	Teenager
1. learned to ride a horse	✓	☐
2. broke his leg	☐	✓
3. got a dog	☐	✓
4. cousin visited his school	✓	☐
5. joined a basketball team	☐	✓
6. moved to Ponce	✓	☐

3 Word power

A Create a verb phrase by adding a word or phrase from the box to each verb.
Then check (✓) the things that you have done or experienced. *(Answers will vary for the things students check.)*

☐ American food	☐ an award	☐ a sports team	☐ English	✓ my leg
☐ a musical instrument	☐ a pet	☐ a trip	☐ my best friend	☐ the city

- ☐ broke _my leg_
- ☐ moved to _the city_
- ☐ learned to play _a musical instrument_
- ☐ learned _English_
- ☐ met _my best friend_

- ☐ joined _a sports team_
- ☐ ate _American food_
- ☐ won _an award_
- ☐ went on _a trip_
- ☐ got _a pet_

B Write about events in your life. Use events from Part A or your own ideas. *(Answers will vary.)*

When I fell off my bike, I broke my leg.

OR _I broke my leg when I fell off my bike._

1. _____
2. _____
3. _____
4. _____

4 Speaking

Share your events from Exercise 3B with your classmates. Answer their questions.

You When I fell off my bike, I broke my leg.
Classmate 1 How old were you?
You I was 12.

You I broke my leg when I fell off my bike.
Classmate 2 How old were you?
You I was 12.

Lesson 4

Then and now

1 Language focus

A What was Greg like when he was ten?
Listen and practice.

Dave Is this you, Greg? You look
so different!

Greg Yes. My friend took that picture when
I was ten.

Dave You're so . . . thin now.

Greg Well, I used to be lazy, but I'm not
anymore. Now I exercise every day.

Dave And your hair – it was so short!

Greg I know. I used to like short hair.

Dave And you wore glasses?

Greg Yes. I used to wear glasses, but I don't
anymore. Now I wear contact lenses.

Dave You're a lot taller now, too.

Greg I know. I used to be the shortest person
in my class, but I'm not anymore. Now
I'm the tallest!

> **used to and not anymore**
>
> I **used to wear** glasses, but I **don't anymore**.
> Now I wear contact lenses.
>
> I **used to be** the shortest person in my class, but
> I**'m not anymore**. Now I'm the tallest.

Dave   Greg

B Look at the pictures. What did Greg use to do? What does he do now?
Write sentences. Then listen and check.

 **7 years ago**  **Now**    **8 years ago**  **Now**

1. (play) *He used to play video games,*
but he doesn't anymore. Now he plays
soccer.

2. (take) *He used to take swimming*
lessons, but he doesn't anymore. Now
he takes guitar lessons.

 **4 years ago**  **Now**    **3 years ago**  **Now**

3. (watch) *He used to watch TV, but*
he doesn't anymore. Now he watches
DVDs.

4. (wake up . . . on Saturdays) *He used*
to wake up at 10 a.m. on Saturdays, but he
doesn't anymore. Now he wakes up at 6 a.m.

10   Unit 1

Then and now

This lesson presents and practices used to *and* not anymore.

1 Language focus

This exercise presents and practices *used to* and *not anymore*.

A CD1, Track 11

• Focus students' attention on the picture. Ask: *What are Dave and Greg doing?* (They're looking at a photo album.) *How old do you think they are?* (15 or 16.) *Whose photo is in the album?* (Greg's.) *How old was he when the photo was taken?* (Ten.)

• Have students read the directions. Ask: *What should you read and listen for?* (What Greg was like when he was ten.)

• Have students read the conversation.

• **Optional** Play the recording. Students listen and read along.

Audio script
Same as the conversation in the Student's Book.

• Ask: *Is Greg thinner now than when he was ten?* (Yes.) *Is he lazy now?* (No.) *Does he exercise now?* (Yes.) *Do you think he exercised when he was ten?* (No.) *Is his hair shorter or longer now?* (It's longer.) *Does he wear glasses or contact lenses now?* (Contact lenses.) *Was he the tallest person in the class when he was ten?* (No.)

• Have students read Greg's part of the conversation again and underline four phrases Greg uses to talk about what he was like when he was ten. (I used to be lazy. I used to like short hair. I used to wear glasses. I used to be the shortest person in my class.) Invite volunteers to come to the board to write one of the phrases or sentences they underlined.

• Ask: *Are these phrases about the present or the past?* (The past.) *What else do they have in common?* (They all begin with *I used to*.) Explain that *used to* refers to things that were true in the past or were done regularly in the past.

• Have students look at Greg's part of the conversation again and find two phrases he uses to emphasize that certain things that were true of him in the past are not true in the present. (But I'm not anymore; but I don't anymore.)

• Play the recording or model the conversation. Students listen and repeat.

• **Optional** Have students practice in pairs.

• **Language Chart** Have students study the examples in the language chart. Ask: *What follows* used to, *the past or the simple form?* (The simple form.) Explain that *used to* + simple form does not change, regardless of the subject of the sentence. Give a few examples: *He used to wear contact lenses. She used to like long hair. We used to live in Boston. They used to watch a lot of TV.*

• **Optional** Model the examples, pausing for students to repeat.

B CD1, Track 12

• Give students several minutes to read the directions, look at the pictures, and read the example.

• Have students work individually to write sentences.

• Play the recording. Students listen and verify their answers.

Audio script
Same as the sentences in the Student's Book.

• Check answers with the class. Invite volunteers to read aloud one of the sentences they wrote.

2 Listening

In this exercise, students listen for differences between what someone was like in the past and what he or she is like now.

CD1, Track 13

- Have students read the directions and the words in the chart.
- Tell students that they will listen to Greg and Dave talk about the ways Dave is different now from when he was younger. Students should listen and make notes to complete the chart.
- Focus students' attention on the *Topic* column and predict things Dave may say about the topics. For example: *I used to watch a lot of movies, but I don't anymore. Now I go out a lot. I used to like action movies, but I don't anymore. Now I like thrillers.*
- Play the recording. Students only listen.

Audio script
See page T-205.

- Play the recording again. Students listen and complete the chart.
- Play the recording once again. Students listen and verify their answers.
- Check answers with the class. Copy the chart on the board. Invite volunteers to come to the board to write one of their answers in the chart.

3 Pronunciation *used to*

This exercise practices the reduction of *used to* in conversation.

A   CD1, Track 14

- Explain the concept of informal conversational English pronunciation to students. Tell them that in everyday conversation, Americans tend to speak quickly and the pronunciation of two words often sounds like one word. With *used to*, in normal conversation, the final *-d* sound is dropped and the two words run together so that the pronunciation sounds like "use-tuh."
- Play the recording. Students listen, paying particular attention to the pronunciation of *used to*.

Audio script
Same as the sentences in the Student's Book.

- Play the recording again. Students listen and repeat.

B

- Give students several minutes to practice the three sentences, using the reduced pronunciation of *used to*.
- Ask random students to say one of the sentences, paying attention to the pronunciation of *used to*.
- **Optional** Ask random students to look at Exercise 1A on page 10 and read a sentence with the reduced pronunciation of *used to*.

4 Speaking

This exercise practices *used to* and *not anymore.*

A

- Have students read the directions. Invite several volunteers to suggest how they would complete the first two sentences. For example: *I used to be very shy. I used to watch cartoons on TV.*
- Have students work individually to complete the sentences with their own information.

B

- Ask volunteers to tell their classmates how they are different now from when they were young children, following the example in the speech balloons and using their ideas from Part A.

- **Optional** Have students work in small groups of four or five. Hand out six slips of paper to each student in each group. Students write each of their sentences with *used to* from Part A on the slips of paper, but they do not write their names on the slips. Have one student collect all the slips and mix them up in random order. Students take turns reading the slips of paper and then guessing who in the group wrote each sentence.

Workbook
Assign the exercises on Workbook page 6. (Workbook answers begin on page T-192.)

Extra Grammar
Assign the exercises for the Extra Grammar, Lesson 4.

2 Listening

How was Dave different when he was younger? Listen and complete the chart.

Topic	In the past	Now
Hobbies	_collected comic books_	_collects stamps_
Movies	_used to watch horror movies_	_watches comedies_
Sports	_used to skateboard_	_rides his mountain bike_
Favorite subject	_used to take French_	_takes Spanish_
Getting to school	_used to take the bus to school_	_walks to school_

3 Pronunciation *used to*

A Listen. Notice how *used to* is reduced in conversation. Then listen again and practice.

> I **used to** wear glasses.
>
> He **used to** have short hair.
>
> I **used to** play basketball.
>
> He **used to** be shy.

B Now practice these sentences.

She **used to** play the violin, but she doesn't anymore.
They **used to** study French, but they don't anymore.
You **used to** be shy, but you're not anymore.

4 Speaking

A Think of yourself when you were a young child. What were you like? Complete the sentences with your own information. *(Answers will vary.)*

I used to be _____ .

I used to watch _____ on TV.

I used to play _____ .

I used to wear _____ .

I used to _____ .

I used to _____ .

B Now tell your classmates. Use your ideas from Part A.

> I used to be short, but I'm not anymore. Now I'm tall.

> I used to watch cartoons on TV. Now I watch music shows.

Get Connected
UNIT 1

Read

A **Read the article quickly. Check (✓) the false statements.**

☐ 1. Shawn Johnson is a top gymnast.

☑ 2. She started gymnastics when she was one year old.

☑ 3. She'd like to go back to Beijing and relax.

A Teenage Star

Shawn Johnson seems like an average teenager. She likes to watch TV and listen to her favorite bands. She goes to school and loves English and wants to do well in math. But Shawn isn't just *any* teenager. She's an Olympic athlete, and has to **train** for four hours every day! While her friends were enjoying summer vacation, she was traveling to the Olympic Games in Beijing, China.

But how did this 4-foot, 9-inch teenager become a top **gymnast**? Well, Shawn learned to walk when she was only nine months old. When she was three, her parents took her to a gymnastics class. And Shawn loved it. When she was in elementary school, Shawn wrote in her **scrapbook**: *Shawn is great at gymnastics.*

And she was right. Shawn won four medals at the Olympic Games and quickly became one of America's **best-loved** sports stars! Thousands of people came to see her when she came back from Beijing. "It feels amazing," she said. Now after many interviews and a U.S. tour, she'd like to relax with her family for awhile.

Go to page 122 for the **Vocabulary Practice**.

B 💿 **Read the article slowly. Check your answers in Part A.**

C **Answer the questions.**

1. Does Shawn have to train for four hours every week?
   No, she doesn't. She has to train for four hours every day.

2. What were Shawn's friends doing when she was in Beijing?
   When she was in Beijing, Shawn's friends were enjoying summer vacation.

3. What did Shawn's parents do when she was three?
   When she was three, Shawn's parents took her to a gymnastics class.

4. What did she win at the Olympic Games?
   She won four medals at the Olympic Games.

5. What would Shawn like to do now that she's back from Beijing?
   She'd like to relax with her family for awhile.

Unit 1 · Get Connected

This lesson practices reading, listening, and writing skills.

> **Review of Lesson 4**
> - Write on the board:
>   *Mario used to watch cartoons on TV. He doesn't watch cartoons anymore. He watches soap operas.*
> - Remind students of the last exercise in Lesson 4 where they shared information about how they are different from when they were young children. Ask them to try to remember what two of their classmates said.
> - Have students work individually to write sentences about how two of their classmates are different now from when they were young children, following the example on the board.
> - Have volunteers read their sentences. Classmates say if the information is correct.

Read

This exercise practices reading for information about a sports star.

Note: Tell students that there is a "Get Connected" lesson in each unit. This lesson provides additional practice in reading, listening, and writing. It uses vocabulary and grammar from previous lessons in the unit, and it presents new vocabulary.

A

- Have students read the title of the article and look at the photo. Ask: *Do you know the person in this photo?* (Shawn Johnson.) *Where is she from?* (The United States.) Invite students to tell the class about their favorite Olympic athletes.

> **Culture Note**
> Gymnastics has been part of the modern Olympics since 1896. There has been a lot of controversy about gymnastics. Some people feel that the long and difficult training is harmful for young girls' bodies. Therefore, the age limit for the Olympics was increased to 16 in 1997. People who disagree argue that 15-year-old athletes, for example, who may be ready to compete will have to wait four years until they are 19 to enter the Olympics. By that time, girls may be past their peak ability. The famous gymnast Nadia Comaneci was only 14 when she scored more than one perfect 10 in 1976.

- Invite a volunteer to read the directions and the three statements aloud. Tell students *read quickly* means they read quickly to find the answers, and they should not read every word carefully.
- Have students work individually to read the article quickly and check the false statements. Do not check answers at this point.

B 💿 CD1, Track 15

- Invite a volunteer to read the directions aloud. Tell students *read slowly* means they read slowly and carefully, and concentrate on getting the meaning of the entire text.

- List the new vocabulary words on the board: *train (v.), gymnast, scrapbook, best-loved.* Explain their meaning. (Train [v.]: to practice something to become better at it; gymnast: a person who does gymnastics; scrapbook: a book of blank pages in which you paste pictures, newspaper articles, or other things to help you remember the past; best-loved: favorite or loved best of all.) As an alternative, have students use their dictionaries to find the meanings of the new vocabulary words.
- Have students read the article again.
- Have students check their answers in Part A in pairs.
- **Optional** Play the recording. Students listen and read along.

> **Audio script**
> Same as the article in the Student's Book.

> **Get Connected Vocabulary**
> *Note:* The Get Connected Vocabulary provides extra practice of new vocabulary words (the words in bold) in the Get Connected readings.
> - Have students do the exercise on Student's Book page 122 in class or for homework. (Get Connected Vocabulary answers begin on page T-122.)

C

- Invite a volunteer to read the directions and first question aloud.
- Ask: *Does Shawn have to train for four hours every week?* Elicit the answer. (No. She has to train for four hours every day!)
- Have students work individually to answer the questions.
- Have students check their answers in pairs.
- Check answers with the class.

Listen

In this exercise, students listen for information about training for a sport.

A 🎧 CD1, Track 16

- Focus students' attention on the photo. Ask: *Where are the teens in the photo?* (On the street.) *What are they doing?* (Talking to each other.)

- Tell students that they will listen to two friends, Nick and Julie, talk about how Julie is training for the swim team.

- Have students read the first question and the example answer.

- Explain that students should listen to the conversation and answer the questions.

- Play the recording. Students only listen.

> **Audio script**
> See page T-205.

- Play the recording again. Students listen and answer the questions.

- Play the recording once again. Students listen and verify their answers.

- Check answers with the class. Invite volunteers to read aloud one answer each.

B

- Have students read the directions and the questions.

- Read the first question with the class and elicit answers from several students. Tell students there are no right or wrong answers for this exercise – they are giving their opinions.

- Have students work individually to answer the questions, and give reasons for their answers.

- Have students work in pairs to compare answers, or elicit opinions from volunteers.

··

Write

In this exercise, students answer questions and write a paragraph about a sport they have trained for or a hobby they have worked hard on.

A

- Invite a volunteer to read the directions and the questions aloud.

- Have students work individually to answer the questions. Tell them that they are answering questions based on their own experience.

- **Optional** Have students ask and answer the questions in pairs.

B

- Invite a volunteer to read the directions aloud. Tell students that they will use their answers in Part A to write about the sport or hobby they have trained for or worked hard on.

- Have students work individually to write their paragraphs.

- Invite several volunteers to read their paragraphs to the class.

- **Optional** Have students work in groups of four and read each other's paragraphs. Students should ask questions about anything they do not understand. They can also ask questions to get more information about their classmates' hobbies.

> **Workbook**
> Assign the exercises on Workbook page 7.
> (Workbook answers begin on page T-192.)

We used to . . .

A 🔊 **Nick and Julie talk about swim team training. Listen and answer the questions.**

1. Did Julie answer Nick's phone calls? _No, she didn't._

2. Why does the swim team have to train so hard? _They have a really important swimming competition._

3. Why are Julie's parents not too happy? _She used to get good grades, but she doesn't anymore._

4. What would Julie like to be someday? _She'd like to be a P.E. teacher and a swim coach, too._

5. What are Nick and Julie going to do together? _They're going to play a (video) game._

B **What do you think? Answer the questions. Give reasons.**
(Answers will vary)
1. Do you think doing one thing for three hours a day is too much?

   _____

2. Which is the most important: schoolwork, sports, or friends?

   _____

3. Would you like to be a teacher someday? _____

4. Do you think it's fun to play video games with friends? _____

Your turn

Write

A **Think of a sport you have trained for or a hobby you have worked hard on. Answer the questions.** _(Answers will vary.)_

1. What did you train for or work hard on? _____

2. How many hours a day did you train or work? _____

3. Why did you train or work? _____

4. What happened to your schoolwork and other activities? _____

5. Are you going to continue training or working hard? Why or why not?

   _____

B **Write a paragraph about your experience. Use the answers in Part A to help you.** _(Answers will vary.)_

⬤⬤⬤

_I . . ._

_____

_____

_____

_____

Unit 1 Review

Language chart review

Simple past	Past continuous

What **did** you **do** yesterday?
   I **went** to the mall. I **didn't have**
   school yesterday.
 Did your friends **go**, too?
   Yes, they **did**. / No, they **didn't**.
	What **was** Izzy **doing** yesterday?
	   She **was playing** video games. She
	   wasn't studying history.
	 Were you **studying** English?
	   Yes, we **were**. / No, we **weren't**.

when clauses of time + simple past
My friends gave me a surprise party **when I turned 13**.   **When I got home**, everyone said, "Surprise!"

A Complete the sentences with the simple past or the past continuous.

1. **Todd** I have a joke for you. A girl _was walking_ (walk) down the road when
   she ___saw___ (see) three very large men. They _were standing_ (stand)
   under a very small umbrella. There ___was___ (be) thunder and
   lightning, but the men didn't get wet.
   Sara Why not?
   Todd It _didn't rain_ (not / rain)!

2. **Mona** I ___heard___ (hear) a funny story today. There ___was___ (be) a class
   with a very scary teacher. Every day ___started___ (start) the same way.
   The teacher ___said___ (say), "Good morning, everyone." Then class
   ___began___ (begin). One day, when the teacher _was explaining_ (explain)
   the lesson, the door opened. The students ___looked___ (look) up, but they
   didn't see (not / see) anyone. When the teacher ___looked___ (look) down,
   she ___saw___ (see) Artie Sullivan, a student in her class. He was
   crawling on his hands and knees. "Why are you crawling into class,
   Artie?" the teacher ___asked___ (ask). "On the first day of class, when you
   ___told___ (tell) us the classroom rules, you ___said___ (say), "Never
   walk into my class late!" _answered_ (answer) Artie.

B Write questions to complete the conversation.

A _What did you do yesterday?_
B I bought some joke books yesterday.
A _Where did you buy them?_
B I bought the books at the mall.
A _Did you read them last night?_
B No, I didn't read them. I was studying all night.
A _Were you studying English?_
B No, I wasn't studying English. I was studying history – the history of jokes.

14   Unit 1

Unit 1 Review

This lesson reviews the grammar and vocabulary introduced in Unit 1.

Language chart review

These charts summarize the main grammar presented and practiced in Unit 1.

Note: Explain that there is a "Review" lesson at the end of every unit that reviews the language of the whole unit. Review lessons start with a Language chart review that summarizes the unit grammar. A chart or charts are followed by a series of exercises. Some Review lessons contain two Language chart reviews.

- Books closed. Write on the board:

Simple past	Past continuous
1.	1.
2.	2.

when clauses of time + simple past
1.
2.

What <u>did</u> you <u>do</u> yesterday?	My friends gave me a surprise party <u>when I turned 13</u>.
What <u>was</u> Izzy <u>doing</u> yesterday?	<u>Did</u> your friends <u>go</u>, too?
<u>Were</u> you <u>studying</u> English?	<u>When I got home</u>, everyone said, "Surprise!"

- Focus students' attention on the headings and examples on the board.
- Have students copy the charts and work in pairs to write each example in the correct chart. Explain that they should pay close attention to the underlined words and phrases to "discover" what the sentences illustrate.
- Invite volunteers to come to the front to write their answers on the board.
- Books open. Have students check their answers against the examples in the Language chart review. Then ask them to check the answers on the board.
- Ask: *When do we use the simple past?* (To describe an action or situation that is now finished or that happened at a specific point in the past.) *When do we use the past continuous?* (To refer to an action that was in progress at a specific point in time in the past.)
- Invite volunteers to give more examples of the use of both forms by talking about things that happened in your classroom or in the school.
- Ask: *Where is the* when *clause in the sentence, first or second?* (It can be either first or second.)
- Answer any questions students may have.

....

Exercises A through D (pages T-14 to T-15)

Note: Students can do these exercises for homework or in class. They should do these exercises with minimal teacher input or help. If you choose to do these exercises as homework, briefly review the exercise directions in class. Make sure that students understand what they should do. Check the answers with the class during the next class meeting. If you choose to do the exercises in class, follow the directions below.

Exercise A

- Have students read the directions and the example aloud.
- Have students work individually to complete the sentences with the simple past or the past continuous form of the verb in parentheses.
- Check answers with the class.

Exercise B

- Have students read the directions and the example question.
- Have students work individually to write the questions.
- Check answers with the class.

Language chart review

These charts summarize further grammar presented and practiced in Unit 1.

- Have students study the examples in the charts.
- Remind students to use *(be) going to* to talk about definite plans, *(would) like to* and *want to* to talk about hopes and wishes, and *have to* to talk about obligations. Review *used to* and *not anymore*. Point out that *used to* is used for situations in the past that are not true for the present.
- Answer any questions students may have.

Exercise C

- Have students read the directions and the example.
- Have students work individually to rewrite the sentences, using the ideas in parentheses.
- Check answers with the class. Invite volunteers to read aloud one sentence each.

Exercise D

- Have students read the directions and look at the chart.
- Go over the example sentence and make sure that students understand how to use the information in the chart to write sentences about what these famous people used to do and what they do now.
- Have students work individually to write sentences.
- Check answers with the class.

Take another look!

- Have a volunteer read the directions aloud.
- Students work individually to circle the action that happened first in each sentence and underline the action that happened second.
- Check answers with the class.

Optional Unit Wrap-Up

- If students did the Review exercises for homework, check answers with the class.
- Have students work in pairs to act out the conversations in Exercises A and B. (Partners can take turns role-playing Mona in number 2 of Exercise A.) Then have each pair write a conversation similar to the one in Exercise B, beginning with the question *What did you buy yesterday?* Invite pairs to present their conversations to the class.
- For more practice with Exercise C, have students work in pairs. Each student makes three sentences with his or her own ideas – one with a definite plan, one with a hope or wish, and one with an obligation – and shares them with his or her partner. Invite a few students to share their sentences with the class.
- For more practice with *used to*, have students write sentences like those in Exercise D describing a famous person, but without saying the name. Their classmates try to guess who it is. For example, *This actor used to be on the TV show* Friends. *Now she acts in a lot of movies.* (Jennifer Aniston.)

Theme Project

Note: Explain that the Theme Projects reinforce the unit vocabulary and language structures in a creative way. They also help students connect their English to the world outside the classroom.

- Assign the *At Home* section of the Unit 1 Theme Project on Student's Book page 126.

Workbook

- Assign the Unit 1 Check Yourself on Workbook page 8. (Workbook answers begin on page T-192.)

Extra Practice Worksheets

Note: Explain that these provide extra vocabulary and grammar practice. These worksheets can be done for homework or in class.

- Assign the Unit 1 Extra Practice worksheets starting on page T-142.

Extra Speaking Practice Worksheet

Note: Explain that this provides extra speaking practice. This worksheet can be done for homework or in class.

- Assign the Unit 1 Extra Speaking Practice worksheet on page T-168.

Arcade Activities

Note: Explain that the Arcade provides fun, interactive activities that review and practice vocabulary and grammar.

- Assign the Unit 1 Arcade activities found at: www.cambridge.org/connectarcade

Learning Log

Note: Explain that these provide a way for students to assess their progress for the unit. The Learning Log can be done for homework or in class.

- Assign the Unit 1 Learning Log. This can be downloaded from the Teacher Support Site at: www.cambridge.org/connect2e/teacher

Quiz

- Give the Unit 1 Quiz on page T-178.

Test

- Give the Unit 1 Test (Form A and / or Form B). These can be downloaded from the Teacher Support Site at: www.cambridge.org/connect2e/teacher

Language chart review

<table>
<tr><td>be going to, would like to, want to, and have to</td><td>used to and not anymore</td></tr>
<tr><td>Definite plans: We're going to play soccer after school today.
Hopes and wishes: I'd like to visit Japan someday.
I want to learn Japanese.
Obligations: We have to wear sneakers in the gym.</td><td>We used to live in an apartment, but we don't anymore. Now we have a house.</td></tr>
</table>

C **Rewrite the sentences with *be going to*, *would like to*, *want to*, or *have to*. Change the meaning, using the ideas in parentheses.**

1. I'd like to start my own fan club.
   (definite plan) *I'm going to start my own fan club.*

2. I'm going to make an exciting Web site for my club.
   a. (hope) *I'd like to / I want to make an exciting Web site for my club.*
   b. (wish) *I'd like to / I want to make an exciting Web site for my club.*

3. I want to work on the Web site today.
   (obligation) *I have to work on the Web site today.*

4. I'd like to start a Jennifer Aniston fan club.
   (definite plan) *I'm going to start a Jennifer Aniston fan club.*

D **Write sentences about what these people used to do and what they do now.**

	Before	Now
1. Liv Tyler	was a model	is an actor
2. Elijah Wood	acted in TV commercials	acts in movies
3. Johnny Depp	lived in the United States	lives in France
4. Beyoncé Knowles	sang with the group Destiny's Child	sings alone

1. *Liv Tyler used to be a model, but she's not anymore. Now she's an actor.*

2. *Elijah Wood used to act in TV commercials, but he doesn't anymore. Now he acts in movies.*

3. *Johnny Depp used to live in the United States, but he doesn't anymore. Now he lives in France.*

4. *Beyoncé Knowles used to sing with the group Destiny's Child, but she doesn't anymore. Now she sings alone.*

Take another look!

Read the sentences. Circle the actions that happened first. Then underline the actions that happened second.

1. When Dad came home, we were watching TV.
2. When the phone rang, my mother answered it.

Go to page 126 for the Theme Project.

Predictions

1 Language focus

💿 **A** Read Professor Pete's Web site. Complete the predictions with *will* or *won't*. Listen and check. Then practice.

Future with *will* and *won't*

Robots **will** help us.
They**'ll** also clean.
Robots **won't** replace humans.

Will robots cook?
Yes, they **will.**
No, they **won't.**

I'll = I will   he'll = he will   we'll = we will
you'll = you will   she'll = she will   they'll = they will

won't = will not

Professor Pete's Predictions for 2030

1. Robots will help us in our homes. Will they cook? Yes, they will. They'll also clean and go shopping. But robots won't replace humans.

2. People ___won't___ have to think about what to wear. "Smart" clothes ___will___ tell them if they look good or not.

You look great!

3. Sleeping machines ___will___ help us sleep well. We ___won't___ have bad dreams or nightmares. We ___'ll___ only have sweet dreams.

4. People ___will___ drive around the world on superhighways. The superhighways ___will___ connect the seven continents.

5. Students ___won't___ stay in the classroom all the time. They ___'ll___ travel to space for their science class.

6. Schools ___will___ be open 24 hours a day. ___Will___ students come to school at the same time every day? No, they ___won't___ .

Open 24 hours

B Which of Professor Pete's predictions do you think will come true? Ask a classmate. Use the first sentence of each prediction.

> What do you think? Will robots help us in our homes?

> Yes, they will. OR No, they won't.

Lesson 5 Predictions

This lesson presents and practices the future with will *and* won't.

1 Language focus

This exercise presents and practices the future with *will* and *won't*.

A 🖸 CD1, Track 17

- Focus students' attention on the name of the Web site and the pictures. Ask: *Who created this site?* (Professor Pete.) Ask: *Is the site about past events or future events?* (Future events.) *Whose opinions does the text show?* (Professor Pete's opinions.)

- Have students read text 1. Ask: *In Professor Pete's opinion, what will robots do for us?* (Cook, clean, and go shopping.) Elicit or explain the meaning of *replace*, or use it in a sentence. Ask: *Will robots replace humans?* (No.)

- Have students study the examples in the left-hand side of the language chart. Ask: *What comes after* will *or* won't *in the statements?* (A verb in the simple form or the adverb *also*.)

- Have students study the examples in the right-hand side of the chart. Ask: *Where does* will *go in the question?* (At the beginning.) *Where does* will *or* won't *go in the short answers?* (At the end.) *Does* will *change according to the subject?* (No, it's always the same.)

- Focus students' attention on the contractions at the bottom of the chart. Ask: *What's the full form of* she'll *and* they'll? (She will, they will.) *What are the two words in* won't? (Will not.) *When do we use* won't? (In negative statements.)

- **Optional** Model the examples, pausing for students to repeat.

- Have students read texts 2–6. Ask: *What is text 2 about?* (Clothes.) *Which text is about where students will study?* (Text 5.) *Which text is about transportation?* (Text 4.) *What is text 6 about?* (School hours.) *Which text is about sleeping machines?* (Text 3.)

- Have students read the directions.

- Have students work individually to complete texts 2–6.

- Play the recording. Students listen and verify their answers.

> **Audio script**
> Same as the Web site in the Student's Book.

- Check answers with the class. Invite volunteers to read aloud one of the sentences they completed.

- Play the recording again or model the sentences. Students listen and repeat.

B

- Have students read the directions and the example conversation. Ask: *Which sentence from each text should you use to make the questions?* (The first sentence in each of the six texts.)

- Invite two volunteers to demonstrate the task.

- Have students work with a classmate to take turns asking and answering questions about Professor Pete's predictions, following the example in the speech balloons.

This unit introduces language to talk about future plans, probabilities, and possibilities.

C 🔊 CD1, Track 18

- Have students read the directions, look at the picture, and read the ad. Ask: *What's the ad for?* (A new computer game.) *What does the game do?* (It makes predictions about the future.)
- Have students work individually to complete the ad.
- Play the recording. Students listen and verify their answers.

- Check answers with the class. Invite volunteers to read aloud one of the sentences they completed.
- **Optional** Invite volunteers to ask their classmates the first two questions in the ad. Students give their own predictions using short answers with *will* or *won't*.

----

2 Listening

In this exercise, students listen for predictions and the reasons for them.

🔊 CD1, Track 19

- Have students read the directions and items 1–5. Ask: *What are the two teens doing?* (Playing the prediction game.) *When are the predictions for?* (2030.) *What should you do?* (Check Agree or Disagree according to whether Professor Pete agrees or disagrees with each prediction.)
- Play the recording. Students only listen.

- Play the recording again. Students listen and check the correct boxes.
- Play the recording once again. Students listen and verify their answers.
- Check answers with the class. Read the predictions aloud and invite volunteers to call out *Agree* or *Disagree* based on what they heard in the conversation.

----

3 Speaking

This exercise practices *will* and *won't*.

A
- Have students read the directions.
- Have students work individually to complete the chart with their own predictions for 2030, using the word *will*.

B
- Have students read the directions and the example in the speech balloons.
- Have students walk around the classroom and find one student who agrees with each prediction. Have them write those students' names in the chart.
- **Optional** In larger classes, have students do this activity in groups of six or seven.

- **Optional** Ask volunteers to share several of their predictions and name the classmates who agreed with them. For example: *Raul and I think robots will do students' homework. Patricia and I think most people won't live in outer space.*

C Professor Pete has a new computer game about predictions. Complete the ad about his game with *will* or *won't*. Then listen and check.

Hey, kids! ___Will___ computers replace humans someday? ___Will___ everyone speak the same language? You ___will___ learn the answers to these questions when you play Professor Pete's new computer game. ___Will___ you be bored? No, you ___won't___ . Professor Pete's game ___will___ entertain you for hours. Hurry and buy this game today. You ___won't___ be sorry.

Professor Pete's Prediction Game

2 Listening

Two teens play Professor Pete's prediction game for 2030. Does Professor Pete agree with these predictions? Listen and check (✓) Agree or Disagree.

	Agree	Disagree
1. Students won't use paper and pencils in school.	✓	☐
2. Cell phones will be the size of a credit card.	✓	☐
3. Most people won't shop in stores for food.	☐	✓
4. People will stay on the moon on vacation.	✓	☐
5. People will live below the sea.	☐	✓

3 Speaking

A Write your own predictions for 2030. Use *will*. *(Answers will vary.)*

	Predictions	Names
1. Robots		
2. Most people		
3. Students		
4. Movies		
5. Houses		
6. Cars		
7. TVs		

B Now find classmates who agree with your predictions. Write their names in the chart.

> What do you think? Will robots do students' homework?

> Yes, they will. OR No, they won't.

When I'm older

1 Word power

A Match each verb phrase to its meaning. Then listen and practice.

1. be famous   _d_
2. be rich   _f_
3. get a driver's license   _g_
4. get a job   _a_
5. get married   _h_
6. go to college   _b_
7. live alone   _c_
8. travel abroad   _e_

a. find a place to work
b. study after graduating from high school
c. not share your living space
d. have many people know who you are
e. visit a country far away from home
f. have a lot of money
g. pass a test to drive a car
h. become a husband or a wife

B What do you want to do or have happen before you are 25?
Complete the sentences. *(Answers will vary.)*

I want to _____ .   I want to _____ .

I want to _____ .   I want to _____ .

2 Language focus

A Jen and her father talk about the future. Listen and practice.

Jen Well, Dad, I probably won't be famous!
I didn't win the singing competition
at school today.

Mr. Wood That's OK, Jen. You have many other
talents. You'll probably get a great
job someday.

Jen Do you think so? I guess I *am* a good writer.

Mr. Wood Yes, you are. And you speak French well, too.
You'll probably work for a French
magazine someday.

Jen Gee. That sounds interesting. I'll also
probably travel abroad . . . maybe to France.

Mr. Wood Anything is possible.

Jen And I'll probably get married to
a handsome . . .

Mr. Wood OK, OK, Jen. Don't get too excited.
You have to finish school first!

Jen Oh, I know. But it's good to have
dreams, right?

Lesson 6 When I'm older

This lesson presents and practices verb phrases related to future goals and future probability with will probably / probably won't.

> **Review of Lesson 5**
> - Write on the board:
>
>   *Predictions*
>   *Pens will take photographs. OR Pens won't take photographs.*
>   *1. planes / fly in outer space   4. children / study in their sleep*
>   *2. people / work seven days a week   5. bikes / fly*
>   *3. older people / look young   6. money / disappear*
>
> - Give students several minutes to write their predictions for the future using cues 1–3 on the board.
> - Invite volunteers to read aloud one sentence each. After each sentence, ask if any students disagree and, if so, ask them to read their version of the sentence.
> - Have students work in small groups and take turns asking and answering *will* questions based on cues 4–6.

1 Word power

This exercise presents and practices some verb phrases related to future goals.

A 🔊 CD1, Track 20
- Give students several minutes to read the directions and the verb phrases and their meanings.
- Tell students that they should match the verb phrases in the left-hand column to the appropriate meaning in the right-hand column.
- Have students work individually to match the verb phrases to their meanings.
- Check answers with the class. Invite volunteers to read their answers aloud.
- Play the recording. Students listen and repeat.

> **Audio script**
> See page T-206.

B
- Have students read the directions.
- Give students several minutes to complete the sentences.
- Invite volunteers to share one of their sentences with the class. After each sentence, ask students who completed the sentence in the same way to raise their hands.

2 Language focus

This exercise presents and practices future probability with *will probably / probably won't.*

A 🔊 CD1, Track 21
- Ask students to read the directions and look at the picture. Ask: *What are Jen and her father talking about?* (Jen's plans for the future.)
- Have students read the conversation.
- **Optional** Play the recording. Students listen and read along.

> **Audio script**
> Same as the conversation in the Student's Book.

- Ask: *Does Jen think she'll be famous in the future?* (No.) *How do you know? What does she say?* (I probably won't be famous.) *Why does she think she won't be famous?* (She didn't win the singing competition.)

- Have students read the conversation again and underline all the sentences with predictions.
- Invite volunteers to read aloud one underlined sentence each. After each sentence, ask them to justify the prediction. For example, after "You'll probably get a great job someday," ask: *Why does Mr. Wood think Jen will get a great job?* (She has many talents.)
- To finish, ask: *What are some of your dreams? Do you think it's good to have dreams?*
- Play the recording or model the conversation. Students listen and repeat.
- **Optional** Have students practice in pairs.

B 💿 CD1, Track 22

- **Language Chart** Have students study the examples in the language chart. Ask: *Which word shows the speakers are not sure what will happen?* (Probably.) *Does probably go before or after* will*?* (After.) *Does probably go before or after* won't*?* (Before.)

- **Optional** Model the examples, pausing for students to repeat.

- Focus students' attention on sentence 1 under the chart. Ask: *Do you agree with the prediction about Max? Is it logical? Why?* (He loves children, so he'll probably have a big family.)

- Have students work individually to write the sentences.

- Play the recording. Students listen and verify their answers.

Audio script
Same as the sentences in the Student's Book.

- Check answers with the class. Invite volunteers to read their answers to the class.

- **Optional** Ask students to make follow-up predictions about each of the people in the sentences. Say: *Max will probably have a big family. They'll probably live in a big house or apartment.*

---

3 Pronunciation Contracted form of *will*

This exercise practices the contracted form of *will*.

A 💿 CD1, Track 23

- Remind students that in conversation *will* is usually contracted when it follows a pronoun so that the pronoun and *will* become one word. For example, *she will* becomes *she'll*.

- Play the recording. Students listen, paying particular attention to the contracted form of *will*.

Audio script
Same as the sentences in the Student's Book.

- Play the recording again, pausing after each sentence for students to repeat.

B

- Give students several minutes to practice saying the sentences they wrote in Exercise 2B, making sure they use the contracted form of *will*.

- Invite volunteers to say one of the sentences with the contracted form of *will*.

---

4 Speaking

This exercise practices future probability with *will probably / probably won't*.

- Have students read the directions and the example in the speech balloon.

- Have students work individually to write four things they will probably do or probably won't do before they are 25.

- Have students work in pairs to read their predictions to each other.

- Invite volunteers to tell the class their predictions. Encourage the class to ask follow-up questions.

  Classmate 1: *I'll probably get married.*

  Classmate 2: *Will you have a lot of children?*

- **Optional** In large classes, have students do this activity in groups of three or four.

Workbook
Assign the exercises on Workbook page 10. (Workbook answers begin on page T-192.)

Extra Grammar
Assign the exercises for the Extra Grammar, Lesson 6.

B Study the chart. Then read about Jen's classmates. What do you think they will probably do in the future? Write sentences. Then listen and check.

Future probability with *will probably / probably won't*	
I**'ll probably** live abroad.	I **probably won't** be famous.
You**'ll probably** get a great job.	She **probably won't** be famous.

1. Max loves children. (have a big family) <u>He'll probably have a big family.</u>
2. Alicia isn't a star. (be famous) <u>She probably won't be famous.</u>
3. Janet wants to study medicine. (go to college) <u>She'll probably go to college.</u>
4. Kate and Dave don't like animals. (get a pet) <u>They probably won't get a pet.</u>
5. Emma doesn't like to drive. (get a driver's license) <u>She probably won't get a</u> <u>driver's license.</u>
6. George likes to read about different countries. (travel abroad) <u>He'll probably</u> <u>travel abroad.</u>

3 Pronunciation   Contracted form of *will*

A Listen. Notice how contracted forms of *will* are pronounced. Then listen again and practice.

I will probably travel to England.	I'll probably travel to England.

She will probably be a good writer.	She'll probably be a good writer.

B Practice the sentences you wrote in Exercise 2B.

4 Speaking

Write four things you will probably do or probably won't do before you are 25. Use the cues in Exercise 1B or your own ideas. Tell your classmates. *(Answers will vary.)*

1. _____
2. _____
3. _____
4. _____

> I'll probably travel abroad. I probably won't get married.

Mini-review

1 Language check

A Look at the pictures from a class yearbook. Then write two sentences about each person. Use *will probably* and *probably won't*.

Ben Taylor

Ben is a great guitar player. He doesn't like to study.

Cho Park

Cho loves children. She doesn't like to travel abroad.

Javier Lopez

Javier doesn't like drama class. He loves cars.

Carolyn Davis

Carolyn doesn't like animals. She's a very good student.

Lucy Romero

Lucy likes to write. She doesn't like the news.

Bert Talbot

Bert doesn't like school. He likes to cook.

1. Ben (be a famous rock star / go to college)
   Ben will probably be a famous rock star.
   He probably won't go to college.

2. Cho (become a teacher / go to Spain on vacation)
   Cho will probably become a teacher.
   She probably won't go to Spain on vacation.

3. Javier (become an actor / get his driver's license next year)
   Javier probably won't become an actor.
   He'll probably get his driver's license next year.

4. Carolyn (get a cat or a dog / win a prize at graduation)
   Carolyn probably won't get a cat or a dog.
   She'll probably win a prize at graduation.

5. Lucy (write books / work for a news magazine)
   Lucy will probably write books.
   She probably won't work for a news magazine.

6. Bert (be a teacher / open a restaurant)
   Bert probably won't be a teacher.
   He'll probably open a restaurant.

This lesson reviews the language presented and practiced in Lessons 5 and 6.

1 Language check

This exercise reviews the structures presented so far in this unit.

A

- Focus students' attention on the photos and their captions. Ask a few questions, such as *Who loves cars?* (Javier Lopez.) *Does Carolyn like animals?* (No, she doesn't.)

- Focus students' attention on the example sentences. Explain that the captions give the reasons for the answers. (Ben will probably be a famous rock star because he is a great guitar player.)

- Invite a volunteer to read aloud the second example sentence about Ben. Elicit the reason for the answer. (Ben probably won't go to college because he doesn't like to study.)

- Have students work individually to write sentences about the other people with *will probably* and *probably won't*.

- Have students work in pairs to read their answers.

- Check answers with the class. Invite several pairs to read their answers aloud.

> **Teaching Tip**
> When you think an exercise might be challenging for some students, have students do the exercise in pairs. Pair stronger students with weaker ones. Such pairing helps weaker students keep up with the lesson. Stronger students benefit from having to explain language to a classmate.

B

- Have students look at the photos. Explain that the photos illustrate predictions for the future.
- Give students several minutes to think of two predictions for each photo, one with *will* and one with *won't*. Possible predictions:

  First photo: *We'll use our fingerprints to get money. We won't use money.*

  Second photo: *We'll speak to our computers. We won't have to type the words.*

  Third photo: *Cars will drive by themselves. We won't drive ourselves.*

  Fourth photo: *We'll have robot dogs. We won't have real dogs.*

  Fifth photo: *Older people will play a lot of sports. Older people won't become weak.*

- Have students read the directions.
- Focus students' attention on the example in the first text. Ask: *Why do we use* won't*?* (Because this is a negative prediction.)
- Have students read the texts and find out whether the predictions in the texts are similar to the predictions they thought of.

- Have students work individually to complete the texts with the correct form of *will* and *won't*.
- Check answers with the class.
- **Optional** Explain that you will read aloud the complete texts, but now and again you will make a mistake. Students have to listen and call out *Wrong!* when you make a mistake. Read the completed texts. Make a mistake every three or four blanks. For example, say: *People won't use money or credit cards anymore. Special machines will read our fingerprints. We won't pay for things that way.* At this point, the class should call out *Wrong!*

Teaching Tip Vary the way in which you check answers to exercises so that procedures do not become too predictable. The technique suggested above works well with exercises in which checking answers involves reading aloud a rather long text or set of sentences.

2 Listening

In this exercise, students listen for predictions and decide if the speaker agrees or disagrees with the predictions.

CD1, Track 24

- Tell students they will listen to a boy and a girl talking about more predictions for the future. The girl talks about whether she thinks the predictions will come true. For each statement, students should listen and check the box under *Agree* or *Disagree*.
- Have students read the directions and the four predictions.
- Focus students' attention on prediction 1. Ask: *Do you think Kim will agree with this prediction? Why? Why not?* Elicit as many answers as possible. Follow the same procedure with the other three predictions.
- Play the recording. Students only listen.

Audio script
See page T-206.

- Play the recording again. Students listen and check the correct boxes.

- Play the recording once again. Students listen and verify their answers.
- Check answers with the class. In each case, ask students if they remember the reason or reasons the predictions will or will not happen. (1. There will be too much traffic in the sky. 2. Houses will be easy to move. 3. Computers will help people speak many languages. 4. It's a crazy idea.)

Workbook
Assign the exercises on Workbook page 11. (Workbook answers begin on page T-192.)

Game
Assign the game on Student's Book page T-115.

B Read these interesting predictions students put on the Internet.
Complete the texts with the correct forms of *will* and *won't*.

Our Favorite Predictions from the Internet

1. People __won't__ use money or credit cards anymore. Special machines __will__ read our fingerprints. We __'ll__ pay for things that way. –*Lisa*

2. We __won't__ have to type on computers. Instead, we __'ll__ say the words, and the computer __will__ type them. –*Andrea*

3. Cars __will__ drive themselves. We __'ll__ just tell the cars where to go. So kids my age __will__ be able to drive. –*Sam*

4. I __'ll__ have a pet robot dog. I __won't__ have to feed it, and I __won't__ have to walk it. The dog __will__ only need batteries! –*Justin*

5. People __will__ live longer, and they __'ll__ be active longer. People __won't__ get sick anymore. There __will__ be many more ways to cure sickness. –*Grace*

2 Listening

Students talk about other predictions. Does Kim agree or disagree with these predictions? Listen and check (✓) the correct boxes.

	Agree	Disagree
1. People will travel from place to place in small airplanes.	☐	✓
2. People will take their houses with them when they move.	✓	☐
3. People won't need to learn foreign languages.	✓	☐
4. People won't need to cook.	☐	✓

Go to page 115 for the Game.

The Future **21**

Teen Center

1 Word power

A What activities are these students going to do at the Teen Center?
Listen and practice.

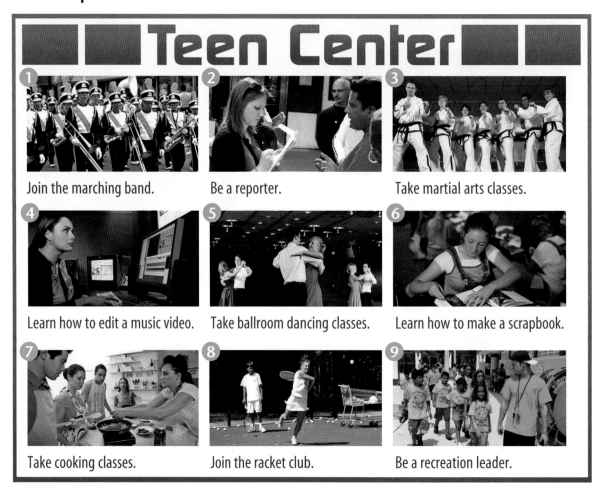

Teen Center

1. Join the marching band.
2. Be a reporter.
3. Take martial arts classes.
4. Learn how to edit a music video.
5. Take ballroom dancing classes.
6. Learn how to make a scrapbook.
7. Take cooking classes.
8. Join the racket club.
9. Be a recreation leader.

B Write each activity in Part A next to the correct description.

1. Students will need their own video cameras. _Learn how to edit a music video._
2. Learn how to make all kinds of food. _Take cooking classes._
3. Learn the rumba and the samba. Please sign up with a partner. _Take ballroom dancing classes._
4. Learn karate and judo with your friends. _Take martial arts classes._
5. Be in the school parade. Play in competitions. _Join the marching band._
6. Play tennis and badminton. Beginner students are welcome. _Join the racket club._
7. Write articles for the school newspaper. _Be a reporter._
8. Bring your favorite photos to class. _Learn how to make a scrapbook._
9. Play games with young children. Have fun. _Be a recreation leader._

Lesson 7 | Teen Center

This lesson presents and practices the names of some activities offered at a teen center and future possibility with might / might not.

> ### Review of Lesson 6
> - Remind students of the Speaking exercise at the end of Lesson 6. Give students a few minutes to write three sentences about what their classmates said they will probably do before they are 25.
> - Invite volunteers to read aloud one of the sentences they wrote. The students that the sentences are about say whether the sentences are right or wrong. They should correct wrong sentences.
>
>   Classmate 1: *Fred will probably get married before he's 25.*
>   Fred: *That's wrong. I probably won't get married before I'm 25.*

1 Word power

This exercise introduces and practices the names of some activities offered at a teen center.

A CD1, Track 25

- Give students several minutes to read the directions and look at the photos. Explain the meaning of *teen center*. Ask students if their school or town has a teen center. Also ask students if they have spent any time at a teen center. If so, what did they do there?
- Have students read the nine teen center activities.
- Point to a photo on the Teen Center poster. Students respond with the appropriate activity.
- Play the recording. Students listen and repeat.

> **Audio script**
> Same as the captions in the Student's Book.

B

- Have students read the directions and the example. Ask: *What should you do?* (Write each activity in Part A next to the correct description.)
- Focus students' attention on description 1. Ask: *Which words in the description tell you which activity goes in the blank?* (Video cameras.)
- Have students work individually to complete the activity.
- Check answers with the class. Invite volunteers to read one of the descriptions they completed. They should say which word(s) helped them find the right activities. (2. Food. 3. Rumba, samba. 4. Karate, judo. 5. School parade, competitions. 6. Tennis, badminton. 7. Articles, school newspaper. 8. Photos. 9. Play games, have fun.)

> **Culture Note**
> Teen centers are popular throughout the U.S., especially in larger cities where outdoor activities can be limited by crime, bad weather, or lack of parks or recreational areas. The centers offer teens a safe and positive environment to meet new friends, participate in fun and interesting activities, get help with homework, and even find part-time jobs.

2 Language focus

This exercise presents and practices future possibility with *might / might not*.

A 🔊 CD1, Track 26

- Have students read the directions and look at the photo.

- Have students read the conversation to find out the Teen Center activities Pam and Marla talk about. (Take ballroom dancing classes, take martial arts classes, be a reporter, be a recreation leader.)

- **Optional** Play the recording. Students listen and read along.

Audio script

Same as the conversation in the Student's Book.

- Ask: *Are Pam and Marla sure about what they're going to do, or are they still thinking about it?* (They're still thinking about it.) *Who would like to take ballroom dancing classes?* (Pam.) *Does she have a lot of time for that?* (No.) *Why not?* (She's really busy this year.) *What two possibilities is Marla thinking about?* (Taking a martial arts class or being a reporter.) *What other possibility is Pam thinking about?* (Being a recreation leader.) *Why?* (She wants to help out at the center.)

- Have students read the conversation again and underline four sentences about possibilities. (My friends and I might take ballroom dancing classes. I might not have time. I might take martial arts classes or be a reporter for the center's newspaper. I might be a recreation leader.)

- Play the recording or model the conversation. Students listen and repeat.

- **Optional** Have students practice in pairs.

Teaching Tip Use the context to highlight the meaning of the new language and guide students so that they find examples of the new language by themselves. This discovery process helps them understand and remember the new language.

- **Language Chart** Have students study the examples in the language chart. Ask: *Which word shows the speaker is still thinking about the possibility of taking ballroom dancing classes?* (Might.) *Which word do you add to make a negative statement?* (Not.)

- Focus students' attention on the contraction at the bottom of the chart. Explain that *maybe I'll* is short for *maybe I will*, which is another more casual way to show future possibility.

- **Optional** Model the examples, pausing for students to repeat.

B 🔊 CD1, Track 27

- Ask students to read the directions and the e-mail.

- Read these sentences aloud. Students tell you whether they are true or false.

   Juan is sure about which activities he's going to do at the Teen Center. (False.)

   He's thinking about three different possibilities. (True.)

   He has a partner for ballroom dancing classes. (False.)

   He knows Diana has a lot of free time. (False.)

   Juan won't have a lot of free time next week. (True.)

- Have students work individually to complete the e-mail.

- Play the recording. Students listen and verify their answers.

Audio script

Same as the e-mail in the Student's Book.

- Check answers with the class. Invite volunteers to read aloud one answer each.

3 Listening

In this exercise, students listen for ten teenagers' possible future plans.

🔊 CD1, Track 28

- Have students read the directions and items 1–5. Ask: *How many people will you listen to?* (Ten.) *What are they talking about?* (The activities they might or might not do.) *What should you write next to the names?* (Might or might not.)

- Play the recording. Students only listen.

Audio script

See page T-206.

- Play the recording again. Students listen and write *might* or *might not* next to the names.

- Play the recording once again. Students listen and verify their answers.

- Check answers with the class. Invite volunteers to read aloud the answers they wrote.

- To finish, invite volunteers to tell the class about activities they might do this year. They can use ideas from this lesson or their own ideas.

Workbook

Assign the exercises on Workbook page 12. (Workbook answers begin on page T-192.)

Extra Grammar

Assign the exercises for the Extra Grammar, Lesson 7.

2 Language focus

Future possibility with *might / might not*

My friends and I **might** take ballroom dancing classes.
I **might not** have time.

I might = maybe I'll

A Pam and Marla talk about what they will do at the Teen Center. Listen and practice.

Pam Hi, Marla. Are you going to sign up for any activities at the Teen Center?

Marla Sure. I'm trying to decide what to do.

Pam Me, too. My friends and I might take ballroom dancing classes, but I'm really busy this year. I might not have time.

Marla I want to do something new this year. I'm not sure what to do. I might take martial arts classes or be a reporter for the center's newspaper.

Pam Hmm. I'd like to help out at the center. I might be a recreation leader. They play games with young kids. Why don't you do that, too? We can work together.

Marla Well, I'm not very good with young children.

Pam Oh, sure you are, Marla. It'll be a lot of fun.

B Juan writes an e-mail to his friend Mark. What might he do this year? Complete the sentences with *might* or *might not*. Then listen and check.

Hi, Mark!

How are you? I'm fine. This year is going to be fun. I'm going to do some things at the Teen Center. I'm not sure what I'll do. I ___might___ take martial arts classes, or I ___might___ learn how to edit a music video. I'd like to take ballroom dancing classes, but I don't have a partner. I'm shy, but I ___might___ ask another student to join me. I'd like to ask Diana, but she's really busy, so she _might not_ have time.

Next week, I'm also going to be very busy – with school! I won't have a lot of free time, so I _might not_ e-mail you. Anyway, have a great week.

–Juan

3 Listening

Listen to the conversations. Who might do the activities? Who might not? Write *might* or *might not* for each student.

1. take cooking classes	Amy	_might_	Sam	_might not_
2. join the marching band	José	_might not_	Anna	_might not_
3. learn how to edit a music video	Staci	_might_	John	_might not_
4. learn how to make a scrapbook	Felicia	_might not_	Laura	_might not_
5. be a reporter	Paul	_might_	James	_might not_

After high school

1 Language focus

A What are these students' plans after high school? Match the first sentence to the rest of the text. Then listen and practice.

Simon, 15, China	Moira, 17, Ireland	Andrea, 16, Argentina
I'll travel for a couple of months. _2_	After high school, I'm going to go to college. _3_	I won't go to college right after high school. _1_

1 I'm going to get a job and make some money. I might get a job at an international hotel. I'll probably have to use my English.

2 I'll go with two friends. We'll probably go to the U.S. and Canada first. If we have time, we might backpack around Europe.

3 I'll probably go to City College. I might study computer programming, or I might study history. I can't decide.

B Study the chart. Then read the statements. Check (✓) D (definite plans) or P (probable / possible plans). Then listen and check.

> **Definite plans with *will* and *be going to* / Probable plans with *will probably* / Possible plans with *might***
>
> I**'ll** travel for a couple of months.   We**'ll probably** go to the U.S.
> I**'m going to** go to college.   I **might** study computer programming.

	D	P
1. Simon is going to take a trip.	✓	☐
2. Simon will travel with friends.	✓	☐
3. Simon will probably visit the U.S.	☐	✓
4. Moira will go to college.	✓	☐
5. Moira might study computer programming.	☐	✓
6. Andrea will make some money.	✓	☐
7. Andrea will probably use her English.	☐	✓
8. Andrea might work at a hotel.	☐	✓

After high school

This lesson contrasts and practices will, (be) going to, will probably, *and* might *for future plans and presents and practices verb phrases related to activities people do after graduating from high school.*

Review of Lesson 7
The grammar introduced in Lesson 7 is reviewed in the Language focus below.

1 Language focus

This exercise contrasts and practices definite plans with *will* and *(be) going to*, probable plans with *will probably*, and possible plans with *might*.

A 💿 CD1, Track 29

- Focus students' attention on the photos and the sentences. Ask students to cover the numbered texts.

- Explain that Simon, Moira, and Andrea are talking about their plans for the future. Have students read the sentences under the photos. Ask: *Who might talk about studying and careers?* (Moira.) *Who might talk about countries and interesting places to visit?* (Simon.) *What might Andrea talk about?* (What she's going to do between high school and college.)

- Have students read the texts and match the first sentences to the rest of the texts.

- Check answers with the class. Invite volunteers to say which words and phrases in the texts helped them match the texts to their respective first sentences.

- Play the recording. Students listen and repeat.

Audio script
Same as the texts in the Student's Book.

B 💿 CD1, Track 30

- **Language Chart** Have students study the examples in the language chart. Ask: *What's the difference between the plans in the left-hand column and the plans in the right-hand column?* (The plans on the left are definite. The plans on the right are probable or possible.)

- Draw students' attention to the words *probable* and *possible*. Explain that *probable* means that it is likely or that there is a good chance that a plan or an event will happen. *Possible* indicates that it is less likely that a plan or an event will happen.

- **Optional** Model the examples, pausing for students to repeat.

- Have students read the directions and sentences 1–8. Ask: *Are all the sentences about plans?* (Yes.) *Are all the plans definite?* (No. Some are probable or possible.) *What should you do?* (If the plans are definite, check the box in the D column. If they are probable or possible, check the box in the P column.)

- Have students work individually to check the correct boxes.

- Play the recording. Students listen and verify their answers.

Audio script
See page T-207.

- Check answers with the class. Read the future plans. Students call out *D* or *P.*

Culture Note
In the year 2000, nearly 2,600,000 students were enrolled as seniors in high schools across the U.S. Of those enrolled seniors, 91.5 percent graduated. Of those graduating students, 65.9 percent went on to study at a two- or four-year college; 8.1 percent went on to enroll in technical programs; and the remaining 26 percent either joined the military, went to work, traveled, or had not yet decided what to do with their lives.

C ⊙ CD1, Track 31

- Have students read the directions and the conversation.
- Have students find a sentence that introduces Will's probable or possible plans. (I'm not sure.) Ask: *What are his probable or possible plans?* (Go to college, visit Spain.) Ask: *How does Diana plan to make some money?* (Help her mom with chores.) *Is she sure her mom will pay?* (No.) *How do you know?* (She says, "I hope so.")

Teaching Tip ....
Before having students complete an exercise, check that they understand the content. You can do this by asking specific questions, by giving students *True / False* statements about the content, or simply by asking students to tell you what is going on in the conversation or text.

- Ask: *Which expressions can you use for probable or possible plans?* (Might, I'll probably.) *How do you know which one to use?* (If *I* appears before a blank, you should use *might*. If not, you should use *I'll probably*.)
- Ask: *Which expressions do you use for definite plans?* (Will, going to.) *How do you know which one to use?* (If *I* or *you* and a form of the verb *be* appears before a blank, you should use *going to*. If not, you should use *will*.)

- Have students work individually to complete the conversation.
- Play the recording. Students listen and verify their answers.

Audio script
Same as the conversation in the Student's Book

- Check answers with the class. Invite volunteers to read aloud one of the sentences they completed.
- **Optional** Have students practice the conversation in pairs.

Teaching Tip ....
Part C of the Language focus in this lesson involves repeated shifts in focus, from meaning to form and vice versa. In these cases, make sure you help students decide when to focus on meaning and when to focus on form. The teacher's questions suggested in these teacher's notes serve this purpose.

2 Word power

This exercise presents and practices verb phrases related to future plans students might have after graduating from high school.

- Have students read the directions, the verb phrases in the box, and the column headings. Ask students to call out any words or phrases they do not understand. Explain them by using them in sentences or by miming them.
- Have students work individually to complete the columns.

- Check answers with the class. Write the three headings on the board and invite volunteers to come to the board to write a verb phrase under one of the headings. Then invite other volunteers to say one of the extra verb phrases they wrote.

3 Speaking

This exercise practices *will*, *(be) going to*, *will probably*, and *might* for future plans.

- Have students read the directions and sentence beginnings 1–6. Ask: *Which beginnings are for definite plans?* (1, 2, 5, and 6.) *Which ones are for probable or possible plans?* (3 and 4.)
- Have students work individually to complete the sentences with ideas from Exercise 2 or their own ideas.
- Divide the class into groups of three to share their completed sentences with one another.
- **Optional** Have students work in groups of four or five. Hand out six slips of paper to each student in each group. Students write each of their six completed sentences on the slips of paper, but they do not write their names on the slips. Have one student collect all the slips and mix them up. Students take turns reading the slips of paper and then guessing who in the group wrote each sentence.

Workbook
Assign the exercises on Workbook page 13. (Workbook answers begin on page T-192.)

Extra Grammar
Assign the exercises for the Extra Grammar, Lesson 8.

C Will and Diana talk about their plans after high school.
Complete the conversation with *will, (be) going to, I'll probably,*
or *might.* Then listen and check.

Will So, what are you _going to_ do after high school?

Diana Well, first I'm _going to_ take a long vacation.

Will _Will_ you go to college someday?

Diana Yes, definitely. What are you _going to_ do
after high school?

Will I'm not sure. I _might_ go to college,
or I _might_ visit Spain. So _I'll probably_
take Spanish lessons.

Diana Great! I can help you with Spanish. How are
you _going to_ pay for the lessons?

Will Well, my dad is very busy in his store.
I'll probably help him. He's _going to_
pay me.

Diana Great idea! I really need money, too. I'm
going to ask my mom if I can help
her with chores at home. She _might_
pay me. I hope so.

2 Word power

Write the verb phrases in the correct columns. Then write one more verb
phrase in each column. *(The order of the answers may vary.)*

☐ get a job   ☐ make money   ☐ take English classes
☐ go around the world ☐ see the U.S.   ☐ take a trip to Europe
☑ go to college   ☐ study computer programming   ☐ work in an office

School	Travel	Work
go to college	go around the world	get a job
study computer programming	see the U.S.	make money
take English classes	take a trip to Europe	work in an office
(Answers will vary.)	(Answers will vary.)	(Answers will vary.)

3 Speaking

What are you going to do after high school? Complete the sentences with the verb
phrases from Exercise 2 or your own ideas. Then share your plans with three classmates.
(Answers will vary.)

1. I'm going to _____ .
2. I'm not going to _____ .
3. I might _____ .
4. I'll probably _____ .
5. I'll _____ .
6. I won't _____ .

Get Connected

Read

A Read the Web site quickly. Check (✓) one thing the Web site does *not* talk about.

- ☐ a flying car
- ☐ electricity from the sun
- ☐ newspapers
- ☐ medicines
- ☑ virtual reality glasses

An Exciting Future

"First **Flying** Car Made," say the newspaper **headlines**! Do we have flying cars today? No, we don't. But in the future, that might be a newspaper headline. However, we probably won't have newspapers in the future. We'll get all our news on video cell phones.

So what will our world look like 10, 20, or 50 years from now? One Web site makes predictions about the future and writes articles about the future. Its prediction for August 23, 2025, reads: *The first hotel on the moon finally opens*. But predictions about the future are difficult. Will people go to the moon for their vacations? They might. Will we find new **medicines** and **cure** terrible sicknesses? We probably will. Will our homes use electricity from the sun and wind? Yes, they will. And *we* won't clean our houses – robots will do this – and cars won't need **gas** anymore.

We don't know these things for sure. But one thing is **certain** . . . our lives in the future will be different from now. And that's very exciting!

Go to page 122 for the **Vocabulary Practice**.

B 🔊 Read the Web site slowly. Check your answer in Part A.

C Circle the correct words to complete the sentences or the correct answers.

1. In the future we probably won't have (**newspapers**)/ video cell phones / new medicines).

2. A headline for 2025 predicts we will have (flying cars / terrible sicknesses / **hotels on the moon**).

3. In the future our homes will get electricity from (**the sun and wind**)/ the moon / robots).

4. In the future we won't (drive our cars /**clean our homes**)/ use medicines).

5. Will our lives be different in the future? (Yes, probably. / No. Not at all. / **Yes, they will.**)

This lesson practices reading, listening, and writing skills.

Review of Lesson 8
* Write on the board:

  Definite plan: (will) _____

                         ([be] going to)_____

  Probable plan: (will probably) _____

  Possible plan: (might) _____

* Invite volunteers to come to the board to write one sentence each to illustrate the use of the words in parentheses to talk about plans.

* On one side of a slip of paper, have students write three sentences: one about a definite plan, one about a probable plan, and one about a possible plan. On the other side, they should write their name.

* Collect all the slips of paper, and put them in a bag. Invite volunteers to pick a slip from the bag and read the sentences, but not who wrote them. The class guesses who wrote the sentences.

Read

This exercise practices reading for information about the future.

A

* Have students read the title of the Web site and look at the photos. Ask: *Do these photos show things happening in the future or now?* (In the future.)

Culture Note
      The spacecraft in the photo is one being developed by a company called Virgin Galactic owned by entrepreneur Richard Branson. He plans to be the first person to offer tourists trips into space. However, the first spaceships will only go to the edge of space, the boundary between the earth's atmosphere and space. They will not go into orbit around Earth. The flights will last about 2.5 hours. At the highest point, passengers will experience weightlessness for about six minutes and be able to float around the cabin.

* Invite a volunteer to read aloud the directions and the five items. Remind students that they should read quickly to find the answers and that they should not read every word carefully.

* Have students work individually to read the Web site quickly and check the one thing the Web site does not talk about. Do not check the answer at this point.

B 💿 CD1, Track 32

* Invite a volunteer to read the directions aloud. Remind students that they should read slowly and carefully, and concentrate on getting the meaning of the entire text.

* List the new vocabulary words on the board: *flying, headline, medicine, cure (v.), gas, certain.* Explain their meaning. (Flying: moving through the air, like a bird or a plane; headline: the title of a newspaper article set in large type; medicine: a drug used to treat an illness; cure [v.]: to make you well; gas: gasoline used in cars to make them go; certain: sure to happen.) As an alternative, have students use their dictionaries to find the meanings of the new vocabulary words.

* Have students read the Web site again.

* Have students check their answer in Part A in pairs. Elicit the answer from one pair. Ask the pair to read the one thing the Web site does not talk about.

* **Optional** Play the recording. Students listen and read along.

Audio script
Same as the Web site in the Student's Book.

Get Connected Vocabulary
Have students do the exercise on Student's Book page 122 in class or for homework. (Get Connected Vocabulary answers are on page T-122.)

C

* Invite a volunteer to read the directions and first sentence aloud.

* Have students work individually to circle the correct words to complete the sentences or the correct answers.

* Check answers with the class. Invite volunteers to read aloud one answer each.

Listen

In this exercise, students listen for ideas about what the future will be like.

A 💿 CD1, Track 33

- Focus students' attention on the photos. Ask: *Who's in the photo?* (A man and a robot.)
- Tell students that they will listen to two friends, Rosa and Jeff, talk about how robots and computers will make our lives different in the future.
- Have students read the first statement and the example answer.
- Explain that students should listen to the conversation and write *True* or *False* for each statement. Tell students not to correct the false statements at this stage.
- Play the recording. Students only listen.

> **Audio script**
> See page T-207.

- Play the recording again. Students listen and write *True* or *False*.
- Check answers with the class. Invite a volunteer to read his or her answers aloud.

- Tell students that they should now correct the false statements. If necessary, play the recording to help them.
- Play the recording once again. Students listen and verify their answers.
- Check answers with the class. Invite volunteers to read their answers aloud.

B

- Have students read the directions and the questions.
- Read the first question with the class and elicit answers from several students. Remind students that there are no right or wrong answers for this exercise – they are giving their opinions.
- Have students work individually to answer the questions, and give reasons for their answers.
- Have students work in pairs to compare answers, or elicit opinions from volunteers.

....

Write

In this exercise, students complete a word web and write an article about their predictions for the future.

A

- Invite a volunteer to read the directions aloud.
- Focus students' attention on the example word web about cars. Ask: *What does this person predict about cars in the future?* Elicit answers based on the information in the word web. (They will fly; they won't use gas; they won't be very big; they will be made of plastic.) Point out that in a word web, students should write only words or phrases, not complete sentences.
- Have students work individually to choose a topic and create a word web for it.
- **Optional** Have students compare their word web with the word web of another student who chose the same topic.

B

- Invite a volunteer to read the directions aloud. Tell students that they will use the word web they created in Part A to help them write about their predictions for the future.
- Have students work individually to write their articles.
- Invite several volunteers to read their articles to the class.
- **Optional** Have students work in groups of four and read each other's articles. Then have each group report two of its predictions to the class. Write these on the board. Ask the class to rate the predictions from 1 to 5 using this scale: 1 = It won't happen. 2 = It probably won't happen. 3 = It might happen. 4 = It probably will happen. 5 = It will happen.

> **Workbook**
> Assign the exercises on Workbook page 14.
> (Workbook answers begin on page T-192.)

Computers will . . .

A 🔊 **Rosa and Jeff talk about the future. Listen and write** *True* **or** *False*.
Then correct the false statements.

1. Rosa wants to go to the movies with Jeff.
   True.

2. Jeff and Rosa think that robots won't do students' homework
   in the future. *False.*   *Jeff and Rosa think that robots will*
   do students' homework in the future.

3. A magazine article says that computers won't be amazing.
   False.   *A magazine article says that computers will be amazing.*

4. In the future computers will type what people are thinking.
   True.

5. Someday people will connect computers to their brains.
   True.

B **What do you think? Answer the questions. Give reasons.** *(Answers will vary.)*

1. Would you like robots to do anything for you? What? _____

2. Do you think computers will be smarter than people? _____

3. Do you think computers will be able to type what we are thinking in the future?
   _____

4. Would you like to connect a computer to your brain? _____

Your turn

A **What do you think the future will be like? Write** *clothes, computers, food,*
houses, **or** *schools* **to start a web about your own predictions.** *(Answers will vary.)*

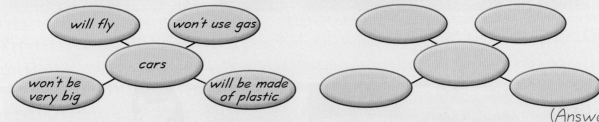

(Answers will vary.)

B **Write an article about your future predictions. Use the web in Part A to help you.**

In the future, . . .

_____

_____

_____

Language chart review

Future with *will* and *won't*

Robots **will** be very smart.
They**'ll** be powerful.
They **won't** think for us.
Will robots have feelings?
Yes, they **will.** / **No,** they **won't.**

Future probability with *will probably* / *probably won't*

I**'ll probably** drive a small car.
I **probably won't** ride a bicycle.

Future possibility with *might* / *might not*

I **might** work at Leo's Drugstore this year.
I **might not** have much free time.

A Look at the pictures. Write sentences with the verb phrases in the box.
Use *probably* or *might* to make guesses about future probability.

☐ drink the milk / drink orange juice
☐ go out in those shoes / wear her other shoes
☐ go to the movie / go to a café
☑ ride his bike / walk to school

1. *He won't ride his bike. He'll*
   probably walk to school.

2. *They won't drink the milk. They'll*
   probably / They might drink the orange juice.

3. *They won't go to the movie. They'll*
   probably / They might go to a café.

4. *She won't go out in those shoes. She'll*
   probably / She might wear her other shoes.

Unit 2 Review

This lesson reviews the grammar and vocabulary introduced in Unit 2.

Language chart review

These charts summarize the main grammar presented and practiced in Unit 2.

- Books closed. Write on the board:

Future with <u>will</u> and <u>won't</u>	*Future probability with <u>will</u> <u>probably</u> / <u>probably won't</u>*	*Future possibility with <u>might</u> / <u>might not</u>*

- Focus students' attention on the headings on the board.
- Invite volunteers to give sentence examples of each of the structures. Write appropriate examples in the correct sections of the charts.
- Books open. Have students compare the examples on the board with the examples in the Language chart review. Ask if the examples on the board are all correct. Have the class suggest how to make any necessary corrections.
- Focus students' attention on the contractions *I'll* and *won't*. Invite volunteers to give the full form. (I will; will not.)
- Answer any questions students may have.

....

Exercises A through D (pages T-28 to T-29)

Note: Students can do these exercises for homework or in class. They should do these exercises with minimal teacher input or help. If you choose to do these exercises as homework, briefly review the exercise directions in class. Make sure that students understand what they should do. Check the answers with the class during the next class meeting. If you choose to do the exercises in class, follow the directions below.

Exercise A

- Have students read the directions and the example sentences.
- Focus students' attention on the pictures.

- Have students work individually to write sentences with the verb phrases in the box and *probably* or *might* to make guesses about future probability.
- Check answers with the class.

Exercise B

- Have students read the directions and the example question and answer.
- Have students work individually to write questions and answers with *will,* using the pictures in Exercise A.
- Check answers with the class. Invite pairs to read aloud one question and answer each.

Language chart review

This chart summarizes further grammar presented and practiced in Unit 2.

- Have students study the examples in the chart.
- Remind students they can use either *will* or *(be) going to* to talk about definite plans in the future. *Probably* indicates a plan is not definite, but probable. *Might* indicates a plan is possible and is the least definite of the three verb forms.
- Answer any questions students may have.

Exercise C

- Have students read the directions and the example.
- Have students work individually to match the two parts of each sentence to complete the conversation.
- Check answers with the class.

Exercise D

- Have students read the directions and the example.
- Have students work individually to write the questions from Exercise C and answer them with their own information.
- Check the questions with the class. Invite several pairs of volunteers to read the questions and answers aloud.

Take another look!

- Have a volunteer read the directions aloud.
- Students work individually to circle the correct answers.
- Check answers with the class.

Optional Unit Wrap-Up

- If students did the Review exercises for homework, check answers with the class.
- Have students look at the pictures in Exercise A again. Invite students to come up with additional ideas for what the people *will probably do* or *might do* in each situation. For example, in number 1, the boy might take the bus. Then have students ask and answer questions with *will* as in Exercise B. (*Will he take the bus? Yes, he will,* or *No, he won't.*)
- Have students work in pairs to ask and answer the questions in Exercise C.
- Have students work in pairs to ask and answer the questions in Exercise D with their own information.

Theme Project

- Assign the *At Home* section of the Unit 2 Theme Project on Student's Book page 127.

Workbook

- Assign the Unit 2 Check Yourself on Workbook page 15. (Workbook answers begin on page T-192.)

Extra Practice Worksheets

- Assign the Unit 2 Extra Practice worksheets starting on page T-143.

Extra Speaking Practice Worksheet

- Assign the Unit 2 Extra Speaking Practice worksheet on page T-169.

Arcade Activities

- Assign the Unit 2 Arcade Activities found at: www.cambridge.org/connectarcade

Learning Log

- Assign the Unit 2 Learning Log. This can be downloaded from the Teacher Support Site at: www.cambridge.org/connect2e/teacher

Quiz

- Give the Unit 2 Quiz on page T-179.

Test

- Give the Unit 2 Test (Form A and / or Form B). These can be downloaded from the Teacher Support Site at: www.cambridge.org/connect2e/teacher

B Look at the pictures in Part A again. Write questions with *will*.
Then answer the questions.

1. he / fix the bike

   Q: _Will he fix the bike?_

   A: _Yes, he will._

2. they / drink the milk

   Q: _Will they drink the milk?_

   A: _No, they won't._

3. they / go to a café

   Q: _Will they go to a café?_

   A: _Yes, they will._

4. she / wear other shoes

   Q: _Will she wear other shoes?_

   A: _Yes, she will._

Language chart review

> **Definite plans with *will* and *be going to* / Probable plans with *will probably* / Possible plans with *might***
>
> I'**ll study** tomorrow night. I'**m going to** stay up late.
> They'**ll probably** travel together.
> We **might** spend a week in Rio.

C Match the two parts of each sentence to complete the conversation.

A What are you going to do   _c_

B I'll probably go   _e_

A Do you think you'll be   _d_

B I don't think I'll make   _a_

A At what age do you think you'll get   _f_

B I might not get   _b_

a. a lot of money.

b. married at all.

c. after high school?

d. rich and famous?

e. to college to study medicine.

f. married?

D Write the questions from Part C. Then answer them with your
own information. (Answers will vary.)

1. **Q:** _What are you going to do after high school?_

   A: _____

2. **Q:** _____

   A: _____

3. **Q:** _____

   A: _____

Take another look!

Circle the correct answers.

1. Which sentence means the same as "I might learn French"?

   a. Maybe I'll learn French.   b. I'm going to learn French.

2. Which sentence talks about definite plans?

   a. I might not go swimming.   b. I won't go swimming.

Go to page 127
for the
Theme Project.

Weekend plans

1 Word power

A **Match each verb or verb phrase to its meaning. Then listen and practice.**

1. amaze _f_
2. come back _c_
3. expect _a_
4. explore _b_
5. head for _h_
6. rescue _g_
7. take off _e_
8. try out _d_

a. think that something will happen
b. travel around a place to learn about it
c. return
d. test something by using it
e. leave the ground and start flying
f. surprise very much
g. save someone in danger
h. move toward a place

B **Complete the description of each weekend event with a pair of verbs or verb phrases in the box.**

- ☐ expect / try out   ☐ head for / amaze
- ☑ explore / rescue   ☐ take off / come back

① Go on a cave tour!

You can spend an exciting hour here! You can ___explore___ one of many caves. You'll probably see bats, and you might get lost. But don't worry, we'll ___rescue___ you.

Friday and Saturday
9:00 a.m. – 10:00 p.m.
Carl's Caves

② See a circus show!

At 2:00 p.m., ___head for___ the Big City Circus Tent and see the Flying Vitale Family. They will ___amaze___ you as they fly through the air on the trapeze.

Saturday and Sunday
2:00 p.m. and 8:00 p.m.
Big City Circus Tent

③ Visit Futureland!

Come to the grand opening of Futureland. Try our newest virtual reality ride – Rocket Ship. You'll ___take off___ , visit the moon, and never want to ___come back___ .

Sunday
9:00 a.m. – 11:00 p.m.
Futureland

Rocket Ship

④ Drive go-carts!

You can ___expect___ an exciting ride at Go-Carts Galore. First drive the latest go-carts on our superfast track. After that, you can ___try out___ our three brand-new racing tracks.

Saturday
4:00 p.m. to 9:00 p.m.
Go-Carts Galore

Lesson 9 Weekend plans

This lesson presents and practices some verbs and verb phrases related to weekend events and Would you like to . . . ? *for invitations.*

1 Word power

This exercise presents and practices verbs and verb phrases related to weekend events.

A 🔘 CD1, Track 34

- Give students several minutes to read the directions, the verbs or verb phrases, and the meanings.
- Tell students that they will match each of the verbs or verb phrases in the left-hand column to the appropriate meaning in the right-hand column.
- Have students work individually to match the verbs or verb phrases to their meanings.
- Have students check their answers in pairs.
- Check answers with the class. Invite volunteers to read their answers aloud.
- Play the recording. Students listen and repeat.

> **Audio script**
> See page T-208.

B

- Have students read through the texts quickly, look at the pictures, and say what the events have in common. (They're fun. They all take place on the weekend.)
- Explain to students that these are some popular weekend events for American teens. Ask students to talk about their favorite weekend events. Ask if any of the students have participated in the weekend events in Part B. Did they enjoy them? Why? Why not?
- Focus students' attention on event number 1. Ask: *How long does the tour take?* (An hour.) *What will you probably see?* (Bats.) *What might happen to you?* (You might get lost.) *What happens if you get lost?* (They'll rescue you.) *Where's the cave tour?* (At Carl's Caves.)
- Focus students' attention on number 2. Ask: *What's the name of the trapeze act?* (The Flying Vitale Family.) *At what times can you see the trapeze act?* (At 2:00 p.m. and 8:00 p.m.)

- Focus students' attention on event number 3. Ask: *What's the name of the virtual reality ride?* (Rocket Ship.) *What can you visit on this ride?* (The moon.)
- Focus students' attention on event number 4. Ask: *What's interesting about the track?* (It's superfast.) *How many new racing tracks are there?* (Three.) *How long can you stay on a Saturday?* (Five hours.)
- Have students work individually to complete each text with a pair of verbs or verb phrases in the box.
- Check answers with the class. Invite volunteers to read aloud one of the sentences they completed.
- **Optional** Have students work in groups of four to five to write their own descriptions of weekend events they enjoy, using some of the words in the box. Invite volunteers from each group to read their descriptions aloud. Take a vote to see which event students think would be the most fun.

> **Culture Note**
> Circus acts are often a family affair. One of the most famous circus families is the Flying Wallendas. They are high-wire or tightrope artists. Karl Wallenda began the act in 1922. He continued performing all his life. He was killed when he fell from the wire in 1978 at the age of 73. Today, several of Karl's grandchildren continue the Wallenda tradition. Another act, The Flying Tabares Family, performs on the flying trapeze. This act was created by two brothers, Nelson and Alberto Quiroga. They are the fourth generation of circus performers in their family. They perform with a small California circus called Circus Vargas.

This unit introduces vocabulary and expressions for making invitations and requests, asking permission, making hypotheses about the future, and describing future plans.

2 Language focus

This exercise presents and practices using *Would you like to . . . ?* for invitations.

A 💿 CD1, Track 35

- Ask students to read the directions and look at the photos. Ask: *What does Nina want to do?* (Go on the cave tour.)
- Have students read the conversation.
- **Optional** Play the recording. Students listen and read along.

> **Audio script**
> Same as the conversation in the Student's Book.

- *Ask: Does Becky accept the invitation the first time Nina asks?* (No.) *Why not?* (She has to babysit her little sister on Saturday morning.) *Does she accept when Nina invites her for Saturday afternoon?* (Yes.) *What does Becky invite Nina to do?* (See the Flying Vitale Family.) *When?* (On Sunday afternoon.) *Does Nina accept?* (Yes.)
- Play the recording or model the conversation. Students listen and repeat.
- **Optional** Have students practice in pairs.
- **Language Chart** Have students study the examples in the language chart. Focus students' attention on the top of the chart. Ask: *What form of the verb do you use after Would you like to . . . ? – the simple form or the -ing form?* (The simple form.)
- Focus students' attention on the bottom part of the chart. Ask: *How many ways of accepting are there?* (Two.) *How would you combine the words to make two more examples?* (Yes, I'd like to. Sure, I'd love to.) *Which are the expressions for refusing?* (I'm sorry, but I can't. I'd love to, but I can't.) Ask: *Is* I have to babysit *a prediction or a reason?* (It's a reason.)
- **Optional** Model the examples, pausing for students to repeat.

B 💿 CD1, Track 36

- Ask students to read the directions and the example. Ask: *Which words in the response tell you which event it is?* (The Flying Vitale Family.)
- Have students read the responses to numbers 2 and 3 and find the words that help determine which event it is. (2. Fast and exciting things. 3. Try the Rocket Ship.)
- Have students work individually to write the invitations for numbers 2 and 3. Remind them to use two different expressions.
- Play the recording. Students listen and verify their answers.

> **Audio script**
> Same as the questions and answers in the Student's Book.

C

- Have students work individually to write refusals to invitations 2 and 3 in Part B. Tell them to use a different refusal each time.
- Check answers to Parts B and C with the class. Invite groups of three volunteers to role-play one of the situations: Volunteer 1 makes the invitation, volunteer 2 accepts, and volunteer 3 refuses.

> **Teaching Tip**
> When an exercise has more than one part, it may be more effective to check the answers to two or more parts together. As in Parts B and C above, students can combine the language practiced in both parts to produce more meaningful and complex exchanges.

3 Speaking

This exercise practices extending an invitation with *Would you like to . . . ?*

- Give students a minute to think of three fun events they would like to participate in this weekend. Explain that they should write three invitations, one for each of the activities or events they thought of. For example: *Would you like to go shopping on Sunday?*
- Have students work individually to write their invitations.
- Focus students' attention on the example conversation. Have volunteers invite classmates to do things with them this weekend. Classmates may accept or refuse. Those who refuse should give a reason. When invitations are refused, volunteers continue inviting other classmates until someone accepts.

> **Workbook**
> Assign the exercises on Workbook page 16. (Workbook answers begin on page T-192.)

> **Extra Grammar**
> Assign the exercises for the Extra Grammar, Lesson 9.

2 Language focus

A Nina invites Becky to go on the cave tour.
Listen and practice.

Would you like to...? for invitations

Would you like to go on a cave tour?
Accepting: **Yes, I'd love to.**
            Sure, I'd like to.
Refusing: **I'm sorry, but I can't. I have to** babysit.
            I'd love to, but I can't.

Nina Hi, Becky. Would you like to go on the
cave tour with me on Saturday morning?
Becky Oh, Saturday morning? I'm sorry,
but I can't. I have to babysit my little sister.
Nina Well, would you like to go in the afternoon instead?
Becky Sure, I'd like to. But, uh, there might be bats in the cave.
They're scary.
Nina There are *supposed* to be bats in a cave! Come on, Becky.
It'll be fun.
Becky Well, OK. Oh! I almost forgot. My family is going
to see the Flying Vitale Family on Sunday afternoon.
Would you like to go with us?
Nina Wow! Yes, I'd love to. We're going to have a great
weekend. I can't wait.

B Write invitations to the events in Exercise 1B. Use the responses as
clues. Then listen and check.

1. *Would you like to see the circus show?*
   Yes, I'd love to. The Flying Vitale Family is amazing.

2. *Would you like to drive go-carts?*
   Sure, I'd like to. I like fast and exciting things.

3. *Would you like to visit Futureland?*
   Yes, I'd love to. I want to try the Rocket Ship.

C Now refuse invitations 2 and 3 in Part B. Use different expressions. *(Answers will vary.)*

1. _____
2. _____

3 Speaking

Invite classmates to do things with you this weekend. Write three
invitations. Then find a classmate who accepts each invitation. *(Answers will vary.)*

1. _____
2. _____
3. _____

You Would you like to go to a movie on Saturday afternoon?
Classmate 1 I'm sorry, but I can't. I have to study for a test.
You Would you like to go to a movie on Saturday afternoon?
Classmate 2 Sure, I'd love to.

Evening plans

1 Language focus

A Matt asks his mom some favors. Listen and practice.

Matt Hey, Mom. Could you buy me a new digital camera today? Mine is broken, and Alex wants me to take pictures at his party tonight.

Mrs. Hays No, I'm sorry. I can't, Matt.

Matt Oh, Mom. Well, can I stay out until 10:00?

Mrs. Hays Yes, all right. But be home at 10:00 sharp!

Matt OK. And, uh, can John sleep over after the party?

Mrs. Hays Sure, that's fine. But we have to get up early, remember? We're going to go visit Aunt Becky.

Matt Oh, yes! I forgot. And, um, Mom, could you lend me $15?

Mrs. Hays $15? No, I can't. Sorry.

B Study the chart. Complete the questions with *Can I* or *Could you*. Then listen and check.

Can / Could for permission and requests	
Asking permission	**Making requests**
Can I stay out until 10:00? **Yes, all right. / No, I'm sorry.**	**Could you** buy me a digital camera? **No, I'm sorry. I can't.**
Can John sleep over? **Sure, that's fine.**	**Could you** lend me $15? **Yes, of course. / No, I can't. Sorry.**
Note: Young children often use *can* for both permission and requests. *Can* may be used for requests, but it is less formal.	

1. _Can I_ borrow your favorite shirt?
2. _Could you_ buy me a pet for my birthday?
3. _Can I_ stay out late on Friday?
4. _Could you_ clean my room, please?
5. _Can I_ go to the movies this weekend?
6. _Can I_ sleep over at Ken's house tonight?
7. _Could you_ make my bed?

Lesson 10 Evening plans

This lesson presents and practices Can / Could for permission and requests.

Review of Lesson 9

- Write on the board the names of four movies playing in your area and the names of four interesting places to visit.
- Ask students to choose a movie and a place from the list.
- Explain that students will invite classmates to see the movie or go to the place they chose. Classmates who chose the same movie or place will accept the invitations. Those who did not will refuse and give an excuse.
- Invite three volunteers to model the task.

  A: *Would you like to see* Fast Cars?

  B: *I'm sorry, but I saw it yesterday.*

  A: *Would you like to go to the video arcade?*

  C: *Sure, I'd love to.*

- Have students take turns making, accepting, and refusing invitations.

1 Language focus

This exercise presents and practices *Can / Could* for permission and requests.

A 💿 CD1, Track 37

- Have students look at the picture and read the directions. Ask: *What should you read and listen for?* (What Matt's mother says when he asks her some favors.)
- Have students read the conversation.
- **Optional** Play the recording. Students listen and read along.

> **Audio script**
> Same as the conversation in the Student's Book.

- Ask: *Does Matt's mother say yes to the first favor he asks?* (No.) *What's wrong with the digital camera?* (It's broken.) *What time can Matt stay out until?* (10:00.) *Who are Matt and his mother going to visit?* (Aunt Becky.) *How much money does Matt want to borrow from his mother?* ($15.)
- Have students read Matt's part of the conversation again and underline the four questions Matt uses to ask some favors. (Could you buy me a new digital camera today? Can I stay out until 10:00? Can John sleep over after the party? Could you lend me $15?)
- Write *Ask for Permission / Make a Request* on the board. Explain to students that when you ask for permission, you are asking to be allowed to do something. When you make a request, you are asking for a favor or a privilege or for someone to do something.
- Play the recording or model the coversation. Students listen and repeat.
- **Optional** Have students practice in pairs.

B 💿 CD1, Track 38

- **Language Chart** Have students study the examples in the language chart. Focus students' attention on the left-hand side of the chart. Ask: *Which word is used to ask for permission?* (Can.) Explain that *can* does not change, regardless of the subject of the sentences. Ask: *What form of the verb is used after the subject?* (The simple form.)
- Focus students' attention on the right-hand side of the chart. Ask: *Which word is used to make requests?* (Could.) Explain that like *can, could* does not change, regardless of the subject of the sentences. Ask: *What form of the verb is used after the subject?* (The simple form.)
- Draw students' attention to the Note. Ask: *Who often uses* can *for both permission and requests?* (Young children.) *Which is less formal,* can *or* could? (Can.)
- **Optional** Model the examples, pausing for students to repeat.
- Have students work individually to complete the questions.
- Play the recording. Students listen and verify their answers.

> **Audio script**
> Same as the questions in the Student's Book.

- Check answers with the class. Ask: *Which questions ask for permission?* (1, 3, 5, and 6.) *What did you use to complete them?* (Can I.) *What about the others?* (They're requests.) *What did you use to complete them?* (Could you.)

C

- Have students read the directions and the questions in the survey. Ask: *Which of the questions ask for permission and which ones are requests?* (1, 2, 3, 4, 6, and 7 ask for permission; 5 and 8 are requests.) *What can you find out with this survey?* (If your parents are easygoing, average, or strict.) *What should you write first?* (Write the answers your parents would give to each question in the *Response* column.) *Can you write any answer?* (No. You have to choose one of the four answers

at the top of the survey.) *What should you do next?* (Write the points for each answer in the *Points* column, and then add them up. Then check the results at the bottom of the survey.)

- Have students work individually to take the survey.

- To finish, find out whether most of the students' parents are easygoing, average, or strict. To do this, ask for a show of hands for each of the categories.

---

2 Pronunciation *Could you*

This exercise practices the reduced form of *Could you*.

A 💿 CD1, Track 39

- Remind students that Americans often pronounce two words as one when they speak. In informal conversation, the pronunciation of *Could you* sounds like "couldja."

- Play the recording. Students listen, paying special attention to the pronunciation of *Could you*.

> **Audio script**
> Same as the questions in the Student's Book.

- Play the recording again. Students listen and repeat.

B

- Give students several minutes to practice saying the questions in Exercises 1B and 1C on pages 32–33, making sure they use the reduced form of *Could you*.

- Ask random students to say one of the questions they practiced, using the reduced form of *Could you*.

- **Optional** Before you move on to Part B, say some of the questions in Exercises 1B and 1C yourself. Use the full form for some of them and the reduced form for others. Students raise their right hand when they hear the reduced form and their left hand when they hear the full form.

---

3 Listening

In this exercise, students listen to teens asking for permission and making requests.

A 💿 CD1, Track 40

- Have students read the directions. Ask: *What are you going to listen to?* (Some teens talking to their parents.) *How many conversations are there?* (Four.) *What should you do?* (Decide whether the teens are asking for permission or making requests.)

- Play the recording. Students only listen.

> **Audio script**
> See page T-208.

- Play the recording again. Students listen and check the correct boxes.

- Play the recording once again. Students listen and verify their answers.

B 💿 CD1, Track 41

- Tell students you will play the recording again for them to write *Yes* or *No* next to numbers 1–4, depending on what they hear in the conversations.

- Play the recording. Students listen and write *Yes* or *No* next to the numbers.

> **Audio script**
> Same as the script in Part A.

- Check answers to Parts A and B with the class. Play the recording and pause after the first conversation. Ask: *Is the girl asking for permission or making a request?* (Asking for permission.) *What does she want to do?* (Have her friend sleep over.) *Does her mother say yes or no?* (She says "Yes.") *Why?* (She thinks it's a great idea, and they can all watch some movies together.) Follow the same procedure with the other conversations.

> **Workbook**
> Assign the exercises on Workbook page 17. (Workbook answers begin on page T-192.)

> **Extra Grammar**
> Assign the exercises for the Extra Grammar, Lesson 10.

C Read the survey. Which of the four responses would your parents give to each question? Complete the chart. Then total the points. Are your parents easygoing, average, or strict? *(Answers will vary.)*

Yes, of course. (1 point) 😀   No, I'm sorry. 😮 (3 points)

Maybe. 😊 Let me think about it. (2 points)   😔 Absolutely not. (4 points)

	Response	Points
1. Can I have a party at home this weekend?	_____	____
2. Can I watch TV tonight?	_____	____
3. Can I use your new DVD player?	_____	____
4. Can I go downtown with my friends now?	_____	____
5. Could you help me with my homework?	_____	____
6. Can I stay out until midnight tomorrow?	_____	____
7. Can I buy an electric guitar?	_____	____
8. Could you lend me $20?	_____	____

Total points: ☐

My parents are:

■ easygoing (8–16 points)   ■ average (17–24 points)   ■ strict (25–32 points)

2 Pronunciation *Could you*

A Listen. Notice how *Could you* is reduced in conversation. Then listen again and practice.

Could you close the door, please?   **Could you** lend me some money?

Could you help me?   **Could you** bring me some water, please?

B Now practice the *Could you* questions in Exercises 1B and 1C.

3 Listening

A Some teens talk to their parents. Are they asking permission or making requests? Listen and check (✓) Permission or Request.

	Permission	Request
1.	✓	☐
2.	☐	✓
3.	✓	☐
4.	✓	☐

B Listen again. Do their parents say yes or no? Write *Yes* or *No*.

1. _Yes_   2. _Yes_   3. _No_   4. _Yes_

Mini-review

1 Language check

A Match the questions to the correct responses.

1. Would you like to go out to eat? _c_
2. Could you help me make dinner? _d_
3. Would you like to play chess? _e_
4. Can I go to the mall tonight? _a_
5. Could you order a pizza? _b_

a. Yes, all right. But be back by 9:00.
b. Sure. What's the phone number?
c. I'm sorry, but I can't. I just ate.
d. Yes. I'll cut the vegetables.
e. I'd love to, but I can't. I don't know how to play.

B Write questions. Use the verb phrases in the box and *Would you like to, Can I,* or *Could you.*

☑ borrow your CD ☐ go shopping at the mall ☐ help me with this math problem
☐ come to my party ☐ have a cookie ☐ lend me your skateboard

1. **Q:** _Can I borrow your CD?_
   A: Yes, of course. But give it back to me tomorrow.

2. **Q:** _Could you lend me your skateboard?_
   A: Absolutely not. I want to go skateboarding today.

3. **Q:** _Would you like to come to my party?_
   A: Thanks. I'd love to come. Do you want me to bring anything?

4. **Q:** _Could you help me with this math problem?_
   A: Sure. Show it to me.

5. **Q:** _Would you like to go shopping at the mall?_
   A: No, I can't. Sorry. I have to finish my homework.

6. **Q:** _Would you like to have a cookie?_
   A: I'd love to. They look delicious.

C Read the invitations. Accept or refuse each one.
Use a different answer each time. (*Answers will vary.*)

1. **Q:** Would you like to study English with me tonight?
   A: _____

2. **Q:** Would you like to go swimming with me on Saturday?
   A: _____

3. **Q:** Would you like to go to the movies this weekend?
   A: _____

4. **Q:** Would you like to run in the park with me tomorrow?
   A: _____

This lesson reviews the language presented and practiced in Lessons 9 and 10.

1 Language check

This exercise reviews the structures presented so far in this unit.

A

- Have students read the directions, the questions, and the responses. Ask: *Which of the questions are invitations?* (1 and 3.) *Which one asks for permission?* (4.) *What are questions 2 and 5?* (Requests.)

- Have students work individually to match the questions to the correct responses.

- Check answers with the class. Ask pairs of students to read one of the questions and the correct response.

B

- Have students read the directions and the example question. Ask: *What should you do?* (Write questions for the responses using the verb phrases in the box.) *What should you use when the question is an invitation?* (Would you like to.) *What should you use for a request?* (Could you.) *What should you use* Can I *for?* (Permission.)

- Have students read the response to question 2. Ask: *Is the person who is asking the question offering something or asking to borrow something?* (Asking to borrow something.) *What does the person want to borrow?* (A skateboard.) Follow the same procedure with the rest of the responses.

- Have students work individually to write the questions.

- Check answers with the class. Ask several pairs of volunteers to read the questions and answers aloud.

C

- Have students read the directions. Ask: *Should you accept each invitation?* (No. You should refuse some of them.) *Should you use the same answer each time?* (No. You should use a different answer each time.)

- Have students work individually to write answers for each invitation.

- Check answers with the class. Ask several pairs of volunteers to read the questions and answers aloud.

- **Optional** Have students work in pairs. Have them choose one of the items in the exercise and extend the conversation. For example:

  A: *Would you like to go swimming with me on Saturday?*

  B: *I'd like to, but I can't. I have to visit my grandmother.*

  A: *Well, can you go on Sunday?*

  B: *Yes, I can.*

  A: *Great! Let's meet at one o'clock.*

D

- Invite a volunteer to read the directions and the first situation aloud. Ask: *Are you going to make a request or ask for permission?* (Ask for permission.)

- Have two students read the example conversation. Elicit that the example uses *Can I* because the person is asking for permission.

- Have students work individually to write the questions and answers. Point out that their answers may vary slightly. For example, to answer no, students could say *No, I'm sorry . . .* or *Absolutely not!*

- Check answers with the class.

- **Optional** Have students practice asking and answering the questions in pairs. Then have each pair create an original conversation to present to the class. The class should say if the conversation makes a request or asks for permission.

2 Listening

A CD1, Track 42

- Have students read the directions.

- Focus students' attention on the chart and the example answer. Play the first conversation. Ask: *What does Junko ask David?* (If he can go to the museum tomorrow night.) *Does David accept the invitation?* (No.) *Why not?* (He has a lot of homework to do.)

- Play the rest of the recording. Students only listen.

> **Audio script**
> See page T-208.

- Play the recording again. Students listen and check the correct boxes.

- Play the recording once again. Students listen and verify their answers.

B CD1, Track 43

- Have students read the directions and the example.

- Play the recording again. Students listen and write short answers.

- Check answers to Parts A and B with the class.

- **Optional** For Part B of this listening, invite students to write the answers to questions 2–4 in pencil *before* you play the recording. Then have students listen and verify their answers.

> **Audio script**
> Same as the script in Part A.

> **Workbook**
> Assign the exercises on Workbook page 18.
> (Workbook answers begin on page T-192.)

> **Game**
> Assign the game on Student's Book page 116.

D Write conversations for these situations. *(Answers may vary.)*

1. You ask your father for permission to go hiking on Saturday. Your father says yes, and to have a good time.

   Q: *Can I go hiking on Saturday?*

   A: *Sure, that's fine. Have a good time.*

2. You ask your mother for permission to go to your friend Angelo's house after school. She says no because you have to practice for your piano lesson.

   Q: *Can I go to Angelo's house after school?*

   A: *No, I'm sorry. You have to practice for your piano lesson.*

3. You ask a friend to help you with your math homework. Your friend says yes and suggests going to the library.

   Q: *Could you help me with my math homework?*

   A: *Yes, of course. Let's go to the library.*

4. You ask a friend to lend you his bike. He says no because his bike is broken.

   Q: *Could you lend me your bike?*

   A: *No, I'm sorry. I can't. My bike is broken.*

2 Listening

A Listen to the conversations. Are the people in the conversations offering an invitation, asking permission, or making a request? Check (✓) the correct answers.

Invitation	Permission	Request
1. ✓	☐	☐
2. ☐	✓	☐
3. ☐	☐	✓
4. ✓	☐	☐

B Listen again and answer the questions.

1. Can David go to the museum?

   No, he can't.

2. Does Billy have to take the history test today?

   Yes, he does.

3. Will Sally clean Alex's room?

   Yes, she will.

4. Would Miranda like to go white-water rafting?

   Yes, she would.

Go to page 116 for the Game.

Making plans

1 Language focus

A Pedro and Juan make plans for the next day. Listen and practice.

If the weather is nice, I**'ll** ride in the park.

If it doesn't rain, we**'ll probably** go to the beach.

We **might** go to the movies **if** it rains.

I **won't** ride my bike **if** it rains.

Pedro So, Juan, what are you going to do tomorrow?

Juan I really want to go for a ride on my new bike. If the weather is nice, I'll ride in the park. How about you? Do you have any plans?

Pedro I'm going to hang out with my cousin, David.

Juan What are you and David going to do?

Pedro Well, I'm not sure. It depends on the weather. If it doesn't rain, we'll probably go to the beach.

Juan And if it rains?

Pedro We might go to the movies if it rains. Would you like to join us?

Juan I'd love to. I won't ride my bike if it rains.

Pedro Good. But I hope it's sunny. I really want to go to the beach.

B Complete the sentences with the correct forms of the verbs. Then listen and check.

1. If the Larsons _don't go_ (not go) to the concert, they _'ll probably stay_ (probably stay) home.

2. If it _rains_ (rain) on the weekend, Kelly _won't play_ (not play) tennis.

3. _I'll be_ (I / be) in the library if you _need_ (need) my help.

4. If Nick _runs_ (run), he _might not be_ (might / not be) late for class.

5. We _might eat_ (might / eat) at an outdoor café if it _'s_ (be) sunny on Sunday.

6. If I _don't have_ (not have) extra money, I _won't buy_ (not buy) your ticket.

7. If we _don't have_ (not have) time tonight, we _'ll do_ (do) it tomorrow.

8. They _probably won't walk_ (probably / not walk) to school if it _isn't_ (not be) warm.

Lesson 11 Making plans

This lesson presents and practices if with will / will probably / won't / might and verb phrases related to activities for sunny and rainy days.

Review of Lesson 10

- Write on the board:

  A: Can I borrow your blue shirt for the party tonight?

  B: Sure. That's fine.

  A: Could you clean my shoes for the party?

  B: No, I can't. I'm busy.

- Have students work in pairs to practice asking for permission and making requests, as in the example.

1 Language focus

This exercise presents and practices *if* with *will / will probably / won't / might*.

A 💿 CD1, Track 44

- Have students read the directions and look at the photo.

- Give students several minutes to read the conversation.

- **Optional** Play the recording. Students listen and read along.

> **Audio script**
> Same as the conversation in the Student's Book.

- Ask: *What do Pedro's and Juan's plans depend on?* (The weather.) *What will Juan do if the weather is nice?* (He'll ride his bike in the park.) *Will he ride his bike if it rains?* (No.) *What will Pedro and David do if it doesn't rain?* (They'll probably go to the beach.) *Will they go to the beach if it rains?* (No, they won't.) *Is Pedro sure what they'll do if it rains?* (No.) *Where might they go?* (They might go to the movies.) *Will Juan go with them if they go to the movies?* (Yes.)

- Play the recording or model the conversation. Students listen and repeat.

- **Optional** Have students practice in pairs.

- **Language Chart** Have students study the examples in the language chart. Focus their attention on the first example. Ask: *Who said this sentence in the conversation?* (Juan.) *What condition is necessary for Juan to ride his bike in the park?* (The weather needs to be nice.) *Does this condition occur after* if *or after* I'll? (After *if*.) Follow the same procedure with the other three examples. Then ask: *Which part of the sentence is always in the simple present, the* if *clause or the other clause?* (The *if* clause.) *Are there always commas in the middle of sentences with* if *clauses?* (No, only when the *if* clause is at the beginning of the sentence.)

- **Optional** Model the examples, pausing for students to repeat.

B 💿 CD1, Track 45

- Ask students to read the directions and the examples.

- Have students work individually to complete the sentences with the correct forms of the verbs in parentheses.

- Have students work in pairs to check their answers.

- Play the recording. Students listen and verify their answers.

> **Audio script**
> Same as the sentences in the Student's Book.

- Check answers with the class. Divide the board into two sections. Invite pairs of volunteers to come to the board to write one of the sentences they completed. The first pair writes sentences 1 and 2 in one section, the second pair writes 3 and 4 in another section, and so on. After each pair finishes writing, discuss with the class whether the sentences are correct.

> **Teaching Tip** When practicing more complex sentences, you may want to write the answers on the board. Though this can be time-consuming, it is a useful way to review the Language focus. To save time, have pairs or groups of three students write simultaneously on the board, as suggested above.

2 Word power

This exercise presents and practices verb phrases related to activities for sunny and rainy days.

A

- Remind students that in Lesson 8 they practiced some verb phrases to describe long-term plans. Invite volunteers to say any verb phrase they may remember from that lesson. (*Get a job, go around the world, go to college, make money, see the U.S., study computer programming, take English classes, take a trip to Europe, work in an office.*) Explain that in this lesson they will practice some verb phrases for short-term plans.

- Ask students to read the directions, the verb phrases in the box, and the column headings.

- Have students call out any words or verb phrases they do not understand. Explain them by using them in sentences or by miming them.

- Have students work individually to write the verb phrases that belong in each column.

- Check answers with the class. Write the two headings on the board and invite volunteers to come to the board to write a verb phrase under one of the headings. Then invite other volunteers to say one of the extra verb phrases they wrote.

Teaching Tip
Constant reviewing is essential for successful vocabulary building. Review vocabulary as often as possible, even if it is by simply eliciting words students already know, as suggested above.

B

- Have students read the directions and the sentence beginnings and endings. Ask: *Do the beginnings and endings tell you what will, will probably, won't, or might happen, or do they describe conditions?* (They describe conditions.) *So what's missing in each sentence?* (What will, will probably, won't, or might happen.)

- Have students work individually to complete the sentences with ideas from Part A or their own ideas.

- Check answers with the class. Invite volunteers to read one of their sentences aloud.

3 Speaking

This exercise practices *if* with *will / will probably / won't / might*.

- Ask students to read the directions and the example conversations. Ask: *What should you do?* (Use the sentences in Exercise 2B to find classmates with the same plans.)

- Invite two volunteers to come to the front to demonstrate the activity with you. Ask the question in the example and have the volunteers read the classmates' responses.

- **Optional** Invite three volunteers to come to the front to demonstrate the activity again.

- Explain how you want students to carry out the activity. You may want them to mingle (walk around the room talking to different classmates) or to remain seated and talk only to classmates sitting close to them. Explain that whenever they find a classmate with the same plan, they should write that student's name next to the corresponding sentence in Exercise 2B.

- Have students carry out the activity.

- To finish, invite volunteers to report on their findings. Model the task. Say: *If it doesn't rain, Laura and I will walk our dogs in the park.* Or *Laura and I will walk our dogs in the park if it doesn't rain.*

Workbook
Assign the exercises on Workbook page 19. (Workbook answers begin on page T-192.)

Extra Grammar
Assign the exercises for the Extra Grammar, Lesson 11.

2 Word power

A Which activities are good for a sunny day? Which are good for a rainy day? Write the verb phrases in the correct columns. Then write one more verb phrase in each column.

☑ play computer games   ☐ rent a DVD
☐ fly a kite   ☐ go biking
☐ have a barbecue   ☐ clean my room
☐ go to an outdoor concert   ☐ visit a museum

Activities for a sunny day	Activities for a rainy day
fly a kite	play computer games
have a barbecue	rent a DVD
go to an outdoor concert	clean my room
go biking	visit a museum
(Answers will vary.)	(Answers will vary.)

B Imagine you have a free day tomorrow. What will you do?
Complete the sentences with ideas from Part A or your own ideas. *(Answers will vary.)*

1. If it doesn't rain tomorrow, _____ .
2. If I go downtown on Saturday, _____ .
3. _____ if it rains in the morning.
4. If I have some extra money, _____ .
5. _____ if we don't have any homework today.
6. If I stay home, _____ .
7. If I'm not tired tonight, _____ .
8. _____ if my friend isn't busy tomorrow.

3 Speaking

Look at Exercise 2B. What are your plans for your free day?
Find a classmate who has the same plans as you.

You If it doesn't rain,
I'll go to the beach.
How about you?
Classmate 1 If it doesn't rain,
I might play volleyball.

You If it doesn't rain,
I'll go to the beach.
How about you?
Classmate 2 If it doesn't rain,
I'll go to the beach, too.

Lesson 12 Vacation plans

1 Language focus

A Jessica is going on vacation. Read her e-mail message to Will. Then listen and practice.

Clauses of time with *before / while / after*

Before I go, I have a lot to do.
While I'm in Hawaii, I'm going to have fun.
I'm going to go to the beach **while** I'm there.
Let's get together **after** I get back.

Hi, Will!

I'm so excited. I'm going to Hawaii tomorrow. Can you believe it?

Before I go, I have a lot to do. I have to finish my book report before I go! It's OK, because while I'm in Hawaii, I'm going to have fun. There are so many things to do on the island of Oahu. I'm going to go to the beach with my cousin while I'm there. She'll probably take me sightseeing, too. And we'll snorkel at Hanauma Bay after I buy some snorkel gear.

I hope you have a great vacation. Let's get together after I get back.

Take care!
Jessica

B Match the two parts of each sentence. Then listen and check.

1. Before I leave, _d_
2. I'm going to pack my bags _e_
3. While I'm there, _c_
4. I'll take lots of pictures _b_
5. I'll call you _a_

a. after I get back.
b. while I'm there.
c. I'll probably take surfing lessons.
d. I might stop by to say good-bye.
e. before I go to bed tonight.

C Imagine you are going on vacation. Complete the sentences with your own information. (*Answers will vary.*)

1. Before I leave, I might _____ .

2. I'll _____ before I leave.

3. I'll probably _____ while I'm there.

4. While I'm there, I'm going to _____ .

5. I might _____ after I get back.

Lesson 12 Vacation plans

This lesson presents and practices clauses of time with before / while / after.

1 Language focus

This exercise presents and practices clauses of time with *before / while / after*.

A 💿 CD1, Track 46

* Ask students to read the directions and look at the photos. Ask: *Where do you think this beach is?* (Answers will vary.) Explain the meanings of *snorkel* (v.) and *snorkel gear*. Say: *Imagine you're about to go on vacation to this place. You send an e-mail message to a friend before you leave. What would you tell your friend?* (Answers will vary.)

* Give students several minutes to read the e-mail message.

* **Optional** Play the recording. Students listen and read along.

> **Audio script**
> Same as the e-mail message in the Student's Book.

* Ask: *Does Jessica mention any of the things you suggested?* (Answers will vary.) *Where's Jessica going to spend her vacation?* (Hawaii.) *Does she have a lot to do before she goes?* (Yes.) *What does she have to do?* (Finish her book report.) *Who's she going to get together with after she gets back?* (Will.)

* Play the recording or model the sentences. Students listen and repeat.

* **Language Chart** Have students study the examples in the language chart. Ask: *Where does the* while *phrase go, in the first part or in the second part of the sentence?* (It can go in either place.) *When do you add a comma?* (When *while* is in the first part or at the beginning of a sentence.) Explain that in many cases, *before* and *after* phrases can go in the first or in the second part of the sentence. For example, you can say *I have a lot to do before I go.*

* Draw a time line on the board:

```
———————— X ———— X ————
   Jessica arrives   Jessica goes
    in Hawaii.        back home.
```

* Ask random students to come to the board to write the words *after*, *before*, and *while* in the correct places on the time line. The time line should look like this:

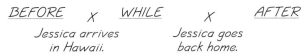

```
BEFORE    X    WHILE    X    AFTER
        Jessica arrives      Jessica goes
         in Hawaii.           back home.
```

* **Optional** Model the examples, pausing for students to repeat.

B 💿 CD1, Track 47

* Ask students to read the directions and the example.

* Have students work individually to match the two parts of the sentences.

* Play the recording. Students listen and verify their answers.

> **Audio script**
> Same as the sentences in the Student's Book.

* Check answers with the class. Invite volunteers to read aloud one answer each.

C

* Ask students to read the directions. Explain that they will imagine they are going on vacation. They can choose any vacation destination.

* Have students work individually to complete the sentences with their own information.

* Invite several volunteers to share their sentences with the class. After each sentence, ask students to raise their hands if they completed the sentence in the same way.

2 Listening

In this exercise, students listen for information about when a teenager will do activities related to her vacation plans.

💿 **CD1, Track 48**

- Tell students that they will listen to Carla and Jessica talk about Carla's plans for her vacation to Disney World. Students should listen and check when Carla is going to do each of the activities.
- Play the recording. Students only listen.

> **Audio script**
> See page T-208.

- Play the recording again. Students listen and check the boxes in the correct columns.
- Play the recording once again. Students listen and verify their answers.
- Check answers with the class. Read each item. Students respond with *before she leaves*, *while she's there*, or *after she gets home*.

3 Speaking

This exercise practices clauses of time with *before / while / after*.

A

- Focus students' attention on the photos. Have them choose a vacation they would like to go on and complete the sentence *I'm going to take . . .* with the name of the vacation.
- Focus students' attention on the chart under the question *What are you going to do . . . ?* and have them read the headings.
- Give students a few minutes to think about what they will or might do at each of the times: before they leave, when they arrive, and so on. They should make notes in the chart using verb phrases. They do not have to use complete sentences.

B

- Have students tell a classmate about their vacation plans, as in the example in the speech balloon.
- To finish, invite volunteers to tell the class about their classmate's plans. For example: *Lisa is going to take a cruise. Before she leaves, she's going to buy sunscreen.*

> **Teaching Tip** Part A of the Speaking exercise above is for students to brainstorm ideas that they can talk about in Part B. The purpose is to ensure that students will have things to say when called upon to speak. Students should be made aware of the purpose of this preparatory stage. Otherwise, they may easily conclude that Part A is a sentence-writing exercise and that Part B is a checking stage in which they should simply read aloud the sentences they wrote.

> **Culture Note** While most American students have two months off from school for summer vacation, their parents only get two or three weeks off from work each year. Therefore, families usually plan their vacations for only a week or so at a time. Some popular American vacation spots include Orlando, Florida (to visit theme parks, such as Disney World, Universal Studios, or Sea World); Branson, Missouri (to see famous musicians and singers perform in one of the 30 theaters); Las Vegas, Nevada (to stay at interesting hotels, such as the one that looks like an Egyptian pyramid or the one that has a roller coaster on its roof); Los Angeles, California (to see where famous American TV shows are filmed and where stars live); or New York City (to visit museums and see Broadway shows).

> **Workbook**
> Assign the exercises on Workbook page 20. (Workbook answers begin on page T-192.)

> **Extra Grammar**
> Assign the exercises for the Extra Grammar, Lesson 12.

2 Listening

Carla is going on vacation to Disney World with her family. When will she do these things? Listen and check (✓) the correct columns.

	Before she leaves	While she's there	After she gets home
1. buy a camera	✓	☐	☐
2. go shopping	☐	✓	☐
3. get a haircut	✓	☐	☐
4. read a travel book	☐	✓	☐
5. write postcards	☐	☐	✓
6. call her friend	☐	☐	✓

3 Speaking

A Choose one of the vacations below. Then complete the chart. *(Answers will vary.)*

a beach vacation

a cruise

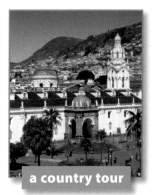
a country tour

a ski vacation

Vacation Planner

I'm going to take _____ .

What are you going to do . . . ?

before you leave	when you arrive	while you are there
_____	_____	_____
_____	_____	_____

if the weather is bad	after you get home
_____	_____
_____	_____

B Tell a classmate about your vacation plans.

I'm going to take a ski vacation. Before I leave, I'm going to buy ski pants.

Get Connected

Read

A Read the article quickly. Check (✓) the main idea.

☐ 1. Teenagers are very social these days.

☐ 2. Teenagers make plans with their friends after school because it's convenient.

☑ 3. Most teenagers use modern technology for their social plans.

WAYD 2nite?

What do you do when you want to go out with your friends? Do you call them on your phone? Maybe. But these days, most teenagers use their phones for **texting**, and they'll probably text this message: *WAYD 2nite?* (What are you doing tonight?) Texting is very **convenient**. You can send messages from the mall, the bus – anywhere.

Teens also like to go online to make plans. They often send **e-vites** – electronic invitations – or use **social networking Web sites**. On Web sites like these, you can make plans with all your friends at the same time.

You can make **fuzzy** plans (plans that might happen), like: "If the weather is nice, I'll probably go to the park," or "We might go to the movies tonight if class doesn't finish late." You can also make **firm** plans (plans that will happen), like: "I'm going to the zoo on Saturday. Do you want to come?" If your friends go on the site, they'll see your plans. They might send you a reply online, or text you a short reply. For example: *XLNT idea* (Excellent idea). Or *IMS 2BZ* (I'm sorry. I'm too busy).

Go to page 123 for the Vocabulary Practice.

B 💿 Read the article slowly. Check your answer in Part A.

C Are these statements true or false? Write *True* or *False*. Then correct the false statements.

1. A lot of teenagers use texting for their social plans. ___*True.*___ _____

2. Texting isn't convenient when you're on the bus or at the mall.
   ___*False.*___ ___*You can send messages from the mall, the bus - anywhere.*___

3. E-vites are invitations you send online. ___*True.*___ _____

4. Fuzzy plans are plans that won't happen. ___*False.*___ ___*Fuzzy plans are plans that might happen.*___

5. Friends can't reply to your online plans. ___*False.*___ ___*Friends might send you a reply online.*___

This lesson practices reading, listening, and writing skills.

Review of Lesson 12

- Write on the board:

before / while / after

1.	*4.*
2.	*5.*
3.	

- Ask students to copy the list of numbers into their notebooks.

- Explain that you will read five incomplete sentences. There is a word missing in each sentence. Instead of the missing word, you will say *blank*. Students should listen to the sentence, decide whether the missing word is *before*, *while*, or *after*, and write it next to the number of the sentence in their notebooks.

- Read each sentence twice. Give students time to write the missing words in their notebooks.

  1. *I like watching the news on TV in the evening. [Blank] I watch the news, I go to bed.*

  2. *I usually have breakfast [blank] I go to school.*

  3. *[Blank] I'm in class, I switch off my cell phone.*

  4. *[Blank] I leave for the beach, I have a lot of things to do.*

  5. *I'll show you my vacation photos [blank] I get back.*

- Check answers with the class. Invite volunteers to come to the board and write the correct words next to the numbers of the sentences. (1. After 2. before 3. While 4. Before 5. after.)

Read

This exercise practices reading for information about how teenagers make social plans with their friends.

A

- Focus students' attention on the title of the article and the photos. Ask: *What are these teens doing?* (Texting.)

- Invite a volunteer to read the directions and the sentences aloud. Remind students that they should read quickly to find the answer and that they should not read every word carefully.

- Have students work individually to read the article quickly and check the main idea. Do not check answers at this point.

B 💿 CD1, Track 49

- Invite a volunteer to read the directions aloud. Remind students that they should read slowly and carefully, and concentrate on getting the meaning of the entire text.

- List the new vocabulary words on the board: *texting, convenient, e-vite, social networking Web site, fuzzy, firm (adj.).* Explain their meaning. (Texting: sending short messages to someone's cell phone; convenient: not taking too much effort to do; e-vite: an invitation sent by computer or cell phone; social networking Web site: an Internet site that allows people to communicate with friends and others online; fuzzy: not clear; firm (adj.): definite.) As an alternative, have students use their dictionaries to find the meanings of the new vocabulary words.

- Have students read the article again.

- Have students check their answer in Part A in pairs. Elicit the answer from one pair.

- **Optional** Play the recording. Students listen and read along.

Audio script

Same as the article in the Student's Book.

Get Connected Vocabulary

- Have students do the exercise on Student's Book page 123 in class or for homework. (Get Connected Vocabulary answers are on page T-123.)

C

- Invite a volunteer to read the directions and first statement aloud.

- Ask: *Do a lot of teenagers use texting for their social plans?* (Yes.) Ask: *So is the statement true or false?* (True.)

- Have students work individually to write *True* or *False*, and then correct the false statements.

- Have students check their answers in pairs.

- Check answers with the class. Invite volunteers to read aloud one answer each.

Listen

In this exercise, students listen for teenagers' ideas about new technology.

A 💿 CD1, Track 50

- Focus students' attention on the photo. Ask: *What are the boy and girl looking at?* (A cell phone.)
- Tell students that they will listen to two friends, Olivia and Carlos, talk about using new technology to make social plans.
- Have students read the first question and the example answer.
- Explain that students should listen to the conversation and answer the questions.
- Play the recording. Students only listen.

> **Audio script**
> See page T-209.

- Play the recording again. Students listen and answer the questions.
- Play the recording once again. Students listen and verify their answers.
- Check answers with the class. Invite several pairs of volunteers to read the questions and answers aloud.

> **Culture Note**
> The first text message was sent by Neil Papworth of the UK on December 2, 1992. He sent it to his friend Richard Jarvis and it said, "Merry Christmas." They had no idea at the time that texting, or SMS (Short Message Service), would become so popular all over the world. In fact, Papworth had to type the message on a computer because they still had not developed the technology to type on a telephone keypad. Today, more than 2 billion people send text messages on their phones. That is about 75 percent of all cell phone users.

B

- Have students read the directions and all the statements.
- Remind students that *I agree* means you think something is right, *I disagree* means you think something is not right, and *I'm not sure* means you cannot say if you think it is right or not. Tell students that there are no right or wrong answers for this exercise – they are giving their opinions.
- Have students work individually to write whether they agree, disagree, or are not sure, and give reasons for their answers.
- Have students work in pairs to compare answers, or elicit opinions from volunteers.
- **Optional** Take a class poll. Read each statement and ask for a show of hands. Say: *Raise your hand if you agree. Now raise your hand if you disagree. Now raise your hand if you're not sure.* Invite each group to record its results in a chart or graph. Then have two groups work together to share their results.

Write

In this exercise, students answer questions and write a paragraph about how they use technology in daily life.

A

- Invite a volunteer to read the directions and all the questions aloud.
- Have students work individually to answer the questions and give reasons for their answers.
- Have students ask and answer the questions in pairs, or elicit opinions from volunteers.

B

- Invite a volunteer to read the directions aloud. Tell students that they will use the information that they wrote in Part A to help them write about how they use technology in their daily life.

- Have students work individually to write their paragraphs.
- Invite several volunteers to read their paragraphs to the class.
- **Optional** Have students work in pairs to read each other's paragraphs. Students should ask questions about anything they do not understand. They can also ask questions to get more information.

> **Workbook**
> Assign the exercises on Workbook page 21.
> (Workbook answers begin on page T-192.)

Can you come to my party?

A 🎧 **Olivia and Carlos talk about texting and technology. Listen and answer the questions.**

1. Why does Olivia ask Carlos for help?
   She can't understand the text messages on her phone.

2. What does Carlos say to Olivia about learning texting?
   He says it's really easy.

3. Does Olivia think technology is wonderful?
   No, she doesn't.

4. Do Olivia and Carlos agree that technology is convenient?
   Yes, they do.

5. Does Olivia spend more time doing homework or learning technology?
   She spends more time learning technology.

B **What do you think? Write _I agree_, _I disagree_, or _I'm not sure_. Give reasons.**
(Answers will vary.)

1. People should talk face-to-face more. _____

2. I think technology is convenient and fun. _____

3. New technology can be difficult to learn. _____

4. Technology makes the world a better place. _____

Your turn
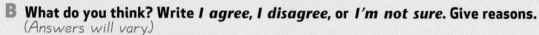

A **How important is technology in your life? Answer the questions. Give reasons.**
(Answers will vary.)

1. How often do you use technology? _____

2. What's your favorite way to keep in touch with friends? _____

3. Do you use a social networking site? _____

4. How often do you text your friends? _____

5. Is it easy for you to learn how to use new technology? _____

B **Write a paragraph about technology in your life. Use the answers in Part A to help you.**
(Answers will vary.)

⬤⬤⬤

I use my . . .

_____

_____

_____

Language chart review

Would you like to . . . ? for invitations	Can / Could for permission and requests	
	Asking permission	Making requests
Would you like to see a movie? 　Yes, I'd love to. / Sure, I'd like to. 　I'm sorry, but I can't. / I'd love to, 　but I can't. **I have to** clean my room.	**Can I** use your pen? 　Yes, all right. 　No, I'm sorry.	**Could you** give me a pen? 　Yes, of course. 　No, I can't. Sorry.

Clauses of time with *before* / *while* / *after*
Before he goes to bed, he has to take out the trash. **While I'm at the mall**, I'm going to look for some T-shirts. They'd like to see that movie **after it comes out on DVD**.

A Mario and his dad are talking. Complete their conversation with *would you like to*, *can I*, and *could you*.

Mario 　*Can I* ＿＿＿＿＿＿ have a birthday party this year?

Dad 　Sure. *Would you like to* ＿ have the party next Saturday?

Mario 　Yes, I'd love to. *Can I* ＿＿＿＿＿ invite all my friends?

Dad 　OK. How many friends? *Could you* ＿＿＿ give me an idea?

Mario 　Yes, of course. There's Marisa, Gavin, Brenda, Min-ho, and Ashton. And ＿＿＿＿ *can I* invite some other friends from school, too?

Dad 　Yes, all right. *Would you like to* ＿ have the party here, or somewhere else?

Mario 　Here. *Can I* ＿＿＿＿＿＿ start calling everyone now?

Dad 　Everyone?

B Mario is planning his party. Write sentences.

1. have to do a lot / before / his friends arrive
   　Mario has to do a lot before his friends arrive.
2. before / Mario's friends play games / eat dinner
   　Before Mario's friends play games, they're going to eat dinner.
3. while / eat dinner / his friends talk
   　While they eat dinner, his friends are going to talk.
4. his friends / dance / after / eat dessert
   　His friends are going to dance after they eat dessert.

Unit 3 Review

This lesson reviews the grammar and vocabulary introduced in Unit 3.

Language chart review

These charts summarize the main grammar presented and practiced in Unit 3.

- Books closed. Write on the board:

A	B
1. Inviting	a. Can I . . . ?
2. Asking for permission	b. Would you like to . . . ?
3. Making requests	c. Could you . . . ?

- Have students work in pairs to match the functions in column A with the question beginnings in column B.
- Check answers with the class. (1.b 2.a 3.c.)
- Give pairs a few minutes to write three questions using the beginnings they just matched.
- Invite three volunteers to read one of the questions they wrote. As they do so, complete the questions on the board.
- Elicit possible responses to the questions on the board. Be sure to elicit both positive and negative responses. Write them on the board.
- Books open. Have students compare the chart on the board against the top chart in the Language chart review.
- Answer any questions students may have.
- Focus students' attention on the second chart. Remind students of the meanings of *before, while,* and *after.* You may wish to draw a time line on the board to clarify the meanings further.
- Invite volunteers to give other examples of clauses of time.
- Answer any questions students may have.

....

Exercises A through C (pages T-42 to T-43)

Note: Students can do these exercises for homework or in class. They should do these exercises with minimal teacher input or help. If you choose to do these exercises as homework, briefly review the exercise directions in class. Make sure that students understand what they should do. Check the answers with the class during the next class meeting. If you choose to do the exercises in class, follow the directions below.

Exercise A

- Focus students' attention on the top picture. Ask: *Where are Mario and his dad?* (At home or in the kitchen.) *What are they doing?* (Eating lunch / sandwiches.)
- Have students read the directions and the example question.
- Have students work individually to complete the conversation between Mario and his dad.
- Check answers with the class.

Exercise B

- Focus students' attention on the bottom picture. Ask: *What's Mario doing?* (Writing a list of things he has to do before the party.)
- Have students read the directions and the example sentence.
- Have students work individually to write sentences with the words or cues given.
- Check answers with the class. Invite volunteers to read aloud one answer each.

Language chart review

This chart summarizes further grammar presented and practiced in Unit 3.

- Have students study the examples in the chart.
- Remind students to use the simple present in the *if* clause when they are talking about future plans.
- Answer any questions students may have.

Exercise C

- Have students read the directions and the example.
- Have students work individually to complete the sentences with the correct forms of the verbs.
- Check answers with the class.

Take another look!

- Invite a volunteer to read the directions aloud.
- Students work individually to circle the correct answers.
- Check answers with the class.

Optional Unit Wrap-Up

- If students did the Review exercises for homework, check answers with the class.
- Have students practice the conversation in Exercise A in pairs.
- Have students work in small groups and imagine they have to plan a class party. They will write a To-Do List. Students write sentences such as those in Exercise B with *before, after,* or *while* using the To-Do List. For example, *After we plan the games, we're going to decorate the classroom. While the girls are decorating the classroom, the boys will plan the games.*
- Have students continue playing the "If" game as in Exercise C. Start them off with one *if* clause. See how many sentences the class can make. Here are some ideas for starter *if* clauses: *If I take ballroom dancing classes, If I go to Hawaii for a vacation, If I learn how to play chess, If I join the drama club, If I have to babysit my little brother tomorrow.*

Theme Project

- Assign the *At Home* section of the Unit 3 Theme Project on Student's Book page 128.

Workbook

- Assign the Unit 3 Check Yourself on Workbook page 22. (Workbook answers begin on page T-192.)

Extra Practice Worksheets

- Assign the Unit 3 Extra Practice worksheets starting on page T-147.

Extra Speaking Practice Worksheet

- Assign the Unit 3 Extra Speaking Practice worksheet on page T-170.

Arcade Activities

- Assign the Unit 3 Arcade activities found at: www.cambridge.org/connectarcade

Learning Log

- Assign the Unit 3 Learning Log. This can be downloaded from the Teacher Support Site at: www.cambridge.org.connect2e/teacher

Quiz

- Give the Unit 3 Quiz on page T-180.

Test

- Give the Unit 3 Test (Form A and / or Form B). These can be downloaded from the Teacher Support Site at: www.cambridge.org.connect2e/teacher

Language chart review

If I have homework, I'**ll** do it after dinner.	We **might** go to a movie **if** we have time.
They'**ll probably** go biking **if** they don't have homework.	I **won't** go to school **if** I'm sick.

C Mario's friends are at his party. They are playing the "If" game.
Complete their sentences with the correct forms of the verbs.

1. **Ashton**   I'll go first! If Pandora, my favorite band, _comes_ (come) to our
town, _they'll probably play_ (they / probably play) at the stadium.

2. **Min-ho**   If Pandora _plays_ (play) at the stadium, Ashton
will go (go) to the concert.

3. **Brenda**   He _might buy_ (might / buy) tickets if he _has_ (have)
some extra money.

4. **Mario**   If Marisa _goes_ (go) to the concert, she'll _leave_ (leave)
her dog at home.

5. **Marisa**   _I'll probably have_ (I / probably / have) a problem if I _don't leave_ (not leave)
my dog at home.

6. **Gavin**   Why _will Marisa have_ (Marisa / have) a problem if she _takes_ (take)
her dog to the concert?

    Mario   Her dog hates rock music!

Take another look!

Circle the correct answers.

1. The word *if* can go _____ of a sentence.
   - a. only at the beginning
   - b. only in the middle
   - c. at the beginning or in the middle

2. In which sentence is the speaker sure she will go out?
   - a. I'll go out if it stops raining.
   - b. I'll go out when it stops raining.
   - c. I might go out after the rain stops.

Go to page 128 for the Theme Project.

Teens online

1 Language focus

A How do teens use the Internet? Read the information.
Then listen and practice.

- Finding information for schoolwork is a popular online activity.
- Teens also like chatting with their friends online.
- Downloading music is popular with teens, too.
- E-mailing is popular, but most teens enjoy chatting online more than e-mailing.
- Playing games and watching videos are popular online activities for some teens.
- Shopping online isn't very popular with teens. Maybe that's because they enjoy hanging out at the mall.

The number of teens who use the Internet for:	
Finding information for schoolwork	57%
Chatting with friends online	34%
Downloading music	33%
E-mailing	32%
Playing games	19%
Watching videos	14%
Shopping	6%

Source: CBSNews.com

B Study the chart. Complete the sentences with the correct forms of the verb phrases in the box. Then listen and check.

Gerunds as subjects	Gerunds as objects
Finding information for schoolwork is the most popular online activity.	Teens also like **chatting** with their friends online.
Downloading music is popular with teens, too.	Do teens enjoy **shopping** online? Yes, they do. / No, they don't.

☐ do crossword puzzles ☐ find information ☑ play chess
☐ download music ☐ get sports scores ☐ shop for clothes

1. *Playing chess* online is my favorite thing to do.

2. I like *doing crossword puzzles* in English online. I learn new words.

3. Ellie buys all of her T-shirts online. She enjoys *shopping for clothes* online.

4. *Downloading music* online is easy. I can buy many songs.

5. *Finding information* online is faster than going to the library.

6. I like *getting sports scores* for all my favorite teams online.

UNIT 4 People

44

Lesson 13 Teens online

This lesson presents and practices gerunds as subjects and objects, and gerunds formed with doing, going to, *and* playing.

1 Language focus

This exercise presents and practices gerunds as subjects and objects.

A CD2, Track 2

- Ask students to read the directions and the information in the graph.
- **Optional** Play the recording. Students listen and read along.

> **Audio script**
> Same as the information in the Student's Book.

- Ask: *What does this text discuss?* (How teens use the Internet.) *Which online activity is more popular: chatting with friends online or playing games?* (Chatting with friends online.) *What percentage of teens like chatting with friends?* (34 percent.) *How many teens like playing games?* (19 percent.) *Which activity is less popular: finding information for schoolwork or downloading music?* (Downloading music.) *Which activities are not very popular?* (Watching videos and shopping.) *What percentage of teens listed e-mailing as most popular?* (32 percent.)
- Ask: *Do you think the percentages in this graph are true for teens you know? Why or why not?*
- Play the recording or model the sentences. Students listen and repeat.

B CD2, Track 3

- **Language Chart** Have students study the examples in the language chart. Remind students about the placement of subjects and objects in sentences. Write some simple sentences on the board and have students identify the subjects and objects.
- Focus students' attention on the language chart headings. Explain that a *gerund* is the *-ing* form of a verb used as a noun. Ask: *What's the simple form of the verb in the phrase* finding information for schoolwork? (Find.) *What's the gerund form of* play? (Playing.) If students ask, explain that the *-ing* form is not called a gerund when it is used with *be* in the present continuous and past continuous.
- Explain that gerunds often form phrases with other words, for example, *finding information* or *downloading music*. These are called gerund phrases. Invite volunteers to suggest other gerund phrases – for example, *playing tennis* or *talking on the phone*.

- Focus students' attention on the left-hand side of the language chart. Ask: *Where are gerunds placed, at the beginning or at the end of the sentence?* (At the beginning.) Then write on the board:

  1. Baseball is the most popular sport.

  2. Finding information for schoolwork is the most popular online activity.

  Explain that *Finding* is the subject of sentence 2 in the same way as *Baseball* is the subject of sentence 1.
- Now focus students' attention on the right-hand side of the language chart. Ask: *Where are gerunds placed in these examples, at the beginning or at the end?* (At the end.) Explain that gerunds can also be used as objects in sentences. Write on the board:

  1. Lydia uses the Internet every day.

  2. Teens like e-mailing.

  Explain that *e-mailing* is the object of sentence 2 in the same way as *the Internet* is the object of sentence 1.
- **Optional** Model the examples, pausing for students to repeat.
- Focus students' attention on the verb phrases in the box and the exercise. Review the directions.
- Have students work individually to complete the sentences with the correct forms of the verb phrases in the box.
- Play the recording. Students listen and verify their answers.

> **Audio script**
> Same as the sentences in the Student's Book.

- Check answers with the class. Invite volunteers to read aloud one of the sentences they completed.

This unit introduces vocabulary and expressions to talk about everyday activities and people's personality, for agreeing and disagreeing, and for giving and checking information about people.

2 Word power

This exercise presents and practices gerund phrases with *doing, going to,* and *playing.*

A

- Ask students to read the directions, the words in the box, and the list of three gerunds.

- Have students call out any words or phrases they do not understand. Explain them by using the words or phrases in sentences or by miming them.

- Have students work individually to create gerund phrases.

- Check answers with the class. Invite volunteers to read one of the gerund phrases they wrote.

B

- Ask students to read the directions. Ask: *What should you do?* (Complete the sentences with gerund phrases.) *What are the sentences about?* (Likes and dislikes.) *Do you have to use only ideas from Part A?* (No. You can use your own ideas.)

- Have students work individually to complete the sentences.

- Check answers with the class. Ask random students to tell you the different answers they wrote. Write them on the board.

- To finish, have students work in small groups to read and compare their sentences.

Teaching Tip   Give exercises a sense of closure so that students realize that they have finished a part of the lesson and should get ready for the next part. The suggestions following "To finish" serve this purpose.

3 Speaking

This exercise practices using gerunds as objects.

A

- Have students read the directions and the chart.

- Explain that the questions make up a survey about teenage interests. Students should complete the questions with a popular example for each of the categories. To model the task, elicit the names of different types of music that students may use to complete the first question. Make sure students understand that there is no specific right answer.

- Give students several minutes to complete the questions. Students then write *Yes* or *No* in the *You* column according to their interests.

B

- Ask students to read the directions and the example conversation.

- Have students work with a classmate, ask the questions, and write *Yes* or *No* in the *Your classmate* column.

- Ask students to give the correct information for *No* answers.

C

- Invite volunteers to share with the class two interesting things about their classmate, as in the example in the speech balloon.

Workbook

Assign the exercises on Workbook page 23. (Workbook answers begin on page T-192.)

Extra Grammar

Assign the exercises for the Extra Grammar, Lesson 13.

2 Word power

A Create gerund phrases by matching the words in the box to the correct gerunds. (*The order of the answers may vary.*)

> ☐ bed late ☐ classes ☐ soccer
> ☐ board games ☐ crossword puzzles ☐ the movies
> ☑ chores ☐ homework online ☐ the piano

doing	_chores_	_crossword puzzles_	_homework online_
going to	_bed late_	_classes_	_the movies_
playing	_board games_	_soccer_	_the piano_

B Complete the sentences about your likes and dislikes with gerund phrases. Use ideas from Part A or your own ideas. (*Answers will vary.*)

1. _____ on the weekend is fun.
2. I really enjoy _____ with my family.
3. I don't like _____ in the morning.
4. _____ is my favorite activity after school.
5. I don't like _____ on the weekend.

3 Speaking

A Complete the questions about your interests. Then answer them with your own information. (*Answers will vary.*)

What are your interests? Do you . . . ?	You	Your classmate
1. like listening to _____ (a type of) music	___	___
2. enjoy going to _____ (a place)	___	___
3. like watching _____ (a TV show)	___	___
4. enjoy playing _____ (a sport)	___	___
5. like getting up at _____ (a time)	___	___
6. enjoy studying _____ (a school subject)	___	___

B Ask a classmate the questions. Write his or her responses in the chart. For *No* answers, give the correct information.

> Do you like listening to jazz?

> No, I don't. I like listening to rock music.

C Now share two interesting things about your classmate with the class.

> Mario likes getting up at 6 a.m. He doesn't like playing basketball.

Personality types

1 Word power

A Complete the sentences about each person with the words in the box.
Then listen and practice.

☐ bad-tempered ☑ forgetful ☐ independent ☐ outgoing ☐ trustworthy
☐ creative ☐ hardworking ☐ organized ☐ thoughtful

1. Abby doesn't remember things sometimes.

   She's forgetful.

2. Sara often gets angry.

   She's bad-tempered.

3. Jimmy isn't shy and is very friendly.

   He's outgoing.

4. Cindy doesn't want any help doing things.

   She's independent.

5. Ken keeps things in order.

   He's organized.

6. Andy is very honest.

   He's trustworthy.

7. Lynn makes beautiful things.

   She's creative.

8. Colin always does nice things for people.

   He's thoughtful.

9. Dora and Estelle always do many chores at home.

   They're hardworking.

B Complete the sentences with the names of classmates. (*Answers will vary.*)

1. _____ is creative.   3. _____ is outgoing.

2. _____ is hardworking. 4. _____ is thoughtful.

Lesson 14 Personality types

This lesson presents and practices adjectives to describe personality types and too *and* either.

Review of Lesson 13

• Write on the board:

A	B		Examples
do	*bed*	*information*	• *Going to bed late is fun.*
find	*board games*	*music*	• *I like going to bed late.*
go to	*chess*	*soccer*	
listen to	*chores*	*the movies*	• *I don't enjoy sending e-mail.*
play	*crossword puzzles*	*the piano*	• *Sending e-mail is boring.*
send	*e-mail*		

• Focus students' attention on lists A and B and the examples on the board. Explain to students that they are going to give their opinions about different activities. They should make a gerund phrase by using the gerund form of one of the verbs in list A and appropriate words from list B; they can use the gerund phrases as subjects or as objects.

• Invite volunteers to give their opinions about different activities. After a volunteer gives an opinion, ask another student to say the sentence in a different way. If the volunteer used the gerund phrase as the subject, the other student should use the gerund phrase as the object, as in the examples on the board.

1 Word power

This exercise presents and practices adjectives to describe personality types.

A CD2, Track 4

• Give students a minute to read the words in the box. Explain that the words are adjectives to describe people's personality types. Ask students to call out adjectives they already know for describing people's personality – for example, *nice, funny, smart, interesting,* or *popular.*

• Ask students to look at the pictures and read the directions and the sentences. Explain that, in each case, the picture and the sentence give clues about the person's personality type. Focus students' attention on Picture 1. Ask: *Where's Abby?* (At school.) *What's she looking for?* (Her pencil case.) *Where's the pencil case?* (Probably at home.) *So what's Abby's problem?* (She sometimes forgets things.) Say: *Someone who forgets things is* forgetful.

• Ask students to write the numbers 2–9 in their notebooks.

• Have students work individually. Students look at pictures 2–9, read the sentences again, and write the correct adjectives next to the numbers in their notebooks. Explain that if they are not sure, they should just guess.

• Focus students' attention on Picture 2. Ask: *Is Sara feeling happy?* (No.) *How's she feeling?* (Angry.) Say: *Sara gets angry very easily. Which adjective describes her personality?* (Bad-tempered.) Model *bad-tempered.* Students listen and repeat.

• Follow the same procedure with the other pictures, clarifying meaning where necessary.

• Have students work individually to write a sentence for each picture using the correct adjective.

• Check answers with the class. Ask random students to read their answers to the class.

• Play the recording. Students listen and repeat.

Audio script
Same as the sentences in the Student's Book.

B

• Have students read the directions. Ask: *How do you choose the classmates' names to write?* (According to their personality type.) Explain that if they want to write the name of more than one classmate in each sentence, they can write the sentences in their notebooks.

• Have students work individually to complete the sentences.

• Invite several volunteers to read aloud one of the sentences they wrote. After each sentence, ask for a show of hands from students who completed the sentence with the same name or names.

People T-46

2 Language focus

This exercise presents and practices *too* and *either*.

A 💿 CD2, Track 5

- Ask students to read the directions and look at the photo.
- Have students read the conversation.
- **Optional** Play the recording. Students listen and read along.

> **Audio script**
> Same as the conversation in the Student's Book.

- Ask: *Why do Trisha and Patsy talk about their personalities?* (Because they're taking a survey.) *Are their personalities very similar or very different?* (Very similar.) *What does that explain?* (Why Trisha and Patsy are best friends.) *Are they forgetful?* (Yes.) *Are they bad-tempered?* (No.) *Are they outgoing?* (Yes.) *Are they organized?* (No.)
- Ask: *Does Trisha say* I'm forgetful? (No.) *What does she say?* (I don't always remember things.) *How does Patsy say that the same thing happens to her?* (I don't, either.) Explain that Patsy uses *either* to avoid repeating Trisha's complete sentence, *I don't always remember things.* Have students find the next example of *either* in the conversation. (I'm not, either.) Ask: *What would the complete sentence be in this case?* (I'm not bad-tempered.)
- Ask: *Does Trisha say* I'm outgoing? (No.) *What does she say?* (I make friends easily.) *How does Patsy say that the same happens to her?* (I do, too.) Have students find another example of *too* in the conversation. (I am, too.) Ask: *What would the complete sentence be?* (I'm thoughtful, too.)

- Play the recording or model the conversation. Students listen and repeat.
- **Optional** Have students practice in pairs.
- **Language Chart** Have students study the examples in the language chart. Ask: *What do you use to agree with an affirmative sentence,* too *or* either? (Too.) *When do you use* either? (To agree with a negative sentence.)
- Focus students' attention on the responses with *too* and *either.* Ask: *Can you always use contractions in responses with* too *or* either? (No. You can't say, "I'm, too.") *What verb do you use in the response if the main verb in the first sentence is not* be? (Do or don't.)
- **Optional** Model the examples, pausing for students to repeat.

B 💿 CD2, Track 6

- Have students read the directions and the example. Ask: *Which sentences are affirmative and which ones are negative?* (1 and 4 are affirmative, and 2 and 3 are negative.) *Which sentences use the verb* be? (1 and 2.) *Which verbs do the other sentences use?* (Remember, keep.)
- Have students work individually to write the responses to the sentences.
- Play the recording. Students listen and verify their answers.

> **Audio script**
> Same as the conversations in the Student's Book.

- Check answers with the class. Invite several pairs of volunteers to read one of the conversations aloud.

---

3 Speaking

This exercise practices *too* and *either*.

- Have students read the directions and sentences 1–4. Ask: *What do you have to do?* (Choose one of the two options in parentheses to complete the sentences with your own information. Then write one sentence of your own.)
- Have students work individually to complete the sentences.
- Have students read the examples in the speech balloons. Explain that they are going to compare answers with a classmate using *too* or *either* in the responses, as in the examples.

- Have students compare their answers in pairs.
- To finish, ask whether any of the pairs completed all the sentences in exactly the same way.

> **Workbook**
> Assign the exercises on Workbook page 24.
> (Workbook answers begin on page T-192.)

> **Extra Grammar**
> Assign the exercises for the Extra Grammar, Lesson 14.

2 Language focus

🎧 **A** **Trisha and Patsy talk about their personalities. Listen and practice.**

too	
I'm thoughtful.	I am, too.
I make friends easily.	I do, too.

either	
I'm not bad-tempered.	I'm not, either.
I don't always remember things.	I don't, either.

Trisha Hey, let's do this survey on personalities.

Patsy OK. Sounds like fun.

Trisha So, about me. I don't always remember things.

Patsy I don't, either. I forgot my lunch today!

Trisha Another one. I'm not bad-tempered.

Patsy I'm not, either. I hardly ever get angry.

Trisha Oh, I like this one. I make friends easily.

Patsy I do, too. I guess I'm outgoing.

Trisha Here's another. I'm thoughtful. Well, I hope I am.

Patsy I am, too. I like to help people.

Trisha Oh, boy! This one. I'm not at all organized.

Patsy I'm afraid I'm not, either. My room is always a mess!

Trisha Hey, we're a lot alike! I guess that's why we're best friends.

B **Jack and Roy are talking. Roy agrees with Jack. Complete the conversations with *too* or *either*. Then listen and check.**

1. **Jack** I'm outgoing.

   Roy *I am, too.*

2. **Jack** I'm not creative.

   Roy *I'm not, either.*

3. **Jack** I don't remember things.

   Roy *I don't, either.*

4. **Jack** I keep things in order.

   Roy *I do, too.*

3 Speaking

Complete the sentences. Add one sentence of your own. Then compare your answers with a classmate. *(Answers will vary.)*

1. I _____ (am / am not) organized.

2. I _____ (enjoy / don't enjoy) doing things alone.

3. I _____ (have / don't have) a good imagination.

4. I _____ (do / don't do) my homework every night.

5. _____

I'm organized.   I am, too.   I'm not organized.   I'm not, either.

Mini-review

1 Language check

A Mark is a new student in the class. He and Liam are going to work together on a science project. Complete the conversations with *I am, too; I do, too; I'm not, either;* or *I don't, either.*

Lessons 13 & 14 Mini-review

This lesson reviews the language presented and practiced in Lessons 13 and 14.

1 Language check

This exercise reviews the structures presented so far in this unit.

A

- Have students read the directions.

- Focus students' attention on the cartoon strip. Give them several minutes to read the strip. Ask: *What is Mark and Liam's project about?* (The moon.) *Do they do a good job?* (No, they don't.) *What are they going to do about it?* (They're going to start again and work more carefully.)

- Focus students' attention on the example. Elicit that Mark answers *I'm not, either* to show that he agrees with Liam's negative statement.

- Have students work individually to complete the conversation.

- Check answers with the class.

- Ask a few more questions about the comic strip: *How does Liam feel when Mark spills paint on the project?* (He feels angry.) *Is Liam bad-tempered sometimes?* (Yes, he is.) *What does Mark do?* (He cleans up the paint.)

- **Optional** Have students practice the conversation in pairs. Students should use their own names. Invite one or two pairs to act out the conversation for the class. Encourage them to use a lot of expression as they do this.

Teaching Tip It is important to draw students' attention to all the relevant information in a text and not just to the information they need in order to complete the exercise. In the comic strip in Exercise 1A, students can understand the main idea of the story and answer two or three questions before they complete the exercise. This will make the exercise more meaningful, as students will understand how the characters express agreement.

Culture Note In many schools, projects are often an important part of the learning process. Some teachers may be concerned about the noise level related to doing projects in class. However, if students are interested in what they are doing, this is not usually a problem. Projects help students become more independent learners. Students learn how to cooperate with others, how to agree and disagree politely, and how to make a plan and carry it out.

B

- Review the use of the verbs *do, go,* and *play* by calling out a word and inviting volunteers to make a phrase. (For example, *a concert; go to a concert.*)
- Have students read the directions and the example.
- Have students work individually to complete the sentences.
- Have pairs compare answers by reading the completed sentences to each other.
- Check answers with the class.

C

- Have students read the directions and the example question and answer.
- Have students work individually to complete the questions and write the answers.
- Check the questions and answers with the class. Invite pairs of volunteers to read the questions and answers aloud.
- **Optional** Have students ask and answer the questions with a classmate using their own information. Encourage them to add additional information to their answers using gerunds. For example, *I don't like talking with my friends on the phone. I like chatting with them online.*

2 Listening

In this exercise, students practice *too* and *either*.

💿 CD2, Track 7

- Tell students that they will listen to teenagers talking about themselves. They should listen and write responses showing agreement with what the teenagers say, using expressions listed in the directions.
- Play the recording. Students only listen.

> ### Audio script
> See page T-209.

- Play the recording again. Students listen and write the correct responses.
- Play the recording once again. Students listen and verify their answers.

- Check answers with the class. Write the numbers 1–6 as a list on the board. Invite volunteers to come to the board and copy one of the responses they wrote next to the correct number. Play the recording again, stopping after each teenager speaks. Ask the class whether they agree with the responses on the board. They should justify their answers by giving the key sentence in each speech. For example, the first boy says *I really enjoy chatting online.* (2. I don't like to play computer games. 3. I'm very outgoing. 4. I don't like it at all. 5. I guess I'm not very organized. 6. I really love sports.)

> ### Workbook
> Assign the exercises on Workbook page 25. (Workbook answers begin on page T-192.)

> ### Game
> Assign the game on Student's Book page T-117.

B Complete the sentences with the correct form of *do, go,* or *play.*

1. Some students enjoy _____*playing*_____ chess. It's a popular activity at some schools.

2. _____*Doing*_____ crossword puzzles helps you learn new words.

3. Kim loves _____*playing*_____ the piano. It really helps her relax.

4. _____*Going*_____ to bed late isn't good for you. You'll probably be tired the next day.

5. My brother doesn't like _____*doing*_____ chores on the weekend.

6. _____*Going*_____ to the movies is a fun weekend activity. You can see your favorite movie stars.

7. _____*Playing*_____ board games with your family can be fun.

8. Some teens enjoy _____*going*_____ to concerts with their friends.

C Complete the questions with the correct forms of the verbs. Then answer the questions with your information.

1. (watch TV) Do you like _*watching TV*_____ ?
   _Yes, I do._____

2. (hang out at the mall) Do your friends like _*hanging out at the mall*_ ?
   (Answers will vary.)

3. (talk on the phone) Do you enjoy _*talking on the phone*_ with your friends?
   (Answers will vary.)

4. (do homework online) Do your friends like _*doing homework online*_ ?
   (Answers will vary.)

5. (play computer games) Does your best friend enjoy _*playing computer games*_ ?
   (Answers will vary.)

6. (read books) Does your mother enjoy _*reading books*_____ for fun?
   (Answers will vary.)

2 Listening

Teens talk about themselves. Listen and write the correct responses. Use *I am, too; I do, too; I'm not, either;* or *I don't, either.*

1. _I do, too._____
2. _I don't, either._____
3. _I am, too._____
4. _I don't, either._____
5. _I'm not, either._____
6. _I do, too._____

Go to page 117 for the Game.

Unusual people

1 Language focus

A Read about these unusual people. Complete the sentences with the simple present or the simple past. Listen and check. Then practice.

who clauses

Simple present

I have a cousin. She collects spiders.
I have a cousin **who collects spiders**.

Simple past

I know a woman. She lived and worked in an ice hotel.
I know a woman **who lived and worked in an ice hotel**.

Do you know anyone who has an **unusual talent**?
A **strange habit**? An **interesting collection**?
Write and tell us. The best story wins a prize.

1. I have a cousin who _collects_ (collect) spiders. She has more than 40 spiders in her collection.
   —Sarah

2. I know a woman who lived and _worked_ (work) in an ice hotel in Sweden. She slept on a bed made of ice.
   —Connor

3. I had a friend who _was_ (be) a one-man band. He traveled all over the world.
   —Elizabeth

4. I know a man who _rides_ (ride) a horse to work every day. He lives on my street.
   —Kelley

5. I have a friend who _taught_ (teach) in a circus school last year. He's a lion tamer.
   —Michael

6. I know a five-year-old boy who _talks_ (talk) to animals. He says he understands dogs better than people!
   —Antonio

B Who do you think should win the prize for the best story? Tell the class.

I think Connor should win. The story about the ice hotel is cool!

Unusual people

This lesson presents and practices who *clauses with the simple present and the simple past.*

Review of Lesson 14

- Write on the board:

  I am, too.   I'm not, either.
  I do, too.   I don't, either.

- Divide the class into two teams, A and B.

- Explain that students are going to play a game called "Quick Response." Say some sentences about yourself. After each sentence, call out a student's name. The student has five seconds or less to respond to your sentence by showing agreement with one of the expressions on the board. When students give a correct response in five seconds or less, their team scores a point. If they take longer than five seconds or give a wrong response, the other team scores a point. The team with the most points at the end of the game wins.

- Demonstrate the game with a volunteer.

- Play the game with the class. Possible sentences:

I'm bad-tempered.	*I'm not lazy.*
I often get angry.	*I like doing chores and studying.*
I always do nice things for people.	*I don't keep things in order.*
I don't want help doing things.	*I'm not shy.*
I'm independent.	*I'm outgoing.*

1 Language focus

This exercise presents and practices who **clauses with the simple present and the simple past.**

A 💿 CD2, Track 8

- Have students read the directions and the introduction to the Web site article. Ask: *What's the Web site about?* (People with unusual talents, strange habits, or interesting collections.) *What could you do if you know someone like that?* (Make a Web site.) *What happens if your story is the best one?* (You win a prize.)

- Have students look at the photos. Elicit what the interesting or unusual things about the people might be.

- Have students read text number 1.

- Have students then work individually to complete the sentences in texts 2–6.

- Play the recording. Students listen and verify their answers.

  Audio script
  Same as the sentences in the Student's Book.

- Check answers with the class. Invite volunteers to read aloud one of the sentences they completed.

- Play the recording again or model the sentences. Students listen and repeat.

- **Language Chart** Have students study the examples in the language chart under *Simple present.* Ask: *Does the third sentence give the same information as the first two together?* (Yes.) *What are the two pieces of information it gives?* (The speaker has a cousin. The speaker's cousin collects spiders.) *What word links or combines the two pieces of information?* (Who.) Explain that in this example, the *who* clause gives extra information about the speaker's cousin.

- Focus students' attention on the examples under *Simple past.* Ask: *Does the third sentence also give two pieces of information?* (Yes.) *What are the two pieces of information?* (The speaker knows a woman. She lived and worked in an ice hotel.) *What word links or combines the two pieces of information?* (Who.) Explain that in this example, the *who* clause gives extra information about the woman the speaker is talking about.

- **Optional** Model the examples, pausing for students to repeat.

B

- Invite volunteers to tell the class who they think should win the prize, as in the example in the speech balloon.

C 🔊 CD2, Track 9

- Have students read the directions and the sentences.
- Have students work individually to write the combined sentences.
- Play the recording. Students listen and verify their answers.

- Check answers with the class. Invite volunteers to read aloud one of the sentences they wrote.

D

- Write on the board:

  I know a man . . .   I know a boy . . . I have a . . .
  I know a woman . . . I know a girl . . .

- Give students several minutes to think about three people they know who have unusual talents, strange habits, or interesting collections.
- Have students work individually to write combined sentences about the people they chose. They should use one of the sentence beginnings on the board and *who*.
- Invite volunteers to read their three sentences aloud.

---

2 Listening

In this exercise, students listen to identify unusual people.

🔊 CD2, Track 10

- Have students read the directions and look at the pictures.
- Have the class suggest what is interesting about the people in the pictures. (From left to right, first picture: The girl has a big stamp collection. Second picture: The woman is surfing. She's not as young as we usually think surfers are. Third picture: The girl is dancing. She's very young. Fourth picture: The woman has a lot of children.)
- Play the recording. Students only listen.

- Play the recording again. Students listen and number the pictures in the correct order.
- Play the recording once again. Students listen and verify their answers.
- Check answers with the class. As students give you the number of each picture, ask them to give at least one more piece of information about the person in it. (Possible answers. Picture 1: *The girl won a competition. She was only eight.* Picture 2: *The woman is 63.* Picture 3: *She only collected stamps from Taiwan.* Picture 4: *The children are all under 18.*)

---

3 Speaking

This exercise practices *who* clauses with the simple present and the simple past.

- Ask students to read the directions.
- Have students work individually to read the questions and check the correct boxes. Give them several minutes to think about extra information they can give about the people they had in mind for the questions they answered with yes.
- Focus students' attention on the example in the speech balloon. Ask: *What extra information does the speaker give?* (The person's occupation and who the person is.)
- Invite volunteers to share extra information about two of the people.
- To finish, ask volunteers to tell the class the person who they thought was the most interesting or unusual, and why.
- **Optional** In larger classes, have students work in groups of three or four to share information about the people they chose.

Culture Note
Here are some interesting facts about a few unusual young Americans. The youngest person to graduate from medical school was Balamurali Ambati, who was 17 when he graduated in May 1995. The youngest solo rap singer to have a number-one hit was Bow Wow, who was 14 when he released his CD *Beware of Dog* in July 2000. The youngest sports announcer was Zach Spedden, who was ten in 2002 when he announced a nine-inning baseball game on the radio.

Workbook
Assign the exercises on Workbook page 26. (Workbook answers begin on page T-192.)

Extra Grammar
Assign the exercises for the Extra Grammar, Lesson 15.

C Combine the two sentences to make one sentence. Then listen and check.

1. I know a boy. He plays four instruments.

   I know a boy who plays four instruments.

2. I met a woman. She was an Olympic champion.

   I met a woman who was an Olympic champion.

3. I had a friend. She collected butterflies.

   I had a friend who collected butterflies.

4. I sent an e-mail to a man. He is 102 years old.

   I sent an e-mail to a man who is 102 years old.

D Write three sentences about an interesting person you know. (*Answers will vary.*)

1. _____

2. _____

3. _____

2 Listening

Teens talk about unusual people. Who are they talking about? Listen and number the pictures.

 3

 2

 1

 4

3 Speaking

Read the questions. Check (✓) Yes or No. Then tell the class about two people you know. (*Answers will vary.*)

Do you know a person who . . . ?	Yes	No
1. has an unusual job	☐	☐
2. is very good at something	☐	☐
3. lived in a foreign country	☐	☐
4. had an interesting experience last year	☐	☐
5. visited an interesting place recently	☐	☐

> I know a woman who has an unusual job. She's a cartoon artist. She's my mother.

Lesson 16 — Who's that girl?

1 Language focus

A Will and Pedro are talking at a party.
Who are they talking about? Listen and practice.

Will Hey, that's Mary. She's the new student, isn't she?

Pedro Yes, she is. And who's that girl with her?
You know her, don't you?

Will Yes, I do. That's Sarah Dixon. She's Australian.

Pedro They both have boyfriends, don't they?

Will No, they don't. Sarah has a boyfriend, but I don't think Mary does.

Pedro Who are those guys over there? They're friends, aren't they?

Will Yes, they are. One is Pablo, Sarah's boyfriend.

Pedro Oh, right. He lives in Colombia, doesn't he?

Will Yes, he does.

Pedro And the other one? Who's he?

Will That's Tom Crowe.

Pedro You're in his class, aren't you?

Will Yes, I am. Oh, now I remember. Tom is Mary's boyfriend.

Pedro So, they *do* both have boyfriends. Too bad! Mary is cute!

B Study the chart. Complete the tag questions, and write responses for each question. Then listen and check.

Tag questions and answers with *be*	Tag questions and answers with the simple present
She's the new student, **isn't she?** **Yes, she is. / No, she isn't.**	He lives in Colombia, **doesn't he?** **Yes, he does. / No, he doesn't.**
You're in his class, **aren't you?** **Yes, I am. / No, I'm not.**	You know her, **don't you?** **Yes, I do. / No, I don't.**
They're friends, **aren't they?** **Yes, they are. / No, they aren't.**	They have boyfriends, **don't they?** **Yes, they do. / No, they don't.**

1. You're 18, _aren't you_ ? _No, I'm not._ OR _Yes, I am._

2. Your teachers are hardworking, _aren't they_ ? _Yes, they are. OR No, they aren't._

3. Tokyo is in Japan, _isn't it_ ? _Yes, it is._

4. You're a student, _aren't you_ ? _Yes, I am. OR No, I'm not._

5. You speak Spanish, _don't you_ ? _Yes, I do. OR No, I don't._

6. You have a brother or a sister, _don't you_ ? _Yes, I do. OR No, I don't._

Who's that girl?

This lesson reviews words and phrases to describe people, and presents and practices tag questions and answers with be and with the simple present.

Review of Lesson 15

- Write on the board:

A	B	C	Example
had	boy	be	*I had a friend who lived in a tree house.*
have	cousin	collect	
know	friend	live	
met	girl	speak	
	OR other people	OR other verbs	

- Explain to the class that they have to write two sentences about people using a word from column A, a word from column B, and the correct form of one of the verbs in column C or any other appropriate verb. One sentence should be about a real person and the other sentence about an imaginary person.

- Invite volunteers to share the sentences they wrote with the class. The class guesses which sentence is about a real person and which one is about an imaginary person.

---

1 Language focus

This exercise presents and practices tag questions and answers with *be* and with the simple present.

A 💿 CD2, Track 11

- Have students read the directions and look at the photo.
- Give students several minutes to read the conversation.
- **Optional** Play the recording. Students listen and read along.

> **Audio script**
> Same as the conversation in the Student's Book.

- Ask: *Who are Will and Pedro talking about?* (Sarah, Mary, and the girls' boyfriends.)
- Tell students that you will say a series of statements. They should respond *True* or *False* to each. When a sentence is false, students should correct it.

  Mary is Pablo's girlfriend. (False. Sarah is Pablo's girlfriend. Mary is Tom's girlfriend.)

  Sarah's boyfriend lives in Colombia. (True.)

  Mary's boyfriend is Tom. (True.)

  Pedro doesn't like Mary. (False. Pedro likes Mary.)

- Focus students' attention on Will's first speech. Ask: *How does Will find out if Mary is the new student? What does he say?* (She's the new student, isn't she?) Explain that this is a tag question – a statement followed by a short two-word question, the *tag*. Explain that we use tag questions when we want to make sure our information is correct.

- Have students read the conversation again and underline the other tag questions in it. (You know her, don't you? They both have boyfriends, don't they? They're friends, aren't they? He lives in Colombia, doesn't he? You're in his class, aren't you?)

- Check answers with the class. Invite volunteers to read aloud one of the tag questions they underlined.
- Play the recording again or model the conversation. Students listen and repeat.
- **Optional** Have students practice in pairs.

B 💿 CD2, Track 12

- **Language Chart** Have students study the examples in the language chart. Focus students' attention on the left-hand side of the language chart. Ask: *Which part of the tag questions is affirmative, the statement or the tag?* (The statement.) *How about the tag?* (It's negative.) *So if you use* is *in the statement, what do you use in the tag?* (Isn't.) *If you use* are *in the statement, what do you use in the tag?* (Aren't.) *Are the answers like answers to information questions or like answers to* Yes / No *questions?* (They're like answers to *Yes / No* questions.)

- Follow the same procedure to analyze the tag questions in the right-hand side of the language chart.

- **Optional** Model the examples, pausing for students to repeat.

- Have students work individually to complete tag questions 2–6 and write responses for them.

- Play the recording. Students listen and verify their answers.

> **Audio script**
> Same as the tag questions and answers in the Student's Book.

- Check answers with the class. Ask random students to read aloud one of the tag questions they completed along with its response.

2 Pronunciation Intonation in tag questions

This exercise practices intonation in tag questions.

A 💿 CD2, Track 13

- Have students read the directions and the tag questions.
- Play the recording. Students only listen.

> **Audio script**
> Same as the tag questions in the Student's Book.

- Ask: *Does the intonation go up or down in the tag?* (It goes up.)
- Play the recording again or model the tag questions, exaggerating the intonation. Students listen and repeat.

B

- Give students several minutes to practice saying the tag questions in Exercise 1B, making sure they use rising intonation.
- Invite volunteers to say one of the tag questions they practiced.

> **Teaching Tip**
> "Rehearsing" sounds, stress, or intonation patterns individually, as in Part B above, gives students confidence and leads to more accurate performance.

---

3 Word power

This exercise reviews words to describe people.

- Ask students to read the directions, the words in the box, and the column headings.
- Have students call out any words they do not understand. Explain them by using the words in a sentence or by miming them.

- Have students work individually to complete the columns.
- Check answers with the class. Write the three headings on the board and invite volunteers to come to the board to write words from the box under one of the headings.

---

4 Speaking

This exercise practices tag questions and answers with *be* and with the simple present.

A

- Ask students to read the directions and the example. Ask: *What do you have to do?* (Choose four classmates and write their names and a tag question about each one.) *What's the purpose of the question?* (To check if the information about the classmate is correct.) Explain that students should write questions only with the simple present.
- Ask the class to suggest different kinds of questions they may ask. If necessary, give one or more of these examples:

  You're a soccer fan, aren't you?

  Your sister is a doctor, isn't she?

  You live near here, don't you?

  Your best friend works in a bank, doesn't he?

  Your brothers live in Japan, don't they?

- Have students work individually to write the tag questions.

B

- Have students read the directions and look at the example in the speech balloon.
- Invite volunteers to ask one of the tag questions they wrote. Classmates answer, as in the example.
- **Optional** In larger classes, have students do this activity in groups of four or five.

> **Workbook**
> Assign the exercises on Workbook page 27. (Workbook answers begin on page T-192.)

> **Extra Grammar**
> Assign the exercises for the Extra Grammar, Lesson 16.

2 Pronunciation Intonation in tag questions

A Listen. Notice the rising intonation in these tag questions. Then listen again and practice.

She's from Colombia, isn't she?   He lives in the U.S., doesn't he?

You're Brazilian, aren't you?   We don't have homework, do we?

B Now practice the tag questions in Exercise 1B.

3 Word power

Write the words in the correct columns. (*The order of the answers may vary.*)

☐ has a dog   ☐ is creative   ☐ is trustworthy   ☐ makes friends easily
☑ has blue eyes   ☐ is Peruvian   ☐ likes to take risks   ☐ speaks Spanish
☐ has curly hair   ☐ is tall   ☐ lives in the U.S.   ☐ wears glasses

Appearance	Personality	Other
has blue eyes	is creative	has a dog
has curly hair	is trustworthy	is Peruvian
is tall	likes to take risks	lives in the U.S.
wears glasses	makes friends easily	speaks Spanish

4 Speaking

A How much do you know about your classmates? Write their names and tag questions. (*Answers will vary.*)

Classmates	Questions
Carlos	You walk to school, don't you?
1.	
2.	
3.	
4.	

B Ask your classmates the questions in Part A. How many guesses did you get right?

Carlos, you walk to school, don't you?   Yes, I do.

Read

A **Read the article quickly. Circle the correct answers.**

1. ((Oldest or only)/ Middle) children are usually hardworking.

2. (Middle /(Youngest)) children like being the boss at work.

The youngest is the most outgoing.

Taking personality quizzes is a popular thing to do and many people take them, don't they? But now people can discover their personalities – not from a quiz, but from their **birth order**. **Researchers** say that the oldest, **middle**, youngest, and only children in a family will all have very different personalities.

The oldest or only child likes doing well in school. These people are usually hardworking and are **leaders**. Over half of the U.S. presidents were **firstborn** children. They're children who get lots of time and attention from their parents, say researchers.

The middle child is very creative and thoughtful. These children keep **peace** in a family, say researchers. So they're good with words and are friendly and honest. These people enjoy working in creative careers in the arts or in sales.

The youngest child is the most outgoing. These are the children who like going to parties and are not at all shy. And at work, these people are usually the ones who like being the **boss**.

So, what do you think? Are your birth order and personality connected? Only you can decide. But it's really interesting, isn't it?

Go to page 123 for the Vocabulary Practice.

B **Read the article slowly. Check your answers in Part A.**

C **Are these statements true or false? Write *True* or *False*. Then correct the false statements.**

1. People ~~don't like~~ *enjoy* finding out about their personalities. *False.*

2. Birth order and personality ~~aren't~~ *are* connected. *False.*

3. Parents usually give the most attention to their ~~youngest~~ *oldest / firstborn* child. *False.*

4. The middle child in a family likes to keep the peace. *True.*

5. The youngest child in a family enjoys socializing / going out. *True.*

This lesson practices reading, listening, and writing skills.

Review of Lesson 16

- Write on the board:

  Sue is new in the class, _____ ?

  Fred is 15, _____ ?

  You're a basketball fan, _____ ?

  Fred and Sue are brother and sister, _____ ?

  Lisa lives with her parents, _____ ?

  Henry studies a lot, _____ ?

  Fred and Sue go to the same school, _____ ?

- Invite volunteers to come to the board to complete the tag questions with the appropriate tags.

- Give students several minutes to write two tag questions about one of their classmates, one with the verb *be* and the other with another verb.

- Invite volunteers to ask the class the tag questions they wrote. The class answers. The students say whether the answers are correct or not.

Read

This exercise practices reading for information about the effect of birth order on personality.

A

- Have students read the title of the article and look at the photo. Ask: *How many children are there in the family?* (Three.) *Which one do you think is the oldest? The youngest?* (Students' own answers.)

- Invite a volunteer to read the directions and the statements aloud. Remind students that they should read quickly to find the answers and that they should not read every word carefully.

- Have students work individually to read the article quickly and circle the correct answers. Do not check answers at this point.

B 🔊 CD2, Track 14

- Invite a volunteer to read the directions aloud. Remind students that they should read slowly and carefully, and concentrate on getting the meaning of the entire text.

- List the new vocabulary words on the board: *birth order, researcher, middle, leader, firstborn (adj.), peace, boss (n.).* Explain their meaning. (Birth order: the order in which children are born in a family; researcher: someone who studies something in order to find new information about it; middle: not the oldest or youngest child, but in between; leader: someone who is in charge of a country or a group of people; firstborn [adj.]: being the child born first in a family; peace: good relations among people in a group; boss [n.]: the person who makes the decisions at work.) As an alternative, have students use their dictionaries to find the meanings of the new vocabulary words.

- Have students read the article again.

- Have students check their answers in Part A in pairs. Elicit the answers from one pair.

- **Optional** Play the recording. Students listen and read along.

Audio script

Same as the article in the Student's Book.

Get Connected Vocabulary

Have students do the exercise on Student's Book 123 in class or for homework. (Get Connected Vocabulary answers are on page T-123.)

C

- Invite a volunteer to read the directions and first statement aloud.

- Ask: *Do people enjoy finding out about their personalities?* (Yes.) Ask: *So is the statement true or false?* (False.)

- Have students work individually to write *True* or *False*, and then correct the false statements.

- Check answers with the class. Invite volunteers to read aloud one answer each.

Listen

In this exercise, students listen for information about the birth order of children in two families.

A 🔊 CD2, Track 15

- Focus students' attention on the photo. Ask: *Is the girl very happy?* (No, she isn't.)
- Tell students that they will listen to two friends, May and Phillip, talk about their birth order.
- Have students read the first question and the example answer.
- Explain that students should listen to the conversation and answer the questions with short answers.

> **Culture Note**
> Some famous firstborn children include Bill and Hillary Clinton, Oprah Winfrey, Sylvester Stallone, and Winston Churchill, the prime minister of England during World War II. Examples of famous middle children are Madonna, Princess Diana, and Bill Gates. It's interesting that many comedians are youngest children, such as Jim Carrey, Billy Crystal, Steve Martin, and Rosie O'Donnell. Only children are similar to firstborn children, as they also get a lot of adult attention. The famous golfer Tiger Woods is an only child.

- Play the recording. Students only listen.

> **Audio script**
> See page T-210.

- Play the recording again. Students listen and answer the questions.
- Play the recording once again. Students listen and verify their answers.
- Check answers with the class. Invite volunteers to read aloud one answer each.

B

- Have students read the directions and all the statements.
- Remind students that *I agree* means you think something is right, *I disagree* means you think something is not right, and *I'm not sure* means you cannot say if it is right or not. Tell students that there are no right or wrong answers for this exercise – they are giving their opinions.
- Have students work individually to write whether they agree, disagree, or are not sure, and give reasons for their answers.
- Have students work in pairs to compare answers, or elicit opinions from volunteers.

Write

In this exercise, students answer questions and write a paragraph about their birth order.

A

- Invite a volunteer to read the directions and the questions aloud.
- Have students work individually to answer the questions.
- **Optional** Have students ask and answer the questions in pairs.

B

- Invite a volunteer to read the directions aloud. Tell students that they will use the information in Part A to help them write about their birth order.
- Have students work individually to write their paragraphs.

- Invite several volunteers to read their paragraphs to the class.
- **Optional** Have students work in groups of four and read each other's paragraphs. It might be interesting to group students according to birth order, with all the oldest children in their family in one group, all the middle children in another group, and so on. Are their personalities like the ones described in the article? How are they similar? How are they different?

> **Workbook**
> Assign the exercises on Workbook page 28. (Workbook answers begin on page T-192.)

I'm the only boy!

A 🔊 **May and Phillip talk about their birth order. Listen and answer the questions.**

1. Is May angry about her sister getting a cell phone? <u>Yes, she is.</u>

2. Is May the youngest child in her family? <u>No, she isn't.</u>

3. Does Phillip's sister think life is easier for her than Phillip? <u>Yes, she does.</u>

4. Does Phillip have friends who study hard? <u>Yes, he does.</u>

5. Is Phillip an only child? <u>No, he isn't.</u>

B **What do you think? Write *I agree, I disagree,* or *I'm not sure.* Give reasons.**
(Answers will vary.)
1. Youngest children have an easy life. _____

2. Getting a lot of attention from your parents is good. _____

3. Being an only child is great. _____

4. Birth order and personality are connected. _____

Your turn

Write

A **Answer the questions about your birth order.** *(Answers will vary.)*

1. Are you an only, oldest, middle, or youngest child? _____

2. What are some of your personality traits? Do they match traits of your birth order?

   _____

3. What are some good things and bad things about your birth order?

   _____

4. Which is the best: being a youngest, middle, oldest, or only chid? Why?

   _____

B **Write a paragraph about your birth order. Use the answers in Part A to help you.** *(Answers will vary.)*

I'm the	child in my family . . .

Language chart review

Gerunds as subjects	Gerunds as objects
Going online is fun.	My friends and I love **going** online.

Tag questions and answers with *be*	Tag questions and answers with the simple present

You're in my science class, **aren't you**?
  Yes, I am. / No, I'm not.
He's Mexican, **isn't he**?
  Yes, he is. / No, he isn't.
They're cousins, **aren't they**?
  Yes, they are. / No, they aren't.
	You wear glasses, **don't you**?
	  Yes, I do. / No, I don't.
	She studies a lot, **doesn't she**?
	  Yes, she does. / No, she doesn't.
	They live near you, **don't they**?
	  Yes, they do. / No, they don't.

A Complete the questions for a survey.

1. He plays on the basketball team, _doesn't he_ ?

   It's enjoyable, _isn't it_ ?

2. You hang out with friends a lot, _don't you_ ?

   That's fun, _isn't it_ ?

3. She has a job in the school office, _doesn't she_ ?

   It's hard work, _isn't it_ ?

4. You do crossword puzzles, _don't you_ ?

   They're interesting, _aren't they_ ?

5. He does homework on Saturdays, _doesn't he_ ?

   It's awful, _isn't it_ ?

B Look again at the sentences in Part A. Combine the two
sentences to make a question. Use a gerund phrase as the
subject. Then answer the questions with your own information.

1. **Q:** _Playing on the basketball team is enjoyable,_   **A:** _Yes, it is._
   isn't it?

2. **Q:** _Hanging out with friends is a lot is fun, isn't it?_   **A:** _(Answers will vary.)_

3. **Q:** _Having a job in the school office is hard work, isn't it?_   **A:** _(Answers will vary.)_

4. **Q:** _Doing crossword puzzles is interesting, isn't it?_   **A:** _(Answers will vary.)_

5. **Q:** _Doing homework on Saturdays is awful, isn't it?_   **A:** _(Answers will vary.)_

Unit 4 Review

This lesson reviews the grammar and vocabulary introduced in Unit 4.

Language chart review

These charts summarize the main grammar presented and practiced in Unit 4.

- Books closed. Write on the board:

  1. Going online is fun.   *2. My friends and I love going online.*

- Focus students' attention on the examples on the board. Ask: *Which form of the verb is used in the underlined phrases?* (The gerund.)

- Remind students that a gerund phrase can function as a subject or as an object in a sentence. Invite a volunteer to come to the board and write the headings *Subject* and *Object* over the appropriate examples. (Sentence 1. Subject. Sentence 2. Object.)

- Read these statements, one at a time, and invite volunteers to turn them into tag questions by adding an appropriate tag. After each tag question, elicit affirmative and negative answers.

  You're in my science class. (You're in my science class, aren't you?)

  He's Mexican. (He's Mexican, isn't he?)

  They're cousins. (They're cousins, aren't they?)

  You wear glasses. (You wear glasses, don't you?)

  She studies a lot. (She studies a lot, doesn't she?)

  They live near you. (They live near you, don't they?)

- Books open. Have students study the examples in the Language chart review.

- Answer any questions students may have.

Exercises A through D (pages T-56 to T-57)

Note: Students can do these exercises for homework or in class. They should do these exercises with minimal teacher input or help. If you choose to do these exercises as homework, briefly review the exercise directions in class. Make sure that students understand what they should do. Check the answers with the class during the next class meeting. If you choose to do the exercises in class, follow the directions below.

Exercise A

- Invite a volunteer to read the directions and the example aloud.

- Have students work individually to complete the tag questions for the survey.

- Have students check their answers in pairs.

- Check answers with the class. Invite several pairs of volunteers to read the sentences aloud.

Exercise B

- Books closed. Write the two questions from Exercise A, number 1, on the board. Circle the words *plays on* and *the basketball team* in the first question and the word *enjoyable* in the second question. Ask: *How can we combine two questions into one question with a gerund?* (Playing on the basketball team is enjoyable, isn't it?) Explain that students do not need to use all the words in the original questions. (In this example, students use only the words *plays on, the basketball team, is,* and *enjoyable* from the original questions.)

- Have students read the directions and the example.

- Have students work individually to write the questions and answer them with their own information.

- Check answers with the class.

People T-56

Language chart review

These charts summarize further grammar presented and practiced in Unit 4.

- Have students study the examples in the charts.
- Remind students to use *too* to express agreement with affirmative sentences and *either* to express agreement with negative sentences.
- Remind students also to use *who* clauses. Explain that the verb in the *who* clause can be in the simple present or the simple past.
- Answer any questions students may have.

Exercise C

- Have students look at the chart and read the directions.
- Focus students' attention on the example. Tell students that they will find the information for the B answers in the chart.
- Have students work individually to complete the conversations.
- Check answers with the class.

Exercise D

- Books closed. Write on the board: *My cousin is a scientist. He studies the weather.* Ask: *How can we combine these two sentences into one sentence by using the word* who? (My cousin is a scientist who studies the weather.)
- Invite a volunteer to read the directions and the example sentence aloud.
- Students work individually to combine the sentences to make one sentence with a *who* clause.
- Check answers with the class.

Take another look!

- Invite a volunteer to read the directions aloud.
- Have students work individually to mark the sentences *T* (true) or *F* (false).
- Check answers with the class.

- If students did the Review exercises for homework, check answers with the class.
- Have students work in pairs to practice asking and answering the questions in Exercise B. Then ask each pair to write two original questions and short answers using the same pattern.
- Have students work in pairs. They make a chart like the one in Exercise C, but with different words. Refer them to the Word Power on Student's Book page 46 if they need more ideas for adjectives. They complete the chart with their own information and use it to make a conversation using the conversation in Exercise C as a model.
- Ask students for the names of some famous people in their communities. Write the names and occupations or positions on the board. Then ask students to think of something each person has done and make notes on the board. Invite volunteers to make sentences with *who* using the information on the board. For example, *Mario Rivera is the businessperson who opened the new pizza restaurant on Main Street.*

Theme Project

- Assign the *At Home* section of the Unit 4 Theme Project on Student's Book page 129.

Workbook

- Assign the Unit 4 Check Yourself on Workbook page 29. (Workbook answers begin on page T-192.)

Extra Practice Worksheets

- Assign the Unit 4 Extra Practice worksheets starting on page T-148.

Extra Speaking Practice Worksheet

- Assign the Unit 4 Extra Speaking Practice worksheet on page T-171.

Arcade Activities

- Assign the Unit 4 Arcade activities found at: www.cambridge.org/connectarcade

Learning Log

- Assign the Unit 4 Learning Log. This can be downloaded from the Teacher Support Site at: www.cambridge.org/connect2e/teacher

Quiz

- Give the Unit 4 Quiz on page T-181.

Test

- Give the Unit 4 Test (Form A and / or Form B). These can be downloaded from the Teacher Support Site at: www.cambridge.org/connect2e/teacher

Language chart review

too		either	
I'm hungry.	I am, too.	I'm not tired.	I'm not, either.
I read magazines.	I do, too.	I don't play video games.	I don't, either.

who clauses	
Simple present	**Simple past**
I have a friend. She loves studying French.	I read about a man. He collected cars.
I have a friend **who loves studying French.**	I read about a man **who collected cars.**

C Look at the chart. Then complete the conversations.

	A	B
Age	15	15
Organized	no	no
Hardworking	yes	yes
Likes pizza	no	no

1. **A** I'm 15.
   B _I am, too._

2. **A** I'm not organized.
   B _I'm not, either._

3. **A** I'm hardworking.
   B _I am, too._

4. **A** I don't like pizza.
   B _I don't, either._

D Combine the two sentences to make one sentence with a *who* clause.

1. Renata Costa is a Brazilian soccer player. She played in her first World Cup game at 17.

   Renata Costa is a Brazilian soccer player who played in her first World Cup game at 17.

2. Al Gore was a U.S. vice president. He won the Nobel Peace Prize.

   Al Gore was a U.S. vice president who won the Nobel Peace Prize.

3. Yao Ming is a Chinese basketball player. He's 7 feet 6 inches tall.

   Yao Ming is a Chinese basketball player who is 7 feet 6 inches tall.

4. Sally Ride was an astronaut. She was the first American woman in space.

   Sally Ride was an astronaut who was the first American woman in space.

5. Paul McCartney is a British singer. He was a member of the Beatles.

   Paul McCartney is a British singer who was a member of the Beatles.

Take another look!

Read the sentences. Write *T* (true) or *F* (false).

1. Gerunds always end with *-ing*. ___T___
2. In tag questions, the verb (*aren't, doesn't*, etc.) comes after the pronoun (*you, he*, etc.). ___F___

Go to page 129 for the Theme Project.

For fun

1 Language focus

A What have these students done for fun during the week? Listen and practice.

I've been really busy this week. I've read three books, I've hung out with friends at the skate park, and I've played video games at the video arcade. I haven't done all of my homework, though. I haven't had time! My parents aren't very happy about that.   —*Will*

We've been really busy this week, too. We've gone out almost every night. We've seen a couple of movies, and we've gone to a basketball game at school. We've also rented three videos so far. We haven't watched any TV this week, though. We haven't had any time!
—*Diana and Jessica*

B Study the chart. Complete the sentences with the present perfect. Then listen and check.

Present perfect with *I* and *We*	
The present perfect is formed with the verb *have* + the past participle.	
I've been busy this week.	**We've gone out** every night.
I haven't done all of my homework.	**We haven't watched** any TV.

Regular past participles:	play → play**ed**	rent → rent**ed**	watch → watch**ed**

Irregular past participles:	be → **been**	go → **gone**	read → **read**
	do → **done**	hang → **hung**	see → **seen**
	eat → **eaten**	have → **had**	

1. Juan: <u>*I haven't done*</u> (not do) many interesting things this week. Let's see . . . <u>*I've played*</u> (play) video games, and <u>*I've gone*</u> (go) to the mall with my father. But <u>*I haven't seen*</u> (not see) any movies, and <u>*I haven't eaten out*</u> (not eat out) at any restaurants. <u>*I've done*</u> (do) a lot of homework, though!

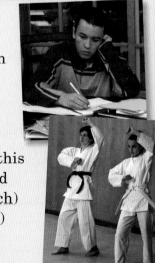

2. Carla and Pedro: <u>*We've been*</u> (be) very busy this week. <u>*We've had*</u> (have) two karate classes, and <u>*we've gone*</u> (go) canoeing. <u>*We've watched*</u> (watch) a tennis match, too. But <u>*we haven't watched*</u> (not watch) soccer on TV, and <u>*we haven't read*</u> (not read) any comic books!

Lesson 17 For fun

This lesson presents and practices phrases with do, make, *and* play, *and the present perfect with* I *and* We.

1 Language focus

This exercise presents and practices the present perfect with *I* and *We*.

A 💿 CD2, Track 16

- Have students read the directions and look at the photos.
- Give students several minutes to read the texts. Explain the meaning of *though*. (Here, it shows contrast in meaning with the sentences that came before.) Explain that *so far* means *up until the present*.
- **Optional** Play the recording. Students listen and read along.

> **Audio script**
> Same as the texts in the Student's Book.

- Ask: *What activity didn't Will have time for?* (His homework.) *Who hung out with friends at the skate park?* (Will.) *Who went to a basketball game at school?* (Diana and Jessica.) *How many videos did Diana and Jessica rent?* (Three.)
- Write on the board:

> *I hung out with my friends at the skate park on Tuesday.*
> *We didn't watch any TV this week.*

- Ask: *What form of the verb is used in these sentences?* (Simple past.) Underline *on Tuesday* and *this week*. Ask: *What day did Will hang out with his friends?* (On Tuesday.) *When didn't Diana and Jessica watch TV?* (This week.) Remind students that the simple past describes a completed action that happened (or did not happen) at some point in the past. When the specific time of an action is mentioned, the simple past is used. Point to the underlined words in the sentences on the board.
- Write on the board:

> *I've hung out with my friends at the skate park.*
> *We've gone to a basketball game at school.*

- Ask: *Do we know when Will hung out with his friends?* (No.) *Do we know when Diana and Jessica went to the basketball game?* (No.) Explain that these sentences are in the present perfect. The present perfect is used to talk about actions completed (or not completed) at some *unspecified* time in the past. The exact time when the action happened is not important.

- Write on the board: *We've gone out almost every night.* Explain that the present perfect is also used to talk about repeated actions at unspecified times in the past. The exact time each repeated action happened is not important.
- Have students read the texts again and find out how many examples of the present perfect there are in each. (6 and 7.)
- Play the recording or model the sentences. Students listen and repeat.
- **Optional** Have pairs read the texts, each student reading one text.

B 💿 CD2, Track 17

- **Language Chart** Have students study the examples in the language chart. Focus students' attention on the words in bold. Ask: *How many verbs do you use to form the present perfect?* (Two.) *What's the first verb?* (Have.) Explain that the form of the second verb is the past participle. Remind students of the different verb forms they know: infinitive, simple present, present / past continuous, gerund, and simple past.
- Focus students' attention on the lists of past participles. Explain that the past participle of regular verbs is the same as the simple past form. Most irregular verbs, however, have different past and past participle forms, for example, *did / done* and *ate / eaten*. Ask students to find two exceptions to this in the lists. (*Had* and *read* are both past and past participle forms.)
- **Optional** Model the examples, pausing for students to repeat.
- Have students read the texts and the example.
- Have students work individually to complete the texts.
- Play the recording. Students listen and verify their answers.

> **Audio script**
> Same as the texts in the Student's Book.

- Check answers with the class. Invite volunteers to come to the board to write one of the sentences they completed.

This unit introduces vocabulary and expressions to talk about everyday activities. It also introduces and practices the present perfect.

2 Word power

This exercise presents and practices phrases with *do, make,* and *play.*

A

- Have students read the directions and the words. Have students call out any words they do not understand. Explain them by using them in sentences or by miming them.
- Have students work individually to make verb phrases.
- Check answers with the class. Invite volunteers to read one of the verb phrases they made.

B

- Have students read the directions and the examples.
- Have students work individually to write the six sentences. Students can use ideas in Part A or their own ideas.
- Have students tell a classmate about what they have done and what they have not done this week. They should note any activities they have in common.
- To finish, invite pairs to share with the class one of the activities they had in common. For example, *(Kim) and I have done a lot of homework.*

3 Speaking

This exercise practices talking about activities using the present perfect with *I* and *We*.

A

- Have students read the directions and look at the Fun-O-Meter. Ask: *How does the Fun-O-Meter work?* (The more fun activities you have done, the higher your temperature.)
- Give students several minutes to think about the fun activities they have done this week and check the corresponding box.
- Have students talk to their classmates to find a classmate for each level on the thermometer, following the examples in the speech balloons, and writing their classmates' names in the chart.

Note: If your class is not too large, you may want your students to mingle for this type of exercise. If your class is large, have students talk to the students seated near them.

B

- Invite volunteers to take turns telling the class about someone who is like them, following the example in the speech balloon.

Teaching Tip Many students find it difficult to understand the meaning of the present perfect. Reassure students that in the next few lessons they will see many other examples of this form and that, little by little, they will understand how it works. Encourage students to think of the form they use in their own language to express the meanings that in English are expressed with the present perfect.

Workbook
Assign the exercises on Workbook page 30. (Workbook answers begin on page T-192.)

Extra Grammar
Assign the exercises for the Extra Grammar, Lesson 17.

2 Word power

A Make verb phrases by adding *do*, *make*, or *play*.

make a cake	_do_ exercises	_do_ homework
_do_ chores	_make_ friends	_make_ money
play the piano	_play_ a game	_make_ plans

B Write three things you have done and three things you have not done this week. Use ideas in Part A or your own ideas. Then tell a classmate. *(Answers will vary.)*

I've made a cake.

I haven't done chores.

1. _____
2. _____
3. _____
4. _____
5. _____
6. _____

> I've made a cake, . . .

3 Speaking

A What have you done this week? Look at the Fun-O-Meter. Check (✓) the sentence that best describes you. Then find a classmate for each level of fun. Write your classmates' names in the chart. *(Answers will vary.)*

What have you done this week?	You	Classmates
I've done lots of fun activities this week.	☐	_____
I've done three or four fun activities this week.	☐	_____
I've done one or two fun activities this week.	☐	_____
I haven't done any fun activities this week.	☐	_____

Really a Lot of Fun
A Lot of Fun
A Little Fun
Not Fun at All

Fun-O-Meter

> I've done three or four fun activities this week. How about you, Sally?

> I've done lots of fun activities this week.

B Now tell the class about someone like you.

> Jane and I have done three fun activities this week. We've been very busy.

Young entertainers

1 Word power

Which five of these activities would you most like to do or have happen? Circle the activities. Then listen and practice. *(Answers will vary.)*

1
become a big star

2
entertain a live audience

3
give interviews

4
have a hit TV show

5
make a movie

6
record a song

7
sign autographs

8
support a charity

9
win a great award

2 Language focus

A Read about these young entertainers. Then listen and practice.

Corbin Bleu
Actor, singer, and dancer
Millions of people have seen Corbin Bleu perform. He's acted, he's sung, and he's danced in many movies. He's been in all of the *High School Musical* movies. Corbin hasn't won an Emmy for his acting, but he'd like to win an Emmy someday.

Haley Joel Osment and Emily Osment, Actors
Brother and sister Haley Joel and Emily Osment have become big stars. Haley Joel has made several movies and he's performed on TV. Emily has been on TV, too. She's also recorded a CD. She hasn't acted with her brother in a movie, but she'll probably do it someday.

Jonah Ellsworth
Cello player
Jonah Ellsworth is only 13, but he's won many awards. He's met the cellist Yo-Yo Ma, and they've given a concert together. But at school, he's like everyone else. He loves to play sports with his classmates. They haven't heard him play the cello, but they might someday!

Lesson 18 — Young entertainers

This lesson presents and practices verb phrases to describe entertainment-related activities. It also presents and practices the present prefect with he, *she,* and they.

Review of Lesson 17

- Say the following verbs and ask students to call out the past participles: *be, eat, go, hang, have, play, read, rent, see, watch.* Write the past participles on the board.
- Have students write a sentence about something they have done and something they have not done this week. For example: *I have seen four movies. I haven't read any books.* One of the sentences should be false.
- Invite volunteers to read the sentences they wrote. The class guesses the false sentences.
- Divide the class into small groups. Give students in each group several minutes to compare things they have done and not done this week.
- Invite a representative from each group to share with the class something they have done and something they have not done this week. For example: *We've watched a lot of TV. We haven't gone out.*

1 Word power

This exercise presents and practices verb phrases to describe entertainment-related activities.

A CD2, Track 18

- Have students read the directions and look at the pictures.
- Have students read the nine entertainment-related activities. Explain the meaning of *live audience*, *hit TV show*, *record* (v.), *support* (v.), and *charity*.
- Call out the activities in random order. Students respond with the appropriate number.
- Have students work individually to circle the activities they would most like to do or have happen.
- Play the recording. Students listen and repeat.

Audio script
Same as the activities in the Student's Book.

- Invite volunteers to read one of the activities they circled. After each volunteer reads an activity, ask for a show of hands of all the other students who chose the same activity.
- To finish, ask the class which are the two most popular activities.

2 Language focus

This exercise presents and practices the present perfect with *he, she* and *they*.

A CD2, Track 19

- Have students cover the three texts and look at the photos. Ask students whether they recognize any of the young entertainers. If so, ask them to share with the class any information they know about them. If not, ask them to guess what the entertainers do.
- Have students read the texts and check if the information they shared or guessed is correct.
- **Optional** Play the recording. Students listen and read along.

Audio script
Same as the texts in the Student's Book.

- Focus students' attention on the first text. Ask: *Has Corbin Bleu been in a lot of movies?* (Yes.) *What is he?* (He's an actor, a singer, and a dancer.) *Has he acted in the* High School Musical *movies?* (Yes.) *Has he won an Emmy?* (No.) *Would he like to win an Emmy?* (Yes.) Follow the same procedure to check comprehension of the other texts.
- Have students read the texts again and underline examples of the present perfect with *he, she,* and *they*. Elicit an example of each.
- Play the recording or model the sentences. Students listen and repeat.
- **Optional** Have students read the texts in groups of three, each student reading one text aloud.

B

- **Language Chart** Have students study the examples in the language chart. Remind students that the present perfect is used to talk about actions completed at some unspecified time in the past. It is also used to talk about repeated actions in the past. The exact time of each repeated action is not important. If a specific time is mentioned, then the simple past is used rather than the present perfect.

- Ask: *What two verbs are used with* he *and* she? (*Has* and a past participle.) *What two verbs are used with* they? (*Have* and a past participle.) Ask: *What's the contracted form of* he has? (*He's.*) *What's the contracted form of* they have not? (*They haven't.*)

- **Optional** Model the examples, pausing for students to repeat.

- Ask students to read the directions and the examples.

- Have them work individually to look through the three texts in Part A again, find the past participles of the verbs, and write them in the blanks.

- Have students check their answers in pairs.

- Check answers with the class. Ask random students to come to the board to write one answer each.

C CD2, Track 20

- Ask students to read the directions and the example.

- Have students work individually to complete the sentences with the verbs in parentheses.

- Play the recording. Students listen and verify their answers.

Audio script

Same as the sentences in the Student's Book.

- Check answers with the class. Invite volunteers to read aloud one of the sentences they completed.

---

3 Listening

In this exercise, students listen for information about the lives of two famous entertainers.

 CD2, Track 21

- Have students read the directions and items 1–6. Tell students that they will listen for information about both Haley Joel Osment and his sister Emily.

- Play the recording. Students only listen.

Audio script

See page T-210.

- Play the recording again. Students listen and check the correct boxes.

- Play the recording once again. Students listen and verify their answers. As they do so, write on the board:

  1. Emily was five years old in 1997.

  2. Both Haley Joel and Emily have made movies.

- Check answers with the class. Invite volunteers to answer one of the questions in the chart, using the sentences on the board as a model.

- To finish, ask the class if they know about any other famous entertainers from the same family.

Culture Note

Many young entertainers do not continue their careers into adulthood. Some decide they want to do other things. One of the most famous child actors of all time, Shirley Temple, made 44 movies before she was 12 years old. She chose to retire in 1949 at the age of 21. Later, she did some work on radio and in TV, but she never made another movie. In later life, however, Shirley Temple became a U.S. ambassador and a diplomat. Other child actors go on to have successful acting careers as adults. Elijah Wood, who is most famous for starring in the *The Lord of the Rings* (2001), began his acting career at the age of eight. He is still working in movies.

Workbook

Assign the exercises on Workbook page 31. (Workbook answers begin on page T-192.)

Extra Grammar

Assign the exercises for the Extra Grammar, Lesson 18.

B Study the chart. Write the past participles from Part A.

Present perfect with *he, she,* and *they*	
He's acted in all of the *High School Musical* movies.	**He hasn't won** an Emmy.
She's recorded a CD.	**She hasn't acted** with her brother.
They've given a concert together.	**They haven't heard** him play the cello.

1. (he / see) _he's seen_
2. (they / act) _they've acted_
3. (she / sing) _she's sung_
4. (they / be) _they've been_
5. (she /win) _she's won_
6. (he / become) _he's become_
7. (they / make) _they've made_
8. (she / perform) _she's performed_
9. (they / record) _they've recorded_
10. (she / meet) _she's met_
11. (he / give) _he's given_
12. (he / hear) _he's heard_

C Complete the sentences with the present perfect. Then listen and check.

1. She _'s appeared_ (appear) in fashion magazines.

2. They _haven't recorded_ (not record) any hit songs.

3. She _'s competed_ (compete) in the Olympic Games twice.

4. He _hasn't acted_ (not act) in any plays on Broadway in New York City.

5. They _'ve won_ (win) a lot of tennis matches this year.

6. They _'ve sold_ (sell) millions of their CDs.

7. He _hasn't made_ (not make) any movies this year.

3 Listening

A radio host interviews a fan about Haley Joel and Emily Osment. Which star is the information about? Listen and check (✓) the correct boxes.

Who . . . ?	Haley	Emily
1. was four years old in 1992	✓	☐
2. made a movie in 1999	☐	✓
3. has worked more in TV	☐	✓
4. hasn't won an Academy Award	✓	☐
5. has made some music videos	☐	✓
6. is going to be in a Broadway show	✓	☐

Mini-review

Lessons 17 & 18

1 Language check

A Complete Ramiro's biography of Kany Garcia. Use the present perfect.

Kany Garcia

- Kany Garcia was born in 1982 in Puerto Rico.

- Her family is very musical. Her brother plays the cello in the Puerto Rican Symphony Orchestra. She _'s studied_ (study) classical cello and the guitar. But she really loves singing, too.

- Kany _has written_ (write) many songs. People call her music intelligent and beautiful. For her, the words of a song are very important.

- She _'s recorded_ (record) an album with Sony Records. She _'s won_ (win) a Gold Album. It _'s sold_ (sell) more than 100,000 copies.

- Kany _has received_ (receive) four Latin Grammy nominations, but she _hasn't won_ (not win) a Grammy.

- She _hasn't recorded_ (not record) an album in English.

- Kany _has supported_ (support) a special charity for children in Puerto Rico.

B Complete the e-mail message. Use the present perfect.

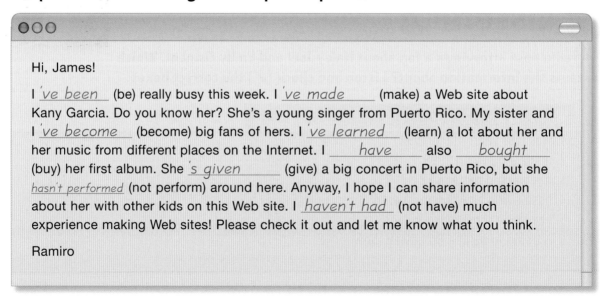

Hi, James!

I _'ve been_ (be) really busy this week. I _'ve made_ (make) a Web site about Kany Garcia. Do you know her? She's a young singer from Puerto Rico. My sister and I _'ve become_ (become) big fans of hers. I _'ve learned_ (learn) a lot about her and her music from different places on the Internet. I _have_ also _bought_ (buy) her first album. She _'s given_ (give) a big concert in Puerto Rico, but she _hasn't performed_ (not perform) around here. Anyway, I hope I can share information about her with other kids on this Web site. I _haven't had_ (not have) much experience making Web sites! Please check it out and let me know what you think.

Ramiro

Mini-review

This lesson reviews the language presented and practiced in Lessons 17 and 18.

1 Language check

This exercise reviews the structures presented so far in this unit.

A

- Focus students' attention on the photo. Ask students if they know Kany Garcia. If so, ask them to share what they know about her with the class. If not, ask them to guess what they think Kany is famous for.

- Have students read the text and check if the information they shared or guessed is correct.

- Have students work individually to complete the sentences.

- Check answers with the class. Invite volunteers to read aloud one of the sentences they completed.

- To finish, have students read the text again and check the two sentences which, in their opinion, describe Kany's most important achievements so far.

- Invite volunteers to share their opinions about Kany's most important achievements with the class.

B

- Have students read the e-mail message. Ask: *What's the connection between this e-mail and the Web site in Part A?* (Both are about Kany Garcia.) *Who's a fan of Kany Garcia, Ramiro or his sister?* (Both of them are.) *Who's made a Web site about her?* (Ramiro.) *Where's Kany Garcia from?* (Puerto Rico.) *What does Ramiro want to do on his Web site?* (Share information about Kany Garcia with other kids.) *Has Ramiro made a lot of Web sites?* (No.)

- Have students work individually to complete the e-mail message using the present perfect.

- Check answers with the class. Invite volunteers to come to the board to write one of the sentences they completed.

C

- Invite a volunteer to read the directions and the example aloud. Point out that students have to complete affirmative sentences about the things Ken, Emily, and Jamie have done and negative sentences about the things they haven't done.

- Have students work individually to complete the sentences.
- Have students work in pairs to read their sentences to their partner.
- Check answers with the class.

2 Listening

In this exercise, students practice the present perfect.

A 💿 CD2, Track 22

- Tell students that they will listen to an interview on the school radio station. The interviewer is interviewing two students, Natalia and Manuel, for the school newspaper.
- Invite a volunteer to read the directions and the example aloud.
- Play the recording. Students only listen.

> **Audio script**
> See page T-211.

- Play the recording again. Students listen and mark each sentence as *T* (true) or *F* (false). Do not check answers at this point.

B 💿 CD2, Track 23

- Play the recording again. Give students several minutes to correct the false statements in Part A.
- Play the recording once again. Students listen and verify their answers.

> **Audio script**
> Same as the script in Part A.

- Check answers with the class. Invite volunteers to read their answers aloud.

> **Workbook**
> Assign the exercises on Workbook page 32. (Workbook answers begin on page T-192)

> **Game**
> Assign the game on Student's Book page 118.

C Ken, Emily, and Jamie have been busy this week. Look at the chart. Then complete the sentences about the things they have done (✓) and the things they haven't done (✗).

	Ken	Emily	Jamie
Do chores	✗	✗	✗
Make plans for Saturday	✗	✓	✗
Play the piano	✗	✓	✓
Hang out with friends	✓	✗	✗
Watch TV	✓	✗	✓
Eat out	✓	✓	✓

1. They *haven't done chores* .
2. Emily *has made plans for Saturday* .
3. Ken and Jamie *haven't made plans for Saturday* .
4. Emily and Jamie *have played the piano* .
5. Ken *hasn't played the piano* .
6. Ken *has hung out with friends* .
7. Emily and Jamie *haven't hung out with friends* .
8. Ken and Jamie *have watched TV* .
9. Emily *hasn't watched TV* .
10. They *have eaten out* .

2 Listening

A A student reporter is interviewing Natalia and Manuel for the school newspaper. Are the sentences true or false? Listen and write *T* (true) or *F* (false).

1. Natalia has learned a lot from her ~~brother~~. *mother* _F_
2. She has climbed Mount Baldy ~~three~~ times. *two* _F_
3. She hasn't visited the Andes. _T_
4. Manuel and Miguel ~~have~~ performed on TV. *haven't* _F_
5. They haven't sold many CDs. _T_
6. Radio stations ~~have~~ played their CD. *haven't* _F_

B Listen again and correct the false statements in Part A.

 **Go** to page 118 for the Game.

Are you a fan?

1 Language focus

Present perfect Yes/No questions with ever

Have you ever gone to a concert?
Yes, I have. / No, I haven't.
Has she ever met Kylie Minogue?
Yes, she has. / No, she hasn't.

A Carla and Pedro are buying tickets for a concert. Listen and practice.

Pedro Hi, Carla. Are you in line for the Kylie Minogue concert?

Carla Yes, I am. I'm so excited!

Pedro Have you ever gone to one of her concerts?

Carla Yes, I have. I've been to ten of her concerts!

Pedro Wow! This will be my first Kylie concert. Have you ever gotten her autograph?

Carla No, I haven't. Have you?

Pedro No, I haven't, but my friend Lily has. She's been to every Kylie concert here.

Carla Has she ever met Kylie?

Pedro Yes, she has. She met her backstage at a concert last year. She always gets invited backstage.

Carla Then let's go with her to the concert. I can't wait to meet Kylie!

B Complete the conversations. Then listen and check.

1. **Sam** ___Have___ you _ever gotten_ (get) a sports star's autograph?
   Maggie Yes, I ___have___ .

2. **Pia** ___Has___ Matt _ever gone_ (go) to a rock concert?
   Beth Yes, he ___has___ .

3. **Kim** ___Has___ your best friend _ever won_ (win) a radio contest?
   Kayla No, she ___hasn't___ .

4. **Tom** ___Have___ you _ever written_ (write) a fan letter?
   Bill No, I ___haven't___ .

5. **Kate** ___Has___ your sister _ever met_ (met) a famous singer?
   Ellen Yes, she ___has___ .

6. **Jack** ___Has___ your brother _ever had_ (have) a girlfriend?
   Matt Yes, he ___has___ . He's had two girlfriends.

Lesson 19 Are you a fan?

This lesson presents and practices present perfect Yes / No *questions with* ever.

Review of Lesson 18

- Write on the board:

  <u>My favorite movie star</u>
  He's made a lot of movies.
  He's appeared on TV.
  He's won an Academy Award.
  He's French.

  <u>My favorite band</u>
  They've sold millions of CDs.
  They've given concerts in many different countries.
  They've recorded in English and in Spanish.
  They're American.

- Point out that the first three sentences in each column on the board use the present perfect. The last sentence in each group uses the simple present.

- Have students work individually to write four sentences about their favorite movie star and four about their favorite band, following the examples on the board.

- Invite volunteers to read one of the sets of sentences they wrote. The class guesses the name of the movie star or the band.

1 Language focus

This exercise presents and practices present perfect Yes / No *questions with* ever.

A 💿 CD2, Track 24

- Have students read the directions and look at the photo. Ask: *What are Carla and Pedro doing?* (They're standing in line to buy tickets.)

- Have students read the conversation.

- **Optional** Play the recording. Students listen and read along.

> **Audio script**
> Same as the conversation in the Student's Book.

- Ask: *Who's giving the concert?* (Kylie Minogue.) Have students share with the class any information they may know about Kylie Minogue.

- Ask: *Who's been to a lot of Kylie's concerts?* (Carla.) *Who else has been to a lot of Kylie's concerts?* (Lily.) *Who's Lily?* (Pedro's friend.) *Has Pedro been to any of Kylie's concerts?* (No.) *Who's been invited backstage at Kylie's concerts, Carla, Pedro, or Lily?* (Lily.) *Why does Carla want to go to the concert with Lily?* (Because Carla wants to be invited backstage.)

- Explain to students that you will give them clues for finding questions in the conversation. After each clue, you will call on random students to say the right question. Read these clues, pausing after each one to give students time to find the question.

  Pedro wants to know if Carla has ever gone to a Kylie concert. (Have you ever gone to one of her concerts?)

  Pedro wants to know if Carla has ever gotten Kylie's autograph. (Have you ever gotten her autograph?)

  Carla wants to know if Lily has ever met Kylie. (Has she ever met Kylie?)

- Ask: *What form is used in the questions?* (The present perfect.) Explain that *ever* means "in my life up to now."

- Play the recording or model the conversation. Students listen and repeat.

- **Optional** Have students practice in pairs.

- **Language Chart** Have students study the examples in the language chart. Focus students' attention on the position of *ever* in the questions and on the position of *have* in the questions and in the short affirmative and negative answers. Remind students that we use *have* with the first person singular (I), the second person singular (you), and the third person plural (they), and that we use *has* with the third person singular (he, she, it).

- **Optional** Model the examples, pausing for students to repeat.

B 💿 CD2, Track 25

- Ask students to read the directions and the example.

- Have students work individually to complete the conversations.

- Play the recording. Students listen and verify their answers.

> **Audio script**
> Same as the conversations in the Student's Book.

- Check answers with the class. Invite pairs of volunteers to read one conversation aloud.

2 Listening

In this exercise, students listen for information about things the speakers have done.

💿 **CD2, Track 26**

- Have students read the directions and questions 1–6.
- Explain to students that they will listen to Diane and Julio talking about Jordin Sparks. Students should listen for what Diane and Julio have done and write *D* for Diane or *J* for Julio.
- Play the recording. Students only listen.

> ### Audio script
> See page T-211.

- Play the recording again. Students listen and write *D* or *J*.
- Play the recording once again. Students listen and verify their answers.
- Check answers with the class. Play the recording again and ask students to call out *Stop!* when they hear the information for each of the questions.

3 Pronunciation Stress in *Have you ever*

In this exercise, students practice *have you ever* questions.

A 💿 **CD2, Track 27**

- Explain to students that in conversation *ever* is usually stressed in *Have you ever* questions.
- Play the recording. Students only listen.

> ### Audio script
> Same as the questions in the Student's Book.

- Play the recording again. Students listen and repeat.

B

- Give students several minutes to practice saying the questions in Exercise 1B on page 64, making sure they stress *ever*.
- Invite volunteers to say one of the questions they practiced.

4 Speaking

This exercise practices asking about past experiences.

A

- Have students read the directions. Demonstrate the example with a volunteer (Classmate A).
- Have students work individually to write the questions.
- Have students ask a classmate the questions and check Yes or No, according to the answers.

B

- Have students read the directions and the example conversation.
- Demonstrate the activity with a volunteer (Classmate B).
- Invite two more volunteers to demonstrate the activity again.
- Have students work in pairs to carry out the activity. Students will make a note of the number of right guesses their partner makes about Classmate A's answers.
- To finish, ask students from several different pairs to say how many right guesses they made.

> ### Workbook
> Assign the exercises on Workbook page 33.
> (Workbook answers begin on page T-192.)

> ### Extra Grammar
> Assign the exercises for the Extra Grammar, Lesson 19.

2 Listening

Diane and Julio are fans of Jordin Sparks. Who has done these things, Diane or Julio? Listen and write *D* (Diane) or *J* (Julio).

Who has . . . ?	
1. gotten Jordin's autograph	D
2. met Jordin	J
3. written a fan letter to Jordin	J
4. received a postcard from Jordin	J
5. bought a Jordin Sparks poster	D
6. gotten a ticket to one of her concerts	D

3 Pronunciation   Stress in *Have you ever*

A Listen. Notice the stress in *Have you ever* questions. Then listen again and practice.

Have you **ever** met a **rock** star?   Have you **ever** won a **ticket**?

Have you **ever** climbed a **mountain**?   Have you **ever** eaten **snails**?

B Now practice the questions in Exercise 1B.

4 Speaking

A Write five *Have you ever* questions. Then ask a classmate (Classmate A) the questions, and check (✓) Yes or No. (*Answers will vary.*)

	Classmate A	
	Yes	No
Have you ever met a sports star?	☐	☐
1. _____	☐	☐
2. _____	☐	☐
3. _____	☐	☐
4. _____	☐	☐
5. _____	☐	☐

B Ask another classmate (Classmate B) the questions in Part A. Classmate B guesses Classmate A's answers. How many did he or she guess right?

You	Has Jake ever met a sports star?
Classmate B	Yes, he has.
You	Right. Has Jake ever studied French?
Classmate B	Yes, he has.
You	Wrong. He hasn't studied French.

1 Language focus

A Are you good at pop culture trivia? Find out. Check (✓) the correct answers. Listen and check. Then practice.

How long has Harrison Ford had a star on the Walk of Fame?
  He's had a star **since May 2003.**
  Since May 2003.
How long has Johnny Depp acted in movies?
  He's acted in movies **for about 25 years.**
  For about 25 years.

1. How long has Harrison Ford had a star on the Walk of Fame?
   ☑ Since May 2003.
   ☐ Since May 1993.

2. How long has Johnny Depp acted in movies?
   ☐ For about 15 years.
   ☑ For about 25 years.

3. How long has Hollywood been the center of the movie industry?
   ☑ Since the 1920s.
   ☐ Since the 1950s.

4. How long has Disneyland been a popular tourist attraction?
   ☑ For about 50 years.
   ☐ For about 75 years.

5. How long have people celebrated New Year's Eve in Times Square?
   ☑ For over 100 years.
   ☐ For over 50 years.

6. How long has MTV shown music videos?
   ☐ Since 1971.
   ☑ Since 1981.

B Write two interesting trivia questions about your life. Ask a classmate the questions. Can your classmate answer correctly? *(Answers will vary.)*

1. _____
2. _____

You How long have I had a pet rabbit?
Classmate You've had a pet rabbit for three years.
You Right.

Lesson 20 Pop culture trivia

This lesson presents and practices How long has / How long have . . . ? *and* since *and* for.

Review of Lesson 19

- Elicit a present perfect *Yes / No* question-and-answer pattern with *ever* such as that found in the Lesson 19 language chart. Write it on the board. Review with students.

- Say the following present perfect statements. Have students convert them into present perfect *Yes / No* questions with *ever*. *Grace has seen a concert.* (Has Grace ever seen a concert?) *They haven't gone to a basketball game.* (Have they ever gone to a basketball game?) *Mr. Lee hasn't eaten sushi.* (Has Mr. Lee ever eaten sushi?) *Lilia has written an e-mail.* (Has Lilia ever written an e-mail?) *Steve has played soccer.* (Has Steve ever played soccer?)

- Play "Toss the Ball." Students toss a ball to the classmate of their choice and ask a present perfect *Yes / No* question with *ever*. The student holding the ball answers the question and then tosses it to another student, continuing the activity.

1 Language focus

This exercise presents and practices *How long has / How long have. . . ?* **and** *since* **and** *for.*

A CD2, Track 28

- Focus students' attention on the name of the lesson. Explain that *trivia* refers to details about celebrities and their lives – for example, the number of movies an actor has made.

- Have students read items 1 and 2. Ask students to share with the class any information they know about Harrison Ford or Johnny Depp. Explain that the Walk of Fame is a sidewalk on Hollywood Boulevard in Hollywood, California. Bronze star-shaped plaques are placed in the sidewalk to honor celebrities for their contributions to show business.

- Draw on the board:

$$X$$
$$\rule{3cm}{0.4pt}\ 2003\ \rule{2cm}{0.4pt}\ NOW$$

- Say: *Harrison Ford got his star in 2003. He's had a star on the Walk of Fame since 2003.*

- Now draw the following on the board. Write the appropriate year to indicate 25 years ago under the X. In this example, the year is 1985.

$$X$$
$$\rule{4cm}{0.4pt}\ 1985\ \rule{4cm}{0.4pt}\ NOW$$
$$25\ years$$

- Say: *Johnny Depp began acting in movies in the mid-1980s. He's acted in movies for about 25 years.*

- Explain that when the present perfect is used with *for* or *since*, it describes actions or situations that started in the past and continue into the present. We use *since* with a specific time in the past and *for* with a period of time.

- Have students read the rest of the questions and check what they think are the correct answers.

- Play the recording. Students listen and verify their answers.

Audio script

Same as the questions and correct answers in the Student's Book.

- Check answers with the class. Invite volunteers to read one of the questions and the answer they checked.

- Play the recording again or model the questions and answers. Students listen and repeat.

- **Language Chart** Have students study the examples in the language chart. Ask: *Which words in the questions ask about a period of time?* (How long.) *What form is used in the questions?* (The present perfect.) *Do you always have to use a long sentence as an answer?* (No. You can give a short answer.) *What words do the short answers begin with?* (Either *since* or *for*.)

- **Optional** Model the examples, pausing for students to repeat.

B

- Invite a volunteer to read the directions aloud. Demonstrate the activity by reading the example conversation with a volunteer.

- Have students work individually to write the questions.

- Have students work with a classmate to take turns asking and answering the questions, following the example conversation.

Entertainment T-66

C CD2, Track 29

- Have students read the directions and the example. Ask: *What do you have to do?* (Complete the questions and answers.) *What words should all the questions begin with?* (How long.) *Should the answers be long or short?* (They can be either long or short.)

- Focus students' attention on question 2. Explain that Grauman's Chinese Theater is famous because many stars have had their handprints and footprints set in cement in front of the theater.

- Have students read the cues for the questions and answers.

- Remind students that *since* is used when indicating the specific time an event began in the past. *For* is used when indicating the duration of an event that started in the past and continues into the present. Ask: *Where will you use* since? (Answers to questions 2 and 5.) *Where will you use* for? (Answers to questions 3 and 4.)

- Have students work individually to write the questions and answers.

- Play the recording. Students listen and verify their answers.

Audio script

Same as the questions and answers in the Student's Book.

- Check answers with the class. Invite several pairs of volunteers to read aloud one of the questions and answers they completed.

- To finish, invite a few volunteers to say which of the trivia questions they found most interesting.

Culture Note

Every year, the Academy for Motion Picture Arts and Sciences presents awards to movies, actors, actresses, directors, costume designers, and others to celebrate excellence in filmmaking. The winners receive a small golden statue nicknamed Oscar. The Academy Awards are held in Los Angeles, California. It is estimated that 40 million people watch the awards in the United States. This award show is also broadcast around the world to 100 countries, where nearly one billion people watch it each year.

---

2 Listening

In this exercise, students listen for the answers to trivia questions.

 CD2, Track 30

- Have students read the directions and items 1–4. Ask the class if they know any of the answers. If they do, write the number of the question(s) and the suggested answers on the board with a question mark next to it.

- Play the recording. Students only listen.

Audio script

See page T-212.

- Play the recording again. Students listen and check the correct answers.

- Play the recording once again. Students listen and verify their answers.

- Check answers with the class. Play the recording again and ask students to call out *Stop!* when they hear the information for each of the questions.

---

3 Speaking

This exercise practices *How long have . . . ?* and *since* and *for*.

A

- Ask students to read the directions and the example.

- Have students work individually to complete question 2 and write question 3.

B

- Have students read the directions.

- Tell them they will make up the answers.

- Have students work in pairs to role-play the interview.

- **Optional** Invite one of the pairs to role-play the interview for the class.

Workbook

Assign the exercises on Workbook page 34. (Workbook answers begin on page T-192.)

Extra Grammar

Assign the exercises for the Extra Grammar, Lesson 20.

C Complete the questions and answers. Then listen and check.

1. the company Paramount Pictures / be / in Hollywood

   Q: *How long has the company Paramount Pictures been in Hollywood?*

   A: *It's been in Hollywood since* 1913. OR *Since* 1913.

2. Jamie Foxx / have / a star on the Hollywood Walk of Fame

   Q: *How long has Jamie Foxx had a star on the Hollywood Walk of Fame?*

   A: *He's had a star on the Hollywood Walk of Fame since / Since* September 14, 2007.

3. people / have / color TVs

   Q: *How long have people had color TVs?*

   A: *They've had color TVs for / For* over 50 years.

4. rock music / be / popular

   Q: *How long has rock music been popular?*

   A: *It's been popular for / For* a long time.

5. actors / receive / Oscars at the Academy Awards

   Q: *How long have actors received Oscars at the Academy Awards?*

   A: *They've received Oscars at the Academy Awards since / Since* 1927.

2 Listening

Jessica, Diana, and Carla appear on a TV game show about pop culture trivia. Listen and check (✓) the correct answers.

1. Broadway Tony Awards
   - ☐ since 1927
   - ☑ since 1947

2. MGM Studios
   - ☑ since 1924
   - ☐ for 100 years

3. CDs
   - ☐ since the 1970s
   - ☑ since the 1980s

4. Grauman's Chinese Theatre
   - ☐ for about 50 years
   - ☑ for about 75 years

3 Speaking

A Imagine you will interview a famous actor. Complete questions 1 and 2. Write question 3. *(Answers will vary.)*

1. *How long have you been* (be) an actor?
2. _____ (live) in Hollywood?
3. _____

B Now role-play the interview with a classmate. Make up the answers.

Read

A Read the article quickly. Check (✓) the main idea of the article.

☐ 1. Reality shows are only for very talented singers.

☐ 2. Reality show performers always become very successful.

☑ 3. You need luck and talent to win on a reality show.

How to Be Rich and Famous

Have you ever watched a **reality show** on TV? Of course you have! They're some of the most popular shows on TV. People have watched reality shows for many years, but they became really popular several years ago with shows like *American Idol*. Millions of **viewers** all over the world have seen this show, and thousands of people have performed on the show. They want to win **recording contracts** and become famous singers. Some of the show's winners have sold millions of CDs, and they now have successful singing **careers**.

So, what kind of reality show do you want to perform on? Have you ever told jokes to people, and have they laughed? Then maybe you can try a reality show for **comedians**. Are you a good dancer? Yes? Then try a reality show for dancers.

Research says that one in seven young people would like to go on a reality show and become famous. So, **go ahead** – **audition** for a show. And if you do . . . good luck!

Go to page 124 for the Vocabulary Practice.

B 💿 **Read the article slowly. Check your answer in Part A.**

C Answer the questions.

1. How long have reality shows been popular? *They've been popular for many years.*

2. Have a lot of people performed on *American Idol*?
   Yes, they have.

3. What do the people on *American Idol* want to win?
   They want to win recording contracts.

4. What has happened to some of the show's winners?
   They have sold millions of CDs.

5. What other kinds of reality shows are there?
   There are reality shows for comedians and dancers.

Unit 5 Get Connected

This lesson practices reading, listening, and writing skills.

Review of Lesson 20

- Write on the board:

  1. _____ a dancer?

  2. _____ in New York?

  3. _____ with the Blue Dance Group?

  4. _____ best friends?

  5. _____ a collection of dance videos?

- Divide the class into small groups.

- Explain that you will twice read a short story about a teenager. Students will listen and try to remember as many events as possible in the story. They cannot make notes.

- Read the following story twice:

  Mandy Perez is a 15-year-old dancer. She started dancing at the age of 5. When Mandy was 10, she moved to New York with her family. Two years after moving to New York, she joined the Blue Dance Group. She met her best friend, Cindy, on the first day of class. Mandy has a great collection of dance videos. She started the collection when she was 11. She has about 30 dance videos now.

- Explain to students that they will write five questions about the story using *How long has / How long have . . . ?* and the endings on the board. They will also write the answers. The group that finishes first wins.

Read

This exercise practices reading for information about reality shows on TV.

A

- Have students look at the top photo. Ask: *Do you know what TV show this photo is from?* (American Idol.)

- Invite a volunteer to read the directions aloud. Remind students that they should read quickly to find the answer and that they should not read every word carefully.

- Have students work individually to read the article quickly and check the main idea. Do not check answers at this point.

B 🔘 CD2, Track 31

- Invite a volunteer to read the directions aloud. Remind students that they should read slowly and carefully, and concentrate on getting the meaning of the entire text.

- List the new vocabulary words on the board: *reality show, viewer, recording contract, career, comedian, go ahead, audition (v.)*. Explain their meaning. (Reality show: a TV program starring real people, not actors; viewer: a person who watches TV; recording contract: an agreement between a singer or group and a record company to record and distribute the singer's song or the group's music; career: an occupation – the kind of work you do; comedian: a person who tells jokes to make people laugh; go ahead: to start to do something; audition [v.]: to perform in front of others who test your ability as a singer, actor, etc., so that you can be on a TV show, in a play, in a movie, etc.) As an alternative, have students use their dictionaries to find the meanings of the new vocabulary words.

- Have students read the article again.

- Have students check their answer in Part A in pairs. Elicit the answer from one pair.

- **Optional** Play the recording. Students listen and read along.

Audio script

Same as the article in the Student's Book.

Get Connected Vocabulary

Have students do the exercise on Student's Book page 124 in class or for homework. (Get Connected Vocabulary answers are on page T-124.)

C

- Invite a volunteer to read the directions and the first question aloud.

- Ask: *How long have reality shows been popular?* Elicit the answer. (They've been popular for many years.)

- Have students work individually to answer the questions.

- Have students check their answers in pairs.

- Check answers with the class. Invite pairs of volunteers to read aloud one question and answer each.

Listen

In this exercise, students listen for information about reality shows.

A 🔊 CD2, Track 32

- Focus students' attention on the photo from the TV show. Ask: *What kind of reality show could this cake be from?* (A cooking show.)

- Tell students that they will listen to two friends, Ricardo and Jill, talk about reality shows.

- Have students read the first question and example answer.

- Explain that students should listen to the conversation and answer the questions.

> **Culture Note**
> Reality TV shows feature ordinary people, as opposed to professional actors, in a variety of situations. Some, like the *Survivor* program, have participants compete against each other in a series of difficult physical challenges. Others have different types of competitions such as singing (*American Idol*) or dancing (*Dancing with the Stars*). There are also somewhat more serious reality programs in which people relive a period of history, such as life in the American West in the 19th century. These programs are not a competition. The purpose is to show what life was like at that time and how people of today react to the challenge of living without modern conveniences.

- Play the recording. Students only listen.

> **Audio script**
> See page T-212.

- Play the recording again. Students listen and answer the questions.

- Play the recording once again. Students listen and verify their answers.

- Check answers with the class. Invite several pairs of volunteers to read the questions and answers aloud.

B

- Have students read the directions and the questions.

- Read the first question with the class and elicit answers from several students. Remind students that there are no right or wrong answers for this exercise – they are giving their opinions.

- Have students work individually to answer the questions, and give reasons for their answers.

- Have students work in pairs to compare answers, or elicit opinions from volunteers.

Write

In this exercise, students answer questions and write a paragraph about winning an imaginary reality show contest.

A

- Invite a volunteer to read the directions and the questions aloud.

- Have students work individually to answer the questions. Tell students that they will write about winning an imaginary reality show, not a real one.

- **Optional** Have students ask and answer the questions in pairs.

B

- Invite a volunteer to read the directions aloud. Tell students that they will use their answers in Part A to help them write about winning an imaginary reality show contest.

- Have students work individually to write their paragraphs.

- Invite several volunteers to read their paragraphs to the class.

- **Optional** Have students work in groups of four and read each other's paragraphs. Students should ask questions about anything they do not understand. When volunteers have finished reading, the class can vote for the most unusual or most interesting reality show.

> **Workbook**
> Assign the exercises on Workbook page 35.
> (Workbook answers begin on page T-192.)

You should go on that show.

A 🔊 **Ricardo and Jill talk about reality shows. Listen and answer the questions.**

1. Who taught Jill everything she knows about cooking?
   Her grandmother taught her everything she knows about cooking.

2. Has Jill ever seen the reality show *Top Chef*?
   No, she hasn't.

3. What do the winners on *Top Chef* win?
   They get $100,000 and a lot of cool prizes.

4. What places have the teams on *Survivor* been to?
   They've been to China, Australia, and Africa.

5. What kind of show would Ricardo like to go on?
   He'd like to go on an eating show.

B **What do you think? Answer the questions. Give reasons.** (*Answers will vary.*)

1. Why do you think reality shows are so popular? _____

2. Have you ever watched any reality shows? Which ones? _____

3. Have you or your friends ever auditioned for a reality show? _____

4. Do you think reality shows are a good way to start a career? _____

Your turn

A **Imagine you have just won a reality show contest. Answer the questions.** (*Answers will vary.*)

1. What kind of reality show is it? _____

2. Were you surprised about winning? _____

3. Was it exciting to win? Why? _____

4. What did you win? _____

5. Has your life changed? How? _____

B **Write a paragraph about winning a reality show contest. Use the answers in Part A to help you.** (*Answers will vary.*)

⬤ ⬤ ⬤

I've just won . . .

_____

_____

_____

_____

◀ ▶

Entertainment   69

Language chart review

Present perfect statements	
Affirmative	**Negative**
I've seen two movies this week.	**I haven't eaten** in a restaurant.
He's had a lot of fun this week.	**He hasn't been** home much.
They've made three new friends.	**They haven't done** their homework.

A Look at Rosie's date book. It's Thursday night. What has she done this week? What hasn't she done? Complete the sentences about Rosie and her friends and family.

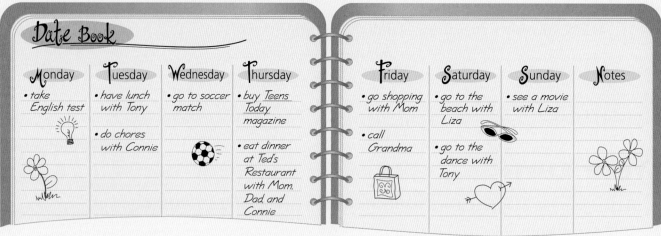

Date Book

Monday
• take English test

Tuesday
• have lunch with Tony
• do chores with Connie

Wednesday
• go to soccer match

Thursday
• buy Teens Today magazine
• eat dinner at Ted's Restaurant with Mom, Dad, and Connie

Friday
• go shopping with Mom
• call Grandma

Saturday
• go to the beach with Liza
• go to the dance with Tony

Sunday
• see a movie with Liza

Notes

1. Rosie _has taken_ an English test.
2. She and her friend Liza _haven't gone_ to the beach.
3. Rosie and her family _have eaten_ at a restaurant.
4. She _has gone_ to the soccer match.
5. She _has bought_ Teens Today magazine.
6. Rosie _hasn't called_ her grandmother.
7. She _hasn't seen_ a movie.
8. Rosie and her little sister Connie _have done_ chores at home.
9. She and her friend Tony _have had_ lunch together.

B Now it's Saturday night. What has Rosie done since Friday? What hasn't she done? Complete the sentences with the present perfect.

I've had (have) an awesome time so far! _I've done_ (do) a lot of interesting things. _I've gone_ (go) shopping with Mom. _I've gone_ (go) to the beach with Liza. Tony and I went to the dance tonight. It was great! _I haven't seen_ (not see) a movie with Liza. I'll do that tomorrow. Uh-oh. I _haven't done_ (not do) any homework!

Unit 5 Review

This lesson reviews the grammar and vocabulary introduced in Unit 5.

Language chart review

This chart summarizes the main grammar presented and practiced in Unit 5.

- Books closed. Write on the board:

  I've seen two movies this week. I haven't eaten in a restaurant this week.

  1. (have) fun

  2. (make) new friends

  3. (be) home a lot / much

  4. (do) homework

- Focus students' attention on the two sentences on the board. Ask: *What form is used in these sentences?* (The present perfect.) *When do you use the present perfect?* (When an action or event happened – or didn't happen – at some unspecified time in the past.)

- Invite volunteers to tell the class about what they have or have not done this week. They will make sentences using the cues on the board.

- Books open. Have students study the Language chart review.

- Answer any questions students may have.

....

Exercises A through C (pages T-70 to T-71)

Note: Students can do these exercises for homework or in class. They should do these exercises with minimal teacher input or help. If you choose to do these exercises as homework, briefly review the exercise directions in class. Make sure that students understand what they should do. Check the answers with the class during the next class meeting. If you choose to do the exercises in class, follow the directions below.

Exercise A

- Have students read the directions and the examples.

- Focus students' attention on Rosie's date book. Tell students that it is now Thursday night. Some events are now in the past, and others are in the future. Ask: *What did Rosie do on Monday?* (She took an English test.) *What is she going to do next Sunday?* (She's going to see a movie with Liza.)

- Have students work individually to complete the sentences.

- Have students check their answers in pairs.

- Check answers with the class.

Exercise B

- Invite a volunteer to read the directions and the example sentence.

- Focus students' attention on Rosie's date book in Part A. Tell students that it is now Saturday night.

- Have students work individually to complete the sentences with the present perfect.

- Check answers with the class. Invite volunteers to read aloud one of the sentences they completed.

Language chart review

This chart summarizes further grammar presented and practiced in Unit 5.

- Have students study the examples in the chart.
- Remind students that in questions in the present perfect, *have / has* goes before the subject. The word *ever* goes before the past participle.
- Remind students also to use *since* + a specific time (*10:00 a.m., Friday,* etc.) and *for* + a length of time (*two days, three years,* etc.).
- Answer any questions students may have.

Exercise C

- Have students read the directions and the texts about the new students at Kennedy Junior High.
- Focus students' attention on the example.
- Have students work individually to complete the questions and answers.
- Check answers with the class. Invite several pairs of volunteers to read the questions and answers aloud.

Take another look!

- Have a volunteer read the directions aloud.
- Students work individually to check all the sentences that are true for Sue.
- Check answers with the class.

Optional Unit Wrap-Up

- If students did the Review exercises for homework, check answers with the class.
- Have students make a date book with several entries like the ones in Exercise A. They should include the present day and one or two days before and after. Remind them to include some activities they are doing with other people, such as friends and family. Students exchange date books with a classmate and write sentences like those in Exercise A about their classmate's activities.
- Have students use their own date books to write a paragraph like the one in Exercise B about the things they have done and have not done.
- Invite several volunteers to answer these questions: *When did you start at this school? What's your favorite memory? What would you like to do in the future?* Make notes of their answers on the board with the person's initials next to the answer. Have students work in pairs to ask and answer questions about their classmates using the information on the board. They use the questions in Exercise C as a model.

Theme Project

- Assign the *At Home* section of the Unit 5 Theme Project on Student's Book page 130.

Workbook

- Assign the Unit 5 Check Yourself on Workbook page 36. (Workbook answers begin on page T-192.)

Extra Practice Worksheets

- Assign the Unit 5 Extra Practice worksheets starting on page T-152.

Extra Speaking Practice Worksheet

- Assign the Unit 5 Extra Speaking Practice worksheet on page T-172.

Arcade Activities

- Assign the Unit 5 Arcade activities found at: www.cambridge.org/connectarcade

Learning Log

- Assign the Unit 5 Learning Log. This can be downloaded from the Teacher Support Site at: www.cambridge.org/connect2e/teacher

Quiz

- Give the Unit 5 Quiz on page T-182.

Test

- Give the Unit 5 Test (Form A and / or Form B). These can be downloaded from the Teacher Support Site at: www.cambridge.org/connect2e/teacher

Language chart review

Present perfect *Yes / No* questions with *ever*	How long has / How long have ... ? since and for

Have you ever lived in an apartment?
  Yes, I have. / No, I haven't.
Has he ever gone to Africa?
  Yes, he has. / No, he hasn't.
	How long have you had your cell phone?
	I**'ve** had it **since Friday**. / **Since Friday**.
	How long has Kimmy lived in London?
	  She**'s** lived in London **for about five years**.
	  For about five years.

C **Read about the new students at Kennedy Junior High. Write questions. Then complete the answers.**

Kaya Morita

Kaya and her family moved here six months ago. She started at Kennedy on Monday. Her favorite memory: She traveled to Australia last year. Her wish for the future: She would love to write a book someday.

Rob and Dave Borelli

Rob and Dave came to Kennedy two weeks ago. Their favorite memory: They met Gustavo Kuerten. Their wish for the future: They want to win a tennis tournament someday.

1. **Q:** (visit Australia) *Has Kaya ever visited Australia?*

   A: *Yes, she has* . Kaya and her family visited Australia last year.

2. **Q:** (be at Kennedy) *How long has she been at Kennedy?*

   A: *Since Monday. / She's been at Kennedy since Monday.* . She just started school.

3. **Q:** (write a book) *Has she ever written a book?*

   A: *No, she hasn't* , but she'd like to write a book someday.

4. **Q:** (win a tennis tournament) *Have they ever won a tennis tournament?*

   A: *No, they haven't* , but they want to.

5. **Q:** (meet a sports star) *Have they ever met a sports star?*

   A: *Yes, they have* . They met Gustavo Kuerten at a tennis match.

Take another look!

Read the sentences. Then check (✓) all the sentences that are true for Sue.

Sue says, "I've lived in Mexico City since June."

a. ☑ Sue lives in Mexico City now.
b. ☐ Sue moved to Mexico City a few years ago.
c. ☑ Sue used to live in another place.
d. ☑ Sue hasn't lived in Mexico City for a very long time.

Go to page 130 for the Theme Project.

Taking risks

1 Word power

A Look at the pictures. Then listen and practice.

dye my hair

explore a cave

ride a motorcycle

go out without permission

go rock climbing

go skydiving

sing karaoke

start a rock band

try new foods

B Complete the sentences with the correct phrases from Part A.

1. He's going to a mountain with big rocks. He might _go rock climbing_ .
2. I love the color blue. I'd like to _dye my hair_ blue.
3. She loves rock music and plays the guitar. Someday, she's going to _start a rock band_ .
4. They love to eat. They always like to _try new foods_ .
5. I'd like to _ride a motorcycle_ . I like to go fast. Do you think my parents will give me permission?
6. He's not shy, and he loves to sing. He'll _sing karaoke_ .
7. They love to fly. Maybe someday they'll _go skydiving_ .
8. My friend's parents say he can't go out on Saturday, but he's going to _go out without permission_ . That's bad.
9. He likes discovering new places. He might _explore a cave_ .

Lesson 21 Taking risks

This lesson presents and practices verb phrases related to taking risks and the present perfect with never.

1 Word power

This exercise presents and practices verb phrases related to taking risks.

A ⊙ CD2, Track 33

- Focus students' attention on the title of the lesson. Explain that *taking risks* means "doing something that doesn't have a definite outcome – the outcome could be good, or it could cause loss or injury."
- Give students several minutes to read the directions and look at the pictures.
- Play the recording. Students listen and repeat.

> **Audio script**
> Same as the verb phrases in the Student's Book.

- **Optional** Invite volunteers to share with the class an experience they have had and one they have not had, choosing from the new vocabulary. For example, *I've dyed my hair, but I haven't explored a cave.*

Culture Note For teens, risk-taking behavior is a way of testing themselves and establishing their identity. Adults often discourage this behavior as dangerous. Now some research shows that teens who engage in positive risk-taking are less likely to do more dangerous things. Examples of positive risk-taking might be social activities such as joining a new club or physical activities such as rock-climbing (done with the proper safety precautions). Even things such as taking a difficult class in school or being on a sports team involve risk. In other words, teens can experience the thrill and challenge of risk without putting their health or lives in danger.

B

- Have students read the directions and the example.
- Have students work individually to complete the sentences with one of the verb phrases from Part A.
- Check answers with the class. Invite volunteers to read aloud one of the sentences they completed. Discuss with the class which word(s) in the incomplete sentences helped them choose the correct phrases. (For example, *mountain* and *big rocks* in sentence 1.)
- **Optional** Have students rewrite one of the sentences so that it is true for them. For example: *I'm not shy, and I love to sing. I'll sing karaoke this weekend.* Invite volunteers to share with the class the sentences they wrote.

Teaching Tip Optional activities can help students retain the new vocabulary by relating it to their own experience. Other ways to enhance retention of new vocabulary include:

<u>Association activities</u> Students associate the new vocabulary with vocabulary they already know. For example:

> *Which words do these phrases make you think of?*
> *dye my hair* (Hairdresser, pink, my cousin.)
> *explore a cave* (Walk, climb, adventure.)

<u>Paraphrasing activities</u> Students explain the meaning of the new vocabulary using known vocabulary. For example:

> *dye my hair* (Make my hair a different color.)
> *explore a cave* (Visit a new place.)

<u>Ranking activities</u> Students rank the new vocabulary according to a given criterion. For example:

> *Number the activities in the pictures from 1 = very risky to 9 = not risky at all.*

UNIT 6 Experiences

This unit introduces vocabulary and expressions for talking about personal experiences.

2 Language focus

This exercise presents and practices the present perfect with *never*.

A 💿 CD2, Track 34

- Ask students to read the directions and look at the photo. Ask: *What are Juan and Will talking about?* (They're talking about taking risks.)
- Have students read the conversation.
- **Optional** Play the recording. Students listen and read along.

> ### Audio script
> Same as the conversation in the Student's Book.

- Ask: *What are the risks Juan and Will talk about?* (Rock climbing, skydiving.) *Is Will going to go on the rock-climbing trip?* (No.) *Is Juan going to go on the rock-climbing trip?* (He probably will, but he doesn't actually say.) *Who's going to go on the skydiving trip?* (Will.)
- Read the following clues. Have students find the sentences in the conversation and call them out.

  Will hasn't had any rock-climbing experience. Find the sentence in which he says this. (I've never gone rock climbing.)

  Find Will's answer to the question "Have you ever gone skydiving?" (No, never.)

  Juan doesn't have any experience jumping from a plane. Find the sentence in which he says this. (I've never jumped from a plane.)

- Ask: *Which word in the sentences you called out means* not at any time *or* at no time? (Never.)
- Play the recording or model the conversation. Students listen and repeat.

- **Optional** Have students practice in pairs.
- **Language Chart** Have students study the examples in the language chart. Focus students' attention on the first two sentences in the chart. Ask: *Where does the word* never *go in affirmative statements?* (After *have* or *has* and before the past participle.) Focus students' attention on the question and the two possible answers. Ask: *Where does the word* ever *go in questions?* (After the subject pronoun and before the past participle.) *What do you say to give a short negative answer?* (No, never.) Focus students' attention on the note. Ask: *Is it correct to say* Have you never gone skydiving? (No.)
- **Optional** Model the examples, pausing for students to repeat.

B 💿 CD2, Track 35

- Ask students to read the directions and the examples.
- Ask: *Who asks the questions?* (Juan.) *Has Will done any of the things Juan asks about?* (No.) Explain to students that they should write Will's answers on the lines.
- Have students work individually to answer the questions.
- Play the recording. Students listen and verify their answers.

> ### Audio script
> Same as the questions and answers in the Student's Book.

- Check answers with the class. Invite several pairs of volunteers to read one question and answer aloud.

---

3 Speaking

This exercise practices talking about risky experiences.

- Have students read the directions and the example in the speech balloons.
- Have students work in pairs to take turns asking and answering the questions in Exercise 2B.

> ### Workbook
> Assign the exercises on Workbook page 37. (Workbook answers begin on page T-192.)

> ### Extra Grammar
> Assign the exercises for the Extra Grammar, Lesson 21.

2 Language focus

🎧 **A** Juan and Will are talking about risks.
Listen and practice.

Juan Hey, Will. Have you ever gone rock climbing?

Will No, I haven't. I've never gone rock climbing. And I don't want to try it.

Juan So, I guess you're not going to go on the school rock-climbing trip?

Will No. But I'm going to go on the skydiving trip. I'm excited!

Juan You're kidding, right? Have you ever gone skydiving?

Will No, never. But there's always a first time. Do you want to come?

Juan No, thanks. I've never jumped from a plane, and I never want to try.

Present perfect with *never*

I**'ve never** gone skydiving.
I**'ve never** jumped from a plane.

Have you **ever gone** rock climbing?
 No, I **haven't**. I**'ve never** gone rock climbing.
 No, never.

Note: *Never* isn't used in questions with the present perfect.

🎧 **B** Juan asks Will more questions about risks he has taken.
Will has not done any of these things. Listen and write his answers.

1. Have you ever ridden on a motorcycle? _No, never._

2. Have you ever sung karaoke? _No, I haven't. I've never sung karaoke._

3. Have you ever had a pet snake? _No, I haven't. I've never had a pet snake._

4. Have you ever taken a trip alone? _No, never._

5. Have you ever dyed your hair? _No, I haven't. I've never dyed my hair._

6. Have you ever eaten worms? _No, I haven't. I've never eaten worms._

7. Have you ever gone out without permission? _No, never._

8. Have you ever started a rock band? _No, I haven't. I've never started a rock band._

3 Speaking

**Work with a classmate. Take turns asking and answering the
questions in Exercise 2B.**

> Have you ever ridden on a motorcycle?

> No, never. Have you ever sung karaoke?

> No, I haven't. I've never sung karaoke. Have you ever . . .

What we've done

1 Language focus

A What have Ally, Matt, and Kristopher done in the last year? Listen and practice.

Ally

I love to travel. I think it's fun. I've been to a lot of places, and I've seen many interesting things since last summer. Last month, I went to London with my parents. We stayed there for two weeks. We did a city tour and saw Big Ben. It's so tall! I was really sad to leave London.

Matt

I started a band called The Green Tomatoes a year ago. We play rock music, and I'm the lead singer. We've practiced in a friend's garage for six months, but we have to find another place to practice soon. Since January, we've played more than 20 shows. It's been fun so far!

Kristopher

I've won two marathons so far this year. In February, I won the school marathon. Last month, I won the city marathon. I've also won three shorter races since the city marathon. I love running. I never want to stop!

B Study the chart. Then read Kristopher's text in Part A again. Write his first four sentences in the correct columns in the chart. Then listen and check.

Simple past		Present perfect	
•—————Now	Time phrases **last month** **a year ago** **in February** **for two weeks**	⌒Now	Time phrases **since last summer** **so far** **for six months**
Last month, I **went** to London with my parents. I **started** a band **a year ago**. We **stayed** there **for two weeks**.		I**'ve seen** many interesting things **since last summer**. We**'ve practiced for six months**. It**'s been** fun **so far**.	
In February, I won the school marathon. *Last month, I won the city marathon.*		*I've won two marathons so far this year.* *I've also won three shorter races since the city marathon.*	

What we've done

This lesson contrasts the simple past and the present perfect.

Review of Lesson 21

- Give students several minutes to write sentences about something they've never eaten, drunk, seen, or done.

- Have students work in small groups and take turns reading the sentences they wrote. Students should take notes about any sentence they may have in common with one or more of their classmates.

- Invite volunteers to report on any similarities they found in their groups. For example, *Pedro and I have never eaten sushi.*

1 Language focus

This exercise contrasts the simple past and the present perfect.

A 💿 CD2, Track 36

- Ask students to cover the texts and look at the photos. Explain that in the texts three teenagers write about things they have done. Have the class suggest topics the teenagers may have written about and write their responses on the board.

- Have students read the texts to check their predictions.

- **Optional** Play the recording. Students listen and read along.

> **Audio script**
> Same as the texts in the Student's Book.

- Ask the following questions to check comprehension of the first text.

  Has Ally traveled a lot since last summer? (Yes.)

  What has she seen since last summer? (She's seen many interesting things.)

  Has she been to London? (Yes.)

  When did she go there? (Last month.)

  Who did she go with? (She went with her parents.)

  How long did they stay there? (For two weeks.)

  How did they get to know the city? (They did a city tour.)

- Have students write two questions about Matt's text and two questions about Kristopher's text.

- Invite volunteers to read one of the questions they wrote. Have other volunteers answer the questions.

- Focus students' attention on Ally's text again. Ask: *Do we know when Ally went to London?* (Yes. Last month.) Remind students that we use the simple past to talk about completed actions at specific times in the past.

- Ask them to find a sentence that uses the present perfect twice, and call it out. (I've been to a lot of places, and I've seen many interesting things since last summer.) Ask: *Do we know about all the places Ally's been to?* (No.) *Do we know exactly when she visited all these places?* (No.) *But when did she start traveling a lot?* (Last summer.) Remind students that the present perfect is used (1) to talk about events completed – or not completed – at some unspecified time in the past, (2) to talk about repeated actions in the past, and (3) with *since* or *for* to describe actions that began in the past and continue into the present.

- Follow the same procedure with the other two texts.

- Play the recording or model the sentences. Students listen and repeat.

B 💿 CD2, Track 37

- **Language Chart** Have students read the directions and study the examples in the language chart. Ask: *Is this chart complete?* (No.) *What do you have to do?* (Complete it with the first four sentences from Kristopher's text.) *Where do you write the sentences?* (Simple past sentences should go in the left-hand column and present perfect sentences in the right-hand column.)

- Review the time phrases with students.

- Have students work individually to complete the chart.

- Play the recording. Students listen and verify their answers.

> **Audio script**
> Same as the chart in the Student's Book.

- Check answers with the class. Invite volunteers to read one of the sentences they added to the chart and to say in which column they wrote it.

- **Optional** Model the examples, pausing for students to repeat.

C   CD2, Track 38

- Invite a volunteer to read the directions and the example sentence aloud.
- Have students work individually to complete the sentences in the texts.
- Play the recording. Students listen and verify their answers.

Audio script
Same as the texts in the Student's Book.

- Check answers with the class. Invite volunteers to read aloud one of the sentences they completed.
- To finish, ask students which of the three people they learned about in Exercise 1A on page 74 has had the most interesting experiences, in their opinion.

---

2   Listening

In this exercise, students listen for the experiences two teenagers have had.

CD2, Track 39

- Have students read the directions and the sentences.
- Tell students that they will listen to Julie and Ray talking about some of their experiences. They should check True or False.
- Play the recording. Students only listen.

Audio script
See page T-212.

- Play the recording again. Students listen and check the correct boxes.
- Play the recording once again. Students listen and verify their answers.
- Check answers with the class. Read the sentences one at a time. Students tell you whether they are true or false.

---

3   Speaking

This exercise practices talking about past experiences using the present perfect and the simple past.

A

- Have students read the directions. Ask: *What do you have to write about?* (Your own interesting experiences.) *Which sentences will use the present perfect?* (The first one on each line.) *What words could go in the last blank in these two sentences?* (Week / month / year.) *Which sentences will use the simple past?* (The second sentence on each line.) *What words could go before* ago *in the second sentence on the first line?* (A day / a week / a month; three weeks / six months / ten years, etc.) *What words can go in the last blank of the last sentence?* (A day of the week; week / month / year.)
- Have students work individually to complete the sentences.
- Have students tell a classmate about their experiences, following the examples in the speech balloons.

B

- Invite volunteers to tell the class about one of their classmate's interesting experiences, following the example in the speech balloon.

Teaching Tip   Nonnative speakers of English often use the simple past where native speakers would use the present perfect. The main difficulty second-language learners often have is with the meaning, rather than the form, of the present perfect. It is important to remind students of the meanings the present perfect conveys, versus the simple past.

Workbook

Assign the exercises on Workbook page 38.
(Workbook answers begin on page T-192.)

Extra Grammar

Assign the exercises for the Extra Grammar, Lesson 22.

C Complete the texts about these students. Use the simple past or the present perfect. Then listen and check.

1. Last year, Cam ___spent___ (spend) six months in Canada on an exchange program. He ___stayed___ (stay) with a Canadian family. He ___came___ (come) back in December. Since then, he *'s e-mailed* (e-mail) his Canadian parents every day. Marc, his Canadian brother, is now staying with Cam and his family. He *'s been* (be) there for five months.

2. We *'ve had* (have) three family reunions since 2000, and I *'ve met* (meet) more than 100 relatives so far at these parties. Last summer, we ___had___ (have) a big picnic near the ocean. I ___went___ (go) scuba diving with my cousins. Two days ago, my mother ___told___ (tell) me that we are going to have another reunion this summer!

2 Listening

Julie and Ray talk about experiences they have had. Are the sentences true or false? Listen and check (✓) True or False.

	True	False
1. Julie saw a skydiving movie when she was eight.	☐	✓
2. She went skydiving four months ago.	✓	☐
3. She's gone skydiving more than 20 times.	☐	✓
4. Ray has collected postcards for about ten years.	✓	☐
5. He got his first postcard from his grandfather.	☐	✓
6. He bought 100 postcards last week.	☐	✓

3 Speaking

A Complete the sentences with your own experiences. Try to think of interesting things. Then tell a classmate about them. *(Answers will vary.)*

I _____ since last _____ . I _____ ago.

I _____ so far this _____ . I _____ last _____ .

> I've read three books in English since last month. I went to Disney World last year.

B Tell the class about one of your classmate's experiences.

> Jack went to South Africa last summer.

Lessons 21 & 22 | Mini-review

1 Language check

A Complete the conversation. Use the present perfect and *ever* or *never*.

Brenda Do you like to try new foods?

Bobby Yes, I do.

Brenda *Have* you *ever tried* (try) Thai food?

Bobby Yes, I love Thai food.

Brenda *Have* you *ever eaten* (eat) at the Thai restaurant on Main Street?

Bobby No, I haven't. I *haven't eaten* (eat) there. Have you?

Brenda No, never. Let's go sometime.

Bobby Good idea. *Have* you *ever been* (be) to a Peruvian restaurant?

Brenda No. I *haven't been* (be) to one. Is there one in our town?

Bobby Yes, there is. There's one next to the library. Come on! Let's go!

B Look at Amanda's calendar. Today is September 14th, and she's at the library. Complete the sentences. Use the simple past or the present perfect, and *for, since, ago,* or *so far*.

SEPTEMBER

Sunday	Monday	Tuesday	Wednesday	Thursday	Friday	Saturday
1 Move to Florida	**2** First day of school. Buy notebooks.	**3** Swimming practice 3:00 p.m.	**4** First piano lesson after school	**5** Swimming practice 3:00 p.m.	**6**	**7** Movie with Sue
8	**9**	**10** Swimming practice 3:00 p.m.	**11** Out to dinner with family	**12** Swimming practice 3:00 p.m.	**13**	**14** Library 10:00 a.m. Study all day. TODAY

1. *She's lived* (live) in Florida _____*since*_____ September 1st.

2. She _*'s been*_ (be) in school _____*for*_____ two weeks.

3. She _____*bought*_____ (buy) some notebooks 12 days _____*ago*_____ .

4. She _*'s been*_ (be) to four swimming practices _____*so far*_____ .

5. She _____*went*_____ (go) out to dinner with her family three days _____*ago*_____ .

6. She _*'s been*_ (be) at the library _____*since*_____ 10:00 a.m. this morning.

7. She _*'s seen*_ (see) one movie _____*so far*_____ .

8. She *hasn't studied* (study) piano _____*since*_____ last week.

This lesson reviews the language presented and practiced in Lessons 21 and 22.

1 Language check

This exercise reviews the structures presented so far in this unit.

A

- Have students read the directions.
- Invite two students to read the first three lines of the conversation, including the example. Ask: *Which word is used in questions – ever or never?* (Ever.) Remind students that *never* is not usually used in questions.
- Have students work individually to complete the conversation.
- Check answers with the class.
- **Optional** Have students practice the conversation in pairs.

B

- Focus students' attention on the calendar. Ask: *What did Amanda do on September 11th?* (She went out to dinner with her family.) *What did she do last Saturday?* (She saw a movie with Sue.) *Where is Amanda now?* (At the library.)
- Invite a volunteer to read the directions and the example sentence aloud. Ask: *What verb tense do you often use with* for, since, *and* so far? (The present perfect.) *What verb tense do you use in sentences with* ago? (Simple past.)
- Have students work individually to complete the sentences.
- Check answers with the class. Invite volunteers to read aloud one of the sentences they completed.

C

- Have students read the directions.
- Ask students to read the e-mail messages and replies, and underline the time phrases in them.
- Focus students' attention on e-mail message 1. Invite a volunteer to call out the time phrase and say which form it is normally used with. (Last month, simple past.) Follow the same procedure with the other two messages and the replies. (E-mail message 2: A month ago, simple past. E-mail message 3: On Saturday, simple past; all weekend, simple past; since I bought it, present perfect; three minutes already, present perfect. First reply: Several times, present perfect. Second reply: Since last summer, present perfect.)

- Ask: *The word* ever *occurs in two of the e-mail messages. What form do you associate it with?* (The present perfect.)
- Have students work individually to complete the e-mail messages and replies. Students then match the messages to the correct replies.
- Check answers with the class. Invite volunteers to read aloud one of the sentences they completed. Finally, ask: *Which e-mail message did you match to the first reply?* (E-mail message 2.) Ask about the other two replies in the same way. (The second reply matches e-mail message 3; the third reply matches e-mail message 1.)

---

2 Listening

In this exercise, students listen for questions in the present perfect and the past.

💿 **CD2, Track 40**

- Have students read the directions and the responses for 1–6.
- Tell students they will listen to people asking questions. Students should choose the correct response for each question.
- Play the recording. Students only listen.

> ### Audio script
> See page T-213.

- Play the recording again. Students listen and check the boxes of the correct responses.

- Play the recording once again. Students listen and verify their answers.
- Check answers with the class. Play the recording once again, stopping after each question. Ask the class to call out the words in the question that helped them choose the correct response.

> ### Workbook
> Assign the exercises on Workbook page 39.
> (Workbook answers begin on page T-192.)

> ### Game
> Assign the game on Student's Book page 119.

C Complete the e-mail messages and replies. Use the simple past or the present perfect. Then match each message to the correct reply.

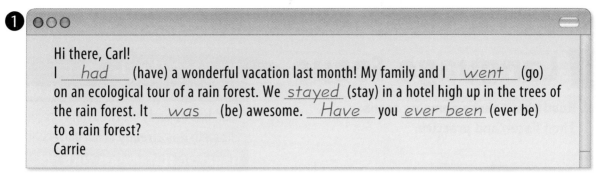

①

Hi there, Carl!
I ___had___ (have) a wonderful vacation last month! My family and I ___went___ (go) on an ecological tour of a rain forest. We ___stayed___ (stay) in a hotel high up in the trees of the rain forest. It ___was___ (be) awesome. ___Have___ you ___ever been___ (ever be) to a rain forest?
Carrie

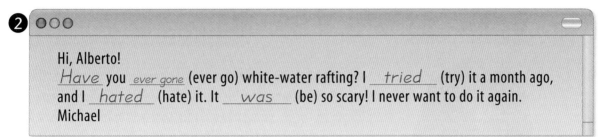

②

Hi, Alberto!
___Have___ you ___ever gone___ (ever go) white-water rafting? I ___tried___ (try) it a month ago, and I ___hated___ (hate) it. It ___was___ (be) so scary! I never want to do it again.
Michael

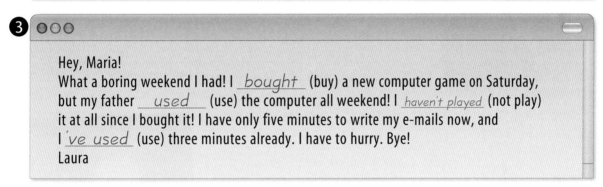

③

Hey, Maria!
What a boring weekend I had! I ___bought___ (buy) a new computer game on Saturday, but my father ___used___ (use) the computer all weekend! I ___haven't played___ (not play) it at all since I bought it! I have only five minutes to write my e-mails now, and I ___'ve used___ (use) three minutes already. I have to hurry. Bye!
Laura

[2] Oh, come on. It's not that bad. My friends and I ___'ve gone___ (go) several times. It ___was___ (be) really exciting.

[3] That's too bad. You need your own computer. I ___'ve had___ (have) mine since last summer, and I use it all the time.

[1] No. I ___'ve never been___ (never be) to one. I'd love to go! Tell me more!

2 Listening

Students ask some questions. Listen and check (✓) the correct responses.

1. ☑ Yes, I have. It was great.
   ☐ Yes, I did. It was great.

2. ☑ Are you kidding? No, I haven't.
   ☐ Are you kidding? No, I didn't.

3. ☐ No, never. I never have.
   ☑ No, I didn't.

4. ☐ For a long time.
   ☑ Last month.

5. ☐ A month ago.
   ☑ Since last spring.

6. ☐ Since last year.
   ☑ A year ago.

Go to page 119 for the Game.

Lesson 23 Amazing teens

1 Language focus

A Read about these amazing teens.
Then listen and practice.

has already / hasn't . . . yet

Affirmative statements with *already*

John **has already** set two world's records.
Elizabeth **has already** taken university classes.

Negative statements with *not . . . yet*

John **hasn't** learned every trick **yet**.
Elizabeth **hasn't** finished high school **yet**.

John Narum

John Narum is 15, and he's a yo-yo champion. Everyone who sees John perform says he's amazing. He knows more than 500 yo-yo tricks. He went to his first yo-yo competition when he was five years old. He's already won a world championship and set two yo-yo world's records. After more than ten years of doing yo-yo tricks, John hasn't learned every trick yet. There are always new ones to learn. John's also a champion chess player. He's already won more than 300 games.

Fifteen-year-old Elizabeth Synge is a math whiz. She was the top middle-school female participant in the 2007 Lockheed Martin MATHCOUNTS® National Competition – a math contest for teenagers in the United States. The contest started with more than 40,000 students from all over the country. Elizabeth has always liked numbers. She was doing simple math problems when she was two years old. She hasn't finished high school yet, but she has already taken several university math classes.

Elizabeth Synge

B Complete the sentences about John and Elizabeth with the correct verbs from Part A. Use *already* or *not . . . yet*. Then listen and check.

1. (two yo-yo world's records) John <u>has already set two yo-yo world's records</u> .

2. (every trick) John <u>hasn't learned every trick yet</u> .

3. (more than 300 chess games) John <u>has already won more than 300 chess games</u> .

4. (a math contest) Elizabeth <u>has already won a math contest</u> .

5. (high school) Elizabeth <u>hasn't finished high school yet</u> .

6. (university math classes) Elizabeth <u>has already taken university math classes</u> .

78 Unit 6

Lesson 23 Amazing teens

This lesson presents and practices statements with has already / hasn't . . . yet *and verb phrases related to important moments and events in a person's life.*

Review of Lesson 22
- Write on the board:

  since (last month)   last (year)

  so far   in (October)

  for (five months)   (two weeks) ago

                          for (nine weeks)

  Example: My sister's been to some exotic places. Two years ago, she went to Tahiti.

- Ask students to think about two relatives or friends who have done interesting or unusual things. Give students several minutes to write sentences with time phrases about their relatives or friends, following the example on the board.

- Have students work in small groups to share the information about their relatives or friends and choose the person who has done the most interesting or unusual things.

- Invite a representative from each group to share with the class the information about the person the group chose.

1 Language focus

This exercise presents and practices statements with *has already / hasn't . . . yet.*

A 💿 CD2, Track 41

- Focus students' attention on the title of the lesson. Ask students if they know any amazing teens and, if so, why the teens are amazing.

- Have students read the texts to find out who is a yo-yo champion (John) and who is a math whiz (Elizabeth).

- **Optional** Play the recording. Students listen and read along.

> **Audio script**
> Same as the texts in the Student's Book.

- Ask: *Who knows more than 500 yo-yo tricks?* (John Narum.) *Who won a math contest for teenagers in the U.S.?* (Elizabeth Synge.) Ask a few more questions like these to check students' understanding.

- Have students find the sentence that tells them about John Narum's yo-yo championship. (He's already won a world championship and set two yo-yo world's records.) Explain that *already* is used with the present perfect to talk about events that happened before now. It usually indicates that the events happened earlier than expected. In this case, it emphasizes that, at 15, John was very young when he won the world championship. Have students find two more sentences with *already*, one in each text. Elicit the reasons for the use of *already*. For example, after students find that Elizabeth *has already taken several university math classes*, ask: *Do high school students usually take university math classes?* (No.)

- Focus students' attention on John's story. Ask: *Has John learned all of the yo-yo tricks in the world?* (No.) *Which sentence gives that information?* (John hasn't learned every trick yet.) Explain that in a negative sentence *yet* means *up to now* or *at this time.* Have students find the sentence with *yet* in the text about Elizabeth Synge. (She hasn't finished high school yet.)

- Play the recording or model the sentences. Students listen and repeat.

- **Language Chart** Have students study the examples in the language chart. Ask: *Which of the words we discussed is used in affirmative statements?* (Already.) *Which word is used in negative statements?* (Yet.) *Where is* already *placed in the sentence?* (Between *has* and the past participle.) *Where is* yet *placed in the sentence?* (At the end.)

- **Optional** Model the examples, pausing for students to repeat.

B 💿 CD2, Track 42

- Have students read the directions, the example, and the cues for the sentences.

- Have students work individually to complete the sentences.

- Play the recording. Students listen and verify their answers.

> **Audio script**
> Same as the sentences in the Student's Book.

- Check answers with the class. Invite volunteers to read aloud one of the sentences they completed.

- To finish, ask the class which of the two teenagers they think is more amazing, and why.

Experiences T-78

2 Listening

In this exercise, students listen for what a teenager has and has not done in her life.

CD2, Track 43

- Focus students' attention on the photo to familiarize students with the American gymnast Shawn Johnson. Ask students if they know any gymnasts like Shawn Johnson in their country.
- Have students read the directions and items 1–5. Ask students to make guesses about the things Shawn has and has not done.
- Play the recording. Students only listen.

Culture Note Female gymnasts are usually younger than male gymnasts. For the Olympics the minimum age to compete in gymnastics is 16. Most of the girls on the teams are between the ages of 16 and 20. It is unusual for women to compete in gymnastics after their early 20s. On the other hand, men are at their best in their mid-20s. Part of the reason for this is that women's gymnastics is more about balance and accuracy. This is easier for younger girls because their bodies are lighter. Men's gymnastics stresses strength and power.

Audio script
See page T-213.

- Play the recording again. Students listen and check the correct boxes.
- Play the recording once again. Students listen and verify their answers.
- Check answers with the class. Invite volunteers to read aloud one of the answers they checked.
- To finish, ask the class if they think Shawn is or will ever be very famous in their country.
- **Optional** Have students work individually to write a complete sentence for each of the items in the exercise. Write the first one on the board as an example:

Shawn has already studied with a famous Chinese gymnast.

3 Word power

This exercise introduces and practices verb phrases related to important moments and events in a person's life.

A

- Ask volunteers to read aloud the directions and the verb phrases in the box. Have students call out any words or verb phrases they do not understand. Explain them by using them in sentences or by miming them.
- Have students work individually to write the verb phrases in the correct columns in the chart. As they do so, copy the chart onto the board.
- Check answers with the class. Invite volunteers to come to the board to write the verb phrases in the correct column in the chart.

B

- Have students read the directions and the example.
- Give students several minutes to write four sentences about themselves using phrases from Part A or their own ideas.
- Check answers with the class. Invite volunteers to read their sentences to the class.

4 Speaking

This exercise practices talking about experiences students have already had or not had yet.

- Have students read the directions and the example.
- Invite two volunteers to come to the front to demonstrate the activity.
- Have students work with a classmate. They take turns comparing their experiences from Exercise 3B, following the example conversation.
- Have students then tell another classmate about their partner's experience, following the examples in the speech balloons.
- **Optional** Ask representatives from several pairs to say whether they found that their experiences were similar to or very different from those of their partner.

Workbook
Assign the exercises on Workbook page 40.
(Workbook answers begin on page T-192.)

Extra Grammar
Assign the exercises for the Extra Grammar, Lesson 23.

2 Listening

American gymnast Shawn Johnson is another amazing teen. What has she already done? What hasn't she done yet? Listen and check (✓) the correct boxes.

Shawn has . . .	Already	Not yet
1. studied with a famous Chinese gymnast.	✓	☐
2. won many gymnastics competitions.	✓	☐
3. won a lot of money.	☐	✓
4. been on television shows.	✓	☐
5. finished high school.	☐	✓

3 Word power

A Write the verb phrases in the box in the correct columns.

✓ decide on a career	☐ get a job	☐ study a foreign language
☐ get a college degree	☐ go to a rock concert	☐ turn 16 years old
✓ get a driver's license	☐ have a boyfriend or a girlfriend	☐ vacation in a foreign country

Personal		School and career	
get a driver's license	turn 16 years old	decide on a career	study a foreign language
go to a rock concert	vacation in a foreign country	get a college degree	
have a boyfriend or a girlfriend		get a job	

B Write sentences about yourself. Use phrases from Part A or your own ideas. *(Answers will vary.)*

I haven't decided on a career yet.

1. _____
2. _____
3. _____
4. _____

4 Speaking

Compare your information from Exercise 3B with a classmate.
Then tell another classmate.

Helen I haven't gotten a driver's license yet.

Ana I've already decided on a career.

Helen hasn't gotten a driver's license yet.

Ana has already decided on a career.

In the spotlight

1 Language focus

A Kira and Leo are studying for a test on the book *The Adventures of Tom Sawyer*. Listen and practice.

Kira Let's review for our English reading test on the first half of *The Adventures of Tom Sawyer*.

Leo OK, Kira. Let's see how much we know. Bret Harte wrote *The Adventures of Tom Sawyer*, didn't he?

Kira No, he didn't. Mark Twain wrote it. He was a famous American writer.

Leo Oh, right. He wrote a lot of books, didn't he?

Kira Yes, he did.

Leo OK. Let's see . . . So far in the book, Tom and his brother Sid have lived with their Aunt Polly for a long time, haven't they?

Kira Yes, they have. Next question: Tom and Sid have always been very different, haven't they?

Leo Yes, they have. Sid has been a good boy, but Tom has often behaved badly.

Kira But Tom has always liked school, hasn't he?

Leo No, he hasn't. He's never liked school.

Kira Oh, yes, I forgot. Anyway, so far Tom has really liked adventures, hasn't he?

Leo Yes, he has. Wait! I have one more question for you. We'll get a good grade on the test, won't we?

Kira Well . . .

B Study the chart. Then complete the sentences with tag questions.

Tag questions with the simple past	Tag questions with the present perfect

He **wrote** a lot of books, **didn't** he?
    Yes, he **did.**
 Bret Harte **wrote** *The Adventures of Tom Sawyer,* **didn't** he?
    No, he **didn't.**
	They**'ve lived** with her for a long time, **haven't** they?
	    Yes, they **have.**
	 Tom **has** always **liked** school, **hasn't** he?
	    No, he **hasn't.**

1. You spoke English yesterday, *didn't you* ?
2. Your friends visited you at home last week, *didn't they* ?
3. You have always lived in the same house, *haven't they* ?
4. You were at school yesterday, *weren't you* ?

Lesson 24 In the spotlight

This lesson presents and practices tag questions with the simple past and the present perfect.

Review of Lesson 23

- Write on the board:

  Maria has already decided on a career. She's going to be a bus driver.

  She hasn't gotten her driver's license yet.

- Remind students of Exercise 4 (Lesson 23) in which they compared experiences with those of a partner. Give students several minutes to try to remember as much as possible about their partner's experiences.

- Have students work with new partners. They share the experiences they found out about in Exercise 4 (Lesson 23). Tell them to use sentences such as the ones on the board.

- Ask volunteers to share with the class one of the experiences they have just talked about.

1 Language focus

This exercise presents and practices tag questions with the simple past and the present perfect.

A CD2, Track 44

- Have students read the directions and look at the photo.
- Give students several minutes to read the conversation.
- **Optional** Play the recording. Students listen and read along.

Audio script

Same as the conversation in the Student's Book.

- Ask: *What are Kira and Leo doing?* (They're studying for a test on the book *The Adventures of Tom Sawyer.*)
- Read the following statements. Students respond true or false. When a sentence is false, ask students to correct it.

  Bret Harte wrote Tom Sawyer. (False. Mark Twain wrote it.)

  Mark Twain wrote a lot of books. (True.)

  Tom and Sid have lived with Aunt Polly for a long time. (True.)

  Tom and Sid are very different. (True.)

  Tom has always liked school. (False. He's never liked school.)

- Focus students' attention on Leo's first speech. Ask: *How does Leo check his idea about the author of* The Adventures of Tom Sawyer? *What does he say?* (Bret Harte wrote *The Adventures of Tom Sawyer,* didn't he?) Ask: *What kind of question is this?* (A tag question.)
- Have students read the conversation again and underline the other tag questions in it. (He wrote a lot of books, didn't he? Tom and his brother Sid have lived with their Aunt Polly for a long time, haven't they? Tom and Sid have always been very different, haven't they? But Tom has always liked school, hasn't he? Anyway, so far Tom has really liked adventures, hasn't he? We'll get a good grade on the test, won't we?)
- Check answers with the class. Ask volunteers to read one of the tag questions they underlined.

- Play the recording or model the conversation. Students listen and repeat.
- **Optional** Have students practice in pairs.

Culture Note *The Adventures of Tom Sawyer* by Mark Twain is considered one of the classics of American literature. Written in 1876, the novel describes the adventures of a young orphan, Tom Sawyer, who is cared for by his loving Aunt Polly. Tom is a mischievous and humorous character. His adventures and friendships reveal much about the social and political conditions in the Southern U.S. in the years just before the American Civil War.

B

- **Language Chart** Have students study the examples in the language chart. Focus students' attention on the left-hand side of the language chart. Ask: *Do we use a negative or an affirmative tag when we ask a question with an affirmative verb?* (A negative tag.) Ask: *What are the answers to tag questions like?* (They are like answers to *Yes / No* questions.) Now focus students' attention on the right-hand side of the language chart. Ask: *If you use* have *in the statement, what do you use in the tag?* (Haven't.)
- **Optional** Model the examples, pausing for students to repeat.
- Have students work individually to complete the sentences with tag questions.
- Check answers with the class. Ask several pairs of volunteers to read one of the tag questions they completed and answer it with their own information.

C ⊙ CD2, Track 45

- Give students several minutes to read the directions, the text, and the example tag question and answer. Ask: *What do you have to do?* (Complete the tag questions and answer them based on the information in the text.)

- Have students work individually to complete the exercise.

- Play the recording. Students listen and verify their answers.

> **Audio script**
>
> Same as the tag questions and answers in the Student's Book.

- Check answers with the class. Ask volunteers to come to the board to write one of the tag questions they wrote and the corresponding answer. Tell students not to write the complete question, just the tag.

- To finish, ask students if they have ever seen a movie with Julia Roberts or her niece Emma. If so, ask them to say what they remember about it and if they liked it or not.

> **Culture Note**
>
> There are a number of famous acting families in the U.S. Here are some of the most recognizable father / son and mother / daughter pairs:
>
> Kirk Douglas and Michael Douglas: Father and son. Kirk was in more than 80 TV shows and movies, including *Spartacus*. Michael, his son, won an Oscar in 1987 for *Wall Street*.
>
> Blythe Danner and Gwyneth Paltrow: Mother and daughter. Blythe has been in more than 70 movies and TV shows. Gwyneth, her daughter, won an Oscar in 1998 for *Shakespeare in Love*.
>
> Judy Garland and Liza Minelli: Mother and daughter. Judy starred in more than 30 movies, including *The Wizard of Oz* and *Meet Me in St. Louis*. Her daughter, Liza, won an Oscar in 1972 for *Cabaret*.

2 Listening

In this exercise, students listen for information about a movie star's life.

A ⊙ CD2, Track 46

- Give students a few minutes to read the directions and sentences 1–6. Ask: *What are Kira and Leo doing?* (Taking a trivia quiz.) *Who's the quiz about?* (Denzel Washington.) Ask students if they have ever heard of Denzel Washington or seen any of his movies.

- Play the recording. Students only listen.

> **Audio script**
>
> See page T-213.

- Play the recording again. Students listen and check T (true) or F (false).

- Play the recording once again. Students listen and verify their answers.

B

- Have students compare answers with a classmate, following the example. They should correct the false sentences.

- Check answers with the class.

3 Pronunciation Intonation in tag questions

In this exercise, students practice intonation in tag questions.

A ⊙ CD2, Track 47

- Have students read the directions and the sample tag questions.

- Play the recording. Students only listen.

> **Audio script**
>
> Same as the tag questions in the Student's Book.

- Ask: *Does the intonation go up or down in the tag?* (It goes up.)

- Play the recording again, or model the tag questions, exaggerating the intonation. Students listen and repeat.

B

- Give students several minutes to practice saying the tag questions in Exercise 1C, making sure they use rising intonation.

- Invite volunteers to say one of the tag questions they practiced.

> **Workbook**
>
> Assign the exercises on Workbook page 41. (Workbook answers begin on page T-192.)

> **Extra Grammar**
>
> Assign the exercises for the Extra Grammar, Lesson 24.

C Read about Julia Roberts and her niece Emma Roberts. Complete the tag questions and answer them. Then listen and check.

> Julia Roberts was born in 1967. She's an actor and has appeared in more than 30 movies and in one Broadway play. Julia's niece, Emma Roberts, has been in several TV shows and she's starred in the movie *Nancy Drew*. Emma's father (Julia's brother), Eric, is also an actor. They've all been very successful.

1. Julia Roberts was born in 1967, _wasn't she_ ? _Yes, she was._
2. She's made more than 30 movies, _hasn't she_ ? _Yes, she has._
3. Her niece Emma became a singer, _didn't she_ ? _No, she didn't._
4. Emma starred in the movie *Runaway Bride*, _didn't she_ ? _No, she didn't._
5. Julia, Eric, and Emma have been successful, _haven't they_ ? _Yes, they have._

2 Listening

A Kira and Leo take a trivia quiz about Denzel Washington. Are these sentences true or false? Listen and check (✓) T (true) or F (false).

	T	F
1. Denzel Washington was born in California.	☐	✓
2. He studied drama in college.	✓	☐
3. His first big part was in a musical.	☐	✓
4. He's won two Oscars.	✓	☐
5. He and his wife have four children.	✓	☐
6. He's acted in about 50 movies.	☐	✓

B How many of your answers are correct? Compare with a classmate.

> Denzel Washington was born in California, wasn't he?

> No, he wasn't.

3 Pronunciation Intonation in tag questions

A Listen. Notice the intonation in tag questions. Then listen again and practice.

He studied computer science in college, didn't he?   They were married about 25 years ago, weren't they?

He's acted in about 40 movies, hasn't he?   He was on *General Hospital*, wasn't he?

B Now practice the tag questions in Exercise 1D.

Read

A Read the article quickly. Check (✓) the phrases you find.

☐ ate a spider   ☑ lived in a glass box   ☑ stayed under water

☐ jumped out of an airplane   ☑ read people's thoughts   ☑ stood on a 30-meter pole

Incredible!

If you ask most people around the world, "Have you ever heard of David Blaine?" the answer will probably be, "No, never." But ask New Yorkers the same question, and they will probably say, "Yes, we have."

David first became popular for his TV show. Several years ago, on his first show, he walked around the streets of New York and entertained people with amazing tricks. He made money disappear and things appear from nowhere. And he read people's thoughts. Everyone was **amazed**.

But David isn't just an entertainer – he also does **stunts**. Since his first TV show, David has spent 72 hours inside a **block** of ice, he's stayed under water in a huge glass **bowl** for 7 days, he's lived in a glass box for 44 days with no food, and he's stood on a 30-meter **pole** for 35 hours. His audiences have never been disappointed.

He's not 40 yet, but he's already written a book about his life. The title of his book – *Mysterious Stranger* – probably describes him really well. Not everyone knows about David yet, but they will someday.

Go to page 124 for the Vocabulary Practice.

B 📀 Read the article slowly. Check your answers in Part A.

C Answer the questions.

1. Have most New Yorkers heard of David Blaine? <u>Yes, they have.</u>

2. How did he first become popular? <u>He first became popular for his TV show.</u>

3. Has he ever stayed under water for a long time? <u>Yes, he has.</u>

4. Have his audiences ever been disappointed? <u>No, they haven't.</u>

5. Has he ever written a book? <u>Yes, he has.</u>

Unit 6 Get Connected

This lesson practices reading, listening, and writing skills.

> **Review of Lesson 24**
>
> - Choose a well-known sports personality and prepare a set of five or six tag questions in the simple past and present perfect about him or her. For example:
>
>   *[Name of player] started playing tennis when she was four, didn't she?*
>
>   *She's been a professional tennis player for ten years, hasn't she?*
>
> - Ask the questions. Invite volunteers to answer one question each.
>
> - Have students work in small groups to write four tag questions about a celebrity they know well. They should write two questions in the simple past and two in the present perfect. Check with each group to make sure that no two groups write questions about the same celebrity.
>
> - Have a competition. Ask each of the groups to take turns asking another group the questions they wrote. Each correct answer is worth one point. The group with the most points at the end of the game wins.

Read

This exercise practices reading for information about a person who does amazing stunts.

A

- Have students look at the photos. Ask: *Would you do what this man is doing in the top picture? Why or why not? Why do you think he's standing under water?*

- Invite a volunteer to read the directions and phrases aloud. Remind students that they should read quickly to find the answers and that they should not read every word carefully.

- Have students work individually to read the article quickly and check the phrases they find. Do not check answers at this point.

B 💿 CD2, Track 48

- Invite a volunteer to read the directions aloud. Remind students that they should read slowly and carefully, and concentrate on getting the meaning of the entire text.

- List the new vocabulary words on the board: *amazed (adj.), stunt, block (n.), bowl (n.), pole.* Explain their meaning. (Amazed [adj.]: very surprised; stunt: an act that is often risky or dangerous that people do to attract attention; block [n.]: a solid piece of wood, stone, ice, etc.; bowl [n.]: a deep, round dish used to hold food or liquid; pole: a long, thin piece of wood or metal.) As an alternative, have students use their dictionaries to find the meanings of the new vocabulary words.

- Have students read the article again.

- Have students check their answers in Part A in pairs. Elicit the answers from one pair.

- **Optional** Play the recording. Students listen and read along.

> **Audio script**
>
> Same as the article in the Student's Book.

> **Get Connected Vocabulary**
>
> Have students do the exercise on Student's Book page 124 in class or for homework. (Get Connected Vocabulary answers are on page T-124.)

C

- Invite a volunteer to read the directions and first question aloud.

- Ask: *Have most New Yorkers heard of David Blaine?* Elicit the answer. (Yes, they have.)

- Have students work individually to answer the questions.

- Check answers with the class. Invite volunteers to read aloud one answer each.

Listen

In this exercise, students listen for teenagers' ideas about doing motorcycle and skateboard stunts.

A 💿 CD2, Track 49

- Focus students' attention on the photo. Ask: *What are the teens doing?* (They're doing motorcycle stunts.)
- Tell students that they will listen to two friends, Dimitri and Heidi, talk about stunts.
- Have students read the first question and the example answer.
- Explain that students should listen to the conversation and answer the questions.
- Play the recording. Students only listen.

> **Audio script**
> See page T-214.

- Play the recording again. Students listen and answer the questions.
- Play the recording once again. Students listen and verify their answers.
- Check answers with the class. Invite volunteers to read aloud one answer each.

B

- Have students read the directions and the questions.
- Read the first question with the class and elicit answers from several students. Remind students that there are no right or wrong answers for this exercise – they are giving their opinions.
- Have students work individually to answer the questions, and give reasons for their answers.
- Have students work in pairs to compare answers, or elicit opinions from volunteers.

Write

In this exercise, students answer questions and write a paragraph about dangerous hobbies.

A

- Invite a volunteer to read the directions and the questions aloud.
- Invite several volunteers to talk about some dangerous hobbies they have heard about.
- Have students work individually to answer the questions.
- **Optional** Have students ask and answer the questions in pairs.

B

- Invite a volunteer to read the directions aloud. Tell students that they will use the information in Part A to help them write about dangerous hobbies.
- Have students work individually to write their paragraphs.
- Invite several volunteers to read their paragraphs to the class.
- **Optional** Have students work in groups of four and read each other's paragraphs. Students can vote on the most dangerous hobby written about in their group and give reasons for their vote.

> **Workbook**
> Assign the exercises on Workbook page 42.
> (Workbook answers begin on page T-192.)

You've gotten good then, haven't you?

A 🔊 **Dimitri and Heidi talk about stunts. Listen and answer the questions.**

1. Has Heidi ever seen motorcycle stunts on TV? _Yes, she has._
2. What does she think about the stunts? _She thinks the stunts are dangerous._
3. Has Dimitri ever done any stunts? _Yes, he has._
4. Has he ever had any accidents? _Yes, he has._
5. Has Heidi ever been to the skateboard park? _No, she hasn't._

B **What do you think? Answer the questions. Give reasons.** _(Answers will vary.)_

1. Do you think people should do dangerous stunts on TV?

   _____

2. Do you think being a stunt person is a good career? _____

3. Why do you think people choose to do dangerous hobbies? _____

4. What do you think parents should say if their children want to try a dangerous hobby? _____

Your turn

Write

A **Think about some dangerous hobbies. Answer the questions.** _(Answers will vary.)_

1. Have you ever tried a dangerous hobby? Why or why not? _____

2. Do you know anyone who has a dangerous hobby? _____

3. How do you feel when people do dangerous hobbies or stunts? _____

4. Would you like to try something dangerous? What? _____

5. What would your family and friends think if you did? _____

B **Write a paragraph about a dangerous hobby. Use the answers in Part A to help you.** _(Answers will vary.)_

_I_ _____ tried a dangerous hobby because . . ._

Language chart review

Present perfect with *never*	
He**'s never** driven a car. We**'ve never** gone rock climbing.	**Have** they **ever explored** a cave? **Yes**, they **have**. / **No**, they **haven't**. **No, never.** They **'ve never** explored a cave.

has already / hasn't . . . yet	
Affirmative statements with *already*	**Negative statements with** *not . . . yet*
I**'ve already** turned 14.	She **hasn't** decided on a career **yet**.

A Look at the pictures. Then write sentences with *already* or *yet* and the verb phrases in the box.

☐ dye hair purple   ☐ explore a cave   ☑ go skydiving   ☐ start a rock band

1. *He's already gone skydiving.*

2. *He hasn't started a rock band yet.*

3. *She hasn't explored a cave yet.*

4. *She's already dyed her hair purple.*

B Look at the chart. Have Alana and Rick ever done these things? Write questions and answers.

Climb a mountain		Eat worms	
Alana ✓	Rick ✗	Alana ✗	Rick ✓

1. **Q:** *Has Alana ever climbed a mountain?*
   A: *Yes, she has.*

2. **Q:** *Has Rick ever climbed a mountain?*
   A: *No, he hasn't.*

3. **Q:** *Has Alana ever eaten worms?*
   A: *No, she hasn't.*

4. **Q:** *Has Rick ever eaten worms?*
   A: *Yes, he has.*

Unit 6 Review

This lesson reviews the grammar and vocabulary introduced in Unit 6.

Language chart review

These charts summarize the main grammar presented and practiced in Unit 6.

- Books closed. Write on the board:

Present perfect with "never"	
Statements	Questions and Answers

has already / hasn't . . . yet	
Affirmative	Negative

- Read the following sentences aloud. After reading each sentence, invite a volunteer to come to the board and write it in the appropriate section of one of the charts.

  She hasn't decided on a career yet.

  Have they ever explored a cave?

  No, they haven't. They've never explored a cave.

  He's never driven a car.

  I've already turned 14.

  Yes, they have.

  We've never gone rock climbing.

- Books open. Give students a few minutes to study the charts, compare them with the charts on the board, and share with the class any differences they may find.

- Remind students that *never* is not usually used in questions.

- Answer any questions students may have.

....

Exercises A through D (pages T-84 to T-85)

Note: Students can do these exercises for homework or in class. They should do these exercises with minimal teacher input or help. If you choose to do these exercises as homework, briefly review the exercise directions in class. Make sure that students understand what they should do. Check the answers with the class during the next class meeting. If you choose to do the exercises in class, follow the directions below.

Exercise A

- Have students read the directions and look at the pictures.
- Invite a volunteer to read the verb phrases in the box and the example.
- Have students work individually to write sentences with *already* or *yet* and the verb phrases in the box.
- Check answers with the class.

Exercise B

- Have students read the directions and look at the chart.
- Invite a pair of volunteers to read the example question and answer aloud.
- Have students work individually to write questions and answers.
- Have students check their answers in pairs.
- Check answers with the class.

Language chart review

These charts summarize further grammar presented and practiced in Unit 6.

- Have students study the examples in the charts.
- Remind students that we use the simple past for events completed at a specific time in the past and that we use the present perfect for events at unspecified times, repeated actions, and actions begun in the past and completed in the present.
- Review the formation of tag questions with the simple past and the present perfect. Point out how short answers and tag questions are formed in similar ways.
- Answer any questions students may have.

Exercise C

- Have students read the directions and the two postcards.
- Invite a volunteer to read the example sentence. Remind students to look for time phrases beginning with *since* or *for* to help them decide which verb form to use.
- Have students work individually to complete the postcards.
- Check answers with the class. Invite volunteers to read the postcards aloud.

Exercise D

- Have students read the directions and the example.
- Have students work individually to complete the correct tag questions and then write the answers.
- Tell students to look again at the postcards in Exercise C to write the answers to Exercise D.
- Check answers with the class.

Take another look!

- Have a volunteer read the directions aloud.
- Students work individually to write *SP* (simple past), *PP* (present perfect), or *SP & PP* (simple past and present perfect) next to the time phrases.
- Check answers with the class.

Optional Unit Wrap-Up

- If students did the Review exercises for homework, check answers with the class.
- Have students work in pairs. Students use Exercise A as a model and tell each other one unusual thing they have already done and one thing they have not done yet. Ask students to report their partner's answers to the class. Make notes on the board about some of the students' answers. For example, write on the board: *Elena / not horseback riding.*
- Ask students questions about their classmates' activities, using the notes on the board. For example, ask: *Has Elena ever gone horseback riding?* Students answer with short answers as in Exercise B. Put students in pairs to continue practicing asking and answering questions.
- Have students write postcards about imaginary vacations. Use the postcards in Exercise C as a model. Each student then "mails" his or her postcard to another student in the class. Have students read the postcard they received.
- Have students choose a different partner. Students ask and answer questions about the postcards they received. Use the questions and answers in Exercise D as a model.

Theme Project

- Assign the *At Home* section of the Unit 6 Theme Project on Student's Book page 131.

Workbook

- Assign the Unit 6 Check Yourself on Workbook page 43. (Workbook answers begin on page T-192.)

Extra Practice Worksheets

- Assign the Unit 6 Extra Practice worksheets starting on page T-153.

Extra Speaking Practice Worksheet

- Assign the Unit 6 Extra Speaking Practice worksheet on page T-173.

Arcade Activities

- Assign the Unit 6 Arcade activities found at: www.cambridge.org/connectarcade

Learning Log

- Assign the Unit 6 Learning Log. This can be downloaded from the Teacher Support Site at: www.cambridge.org/connect2e/teacher

Quiz

- Give the Unit 6 Quiz on page T-183.

Test

- Give the Unit 6 Test (Form A and / or Form B). These can be downloaded from the Teacher Support Site at: www.cambridge.org/connect2e/teacher

Language chart review

Simple past	Present perfect
I **got** a job **in May**.	I'**ve met** many interesting people **since May**.
He **learned** a lot **last year**.	**Since last spring**, we'**ve made** a lot of money.

Tag questions with the simple past and present perfect

Simple past	Present perfect
You **called** her yesterday, **didn't** you?	You'**ve come** to class every day, **haven't** you?
Yes, I did. / No, I didn't.	**Yes, I have. / No, I haven't.**

C Complete the postcards with the simple past or the present perfect.

Dear Carlos,
<u>We've been</u> (we / be) in New York City since last Friday. Our first hotel <u>was</u> (be) noisy, so we <u>moved</u> (move) to a quieter place. Last night, we <u>ate</u> (eat) at the Hard Rock Cafe, and I <u>saw</u> (see) Miley Cyrus! I <u>took</u> (take) a picture of her with my new camera. She <u>gave</u> (give) me her autograph!
See you soon,
Connie

Hi, Sonia!
<u>I've been</u> (I / be) in New York for almost a week. We <u>got</u> (get) here last Friday. We <u>heard</u> (hear) the buses and cars all night, so we <u>moved</u> (move) to a quieter hotel. The weather <u>has been</u> (be) beautiful. Yesterday we <u>bought</u> (buy) a new camera. I'll e-mail you some pictures this afternoon.
Connie

Sonia Alvarez
432 Park Street
San Francisco, CA 94105

D Look again at the postcards in Part C. Complete the tag questions. Then write the answers.

1. **Q:** Connie bought a new camera in New York City, <u>didn't she</u>?

    A: <u>Yes, she did.</u>

2. **Q:** Their first hotel was noisy, <u>wasn't it</u>?

    A: <u>Yes, it was.</u>

3. **Q:** The weather in New York City has been terrible, <u>hasn't it</u>?

    A: <u>No, it hasn't.</u>

4. **Q:** Connie got Miley's autograph, <u>didn't she</u>?

    A: <u>Yes, she did.</u>

Take another look!

Are these time phrases used with the simple past (*SP*), with the present perfect (*PP*), or both (*SP & PP*)?

1. so far <u>PP</u>   3. for a month <u>SP & PP</u>

2. last Saturday <u>SP</u>   4. a week ago <u>SP</u>

Go to page 131 for the Theme Project.

Teen opinions

Lesson 25

1 Language focus

A Read these teens' opinions about movies and music. Then listen and practice.

good / better / the best
bad / worse / the worst

Action movies are **good**.
Comedies are **better than** action movies.
Science-fiction movies are **the best** movies of all.

I think rap music is **bad**.
Rock music is **worse than** rap music.
Pop music is **the worst** music of all.

Adjective	Comparative	Superlative
good	better	the best
bad	worse	the worst

I'm a big movie fan, so I like all kinds of movies. Action movies are OK, but I think comedies are better than action movies. They make me laugh. Science-fiction movies are the best movies of all. The stories are always interesting. I've seen all of the *Star Trek* movies three times. They're great! – **Andrea**

I only listen to country music and jazz music. They're the only kinds of music I like. I think rap music is bad. I can't understand the words. And rock music is worse than rap music. It's too loud. But take my advice. Pop music is the worst music of all because it's so boring. – **Bart**

B Complete the sentences with the correct words. Then listen and check your answers.

1. I love history. I think it's _the best_ (the best / the worst) subject at school. It's easy for me.
2. Sports are great. Volleyball is a _good_ (good / bad) sport to play with friends, but I think soccer is better than volleyball.
3. I can't stand dramas. The stories are boring. They're _the worst_ (the best / the worst) shows on TV.
4. School uniforms are great. Wearing a uniform is much _better than_ (better than / worse than) wearing your own clothes to school.
5. I don't like doing the dishes. But I think cleaning my room is _worse than_ (better than / worse than) doing the dishes. I don't like chores.
6. I really like pizza, but the pizza at Rocco's is _bad_ (bad / good). It tastes awful. It's the worst pizza in my neighborhood.

UNIT 7 Teen Time

86

Lesson 25 Teen opinions

This lesson reviews adjectives and presents and practices good / better / the best *and* bad / worse / the worst.

1 Language focus

This exercise presents and practices *good / better / the best* and *bad / worse / the worst*.

A 💿 CD3, Track 2

- Ask students to cover the language chart with a sheet of paper.

- Focus students' attention on the title of the lesson. Write these two sentences on the board.

  1. Star Trek is a science-fiction movie.

  2. Star Trek is the best science-fiction movie.

  Ask: *Which sentence is an opinion?* (Sentence 2.) *Can you agree or disagree with an opinion?* (Yes.) Explain that the first sentence is a fact.

- Have students read the two texts quickly. Ask: *Who is talking about movies?* (Andrea.) *What is Bart talking about?* (Music.)

- Have students read the two texts slowly and carefully. While they are reading, draw this chart on the board:

	Comparative	Superlative
good		
bad		

- **Optional** Play the recording. Students listen and read along.

> **Audio script**
> Same as the texts in the Student's Book.

- Focus students' attention on Andrea's text. Ask: *What did Andrea say about action movies? Are they good or bad?* (Good.) *Which kind of movies does she like more, action movies or comedies?* (Comedies.) *Which movies are her favorite?* (Science-fiction movies.)

- Focus students' attention on Bart's text. Ask: *What kinds of music does Bart listen to?* (Country music and jazz.) *What's his opinion of rap?* (It's bad.) *What kind of music does he think is boring?* (Pop.)

- Explain that the words *good* and *bad* have irregular comparative and superlative forms. (Good → better → the best; bad → worse → the worst.) Ask students to find the irregular forms of *good* and *bad* in the texts. Invite four volunteers to come to the board and each write in the chart the comparatives and superlatives they found.

- Play the recording or model the text. Students listen and repeat.

- **Language Chart** Ask students to uncover the language chart. Have them study the examples. Answer any questions students may have.

- **Optional** Model the examples, pausing for students to repeat.

- **Optional** Ask students to produce sentences similar to the examples, replacing the kinds of movies and music with other kinds of movies and music they know.

B 💿 CD3, Track 3

- Ask students to read the directions and the example.

- Have students work individually to complete the sentences with the correct words.

- Play the recording. Students listen and verify their answers.

> **Audio script**
> Same as the sentences in the Student's Book.

- Check answers with the class. Invite volunteers to come to the board to write the word or phrase they used to complete one of the sentences.

UNIT 7 Teen Time

This unit introduces words and expressions for making comparisons, talking about extreme experiences, and making choices.

T-86

2 Word power

This exercise reviews adjectives with positive and negative meanings.

A

- Ask students to read the directions and the adjectives in the box. Have students call out any words they do not understand. Explain the words by using them in sentences or by miming them. Ask: *What do you have to do?* (Write the adjectives in the correct columns according to whether they have positive or negative meanings.)
- Have students work individually to complete the exercise.
- Check answers with the class. Write the two headings on the board and ask random students to come to the board to write a word correctly under one of the two headings.

B

- Ask students to read the directions and the sentences.
- Have students work individually to complete the opinions with the best words from Part A.
- Check answers with the class. Invite volunteers to read aloud one of the sentences they completed.
- **Optional** Have other students say whether they agree or disagree with the opinions.

- **Optional** Read the following sentences, saying *blank* for the missing words. Students say which of the words in the box in Part A that they did not use in Part B goes in the blank.
  1. *He doesn't remember things. He's _____ .* (Forgetful.)
  2. *She works ten hours a day, including Saturdays and Sundays. She's _____ .* (Hardworking.)
  3. *He's the worst player I know. He's _____ .* (Awful.)
  4. *I like to read detective stories. I think they're _____ .* (Thrilling.)
  5. *She's the best actor I know. She's _____ .* (Excellent.)
  6. *There are clothes on the table and books and papers on the floor. This room is _____ .* (Messy.)
  7. *You can believe in his honesty and goodness. He's _____ .* (Trustworthy.)

3 Speaking

This exercise practices discussing opinions.

A

- Invite a volunteer to read the directions aloud.
- Give students a few minutes to study the chart.
- Have students work individually to complete the chart with examples of each thing listed.

B

- Ask students to read the directions and the example opinions.
- Invite volunteers to share one of their opinions with the class, following the example in the speech balloon.

Culture Note   Teenagers in the U.S. can take opinion polls (surveys in which people are asked for their opinions about a topic or a person). These polls may appear in newspapers, on the Internet, and in magazines, but what happens to the information contained in these opinion polls? Most of the time, the information is not used for anything important. Sometimes, however, a U.S. corporation might use the teen opinion surveys to develop fashion trends and marketing strategies for future products. The companies want to know how and where U.S. teens shop, and they benefit from the teens' answers. The teens benefit from taking part in these opinion polls as well – they learn how different companies conduct market research.

Workbook
Assign the exercises on Workbook page 44. (Workbook answers begin on page T-192.)

Extra Grammar
Assign the exercises for the Extra Grammar, Lesson 25.

2 Word power

A Which of these words have positive meanings? Which have negative meanings? Write the words in the correct columns. *(The order of the answers may vary.)*

☑ awful ☐ dangerous ☐ entertaining ☐ forgetful ☐ messy ☐ thrilling
☑ beautiful ☐ difficult ☐ excellent ☐ hardworking ☐ scary ☐ trustworthy

Positive		Negative	
beautiful	*hardworking*	*awful*	*forgetful*
entertaining	*thrilling*	*dangerous*	*messy*
excellent	*trustworthy*	*difficult*	*scary*

B Complete these opinions with the best words from Part A.

1. Roller coasters are the best amusement park rides! I'm never afraid on roller coasters. They're not ___*scary*___ at all.
2. I think skydiving is a bad sport because you can get hurt. It's very ___*dangerous*___ .
3. My math test grade is worse than my English test grade. I think math is very ___*difficult*___ .
4. I think Pink is the best singer right now. She's pretty, too. She has a ___*beautiful*___ face.
5. Comedies are better than thrillers. They aren't as exciting, but they're more ___*entertaining*___ .

3 Speaking

A What's your opinion? Complete the chart with examples of each thing. *(Answers will vary.)*

	Good	Better	The best
Singers			
Actors			
TV shows			
	Bad	**Worse**	**The worst**
Chores			
Movies			

B Share your opinions with the class.

> I think Pink is a good singer. Celine Dion is better than Pink. Jennifer Lopez is the best singer.

Unforgettable moments

1 Language focus

Parasailing is **the scariest** thing I**'ve ever done**.
It's **the most disgusting** food we**'ve ever eaten**.
It's **the weirdest** present he**'s ever received**.

A Read about these teens' unforgettable moments.
Complete the texts with the superlative + *ever*
and the correct form of the verbs. Listen
and check. Then practice.

1. Parasailing is the
scariest thing I've ever
done. I never want to
do it again.

2. We ate crocodile meat
on a safari once. It's
the most disgusting
food we've ever eaten.

3. My brother's friend
gave him a spider for
his birthday. It's the
weirdest present he's
ever received.

4. I got 40 percent on my
math test last week.
It's *the worst* (bad)
grade I've *ever gotten*
(get).

5. Beyoncé is *the best*
(good) singer I've
ever heard (hear). I
went to her concert last
year. It was great.

6. Jenny fell during a
play. It's *the most embarrassing*
(embarrassing)
experience she's
ever had (have).

B Complete the sentences with your opinions. Then tell the class. *(Answers will vary.)*

1. _____ is the scariest thing I've ever done.

2. _____ is / are the most disgusting food I've ever eaten.

3. _____ is the weirdest present I've ever received.

> Riding a roller coaster is the scariest thing I've ever done.

Unforgettable moments

This lesson presents and practices superlative + . . . have ever.

Review of Lesson 25

- Write on the board:

	good	better	the best
sports team			
TV show			

	bad	worse	the worst
sports team			
TV show			

. . . is good.	. . . is better than . . .	. . . is the best.
. . . is bad.	. . . is worse than . . .	. . . is the worst.

- Have students work individually to complete the chart with the names of sports teams and TV shows that they think are representative of each category. Then ask students to write sentences following the cues on the board.

- Invite volunteers to share with the class one of the sentences they wrote.

1 Language focus

This exercise presents and practices superlative + . . . *have ever*.

A CD3, Track 4

- Focus students' attention on the title of the lesson. Explain that *unforgettable* refers to something or someone that is impossible to forget.

- Give students several minutes to read the directions and texts 1–6.

- Read the following statements. Students respond true or false.

Parasailing isn't the scariest thing the girl in Picture 1 has ever done. (False.)

Crocodile meat is the most delicious food the kids in Picture 2 have ever eaten. (False.)

A spider is the weirdest present the boy in Picture 3 has ever received. (True.)

- Have students work individually to complete texts 4–6 with the superlative + *ever*.

- Play the recording again. Students listen and verify their answers.

Audio script
Same as the texts in the Student's Book.

- Check answers with the class. Invite volunteers to read aloud one of the sentences they completed.

- Play the recording again or model the sentences. Students listen and repeat.

- **Language Chart** Have students study the examples in the language chart. Ask: *What is used in the first half of each sentence, the comparative or the superlative?* (The superlative.) *What form is used in the second half of each sentence?* (The present perfect.) *Which word in each sentence means* in my life up to now? (Ever.) *Where is ever placed in the sentence?* (Between the pronoun + has / have and the past participle.) Remind students that we form superlatives by adding *-est* to the end of short adjectives like *scary* and *weird*. If the adjective ends in a consonant + *y*, we change *y* to *i* before adding *-er* or *-est*.

scary ⟶ *scarier* ⟶ *the scariest*
pretty ⟶ *prettier* ⟶ *the prettiest*

We add *the most* before longer words like *disgusting* or *embarrassing*.

- **Optional** Model the examples, pausing for students to repeat.

B

- Give students several minutes to read the directions and the sentence endings. Stress the fact that students have to complete the sentences with their own opinions and experiences.

- Have students work individually to complete the sentences, following the example in the speech balloon.

- Invite volunteers to share with the class one of the sentences they completed.

C CD3, Track 5

- Give students several minutes to read the directions, the sentences, and the words or cues in parentheses. Explain that the sentences students have to write give additional information about each item in the exercise.

- Check that students understand the sentences and the cues in parentheses. Ask the following questions:

  Why was Tom's experience scary? (Because he didn't know the city and it was late at night.)

  What's special about Quest? (It's exciting.)

  Why was the experience in sentence 4 frustrating? (The boy erased his favorite computer files by mistake.)

  What language did Kate find difficult to study? (Japanese.)

  What's special about Silly Stories? (It's funny.)

- Have students work individually to write the sentences.

- Play the recording. Students listen and verify their answers.

> **Audio script**
> Same as the sentences in the Student's Book.

- Check answers with the class. Invite volunteers to come to the board to write one of the sentences they wrote.

- **Optional** Mark the stressed words in the first sentence on the board as follows:

  It's the scáriest expérience he's éver hád.

- Ask students to call out the words they think are stressed in the other sentences. As they do so, mark the stressed words.

  It's the most excíting gáme she's éver pláyed.

  It's the most frústrating thíng he's éver dóne.

  It's the most dífficult lánguage she's éver stúdied.

  It's the fúnniest bóok I've éver réad.

- Give students several minutes to practice saying only the stressed words. Then ask them to practice the complete sentences. After a few minutes, invite volunteers to read aloud one sentence each.

Note: Students often find it difficult to say sentences with the superlative + *have ever* and tend to stress the word *most* rather than the adjective. Making them aware of the stress pattern in sentences like these enables students to say sentences more fluently.

---

2 Listening

In this exercise, students listen for some teenagers' unique experiences.

CD3, Track 6

- Have students read the directions.

- Focus students' attention on the titles of the stories. Have students work with a classmate to suggest what each of the stories may be about. Encourage them to be as imaginative as possible.

- Invite representatives from different pairs to share one of their suggestions with the class.

- Play the recording. Students only listen.

> **Audio script**
> See page T-214.

- Play the recording again. Students listen and number the titles of the stories.

- Play the recording once again. Students listen and verify their answers.

- Check answers with the class.

- **Optional** Play the recording again. Students listen for details of each story. Ask: *What's the title of the first story?* ("The Scariest Moment I've Ever Had.") Elicit the key events in each story. For example: *Story One. What's the story about?* (A cat.) *Where was it?* (In a tree.) *What did the girl try to do?* (Save the cat.) *Why was she scared?* (She was very high up.) *Who helped her?* (Her father.) If necessary, play the recording again.

- To finish, ask students which stories they found the most and least interesting.

---

3 Speaking

This exercise practices discussing personal opinions and experiences.

- Have students read the directions and study the chart.

- Give students several minutes to complete the *You* column.

- Ask students to read the example in the speech balloons.

- Have students work with a classmate, take turns asking questions, and complete the *Your classmate* column.

- Invite volunteers to share one of their findings about a classmate with the class. For example, Silly Stories *is the worst book Maria has ever read.*

> **Workbook**
> Assign the exercises on Workbook page 45.
> (Workbook answers begin on page T-192.)

> **Extra Grammar**
> Assign the exercises for the Extra Grammar, Lesson 26.

C Read the statements and write sentences with the superlative + *ever* and the correct form of the verbs. Then listen and check.

1. I got 100 percent on the test last week.

   (good grade / get) *It's the best grade I've ever gotten.*

2. My friend Tom got lost in a strange city late at night.

   (scary experience / have) *It's the scariest experience he's ever had.*

3. My sister bought *Quest*, a new computer game.

   (exciting game / play) *It's the most exciting game she's ever played.*

4. My brother erased his favorite computer files by mistake.

   (frustrating thing / do) *It's the most frustrating thing he's ever done.*

5. Kate studied Japanese last summer.

   (difficult language / study) *It's the most difficult language she's ever studied.*

6. I spent the weekend reading *Silly Stories*.

   (funny book / read) *It's the funniest book I've ever read.*

2 Listening

Look at these titles and listen to the stories. What is the best title for each one? Listen and number the titles.

Title	Number
"The Most Interesting Place I've Ever Visited"	4
"The Worst Car Ride I've Ever Had"	3
"The Scariest Moment I've Ever Had"	1
"The Most Embarrassing Experience I've Ever Had"	2

3 Speaking

Complete the survey for yourself. Then ask a classmate the questions. (*Answers will vary.*)

What's the . . . ?	You	Your classmate
1. best movie you've ever seen		
2. worst book you've ever read		
3. most interesting place you've ever visited		
4. best vacation you've ever had		

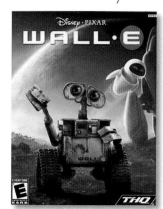

What's the best movie you've ever seen?

WALL • E is the best movie I've ever seen.

Mini-review

1 Language check

A Read the critic's ratings of burger places and online music stores. Then complete the sentences with *better than*, *worse than*, *the best*, or *the worst*.

BURGER PLACES ★ ★ ★ ★

Burger City
★ ★ ★ ★
The burgers here are great. They're big, tasty, and juicy. The french fries are OK. The only problem is the noise. It's always very crowded and very loud.

Burger and Fries
★ ★ ★
The burgers are OK, and the french fries are OK. It sometimes gets crowded, and it's a little loud, but you can usually get a table.

Galaxy Burger
★ ★
The burgers aren't very good at all, but the french fries are delicious. The place usually isn't very crowded, so noise isn't a problem.

ONLINE MUSIC STORES ★ ★ ★ ★

YourTunes
★ ★ ★
This Web site has a big music selection, from rock to jazz. You can find and download almost anything you want. The download time is very fast. The only problem is that the prices are the highest online, and there isn't any free music.

BestTunes
★ ★
This Web site sells a variety of popular music, but there are many songs you can't find on the site. Also the download time on this Web site is really slow. But the prices are really low, and you can get some music for free here.

ClassicTunes
★ ★ ★ ★
This Web site only has classical music and jazz. If that's what you're looking for, you'll find it here. The prices are lower than the prices on YourTunes. This site also offers a lot of information about the music. The other sites don't.

1. The burgers are _the best_ at Burger City.
2. The burgers at Burger City are _better than_ the burgers at Burger and Fries.
3. The burgers are _the worst_ at Galaxy Burger.
4. The fries at Galaxy Burger are _better than_ the fries at Burger and Fries.
5. The fries at Galaxy Burger are _the best_ in town.
6. The noise at Burger City is _worse than_ the noise at Burger and Fries.
7. The music selection at YourTunes is _better than_ the selection at BestTunes.
8. The prices at YourTunes are _the worst_ online.
9. ClassicTunes is _the best_ site for classical music and jazz.
10. The download time at BestTunes is _worse than_ the download time at YourTunes.

This lesson reviews the language presented and practiced in Lessons 25 and 26.

1 Language check

This exercise reviews the structures presented so far in this unit.

A

- Give students several minutes to read the directions and the texts. Explain that a *critic* is someone who expresses opinions about things like books, movies, plays, restaurants, and so on.

- Ask: *What do the first three texts compare?* (Burger places.) *What do the other texts compare?* (Online music stores.) *Can you tell how good these places are without reading the texts?* (Yes.) *How?* (By looking at the number of stars they have.) *What's the best place for burgers?* (Burger City.) *Which is better, Galaxy Burger or Burger and Fries?* (Burger and Fries.) *Which is the best online music store?* (ClassicTunes.) *Which is better, YourTunes or BestTunes?* (YourTunes.)

- Check students' understanding of the texts about places for burgers. Tell students that you will say a series of statements. Students should say *True* or *False*.

  Burger City has the best burgers. (True.)

  Burger City's fries are not fantastic. (True.)

  The burgers and fries at Burger and Fries are excellent. (False.)

  It's always crowded and noisy at Burger and Fries. (False.)

  The burgers at Galaxy Burger are delicious. (False.)

  The fries at Galaxy Burger are delicious. (True.)

  It's always noisy and crowded at Galaxy Burger. (False.)

- Check students' understanding of the texts about online music stores. Read the following sentences, one at a time. Ask students to say which store each sentence is about.

  This Web site has some free music. (BestTunes.)

  You won't find rock music at this site. (ClassicTunes.)

  The prices here are the lowest. (BestTunes.)

  You can download music very quickly on this site. (YourTunes.)

  On this site you can learn more about the music. (ClassicTunes.)

  This online store has many different kinds of music. (YourTunes.)

- Have students work individually to complete the sentences.

- Check answers with the class. Invite volunteers to read aloud one of the sentences they completed.

> **Teaching Tip** In exercises where students have to manipulate a great deal of potentially confusing information, it is important to check understanding in detail before asking students to carry out the task. Otherwise, they may fail to do the exercise not because they do not know the language required but because they did not understand the information.

B

- Invite a volunteer to read the directions aloud.

- Ask: *What kind of program is this?* (A quiz show.) *What are the questions going to be about?* (Family.)

- Have students read the entire conversation quickly without writing the answers. Ask: *What thrilling experience did Mike's mother have?* (She went skydiving.) *What movie did Joe and Jim see?* (A Clown's Life.) *Where did Katie and Mike's parents go?* (To the Grand Canyon.)

- Have students work individually to complete the conversation.

- Check answers with the class. Invite two volunteers to read portions of the conversation. One reads the Host's line, and the other reads Katie's or Mike's answer.

- **Optional** Have students work in pairs to read the conversation.

....

2 Listening

In this exercise, students listen to find out if Mike and Katie's answers in Part A were correct.

A 🔘 **CD3, Track 7**

- Invite a volunteer to read the directions aloud. Ask: *How much money will Katie and Mike win for each correct answer?* ($1,000.)

- Play the recording. Students only listen.

> **Audio script**
> See page T-215.

- Play the recording again. Students listen and check the boxes. Don't verify answers at this time, as this would give away the answer to the final question in Part B.

B

- Invite a volunteer to read the directions aloud.

- Give students a minute to calculate the answer, according to their answers in Exercise A.

- Have students work in pairs to compare answers.

- Play the recording again. Students verify their answers to Exercises A and B.

- Check answers with the class. Invite a volunteer to explain the correct answer. (Katie's and Mike's guesses for 1, 5, and 6 were incorrect. That leaves three correct answers at $1,000 each for a total of $3,000.)

> **Workbook**
> Assign the exercises on Workbook page 46. (Workbook answers begin on page T-192.)

> **Game**
> Assign the game on Student's Book page 120.

B Katie and Mike are on the quiz show *Do You Know Your Family?* Write answers with the superlative + *ever* and the correct form of the verb.

Host Good evening everyone. Tonight Katie Wilson and her brother Mike are going to answer questions about their family. Katie, has your father ever done anything scary?

Katie Well, he went rock climbing once. I think (scary / did) *it's the scariest thing he's ever done* .

Host OK. Now, Mike. Has your mother ever had a thrilling experience?

Mike Definitely. She went skydiving last month. I think (thrilling experience / have) *it's the most thrilling experience she's ever had* .

Host OK. Now Katie, you and Mike have twin brothers, Joe and Jim. Do they like funny movies?

Katie They love them. They saw *A Clown's Life* last week. I think (funny movie / see) *it's the funniest movie they've ever seen* .

Host And Mike. What about Katie? What's something disgusting she has eaten?

Mike Oh, once some kids made her eat a worm. I think (disgusting thing / eat) *it's the most disgusting thing she's ever eaten* .

Host And a question for you, Katie. Has Mike ever read a bad book?

Katie Oh, yes. He read *How to Be Happy*. I think (bad book / read) *it's the worst book he's ever read* .

Host One more question. Mike, have your mom and dad visited any beautiful places?

Mike Hmm. They loved the Grand Canyon. I think (beautiful place / visit) *it's the most beautiful place they've ever visited* .

2 Listening

A Listen to the rest of the quiz show from Exercise 1B. Were Mike and Katie's answers correct or incorrect? Check (✓) Correct ($1,000) or Incorrect ($0) for each question.

	Correct ($1,000)	Incorrect ($0)
1.	☐	✓
2.	✓	☐
3.	✓	☐
4.	✓	☐
5.	☐	✓
6.	☐	✓

B How much money did Mike and Katie win? Add together the number of correct answers in Part A. Then write the number below.

Mike and Katie won $ *3,000* .

**Go** to page 120 for the Game.

Lesson 27 Are we alike?

1 Language focus

A What do you know about Cole and Dylan Sprouse? Read Elena's Web site about them. Then listen and practice.

Cole and Dylan Sprouse

Welcome to my Sprouse Brothers Web site. I think these brothers are awesome. They're twins, and they're both actors. Cole is as famous as Dylan, but he isn't as old as him. He's 15 minutes younger. People say that Cole is funnier than Dylan. But, I think Dylan is funnier than Cole. Anyway, I hope you enjoy my Web site.

Facts about the Sprouse brothers

They were born in Italy, on August 4, 1992. Their parents are American. They're both talkative and outgoing. Dylan is very artistic. Cole is one inch taller than Dylan. He's 5 feet, 6 inches tall (168 cm).

▼ **And who am I?**
My name's Elena, and I'm a fan of Cole and Dylan Sprouse. Am I as famous as them? No, I'm not. I'm older than they are. Here's my photo and some more information about me.

▼ **Facts about me**
I was born on June 11. I'm 5 feet, 4 inches tall (163 cm). I'm funny, but I'm shy. I'm athletic, but I'm not good at tennis. I have one brother, Dario. He was born on June 11. We're twins, too!

B Study the chart. Rewrite the sentences with informal comparisons. Then listen and check.

Formal comparisons: *as ... as / not as ... as*	Informal comparisons: *as ... as / not as ... as* + object pronoun
Cole is **as famous as** Dylan. Cole is **as famous as** he is.	Cole is **as famous as him**.
I'm **not as famous as** the Sprouse brothers. I'm **not as famous as** they are.	I'm **not as famous as them**.
	Object pronouns: *me, you, him, her, it, us, them*

1. Elena isn't as tall as the Sprouse brothers. *She isn't as tall as them.*

2. Dario is as old as Elena is. *He's as old as her.*

3. Elena isn't as famous as Cole and Dylan are. *She isn't as famous as them.*

4. The Sprouse brothers aren't as old as Dario is. *They aren't as old as him.*

5. Cole Sprouse isn't as short as I am. *He isn't as short as me.*

Lesson 27 Are we alike?

This lesson reviews adjectives to describe people's personalities. It also presents and practices formal comparisons with as . . . as / not as . . . as and informal comparisons with as . . . as / not as . . . as + object pronoun.

Review of Lesson 26

- Write on the board:

bad	disgusting	embarrassing	frustrating	good	sad	weird
difficult	easy	exciting	funny	happy	scary	

Have students work in pairs. They take turns talking about experiences they have had using the adjectives on the board as cues, and a superlative and *ever*. For example, *Jumping from a plane is the scariest thing I've ever done.*

- Have volunteers share with the class any interesting things they learned about their partner.

1 Language focus

This exercise presents and practices formal comparisons with *as . . . as / not as . . . as* and informal comparisons with *as . . . as / not as . . . as* + object pronoun.

A CD3, Track 8

- Have students read the directions and look at the photos.
- Have students read the text.
- **Optional** Play the recording. Students listen and read along.

> **Audio script**
> Same as the Web site in the Student's Book.

- Ask: *Where does this text come from?* (Elena's Web site about Cole and Dylan Sprouse.)
- Read the following phrases. Students say who they refer to – Cole, Dylan, and / or Elena.
  Was born on August 4, 1992. (Cole and Dylan.)
  Is 5 feet 5 inches tall. (Dylan. Cole is one inch taller.)
  Has a twin brother. (Cole, Dylan, and Elena.)
- Ask: *Who do the first two paragraphs compare?* (Cole and Dylan Sprouse.) *Who does the paragraph next to Elena's photo compare?* (Cole, Dylan, and Elena.)
- Have students work individually to underline all the phrases or sentences that make comparisons in the text. While they do so, write these column headings on the board: *-er / more than   as . . . as   not as . . . as*
- Invite volunteers to come to the board to write one of the sentences they underlined under the correct column. The completed chart should look like this:

-er / more than	as . . . as	not as . . . as
He's 15 minutes younger. Cole is funnier than Dylan. Dylan is funnier than Cole. Cole is one inch taller than Dylan. I'm also older than they are.	Cole is as famous as Dylan. Am I as famous as them?	but he isn't as old as him.

- Play the recording or model the text. Students listen and repeat.

B CD3, Track 9

- **Language Chart** Have students study the examples in the language chart. Focus students' attention on the left-hand column. Ask: *Which expression suggests that the two things being compared are similar or the same?* (As . . . as.) *What does* not as . . . as *suggest?* (That the things being compared are different.) Ask: *What's the difference between the first two sentences?* (The first one uses a name – *Dylan* – after *as . . . as* and is not followed by a verb. The second one uses the pronoun *he* after *as . . . as* and is followed by the verb *is*.) Analyze the other two sentences in the same way.

Note: Tell students that it is also correct to say *Cole is as famous as Dylan is,* but this form is not usually used in speaking.

- Focus students' attention on the right-hand column. Ask: *What do you use after* as . . . as *or* not as . . . as *in this version of the sentences?* (An object pronoun.) *Do you use a verb after an object pronoun?* (No.) Explain that the formal comparisons are more likely to be used in writing and the informal ones in speaking. For the object pronouns, say the subject pronoun and elicit the object pronoun – for example: *I – me.*
- **Optional** Model the examples, pausing for students to repeat.
- Have students read the directions and the example.
- Have students work individually to rewrite the sentences with informal comparisons.
- Play the recording. Students listen and verify their answers.

> **Audio script**
> Same as the sentences in the Student's Book.

- Check answers with the class. Invite volunteers to come to the board to write one of the sentences they rewrote.

C

- Give students several minutes to read the directions and the information about Dylan Sprouse.
- Elicit adjectives from students that match Dylan's interests and write them on the board: *snowboarding → athletic; drawing → artistic.* Explain that students can choose either adjective to compare their interests with Dylan's.

- Have students work individually to write comparative sentences about Dylan Sprouse and themselves using *as . . . as* or *not as . . . as.*
- Check answers with the class. Invite volunteers to come to the board to write one of their sentences. If necessary, check that the sentences convey the right information by asking questions such as: *How old is Dylan Sprouse now? How old are you?*

2 Word power

This exercise reviews adjectives to describe people's personalities.

A

- Ask students to read the directions and the words in the list.
- Have students call out any words or phrases they do not understand. Explain them by using them in sentences or by miming them. Ask: *How many categories does the list include?* (Four.) *How many words are in each category?* (Four.) *What do you have to do?* (Check the word in each category that does not belong.)
- Have students work individually to complete the exercise.
- Check answers with the class. Invite volunteers to take turns calling out one of the words they checked.

B

- Ask students to read the directions and the example. Ask: *What kind of word goes in the first blank in the sentence, an adjective or a pronoun?* (An adjective.) *What kind of pronoun goes in the second blank?* (An object pronoun.) *Which are the object pronouns?* (Me, you, him, her, it, us, you, them.)
- Have students work individually to complete the sentences.
- Check answers with the class. Invite volunteers to read one of the sentences they completed. After a sentence is read, ask another volunteer to call out the words that enabled him or her to choose the appropriate adjective for each sentence. (1. *sports*; 2. *draws*; 3. *lazier*; 4. *isn't shy when he meets people*; 5. *telling jokes.*)

3 Speaking

This exercise practices making comparisons between people using *as . . . as* or *not as . . . as.*

- Ask students to read the directions, the words in the chart, and the examples in the speech balloons.
- Give students a few minutes to choose the people in their lives that they want to compare themselves to and think about how they are alike or different.
- Invite volunteers to tell the class how they compare themselves to the people they chose, following the examples in the speech balloons.
- To finish, ask students if there is anyone they want to be like.

Workbook

Assign the exercises on Workbook page 47. (Workbook answers begin on page T-192.)

Extra Grammar

Assign the exercises for the Extra Grammar, Lesson 27.

C Read the information about Dylan Sprouse. How are you alike? How are you different? Write sentences using informal comparisons.

> Dylan Sprouse was born on August 4, 1992. He's 5 feet, 5 inches tall (165 cm). He likes snowboarding and drawing. His favorite school subject is math.

(Answers will vary.)

1. (age) _____

2. (height) _____

3. (interests) _____

2 Word power

A Check (✓) the word in each category that does not belong.

1. sports	☐ athletic	☐ active	☑ artistic	☐ strong
2. school	☑ lazy	☐ serious	☐ smart	☐ hardworking
3. making friends	☐ outgoing	☑ bad-tempered	☐ friendly	☐ funny
4. helping others	☐ thoughtful	☐ trustworthy	☐ kind	☑ forgetful

B Complete the sentences with words from Part A and object pronouns.

1. You're better at sports than me. I'm not as _athletic_ as _you_ .

2. My sister draws well. I do, too. I'm as _artistic_ as _her_ .

3. My brother is lazier than I am. He's not as _hardworking_ as _me_ .

4. My father isn't shy when he meets people. I'm not, either. I'm as _outgoing_ as _him_ .

5. Our neighbors are always telling jokes. No one is as _funny_ as _them_ .

3 Speaking

Compare yourself to people in your life. Tell your classmates.
Use the ideas in the chart or your own ideas.

People	Characteristics	Good at
best friend	artistic	computer games
cousins	musical	math
brother or sister	athletic	cooking
neighbors	outgoing	languages
teacher	creative	making friends
your mom or dad	thoughtful	sports

> My friend Mike is athletic. I am, too. I'm as athletic as him.

> My cousins are good at math. I'm not. I'm not as good at math as them.

I'd rather . . .

1 Language focus

would . . . rather for preferences

Would you **rather** be rich **or** famous?
I**'d rather** be famous.
I**'d rather** be rich **than** famous.

A Carla and Will talk about a survey. Who would rather be famous? Listen and practice.

Carla What are you looking at, Will?

Will This survey. It has some interesting questions. Listen to this one. "Would you rather be rich or famous?"

Carla Oh, that's an easy choice. I'd rather be famous. A famous singer, a famous actor, a famous poet . . . I'd love to be famous all over the world!

Will Well, not me. I'd rather be rich than famous. I'd like to have lots of money to buy anything I want!

Carla Really? I don't think money is important.

Will You don't? Then could you lend me $30?

Carla What? $30? Are you kidding?

Will But, Carla, money isn't important . . .

B Write questions and answer them with your own preferences. Then listen and check.

1. **Q:** (listen to rap / to rock music) _Would you rather listen to rap or rock music?_

    A: _I'd rather listen to rap than rock music._ OR _I'd rather listen to rock music than rap._

2. **Q:** (have a car / a motorcycle) _Would you rather have a car or a motorcycle?_

    A: _I'd rather have a car than a motorcycle._ OR _I'd rather have a motorcycle than a car._

3. **Q:** (swim / run) _Would you rather swim or run?_

    A: _I'd rather swim than run._ OR _I'd rather run than swim._

4. **Q:** (meet an actor / a sports star) _Would you rather meet an actor or a sports star?_

    A: _I'd rather meet an actor than a sports star._ OR _I'd rather meet a sports star than an actor._

5. **Q:** (read a book / a magazine) _Would you rather read a book or a magazine?_

    A: _I'd rather read a book than a magazine._ OR _I'd rather read a magazine than a book._

C Tell your classmates about your preferences.

> I'd rather listen to rap than rock music.

Lesson 28 I'd rather . . .

This lesson presents and practices would . . . rather *for preferences.*

Review of Lesson 27

- Write on the board:

  Name: Juan Carlos Ferrero
  Born: December 2, 1980
  Height: 5 feet, 9 inches
  Weight: 159 pounds
  Likes: Telling jokes

  Name: Amelie Mauresmo
  Born: July 5, 1979
  Height: 5 feet, 7 inches
  Weight: 141 pounds
  Likes: playing tennis

  He's (not) as . . . as her.
  She's (not) as . . . as him.
  I'm (not) as . . . as him / her.

- Give students a few minutes to study the information and the sentence cues on the board. Have students work individually to write three sentences using the information in the chart, one for each of the sentence cues.

- Ask volunteers to share with the class one of the sentences they wrote.

1 Language focus

This exercise presents and practices *would . . . rather* for preferences.

A 💿 CD3, Track 10

- Ask students to read the directions and look at the photo.

- Have students read the conversation.

- **Optional** Play the recording. Students listen and read along.

> ### Audio script
> Same as the conversation in the Student's Book.

- Ask: *How many questions from the survey do Carla and Will discuss?* (One.) *What are the choices in the question?* (Being rich or being famous.) *What's Carla's preference?* (Being famous.) *What's Will's preference?* (Being rich.) *What's funny about the end of the conversation?* (Carla says money is not important, but she does not want to lend Will $30.)

- Focus students' attention on Carla's second speech. Ask: *How does Carla say what her preference is?* (I'd rather be famous.) *How does Will say what his preference is?* (I'd rather be rich than famous.) Explain that *rather* is an adverb used to express preferences.

- Focus students' attention on the survey question. Ask: *Which words in the question introduce the choice?* (Would you rather . . . ?)

- Play the recording or model the conversation. Students listen and repeat.

- **Optional** Have students practice in pairs.

- **Language Chart** Have students study the examples in the language chart. Ask: *Which word is used between the options in the question?* (Or.) *Do you have to mention both choices in the answer, or can you just say what your preference is?* (You can do either one.) *Which word is used between the choices if you mention both in the answer?* (Than.)

- **Optional** Model the examples, pausing for students to repeat.

B 💿 CD3, Track 11

- Have students read the directions, the example, and the choices for each item.

- Ask: *What do you have to do?* (Write questions using *would . . . rather* and the choices in parentheses. Then answer the questions with your own preferences.)

- Have students work individually to write the questions and answer them.

- Play the recording. Students listen and verify their answers.

> ### Audio script
> Same as the questions and answers in the Student's Book.

- Check answers with the class.

C

- Invite volunteers to share one of their preferences with the class, following the example in the speech balloon.

Teen Time T-94

2 Listening

In this exercise, students listen for Diana's and Juan's preferences.

A 🔊 CD3, Track 12

- Give students a few minutes to read the directions and questions in the chart. Ask: *What are Diana and Juan doing?* (They're answering questions for a TV program.) *What do you have to listen for?* (Their preferences.) *What do you have to do?* (Check the correct names.)
- Play the recording. Students only listen.

> **Audio script**
> See page T-215.

- Play the recording again. Students listen and check the correct boxes.
- Play the recording once again. Students listen and verify their answers.
- Check answers with the class.

B

- Have students work individually to write the answers to the questions in Part A, as in the example.
- Check answers with the class. Invite volunteers to come to the board to write one of the answers they wrote.

---

3 Pronunciation   Intonation in questions of choice

This exercise practices intonation in questions of choice.

A 🔊 CD3, Track 13

- Have students read the directions and the questions of choice.
- Play the recording. Students only listen.

> **Audio script**
> Same as the questions of choice in the Student's Book.

- Ask: *Where does the intonation go up, in the first choice or in the second choice?* (In the first choice.) *What happens in the second choice?* (The intonation goes down.)

- Play the recording again, or model the questions of choice, exaggerating the intonation. Students listen and repeat.

B

- Have students work individually or in pairs to practice saying the questions of choice in Exercise 1B on page 94.
- Invite volunteers to say one of the questions of choice they practiced. Make sure they use rising intonation for the first choice and falling intonation for the second choice.

---

4 Speaking

This exercise practices discussing preferences using *would . . . rather.*

A

- Give students a few minutes to read the directions, the verb phrases in the box, and the example in the speech balloons.
- Invite two volunteers to come to the front to demonstrate the activity by reading the example question and answer.
- Have students work with a classmate. They take turns asking and answering questions with the verb phrases in the box or their own ideas, following the examples in the speech balloons.

B

- Invite volunteers to report to the class about their classmate's preferences, following the example in the speech balloon.

> **Workbook**
> Assign the exercises on Workbook page 48. (Workbook answers begin on page T-192.)

> **Extra Grammar**
> Assign the exercises for the Extra Grammar, Lesson 28.

2 Listening

A Diana and Juan answer questions for a TV show.
Who would rather do or be these things?
Listen and check (✓) the correct names.

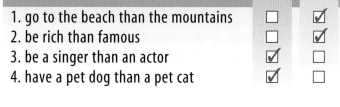

Who would rather . . . ?	Diana	Juan
1. go to the beach than the mountains	☐	☑
2. be rich than famous	☐	☑
3. be a singer than an actor	☑	☐
4. have a pet dog than a pet cat	☑	☐

B Write the answers to the questions in Part A.

1. *Juan would rather go to the beach than the mountains.*

2. *Juan would rather be rich than famous.*

3. *Diana would rather be a singer than an actor.*

4. *Diana would rather have a pet dog than a pet cat.*

3 Pronunciation   Intonation in questions of choice

A Listen. Notice the intonation in questions where there is a
choice. Then listen again and practice.

Would you rather swim or run?   Would you rather be a singer or an actor?

B Practice the questions in Exercise 1B.

4 Speaking

A Work with a classmate. What would your classmate rather do?
Ask questions. Use the verb phrases in the box or your own ideas.

> do chores / homework
> join a theater group / a rock band
> eat meat / vegetables
> buy CDs / clothes
> play video games / a sport
> learn karate / to play a musical instrument

Ricardo, would you rather do chores or homework?

I'd rather do chores.

B Tell the class about your classmate.

Ricardo would rather do chores than homework.

Get Connected

UNIT 7

Read

A Read the Web site quickly. Check (✓) what one teen wrote about a trip.

☐ "It was amazing. It's the most interesting place I've ever been."

☑ "It's one of the greatest experiences I've ever had. It made me a better person."

Amazing Experiences

Would you rather go on a trip next summer or stay at home? That's an easy question for the thousands of teens who have traveled all over the world with AAVE (All About Visiting Earth). They'd rather go on an exciting summer trip with AAVE than stay at home. But AAVE isn't just a travel company. AAVE believes that experiencing a culture is better than only traveling to a country. So, teens who travel with the company do **community work**, study languages, and learn outdoor **wilderness skills**.

Recently, some teens went to China. They walked on the Great Wall, learned about **pandas** at a center for pandas, and worked with **farmers**. They also taught English to children, and they studied Chinese.

On the AAVE blog, teens say summers with the company are the best they've ever had. Many teens think that spending time together is as much fun as traveling. One teen who traveled to Africa wrote, "It's one of the greatest experiences I've ever had. It made me a better person."

One thing is certain: After a **memorable** experience like this, these teenagers aren't the same as they were before.

Go to page 125 for the Vocabulary Practice.

B 💿 Read the Web site slowly. Check your answer in Part A.

C Are these statements true or false? Write *T* (true) or *F* (false). Then correct the false statements.

                           rather go on an exciting AAVE trip

1. Teens who have traveled with AAVE would ~~like to stay home~~. _F_

2. AAVE thinks cultural experiences are better than only traveling to a country. _T_

3. Teens say AAVE trips are the best they've ever had. _T_

                                is

4. AAVE teens think spending time together ~~isn't~~ as much fun as traveling. _F_

                aren't

5. After traveling with AAVE, teens ~~are~~ the same as they were before. _F_

Get Connected

This lesson practices reading, listening, and writing skills.

> **Review of Lesson 28**
> - Write on the board:
>
> *Choices*
>
> | | | |
> |---|---|---|
> | *be a singer or . . .* | *have a car or . . .* | *meet a pop star or . . .* |
> | *buy CDs or . . .* | *have a pet dog or . . .* | *play video games or . . .* |
> | *do chores or . . .* | *join a theater group or . . .* | *read a book or . . .* |
> | *eat meat or . . .* | *learn karate or . . .* | *swim or . . .* |
> | *go to the beach or . . .* | *listen to rap or . . .* | |
>
> *Example*
>
> *A: Would you rather be rich or famous?*
> *B: I'd rather be famous. Would you rather listen to rap or rock music?*
> *C: I'd rather . . .*
>
> - Give students a few minutes to try to remember the choices they discussed in Lesson 28.
> - Divide the class into groups of three. Have the groups play a chain game, as in the example on the board. As they play, students should try to remember their classmates' choices.
> - Have groups play a memory game. Students take turns reporting on their classmates' choices. For example, Student A says: *(Student B) would rather be famous than rich.* Student B confirms if this is correct.

Read

This exercise practices reading for information about a travel program for teens.

A

- Have students read the title of the Web site and look at the photos. Ask: *Where do you think the students are?* (China.) *What kind of animal is in the picture?* (Panda.)
- Invite a volunteer to read the directions and the statements aloud. Remind students that they should read quickly to find the answer and that they should not read every word carefully.
- Have students work individually to read the Web site quickly and check the correct sentence. Do not check the answer at this point.

B 💿 CD3, Track 14

- Invite a volunteer to read the directions aloud. Remind students that they should read slowly and carefully, and concentrate on getting the meaning of the entire text.
- List the new vocabulary words on the board: *community work, wilderness skills, panda, farmer, memorable.* Explain their meaning. (Community work: work you do, such as planting trees or building houses, to help a group of people living in the same area; wilderness skills: training that helps you survive outdoors, such as learning what to do if you get lost in the woods; panda: a black-and-white animal that looks like a bear and lives in China; farmer: a person who lives on a farm and plants food or raises animals; memorable: something you will always remember.) As an alternative, have students use their dictionaries to find the meanings of the new vocabulary words.

- Have students read the Web site again.
- Have students check their answer in Part A in pairs. Elicit the answer from one pair.
- **Optional** Play the recording. Students listen and read along.

> **Audio script**
> Same as the Web site in the Student's Book.

> **Get Connected Vocabulary**
> Have students do the exercise on Student's Book page 125 in class or for homework. (Get Connected Vocabulary answers are on page T-125.)

C

- Invite a volunteer to read the directions and first statement aloud.
- Ask: *Would the teens who have traveled with AAVE like to stay home next summer?* (No, they wouldn't.) Ask: *So is the sentence true or false?* (False.) Ask: *What would they rather do?* (They'd rather go on an exciting AAVE trip.)
- Have students work individually to write *True* or *False*, and then correct the false statements.
- Have students check their answers in pairs.
- Check answers with the class. Invite volunteers to read aloud one sentence they completed.

Listen

In this exercise, students listen for information about a summer trip.

A 🔊 CD3, Track 15

- Focus students' attention on the photo. Ask: *Where do you think the photo was taken?* (Accept any answers and verify later.)
- Tell students that they will listen to two friends, Carlos and Luisa, talk about exciting experiences Carlos is going to have on his next summer vacation.
- Have students read the first question and the example answer.
- Explain that students should listen to the conversation and answer the questions.
- Play the recording. Students only listen.

> **Culture Note**
> In the U.S., teens often look for special activities and experiences during the summer months when school is not in session. There are many choices, from summer camps in rural areas to organizations that sponsor trips abroad for teenagers. Many, like the one in the reading, offer a combination of language learning, adventure, and community service. Other programs are more specialized. Teens may go to a computer camp or an acting or filmmaking camp, for example. Sports camps are also very popular. In all cases, the objective is for the teens to learn and have fun at the same time. In addition, being away from family and friends for an extended period of time helps teens become more independent and mature.

> **Audio script**
> See page T-216.

- Play the recording again. Students listen and answer the questions.
- Play the recording once again. Students listen and verify their answers.
- Check answers with the class. Invite several pairs of volunteers to read the questions and answers aloud.

B

- Have students read the directions and the questions.
- Read the first question with the class and elicit answers from several students. Remind students that there are no right or wrong answers for this exercise – they are giving their opinions.
- Have students work individually to answer the questions, and give reasons for their answers.
- Have students work in pairs to compare answers, or elicit opinions from volunteers.
- **Optional** Review students' answers by inviting a volunteer from one group to report the group's answers to one of the questions. Ask students from the other groups to say if they agree or disagree, and why. Repeat this procedure for the other questions.

Write

In this exercise, students answer questions and write a paragraph about an exciting experience.

A

- Invite a volunteer to read the directions and the questions aloud.
- Have students work individually to answer the questions.
- **Optional** Have students ask and answer the questions in pairs.

B

- Invite a volunteer to read the directions aloud. Tell students that they will use their answers in Part A to help them write their paragraphs about an exciting experience they have had.
- Have students work individually to write their paragraphs.

- Invite several volunteers to read their paragraphs to the class.
- **Optional** Have students work in groups of four and read each other's paragraphs. Students can ask questions about anything they do not understand. They can then vote on their group's most exciting experience.

> **Workbook**
> Assign the exercises on Workbook page 49. (Workbook answers begin on page T-192.)

I'd rather go with you.

A  **Carlos and Luisa talk about an exciting experience.**
Listen and answer the questions.

1. Where's Carlos going on his next vacation? _He's going to Peru._

2. What's one of the most interesting places in Peru? _Machu Picchu is one_
of the most interesting places in Peru.

3. Is Carlos going to study Spanish there? _No, he isn't._

4. What's the most important part of the trip? _The most important part_
of the trip is doing community work.

5. What would Luisa rather do – go to music camp or go on the trip with
Carlos? _She'd rather go on the trip with Carlos._

B **What do you think? Answer the questions. Give reasons.** (*Answers will vary.*)

1. Do you think it's important for young people to travel?

_____

2. Would you rather travel in your own country or travel to other
countries? _____

3. Do you think it's important to learn other languages? _____

4. Do you think it's good to try new things? _____

Your turn

 **Write**

A **Think of an exciting experience you've had (taking a trip, trying an activity).**
Answer the questions. (*Answers will vary.*)

1. What did you do? When? _____

2. How did you feel? _____

3. Was it the best experience you've ever had? _____

4. Would you like to do it again? _____

5. What other experiences would you like to try? _____

B **Write a paragraph about an exciting experience. Use the answers in Part A to help you.**
(*Answers will vary.*)

About _____ _ago, I . . ._

_____

_____

_____

_____

Language chart review

good / better / the best	bad / worse / the worst
Nellie's is a **good** restaurant.	The Hawks are a **bad** baseball team.
Burger Barn is **better than** Nellie's.	The Eagles are **worse than** the Hawks.
Tom's Diner is **the best** restaurant in town.	The Bobcats are **the worst** team in the city.

Superlative + ... have ever ...
He's **the messiest** person she**'s ever met**.
Those are **the most beautiful** flowers I**'ve ever seen**.

A Complete the conversations. Use the correct forms of the words in parentheses.

1. **A** How did you do on the history exam?
   B I got 63 percent. It's _the worst grade I've ever gotten_ (bad grade / get)! How about you?
   A My grade is even worse than yours. I got 55 percent.

2. **A** What a great game!
   B This is _the best game I've ever seen_ (good game / see)!
   A I'm not sure about that. You were at last week's game, weren't you? That game was _better_ (good) than this one. It was really exciting.
   B You might be right.

3. **A** Do you want to go out to eat?
   B Sure. Let's go to Dino's. They have _the best_ (good) pizza in town.
   A I can't go to Dino's. The last time I was there, I dropped my tray in the middle of the restaurant. It was _the most embarrassing thing I've ever done_ (embarrassing thing / do)!

4. **A** I think this movie is _worse_ (bad) than *Action Man*, the movie we saw last week.
   B I agree. It's _the worst movie I've ever seen_ (bad movie / see).
   A It wasn't even _scarier_ (scary) than *Action Man*.
   B I hope the movie we'll see next week will be _better_ (good) than this one.

Unit 7 Review

This lesson reviews the grammar and vocabulary introduced in Unit 7.

Language chart review

These charts summarize the main grammar presented and practiced in Unit 7.

- Books closed. Write on the board:

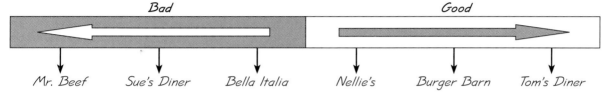

Bad   *Good*

Mr. Beef   *Sue's Diner*   *Bella Italia*   *Nellie's*   *Burger Barn*   *Tom's Diner*

- Focus students' attention on the diagram. Explain that it shows the restaurants in a small town according to their reputation. Have students make sentences comparing the restaurants. For example: *Nellie's is good. Burger Barn is better than Nellie's.*

- Other possible sentences:

  Tom's Diner is better than Burger Barn.

  Tom's Diner is the best restaurant.

  Bella Italia is bad.

  Sue's Diner is worse than Bella Italia.

  Mr. Beef is worse than Bella Italia.

  Mr. Beef is the worst restaurant.

- Books open. Give students several minutes to study the first chart.

- Answer any questions students may have.

- Focus students' attention on the second chart. Ask: *Where does the superlative go, in the first half or in the second half of the sentence?* (In the first half.) *Which word means* in my life up to now? (Ever.)

....

Exercises A through D (pages T-98 to T-99)

Note: Students can do these exercises for homework or in class. They should do these exercises with minimal teacher input or help. If you choose to do these exercises as homework, briefly review the exercise directions in class. Make sure that students understand what they should do. Check the answers with the class during the next class meeting. If you choose to do the exercises in class, follow the directions below.

Exercise A

- Have students read the directions and look at the picture.

- Invite two volunteers to read the example conversation aloud.

- Have students work individually to complete the other conversations with the correct forms of the words in parentheses.

- Check answers with the class.

Language chart review

These charts summarize further grammar presented and practiced in Unit 7.

- Have students study the examples in the charts.
- Remind students about the use of pronouns in comparisons with *as . . . as* or *not as . . . as*. Remind them, too, that formal comparisons end with a noun (for example, a name) or a subject pronoun followed by a verb. Informal comparisons use the object pronoun and no verb.
- Remind students also that *would . . . rather* is used for preferences.
- Answer any questions students may have.

Exercise B

- Have students read the directions and look at the picture.
- Have students work individually to complete the comparisons with *as . . . as* or *not as . . . as*.
- Check answers with the class.

Exercise C

- Have students read the directions.
- Have students work individually to complete the sentences with object pronouns.
- Check answers with the class. Invite volunteers to write one sentence each on the board.

Exercise D

- Have students read the directions and the example.
- Have students work individually to write the questions. Students should answer number 3 with their own information.
- Check answers with the class. Invite several pairs of volunteers to read their questions and answers aloud.

Take another look!

- Invite a volunteer to read the directions aloud. Have students read the questions and the answer choices.
- Students work individually to circle the correct answers.
- Check answers with the class.

- If students did the Review exercises for homework, check answers with the class.
- Have students work in pairs to read the conversations in Exercise A. Then, have them create an original conversation about movies, using the conversation in item number 4 as an example.
- Write these adjectives on the board: *tall, hardworking, athletic, friendly, strong*. Have students work in pairs to compare themselves with someone in their family using sentences with *as . . . as* or *not as . . . as*. They can say things such as: *I'm as tall as my sister. She isn't as hardworking as me.* Use the sentences in Exercises B and C as examples.
- Brainstorm ideas to create a list of some things students often choose between, such as flavors of ice cream or pizza versus hamburgers, etc. Write the options on the board. Use one option and ask a question with *would . . . rather*. Invite a volunteer to answer the question. Students continue asking and answering questions in pairs, using Exercise D as a model.

Theme Project

- Assign the *At Home* section of the Unit 7 Theme Project on Student's Book page 132.

Workbook

- Assign the Unit 7 Check Yourself on Workbook page 50. (Workbook answers begin on page T-192.)

Extra Practice Worksheets

- Assign the Unit 7 Extra Practice worksheets starting on page T-157.

Extra Speaking Practice Worksheet

- Assign the Unit 7 Extra Speaking Practice worksheet on page T-174.

Arcade Activities

- Assign the Unit 7 Arcade activities found at: www.cambridge.org/connectarcade

Learning Log

- Assign the Unit 7 Learning Log. This can be downloaded from the Teacher Support Site at: www.cambridge.org/connect2e/teacher

Quiz

- Give the Unit 7 Quiz on page T-184.

Test

- Give the Unit 7 Test (Form A and / or Form B). These can be downloaded from the Teacher Support Site at: www.cambridge.org/connect2e/teacher

Language chart review

Formal comparisons: *as ... as / not as ... as*	Informal comparisons: *as ... as / not as ... as* + object pronoun
Ines is **as tall as** Tom. Ines is **as tall as** he is. I'm **not as tall as** Ines and Tom. I'm **not as tall as** they are.	She's **as tall as him**. I'm **not as tall as them**. Object pronouns: *me, you, him, her, it, us, them*

would ... rather for preferences

Would you **rather** have a cat **or** a dog?
  I'd rather have a cat.
  I'd rather have a cat **than** a dog.

B **Complete the comparisons of Sally and Jack with**
_as ... as_ or _not as ... as_.

1. Jack is lazy. Sally isn't. Sally is <u>n't as lazy as Jack</u> .
2. Jack is smart, and Sally is, too. Jack is <u>as smart as Sally</u> .
3. Sally is tall, and Jack is, too. Sally is <u>as tall as Jack</u> .

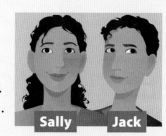

Sally   Jack

C **Complete the sentences about Sally and Jack with object pronouns.**

1. Sally and Jack are very strong, but Jack isn't as strong as <u>her</u> .
2. My friends and I are athletic. Sally and Jack aren't as athletic as <u>us</u> .
3. Jack loves meeting new people. But Sally isn't as friendly as <u>him</u> .
4. Sally and Jack are really tall. I'm not as tall as <u>them</u> .

D **Write questions for numbers 1 and 2. Then answer number 3**
with your own information.

1. **Q:** <u>Would you rather read a book or watch TV?</u>

   A: I'd rather read a book than watch TV.

2. **Q:** <u>Would you rather do a homestay in Canada or England?</u>

   A: I'd rather do a homestay in Canada than in England.

3. **Q:** Would you rather eat at home tonight or go to a restaurant?

   A: <u>(Answers will vary.)</u>

Take another look!

Circle the correct answers.

1. Which sentence means the same as "I'm not as hardworking as him"?
a. I work harder than him. (b.) He works harder than me c. He works as hard as me.

2. Would you rather travel or stay home?
a. I'd rather go to school. b. I'll stay home. (c.) I'd rather stay home than travel.

Go to page 132
for the
Theme Project.

Our dreams

1 Language focus

If clauses with could ... would

A Trish and her classmates were asked about their dreams. Here are their responses. Complete the texts. Listen and check. Then practice.

> **If I could live in any country in the world**, I**'d live** in Italy.
>
> **If Jack could talk to a famous person**, he**'d talk** to Bill Gates.
> ....
> *I'd = I would; he'd = he would*

Check out our dreams!

Do you think they'll come true?
What's your dream?

1. If I _could live_ (live) in any country in the world, _I'd live_ in Italy. It looks beautiful, and I love Italian food.

2. If Jack _could talk_ (talk) to a famous person, _he'd talk_ to Bill Gates. He's one of the richest people in the world, and he's very smart.

3. If Jenny _could buy_ (buy) any house in the world, _she'd buy_ the White House. It's the coolest house she's ever seen.

4. If Hilary _could wear_ (wear) any clothes to school, _she'd wear_ a pink T-shirt, a pink miniskirt, and pink shoes. She loves pink!

5. If he _could be_ (be) good at any sport, _he'd be_ good at basketball. He'd like to play for the Los Angeles Lakers someday.

6. If they _could go_ (go) on a trip anyplace in the world, _they'd go_ to Africa. They want to go on a safari and see wild animals.

Our dreams

This lesson presents and practices if *clauses with* could . . . would.

1 Language focus

This exercise presents and practices *if* clauses with *could . . . would.*

A 💿 CD3, Track 16

- Have students read the directions. Ask: *Who wrote the texts?* (Trish and her classmates.) *What do they write about in the texts?* (Their dreams.)

- Invite a volunteer to read text 1 aloud. Ask: *Where would this teenager like to live?* (In Italy.)

- Have students read texts 2–6. Ask: *Why does Jack want to talk to Bill Gates in text 2?* (Because Bill Gates is one of the richest people in the world, and he's also very smart.) *What house does Jenny think is cool in text 3?* (The White House.) *What's Hilary's favorite color in text 4?* (Pink.) *Would she like to wear pink clothes to school?* (Yes.) *What sport would the teenager in text 5 like to be good at?* (Basketball.) *Where would the people in text 6 like to go to?* (To Africa.)

- Have students work individually to complete the sentences in texts 2–6.

- Play the recording. Students listen and verify their answers.

Audio script
Same as the texts in the Student's Book.

- Check answers with the class. Invite volunteers to read aloud one of the sentences they completed.

- Play the recording again or model the sentences. Students listen and repeat.

- **Language Chart** Have students study the examples in the language chart. Ask: *Where does the If clause go in the sentence, in the first clause or in the second clause?* (In the first clause.) *What modal do you see in this clause?* (Could.) *What separates the If clause from the rest of the sentence?* (A comma.) *What word does the 'd stand for in the second clause in the sentence?* (Would.)

- **Optional** Model the examples, pausing for students to repeat.

UNIT 8 Dreams and Reality

This unit introduces vocabulary and expressions to talk about hypothetical situations, wishes, and special personal experiences.

T-100

B

- Have students read the directions, the ideas in the box, and the example. Ask: *What do you have to write about?* (Your dreams.) Have students call out any words or phrases they do not understand. Explain them by using the words and phrases in a sentence or by miming them.
- Have students work individually to write the sentences.

- Have students work with a classmate to take turns telling each other about their dreams.
- **Optional** Ask students to give reasons for their dreams as they talk to their classmate. For example: *If I could live in any country in the world, I'd live in Finland. I love cold weather.*
- To finish, invite volunteers to share with the class one of the dreams they were told about. For example, *If Sergio could live in any city in the world, he'd live in Helsinki.*

2 Pronunciation Pauses

This exercise practices pauses in *If* clauses.

A CD3, Track 17

- Have students read the directions and the sentences.
- Play the recording. Students only listen.

> **Audio script**
> Same as the sentences in the Student's Book.

- Ask: *Where is the pause in the sentence?* (Immediately before the *would* clause.)
- **Optional** Ask: *Does intonation go up or down in the second clause?* (It goes down.)

- Play the recording again, or model the sentences, exaggerating the pause. Students listen and repeat.

B

- Give students several minutes to practice saying the sentences in Exercise 1B, making sure they pause in the correct place.
- Invite volunteers to read aloud one of the sentences they practiced.

3 Listening

In this exercise, students listen for specific information about teenagers' dreams.

A CD3, Track 18

- Have students read the directions and items 1–4. Focus students' attention on the dreams (phrases a to d). Tell students they will hear four teens describe their dreams. They should listen and match each person to his or her dream.
- Play the recording. Students only listen.

> **Audio script**
> See page T-216.

- Play the recording again. Students listen and write the correct letters next to items 1–4.
- Play the recording once again. Students listen and verify their answers.
- Check answers with the class. Invite pairs of volunteers to ask and answer questions about the teenagers. For example:

  Student A: *Who would like to marry a member of a royal family?*

  Student B: *Liz.*

B CD3, Track 19

- Have students read the directions and items 1–4.
- Play the recording again. Students listen and check the correct sentence for each person.

> **Audio script**
> Same as the script in Part A.

- Check answers with the class. Play the recording again. Ask students to call out *Stop!* when they hear the information to answer one of the questions. Invite volunteers to try to reconstruct what the teenagers say each time they ask you to pause. Then ask the class to confirm what the correct answer is.

Teaching Tip You can follow up a listening activity with a free-writing activity about the same topic. Set a time limit of about five minutes for students to write their ideas.

> **Workbook**
> Assign the exercises on Workbook page 51. (Workbook answers begin on page T-192.)

> **Extra Grammar**
> Assign the exercises for the Extra Grammar, Lesson 29.

B Write sentences about your dreams. Use the ideas in the box or your own ideas. Then tell a classmate. *(Answers will vary.)*

> be good at any sport   look like any person   visit anyplace in the world
> live in any city in the world talk to any famous person   wear any clothes to school

If I could live in any city in the world, I'd live in Miami.

1. _____
2. _____
3. _____
4. _____
5. _____
6. _____

> If I could live in any city in the world, I'd live in Miami.

2 **Pronunciation** Pauses

A Listen. Notice the pause in *If* clauses. Then listen again and practice.

> If I could live anyplace in the world, I'd live in Paris.

> If she could talk to a famous person, she'd talk to Pink.

B Practice your sentences from Exercise 1B.

3 **Listening**

A Some students talk about their dreams. Listen and match the students to their dreams.

1. Carl _b_   a. marry a member of a royal family
2. Rita _d_   b. be a professional athlete
3. Liz _a_   c. win an event at the Olympic Games
4. Mark _c_   d. fly fighter planes

B Listen again. Check (✓) why they have those dreams.

1. Carl ☑ He'd love to travel.   ☐ He'd love to play basketball sometimes.
2. Rita ☐ She loves to travel.   ☑ She loves exciting situations.
3. Liz   ☐ She likes princes.   ☑ She likes people who help others.
4. Mark ☑ He loves horses.   ☐ He has his own horse.

What would you do?

1 Word power

A Match each verb or verb phrase to its meaning. Then listen and practice.

1. eavesdrop _h_
2. cheat on a test _f_
3. break a promise _g_
4. gossip _d_
5. jaywalk _a_
6. lie _b_
7. litter _e_
8. trespass _c_

a. cross the street in the middle of the block
b. say things that are not true
c. enter a private place without permission
d. talk about other people's lives
e. leave paper or garbage around carelessly
f. copy someone's answers
g. not do something you said you'd do
h. listen in secret to someone's conversation

B What are these people doing? Label the pictures.

1. _He's breaking a promise._ 2. _She's littering._ 3. _He's jaywalking._

4. _They're trespassing._ 5. _He's cheating on a test._ 6. _She's eavesdropping._

7. _They're gossiping._ 8. _He's lying._

C Which of these things do you think is the worst behavior? Tell your classmates.

> I think cheating on a test is the worst behavior.

Lesson 30 What would you do?

This lesson presents and practices verbs and verb phrases related to bad behaviors and the unreal conditional with If clauses.

Review of Lesson 29

- Write on the board:

Example: If I could be good at any language, I'd be good at Russian.

Names:				
be good at any musical instrument				
buy a really expensive car				
live on a different planet				
talk to a politician				

- Have students copy the chart.
- Give students several minutes to think about the dreams in the chart and decide what their choice would be in each case. Ask them to think of a sentence like the one in the example on the board for each dream.
- Have students stand up, talk to four different classmates, and compare dreams. They should take turns saying sentences, as in the example on the board. Ask them to write the names of the classmates in the chart and to put a check mark in the correct box each time they have the same dream.
- To finish, invite volunteers to report on common dreams. For example, *If Sergio and I could live on a different planet, we'd live on Mars.*

1 Word power

This exercise presents and practices verbs and verb phrases related to types of bad behaviors.

A   CD3, Track 20

- Give students several minutes to read the directions, the verbs and verb phrases, and the meanings. Ask: *How would you describe the actions the verbs and verb phrases describe? Are they good or bad?* (Bad.) Explain that students should start by matching any verb or verb phrase they may already know to its meaning. They should then guess the rest. At the "guessing" stage, they can also look at the pictures in Part B. Each of the pictures illustrates one of the verbs or verb phrases in Part A.

- Have students work individually to match the verbs or verb phrases to their meanings.

- Check answers with the class. Invite volunteers to say one of the answers like this: *To* eavesdrop *means "to listen in secret to someone's conversation."*

- Play the recording. Students listen and repeat.

Audio script
See page T-216.

B

- Ask students to read the directions and look at the pictures.

- Have students work individually to label the pictures. Remind them to use the present continuous form of the verb phrases in Exercise 1A, as in the example.

- Check answers with the class. Invite volunteers to read one of the labels they wrote.

C

- Ask students to read the example in the speech balloon. Explain that in this example the word *behavior* refers to how you act. Model the example for students to repeat.

- Conduct a class discussion. Invite volunteers to share with the class their opinions about the worst behavior, as in the example. Students may also want to compare types of behavior. For example, *I think gossiping is worse than cheating on a test.*

2 Language focus

This exercise presents and practices the unreal conditional with *If* clauses.

A 🔘 CD3, Track 21

- Have students look at the photo and read the directions. Ask: *What should you read and listen for?* (The name of the game Pedro played.)
- Have students read the conversation.
- **Optional** Play the recording. Students listen and read along.

> **Audio script**
> Same as the conversation in the Student's Book.

- Ask: *What's the name of the game Pedro played?* ("What would you do if . . . ?") *Did Carla play the game, too?* (No.) *Does Pedro remember any of the questions in the game?* (Yes.) *What's the question?* (What would you do if you found $20 at school?) *How does Carla answer at first?* (She'd keep it.) *Why?* (It isn't a lot of money.) *Does she change her mind later?* (Yes.) *So what would she do?* (She'd take the money to the teacher.) *Would Pedro take the money to the teacher, too?* (Yes.) *If Pedro saw a person littering, what would he ask the person to do?* (He'd ask the person to throw the garbage in the trash can.) *What would Carla do?* (She'd pick up the garbage and throw it in the trash can.)
- Play the recording or model the conversation. Students listen and repeat.
- **Optional** Have students practice in pairs.
- **Language Chart** Have students study the examples in the language chart. Ask: *What tense is used in the* If *clause?* (Simple past.) *What word (or modal) is used in the main clause and in the question?* (Would.) *What separates the* If *clause from the main clause?* (A comma.) *Is there a comma in the question?* (No.) *Why do you think the title of the chart is* unreal conditional? (The situation is not real. It's an imaginary situation.) Explain that we use the unreal conditional with *If* clauses to talk about situations that are not real in the present or the future.
- **Optional** Model the examples, pausing for students to repeat.

B 🔘 CD3, Track 22

- Have students read the directions and the clauses in the left- and right-hand columns.
- Have students work individually to match the two parts of each sentence.
- Play the recording. Students listen and verify their answers.

> **Audio script**
> Same as the sentences in the Student's Book.

- Check answers with the class. Invite volunteers to read aloud one sentence each.

C

- Give students several minutes to choose two *If* clauses from the left-hand column in Part B and complete them with their own information.
- Have students work in pairs to take turns reading the sentences they wrote.
- Invite several pairs of volunteers to read their sentences to the class.

3 Speaking

This exercise practices the unreal conditional with *If* clauses to talk about what students would do in some imaginary situations.

- Have students read the directions. Demonstrate the activity by reading the example conversation with two volunteers.
- Invite two other volunteers to come to the front to work with you to demonstrate the activity for the class. Then continue the activity with a student taking your place.
- Have students work in groups of three to talk about what they would do in the situations in Exercise 2B.
- **Optional** Have several volunteers tell the class what they would do in each situation in Exercise 2B.

> **Workbook**
> Assign the exercises on Workbook page 52. (Workbook answers begin on page T-192.)

> **Extra Grammar**
> Assign the exercises for the Extra Grammar, Lesson 30.

2 Language focus

A **What game did Pedro play today?
Listen and practice.**

> **Unreal conditional with *if* clauses**
>
> What **would** you **do if you found** $20?
> **If I found** $20, **I'd take** it to the teacher.
> **I'd keep** it.
>
> *I'd = I would*

Pedro We played a game today called
"What would you do if . . . ?" It
made us think about doing the right thing.
Did you play the game, too?

Carla No, we didn't. But it sounds interesting. Do you
remember any of the questions?

Pedro Yeah. What would you do if you found $20 at school?

Carla I'd keep it, because $20 isn't a lot of money. I mean,
it's not the same as finding $1,000! So, what would
you do if you found $20?

Pedro If I found $20, I'd take it to the teacher. It's not my
money, so it doesn't matter how much it is.

Carla You're right. I'd take it to the teacher, too, I guess.
What would you do if you saw a person littering?

Pedro I'd ask the person to throw the garbage in the trash
can. What would you do?

Carla If I saw a person littering, I'd pick up the garbage
and throw it in the trash can.

B **Match the two parts of each sentence. Then listen and check.**

1. If I found a lot of money on the street, __d__
2. If I saw a classmate cheating on a test, __f__
3. If my sister lied to our parents, __a__
4. If I heard my friends gossiping about me, __b__
5. If I saw my brother jaywalking, __c__
6. If my brother was eavesdropping, __e__

a. I'd tell them about it.
b. I'd ask them not to talk about me.
c. I'd tell him to cross at the corner.
d. I'd take it to the police.
e. I'd ask him to stop listening.
f. I'd tell him or her to stop copying.

C **Write sentences. Choose two *If* clauses from Part B, and complete them
with your own information. Then read your sentences to a classmate.** *(Answers will vary.)*

1. _____

2. _____

3 Speaking

**Talk with two classmates. Look at the situations in Exercise 2B.
What would you do in each situation?**

Maya What would you do if you found a lot of money
on the street, Mike?

Mike If I found a lot of money, I'd take it to the police. How about
you, Carly?

Carly I'd take it to the police, too. What would you do if . . . ?

Mini-review

1 Language check

A Choose the correct words to complete the conversation.

Todd If you ____could____ (could / would) visit
any country in the world, where
____would____ (do / would) you go?

Paula Hmm. If I ____could____ (could / would) visit
any country, I think ____I'd____ (I'll / I'd)
go to Kenya.

Todd What would you do there?

Paula If I ____went____ (went / go) to Kenya,
____I'd____ (I'm / I'd) go on a safari and
see lions in the wild.

Todd Yeah, that would be cool.

Paula What about you? What country would you
visit?

Todd If I ____had____ (have / had) enough
time, I'd ____visit____ (visited / visit)
Mongolia.

Paula Mongolia! Why?

Todd I saw a documentary about Mongolia
on TV. It was beautiful, and the people
were fascinating. If I ____traveled____ (travel / traveled)
to Mongolia, ____I'd____ (I'd / I) ride a horse. I'd love that.

B Number the sentences in the correct order.

__5__ If he gave me his autograph, I'd show it to all of
my friends.

__3__ If I went backstage after the concert, I'd meet David
Archuleta.

__1__ If I could go to any concert, I'd go to a David Archuleta
concert.

__4__ If I met David Archuleta, I'd ask him for his autograph.

__2__ If I went to one of David Archuleta's concerts, I'd go
backstage after the concert.

This lesson reviews the language presented and practiced in Lessons 29 and 30.

1 Language check

This exercise reviews the structures presented so far in this unit.

A

- Focus students' attention on the two photos. Ask: *What places do you think are shown in the photos?* Students may guess Africa, but they probably will not be able to identify Mongolia. (Do not confirm or deny answers at this time.)

- Have students read the conversation quickly. Ask: *What country does Paula talk about?* (Kenya.) Ask: *What country does Todd talk about?* (Mongolia.) If possible, find Kenya and Mongolia on a world map.

- Invite a volunteer to read the directions aloud. Have students read the example sentence. Elicit that *would* is the correct answer for the second blank in this sentence and have students write the answer.

- Have students work individually to complete the conversation.

- Check answers with the class. Invite volunteers to read aloud one sentence each from the conversation.

- **Optional** Have students work in pairs to read the conversation aloud.

B

- Invite a volunteer to read the directions aloud. Point out that one sentence is already numbered as an example.

- Have students work individually to number the rest of the sentences in the correct order. If students find this challenging, point out that the end of the first sentence is used as the beginning of the second sentence, and so on.

- Check answers with the class. Invite five volunteers to read the sentences in the correct order.

- **Optional** Have students work in pairs to take turns reading the sentences to each other in the correct order.

- **Optional** Have students work in pairs to create a similar sentence chain with their own ideas.

C

- Have students read the directions and the clauses in the box and in the survey. Have students call out any words or phrases they do not understand. Explain them by using the words or phrases in a sentence or by miming them.

- Have students work individually to complete the sentences in the survey using the clauses in the box.

- Check answers with the class. Invite volunteers to read aloud one of the sentences they completed.

D

- Give students several minutes to use the four *If* clauses from Part C to write sentences, adding their own information.

- Invite volunteers to share with the class one of the sentences they wrote.

2 Listening

In this exercise, students listen for information about someone's life and future dreams.

CD3, Track 23

- Have students read the directions.

- Explain to students that they are going to listen to Chrissa talk about her life and her future dreams. After Chrissa talks about each of her dreams, students will hear a question. They should answer each question by checking Yes or No.

- Play the recording. Students only listen.

Audio script
See page T-217.

- Play the recording again. Students listen and check Yes or No.

- Play the recording once again. Students listen and verify their answers.

- Check answers with the class. Play the recording again, pausing after each excerpt. In each case, ask students to try to reconstruct what Chrissa said and the question that followed. Then invite a volunteer to say whether the answer is Yes or No and ask the class whether they agree.

Workbook
Assign the exercises on Workbook page 53. (Workbook answers begin on page T-192.)

Game
Assign the game on Student's Book page 121.

C Complete the sentences with the clauses in the box.

- ☐ I'd be a lion
- ☐ I'd be a movie star
- ☐ I'd buy an expensive car
- ☐ I'd study chess
- ☑ If I could change my appearance
- ☐ If I could change my personality
- ☐ If I had a fight with my best friend
- ☐ If I needed help with my schoolwork

What would you do if . . . ?

1. _If I could change my appearance_ , I'd be taller.

2. If I could have any job, _I'd be a movie star_ .

3. If I could learn any new game, _I'd study chess_ .

4. _If I had a fight with my best friend_ , I'd try to be friends again.

5. _If I could change my personality_ , I'd be more outgoing.

6. If I could be any animal, _I'd be a lion_ .

7. If I had a lot of money, _I'd buy an expensive car_ .

8. _If I needed help with my schoolwork_ , I'd ask my older sister.

D Write sentences. Use the four *If* clauses from Part C, and add your own information. (*Answers will vary.*)

1. _____

2. _____

3. _____

4. _____

2 Listening

Chrissa talks about her life and her future dreams. Listen to the questions and check (✓) Yes or No.

	Yes	No		Yes	No
1.	☐	☑	4.	☐	☑
2.	☑	☐	5.	☑	☐
3.	☑	☐	6.	☐	☑

Go to page 121 for the Game.

What I'm going to be

1 Word power

A What do these people do? Complete the sentences with the verb phrases. Use the correct forms of the verbs. Then listen and practice.

- ☐ create programs
- ☑ fly planes
- ☐ help sick animals
- ☐ make discoveries
- ☐ make furniture
- ☐ report on events and people
- ☐ solve mysteries
- ☐ travel in outer space
- ☐ write stories

1. A pilot _flies planes_ .

2. An author _writes stories_ .

3. An astronaut _travels in outer space_ .

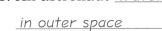

4. A carpenter _makes furniture_ .

5. A detective _solves mysteries_ .

6. A scientist _makes discoveries_ .

7. A journalist _reports on events and people_ .

8. A veterinarian _helps sick animals_ .

9. A computer programmer _creates programs_ .

B Ask a classmate three questions about what people do. Your classmate names the jobs.

Who reports on events and people?   A journalist.

Lesson 31 · What I'm going to be

This lesson presents and practices verb phrases related to occupations and infinitives to give a reason.

Review of Lesson 30

- Write on the board:

  find puppy / street   see / friend shoplifting   my best friend / lie to me

  my best friend / break promise   find snake / my bed   see elephant / flying

  <u>Example 1</u>

  If I found a puppy in the street, I'd keep it.

  <u>Example 2</u>

  A: What would I do if I found a puppy in the street? Keep it or take it to the police?

  B: You'd take it to the police.

  A: That's right. / No, I'd keep it.

- Ask students to choose two of the situations on the list and write sentences about what they would do, as in Example 1.

- Have students work in small groups and play a guessing game, as in Example 2.

1 Word power

This exercise presents and practices verb phrases related to occupations.

A 💿 CD3, Track 24

- Ask students to cover the photos and captions with a piece of paper. Focus students' attention on the verb phrases in the box. Explain that the verb phrases describe what people with different occupations do.

- Give students several minutes to discuss the phrases with a classmate and think about an occupation for each phrase. They should write the occupations in their notebook in the same order as the verb phrases in the box. Encourage them to make up occupations when they do not know the exact word. For example, if they do not know the exact word for someone who *helps sick animals*, they can write *doctor for animals*.

- Call out the verb phrases, one at a time, and ask students to share with the class the occupations they thought about.

- Ask students to uncover the photos, read the captions, and check their guesses.

- Have students work individually to complete the sentences, as in the example.

- Check answers with the class.

- Play the recording. Students listen and repeat.

> **Audio script**
> Same as the sentences in the Student's Book.

B

- Invite pairs of volunteers to ask and answer questions about what people do, following the example in the speech balloons.

> **Teaching Tip**   Being able to use language creatively is one of the characteristics of efficient language learners. At this stage, your students have learned enough English and have had enough language-learning experience to be able to use what they know in a creative way. The suggestion that they should "make up" the names of occupations they do not know is an example of how students can be encouraged to use their creativity.

2 Language focus

This exercise presents and practices infinitives to give a reason.

A 💿 CD3, Track 25

- Ask students to read the directions and the four texts.
- **Optional** Play the recording. Students listen and read along.

> ### Audio script
> Same as the sentences in the Student's Book.

- Ask: *What's a school yearbook?* (A book with information about people and events at school during the past year.) *What do the students write about in this school yearbook?* (They write about what they want to be.)
- Ask students to cover the text. Play a memory game. Ask the class the following questions to see how many they can answer just from having read the text once.

  Who wants to travel in outer space? (Adam and Max.)

  What does Ryoko want to be? (A detective.)

  Who's going to be a veterinarian? (Lisa.)

  Is Dennis going to be a detective? (No.)

- Have students uncover the texts. Focus students' attention on Lisa's text. Ask: *Why is Lisa going to be a veterinarian?* (To help sick animals.) Ask about the other students in the texts in the same way.
- Play the recording or model the sentences. Students listen and repeat.

B 💿 CD3, Track 26

- **Language Chart** Have students study the examples in the language chart. Focus students' attention on the chart heading and the first two examples. Ask: *What's the infinitive used at the end of these sentences?* (To help.) Explain that in this case, the infinitive *to help* gives the reason why the person saying the sentence is going to be a veterinarian. Focus students' attention on the third and fourth examples. Ask: *What infinitive is used at the end of these sentences?* (To report.) *What information does the infinitive give?* (It gives the reason he wants to be a journalist.) Explain that an infinitive to describe a reason answers the question *Why?* For example, Why does he want to be a journalist? He wants to report on events and people.
- **Optional** Model the examples, pausing for students to repeat.
- Have students work individually to write sentences with infinitives.
- Play the recording. Students listen and verify their answers.

> ### Audio script
> Same as the sentences in the Student's Book.

- Check answers with the class. Ask students to cover their sentences. Invite volunteers to say one of the sentences they wrote but replace the name(s) with an appropriate pronoun. For example, for sentence 1, they should say, *She's going to be a carpenter to make furniture.* The class then says who the sentence is about. For example, *That's Emma.*
- **Optional** Give students a few minutes to think about one or two people in their lives and what their wishes are. Invite volunteers to share this information with the class. For example, *My cousin wants to be a chef to make really great food.*

....

3 Speaking

This exercise practices infinitives to give reasons.

A

- Have students work individually to complete the job survey for themselves by checking Yes or No in the *You* columns.
- Have students ask a classmate the survey questions and check Yes or No in the *Your classmate* columns.

B

- Give students a few minutes to think about their classmates' answers to the job survey in Part A and draw conclusions about the most appropriate occupation for them.

- Invite volunteers to share with the class conclusions about the best occupations for their classmates, following the example in the speech balloon. After a volunteer talks about a classmate, ask the classmate whether or not he or she agrees with the conclusion.
- To finish, ask: *What are the class's most popular jobs?*

> ### Workbook
> Assign the exercises on Workbook page 54.
> (Workbook answers begin on page T-192.)

> ### Extra Grammar
> Assign the exercises for the Extra Grammar, Lesson 31.

2 Language focus

A Look at the school yearbook. What does everyone want to be?
Why do they want to have that job? Listen and practice.

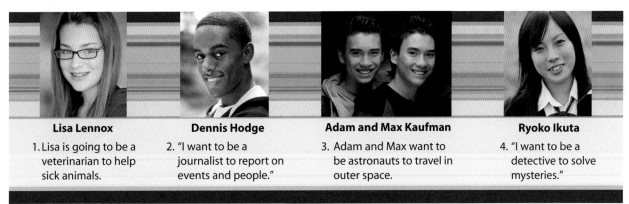

Lisa Lennox
1. Lisa is going to be a veterinarian to help sick animals.

Dennis Hodge
2. "I want to be a journalist to report on events and people."

Adam and Max Kaufman
3. Adam and Max want to be astronauts to travel in outer space.

Ryoko Ikuta
4. "I want to be a detective to solve mysteries."

B Study the chart. Write sentences with infinitives. For numbers 1–3, use
going to. For numbers 4 and 5, use *want to*. Then listen and check.

> ### Infinitives to give a reason
>
> I'm going to be a veterinarian. I want to help sick animals.
> I'm going to be a veterinarian **to help** sick animals.
>
> He wants to be a journalist. He wants to report on events and people.
> He wants to be a journalist **to report** on events and people.

1. (Emma / carpenter) *Emma is going to be a carpenter to make furniture.*
2. (Nick and Sue / pilots) *Nick and Sue are going to be pilots to fly planes.*
3. (Jenny / author) *Jenny is going to be an author to write stories.*
4. (Paul / astronaut) *Paul wants to be an astronaut to travel in outer space.*
5. (Kim and Kelly / scientists) *Kim and Kelly want to be scientists to make discoveries.*

3 Speaking

A Complete the job survey for yourself. Then ask a classmate the questions. *(Answers will vary.)*

Do you like to . . . ?	You		Your classmate				You		Your classmate	
	Yes	No	Yes	No			Yes	No	Yes	No
meet people	☐	☐	☐	☐		take risks	☐	☐	☐	☐
spend time on your own	☐	☐	☐	☐		have fun	☐	☐	☐	☐
make or create things	☐	☐	☐	☐		help others	☐	☐	☐	☐
travel	☐	☐	☐	☐		write a lot	☐	☐	☐	☐

B What do you think your classmate would probably like to be one day? Why?
Choose a job from Exercise 1A, or use your own ideas. Then tell the class.

> Mario would probably like to be a pilot to travel, to have fun, and to meet people.

The past year

1 Language focus

A Juan is interviewing Keiko for the school magazine. Has Keiko had a good year or a bad year? Listen and practice.

Juan So, did you do anything really crazy or special last year?

Keiko Well, I didn't do anything crazy, but I did do something really special. I entered a poetry competition, and I won a prize.

Juan Great! What about this year? Have you been anywhere interesting or unusual?

Keiko Oh, I went somewhere fascinating – Antarctica.

Juan Wow! I'm sure that was an incredible trip.

Keiko Yeah! It was awesome!

Juan And have you met anyone special recently?

Keiko Oh, yes. I met someone really special a few weeks ago – a cute guy.

Juan Really? Where did you meet him?

Keiko Well, we met at a party. Then we started going out together, . . . and then he met my sister. He's going out with her now!

B Study the chart. Complete the conversations with indefinite pronouns. Then listen and check.

Indefinite pronouns		
Questions	**Negative statements**	**Affirmative statements**
Did you do **anything** special?	I didn't do **anything** special.	I did **something** really special.
Is there **anywhere** interesting to visit near the school?	I haven't been **anywhere** interesting.	I went **somewhere** fascinating.
Have you met **anyone** special recently?	I haven't met **anyone** special.	I met **someone** really special.

1. **Sam** Is there _anywhere_ interesting to visit near the school?
   Jill Well, maybe. The planetarium. But I don't know _anything_ about it.
2. **Sam** Have you met _anyone_ interesting recently?
   Jill Yes. I met _someone_ at a party the other day. He's very funny.
3. **Sam** Is there _anything_ special you'd like to do this year?
   Jill Oh, yes. I'd like to go _somewhere_ fun. Maybe Disney World.
4. **Sam** I just read _something_ about the Bahamas. Have you ever been there?
   Jill No. I've never been _anywhere_ outside the U.S.

Lesson 32 The past year

This lesson presents and practices indefinite pronouns.

1 Language focus

This exercise presents and practices indefinite pronouns.

A 💿 CD3, Track 27

* Have students look at the photo and read the directions. Ask: *What's Juan doing?* (He's interviewing Keiko.) *Where's the interview going to appear?* (In the school magazine.) *What do you have to find out?* (If Keiko had a good year or a bad year.)

* Have students read the conversation.

* **Optional** Play the recording. Students listen and read along.

> **Audio script**
> Same as the conversation in the Student's Book.

* Ask: *Has Keiko had a good year or a bad year?* (She's had a good and bad year.) *What are some of the interesting things she's done?* (She entered a poetry competition, and she won. She went to Antarctica. She met a boy at a party.) *What wasn't so good?* (The boy is going out with her sister now.)

* Read the following clues, one at a time. Have students find phrases in Keiko's speeches that have the same meaning as the clues. Write the phrases as a list on the board:

  An action or an event that was special – something really special

  A place that is fascinating – somewhere fascinating

  A person who is really special – someone really special

* Underline *something, somewhere,* and *someone* on the board. Explain that these words are called *indefinite pronouns*. Indefinite pronouns do not refer to a specific person, place, or thing. Ask students to find and underline three other indefinite pronouns in the conversation. (Anything, anywhere, anyone.)

* Check answers with the class. Invite volunteers to call out one of the indefinite pronouns they underlined.

* Play the recording or model the conversation. Students listen and repeat.

* **Optional** Have students practice in pairs.

B 💿 CD3, Track 28

* **Language Chart** Have students study the examples in the language chart. Ask: *When do you use indefinite pronouns beginning with* some? (In affirmative statements.) *When do you use indefinite pronouns beginning with* any? (In negative statements and questions.) *Which indefinite pronouns refer to unspecified actions or events?* (Anything, something.) *Which indefinite pronouns refer to unspecified places?* (Anywhere, somewhere.) *Which indefinite pronouns refer to unspecified people?* (Anyone, someone.)

* **Optional** Model the examples, pausing for students to repeat.

* Ask students to read the directions and the conversations.

* Have students work individually to complete the conversations.

* Play the recording. Students listen and verify their answers.

> **Audio script**
> Same as the conversations in the Student's Book.

* Check answers with the class. Invite several pairs of volunteers to read the completed conversations aloud.

2 Listening

In this exercise, students listen for information about people's special experiences in the past year.

A 💿 CD3, Track 29

- Have students read the directions and look at the photos. Ask: *Who are you going to listen to?* (Lucia, Greg, and Megan.) *What do they talk about?* (Their experiences in the past year.) *What do you have to do?* (Listen and label the photos with the people's names.)
- Play the recording. Students only listen.

> **Audio script**
> See page T-217.

- Play the recording again. Students listen and label the photos.
- Play the recording once again. Students listen and verify their answers.
- Check answers with the class. Invite a volunteer to say which teen goes with which photo. For example, *Number 1 is Megan.*

B 💿 CD3, Track 30

- Have students read the directions and the sentences in the chart. Ask: *What do you have to do?* (Listen and check the correct name or names.)
- Play the recording again. Students listen and check the correct name or names.

> **Audio script**
> Same as the script in Part A.

- Play the recording once again. Students listen and verify their answers.
- Check answers with the class. Invite volunteers to say one sentence each about what the people have and have not done. For example: *Lucia has done something special this year. Lucia has met someone special this year.*

---

3 Speaking

This exercise practices indefinite pronouns.

Note: Make sure to bring a sheet of paper with a list of the names of all the students in your class. You will need the list for Part B of this exercise.

A

- Have students read the directions, the words in the box, and the example. Ask: *What do you have to ask your classmate about?* (About things he or she has done in the past year.)
- Demonstrate the activity with a volunteer, using the words in the box or your own ideas, and following the example in the speech balloons.
- Have students work with a classmate to carry out the activity.

B

- Have students read the directions and the example.
- Invite volunteers to share with the class what they found out about the classmate they talked to, following the example in the speech balloon. Ask the class to pay close attention to the information about each classmate, as they may need it for a later lesson.

- Use the list of names you prepared to keep a record of the information volunteers share with the class. To be able to do this quickly, use the following code. Write the appropriate letter next to each name.

  A – Did something special

  B – Met someone special

  C – Learned something useful

  D – Went somewhere exciting

  E – Tried something new to eat

  F – Read something interesting

- Bring the list to class again for the next lesson.

> **Workbook**
> Assign the exercises on Workbook page 55.
> (Workbook answers begin on page T-192.)

> **Extra Grammar**
> Assign the exercises for the Extra Grammar, Lesson 32.

2 Listening

A Lucia, Greg, and Megan talk about their experiences this past year. Who is talking? Listen and write the correct name below each picture.

Megan

Lucia

Greg

B Listen again and check (✓) the correct name or names.

	Lucia	Greg	Megan
Who has done something special this year?	✓	☐	✓
Who has been somewhere amazing this year?	☐	☐	✓
Who hasn't met anyone special this year?	☐	✓	✓

3 Speaking

A Ask a classmate about things he or she has done in the past year. Use the words in the box or your own ideas.

do something interesting
meet someone special
learn something useful
go somewhere exciting
try something new to eat
read something interesting

> João, have you done anything interesting this year?

> Yes, I have. In June, I learned how to ride a horse. In August, I went . . .

B Tell the class what you found out about your classmate.

> João has done something interesting this year. In June, he learned how to ride a horse. In August, he went somewhere exciting on vacation. He went to Fortaleza. He tried something new to eat. He tried the local food there, crabs. He loved them.

Read

A Read the article quickly. Circle the words you find.

> ambassador cancer community donate foundation
> billion cities cure education skills

If you could do something for the world . . .

What would *you* do if you were rich and famous? Would you stay at home or would you travel? Would you do anything special? Well, some **celebrities** do many special things, and they help millions of people.

Bill Gates, one of the richest people in the world, and his wife, created the Bill and Melinda Gates **Foundation**. It's the largest foundation in the world, and it has $31 **billion** to spend on health and **education** in poor countries.

Angelina Jolie and Brad Pitt, the famous actors, give a lot of money to charity. They sold pictures of their twin babies to a magazine for $14 million! But they gave all the money to charity. And in her **role** as an **ambassador** for the United Nations, Angelina visits the world's poorest countries. She wants everyone to know about problems there.

Lance Armstrong, who has won the Tour de France seven times, is one of the world's greatest cyclists. Lance has survived **cancer** and has made over $250 million and donated some to cancer research.

But you don't have to be rich and famous to help. Everyone can do something. If you could do something for the world, what would you do?

Go to page 125 for the **Vocabulary Practice.**

B 🔊 Read the article slowly. Check your answers in Part A.

C Are these statements true or false? Write *True* or *False*. Then correct the false statements.

1. Bill and Melinda Gates created their foundation to help people in poor countries.
   True.

2. Brad Pitt and Angelina Jolie sold pictures of their house.
   False. *Brad Pitt and Angelina Jolie sold pictures of their twin babies.*

3. Angelina visits many places to talk about problems in the world.
   True.

4. Lance Armstrong donates money to education.
   False. *Lance Armstrong donates money to cancer research.*

5. You can only help people if you're rich and famous.
   False. *Everyone can do something.*

Unit 8 — Get Connected

This lesson practices reading, listening, and writing skills.

Review of Lesson 32

- Write on the board:

  A: *Sue went somewhere exciting this year.*   A: *Paul went somewhere exciting this year.*
  B: *That's right. She went to Bermuda.*   B: *That's wrong. He didn't go anywhere*
                                                 exciting. He met someone special
                                                 at a party.

- Give students several minutes to try to remember as much as possible about the information they shared in Part B of the Speaking exercise in Lesson 32.

- Ask students to read the conversations on the board. Then use your notes from the last class to say sentences about things students have done in the past year. Make sure some of the sentences are right and some wrong.

- After saying each sentence, ask a volunteer to comment on it, as in the examples on the board. Finally, ask a volunteer for the subject of the sentence to confirm that the information is right or to correct it if it is wrong.

Read

This exercise practices reading for information about how famous people help others around the world.

A

- Have students read the title of the article and look at the photos. Ask: *Do you know who any of these people are?* (Bill and Melinda Gates, Brad Pitt and Angelina Jolie, and Lance Armstrong.)

Culture Note
Bill Gates founded the Bill and Melinda Gates foundation in the year 2000. In 2006, Bill Gates stopped his full-time work as head of the Microsoft Corporation in order to devote himself full-time to the foundation. The motto of the foundation is "All lives have equal value." In the U.S., the foundation focuses on building better libraries in schools and improving educational opportunities for low-income students. In Africa there are also projects relating to agriculture and health.

- Invite a volunteer to read aloud the directions and the words in the box. Remind students that they should read quickly to find the answers and that they should not read every word carefully.

- Have students work individually to read the article quickly and circle the words. Do not check answers at this point.

B CD3, Track 31

- Invite a volunteer to read the directions aloud. Remind students that they should read slowly and carefully, and concentrate on getting the meaning of the entire text.

- List the new vocabulary words on the board: *celebrity, foundation, billion, education, role, ambassador, cancer.* Explain their meaning. (Celebrity: famous person or star; foundation: an organization that helps

people; billion: a very large amount – a billion dollars is a lot of money; education: what you learn in school; role: a job or part you play; ambassador: someone who visits a country as a representative of the United Nations or of a government; cancer: a terrible disease in which many bad cells grow.) As an alternative, have students use their dictionaries to find the meanings of the new vocabulary words.

- Have students read the article again.

- Have students check their answers in Part A in pairs. Elicit the answers from one pair.

- **Optional** Play the recording. Students listen and read along.

Audio script
Same as the article in the Student's Book.

Get Connected Vocabulary
Have students do the exercise on Student's Book page 125 in class or for homework. (Get Connected Vocabulary answers are on page T-125.)

C

- Invite a volunteer to read the directions and first statement aloud.

- Ask: *Did Bill and Melinda Gates create their foundation to help people in poor countries?* (Yes.) Ask: *So is the statement true or false?* (True.)

- Have students work individually to write *True* or *False*, and then correct the false statements.

- Check answers with the class. Invite volunteers to read their answers aloud.

Listen

In this exercise, students listen for opinions about having a lot of money.

A 🔊 CD3, Track 32

- Focus students' attention on the photo. Ask: *What do you see in the photo?* (A wallet with a lot of money.)
- Tell students that they will listen to two friends, Laurie and Scott, talk about what they would do if they had a million dollars and if it would make them happy.
- Have students read the first question and the example answer.
- Explain that students should listen to the conversation and answer the questions.
- Play the recording. Students only listen.

> **Audio script**
> See page T-218.

- Play the recording again. Students listen and answer the questions.
- Play the recording once again. Students listen and verify their answers.
- Check answers with the class. Invite several pairs of volunteers to read the questions and answers aloud.

B

- Have students read the directions and the questions.
- Read the first question with the class and elicit answers from several students. Remind students that there are no right or wrong answers for this exercise – they are giving their opinions.
- Have students work individually to answer the questions with their own information or ideas, and give reasons for their answers.
- Have students work in pairs to compare answers, or elicit opinions from volunteers.

Write

In this exercise, students answer questions and write a paragraph about having a million dollars.

A

- Invite a volunteer to read the directions and the first question aloud. Elicit a few possible responses.
- Have students work individually to answer the questions about what they would do if they had a million dollars.
- **Optional** Have students ask and answer the questions in pairs.

B

- Invite a volunteer to read the directions aloud. Tell students that they will use their answers in Part A to help them write about what they would do if they had a million dollars.
- Have students work individually to write their paragraphs.
- Invite several volunteers to read their paragraphs to the class.
- **Optional** Have students work in groups of four and read each other's paragraphs. Students should compare their ideas. Which students had similar ideas? Who had the most unusual idea in the group?

> **Workbook**
> Assign the exercises on Workbook page 56.
> (Workbook answers begin on page T-192.)

If I had a million dollars . . .

A 🎧 **Laurie and Scott talk about being rich. Listen and answer the questions.**

1. Why can't Scott get something nice for his mother? <u>*He doesn't have enough money.*</u>
2. Why doesn't Laurie get a part-time job? <u>*Her parents say studying is more*</u>
   <u>*important than getting a part-time job.*</u>
3. What would Scott do for his parents if he had a million dollars?
   <u>*He'd give half the money to his parents so they wouldn't have to work so hard.*</u>
4. Would he buy anything for himself? <u>*Yes, he would.*</u>
5. Does Laurie need a lot of money to have fun?
   <u>*No, she doesn't.*</u>

B **What do you think? Answer the questions. Give reasons.**
(Answers will vary.)
1. Do you think it's a good idea for students to work part-time?
   _____

2. Do you think parents should give a lot of money to their children?
   _____

3. Do you think it's important to give money to charity? _____

4. Do you agree that you don't need money to have fun? _____

Your turn

A **Imagine you have one million dollars. What would you do? Answer the questions.**
(Answers will vary.)
1. How would you feel if you won a million dollars? _____

2. Would you give any to charity? If yes, which ones? _____

3. Would you give money to anyone? Who? _____

4. What would you buy for yourself? _____

5. Would you save any of the money? Why? _____

B **Write a paragraph about having a million dollars. Use the answers in Part A to help you.**
(Answers will vary.)

⚪⚫⚪

If I had a million dollars, I'd . . .
_____
_____
_____
_____
_____
◀▶

Language chart review

If clauses with *could...would*	Infinitives to give a reason
If I could learn any language, I'**d learn** Japanese. **If he could change the way he looks**, he'**d be** taller.	I'm going to be a detective. I want to solve mysteries. I'm going to be a detective **to solve** mysteries. She wants to be a carpenter. She wants to make furniture. She wants to be a carpenter **to make** furniture.

A Look at the pictures. Then write sentences about the people's dreams with the words in the box.

- ☐ buy anything: video arcade – play games all day
- ☐ have any job in the world: be an astronaut – travel in outer space
- ☐ play any sport: soccer – score a lot of goals
- ☑ visit any city in the world: Paris – see the Eiffel Tower

1. *If she could visit any city in the world, she'd visit Paris. She wants to visit Paris to see the Eiffel Tower.*

2. *If he could buy anything, he'd buy a video arcade. He wants to buy a video arcade to play games all day.*

 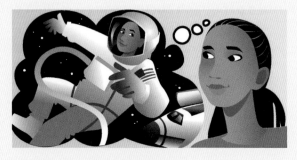

3. *If they could play any sport, they'd play soccer. They want to play soccer to score a lot of goals.*

4. *If she could have any job in the world, she'd be an astronaut. She wants to be an astronaut to travel in outer space.*

This lesson reviews the grammar and vocabulary introduced in Unit 8.

Language chart review

These charts summarize the main grammar presented and practiced in Unit 8.

- Books closed. Write on the board:

A	B
1. If I could learn any language,	a. to solve mysteries.
2. I'm going to be a detective	b. I'd learn Japanese.
3. If he could change the way he looks,	c. to make furniture.
4. She wants to be a carpenter	d. he'd be taller.

- Have students work in small groups to match the phrases in columns A and B.
  (1.b; 2.a; 3.d; 4.c.)
- Check answers with the class.
- Focus students' attention on sentences 1 and 3. Invite volunteers to give more examples of sentences with *If* clauses with *could . . . would.*
- Focus students' attention on sentences 2 and 4. Remind them that infinitives are used to give a reason.
- Books open. Have students study the Language chart review.
- Answer any questions students may have.

Exercises A through C (pages T-112 to T-113)

Note: Students can do these exercises for homework or in class. They should do these exercises with minimal teacher input or help. If you choose to do these exercises as homework, briefly review the exercise directions in class. Make sure that students understand what they should do. Check the answers with the class during the next class meeting. If you choose to do the exercises in class, follow the directions below.

Exercise A

- Have students read the directions and look at the pictures.
- Invite volunteers to read aloud the words in the box and the two example sentences.
- Have students work individually to write the sentences about the people's dreams, using the words in the box. Remind them that they have to write two sentences for each answer.
- Check answers with the class.

Language chart review

These charts summarize further grammar presented and practiced in Unit 8.

- Have students study the examples in the top chart.
- Remind students that sentences with unreal conditions use the simple past in the *If* clause and *would* + verb in the main clause. These sentences never use *would* in the *If* clause.
- Have students study the examples in the bottom chart. Remind students also that we use indefinite pronouns beginning with *any-* in negative statements and questions. We use pronouns beginning with *some-* in affirmative statements.
- Answer any questions students may have.

Exercise B

- Invite students to read the directions and the answers in the example conversation.
- Have students work individually to complete the second conversation.
- Check answers with the class.

Exercise C

- Have students read the directions and the example sentence.
- Have students work individually to complete the book review with indefinite pronouns.
- Check answers with the class. Invite volunteers to read the book review aloud.

Take another look!

- Have students read the directions.
- Students work individually to circle T (true) or F (false).
- Check answers with the class.

Optional Unit Wrap-Up

- If students did the Review exercises for homework, check answers with the class.
- Have students work in pairs to make new sentences with the phrases in Exercise A. For example, they could start a sentence with *If I could buy anything in the world, . . .* and then finish it with their own idea. They should add another sentence as in Exercise A.
- Have students work in pairs to read the conversations in Exercise B. They then make a new conversation with their own ideas.
- Have students write a review of a book they have read or a movie they have seen using Exercise C as a model. They should use different adjectives to express their own opinions.

Theme Project

- Assign the *At Home* section of the Unit 8 Theme Project on Student's Book page 133.

Workbook

- Assign the Unit 8 Check Yourself on Workbook page 57. (Workbook answers begin on page T-192.)

Extra Practice Worksheets

- Assign the Unit 8 Extra Practice worksheets starting on page T-158.

Extra Speaking Practice Worksheet

- Assign the Unit 8 Extra Speaking Practice worksheet on page T-175.

Arcade Activities

- Assign the Unit 8 Arcade activities found at: www.cambridge.org/connectarcade

Learning Log

- Assign the Unit 8 Learning Log. This can be downloaded from the Teacher Support Site at: www.cambridge.org/connect2e/teacher

Quiz

- Give the Unit 8 Quiz on page T-185.

Test

- Give the Unit 8 Test (Form A and / or Form B). These can be downloaded from the Teacher Support Site at: www.cambridge.org/connect2e/teacher

Language chart review

Unreal conditional with *if* clauses

What **would** you **do if you found an expensive ring on the street?**
If I found an expensive ring on the street, I'**d give** it to the police.
I'**d give** it to the police.

Indefinite pronouns

Questions	Negative statements	Affirmative statements
Have you done **anything** crazy?	I haven't done **anything** crazy.	I did **something** crazy.
Have you been **anywhere** fun?	I haven't been **anywhere** fun.	I went **somewhere** fun.
Did you meet **anyone** special?	I didn't meet **anyone** special.	I met **someone** very special.

B **Complete the conversations.**

1. **A** What _would you do_ (you / do) if _you saw_ (you / see) a snake?

   B _I'd scream_ (I / scream)!

2. **A** If _someone asked_ (someone / ask) me to give him the answers to a test,
   I'd say (I / say) no. What _would you_ (you / do)?

   B _I'd say_ (I / say) no, too. Do you think _you'd tell_ (you / tell)
   the teacher?

   A No, _I wouldn't tell_ (I / not tell) the teacher. _I'd tell_ (I / tell) the principal!

C **Complete the book review with *anything, something, anyone, someone,*
anywhere, or *somewhere.***

> Have you read _anything_ interesting this month? Well, I have
> _something_ fun and fascinating for you. It's *How to Be Someone Special*,
> Melissa Costa's new book for teens. I haven't read _anything_ as
> interesting as this in a long time. I don't know _anyone_ who doesn't
> like this book. The writer tells us we don't have to go _anywhere_
> unusual or do _anything_ fascinating to be happy. We just have to use
> our imaginations! Go _somewhere_ quiet and read this book. Then give it
> to _someone_ special.

Take another look!

Circle T (true) or F (false).

1. In the sentence "If I found a lot of money, I'd keep it," *'d* is the
   contraction for *would.* (T)   F

2. Questions with "What would you do if . . . ?" are asking about
   things that can never happen. T (F)

Go to page 133 for the Theme Project.

A What were these people doing one hot afternoon last summer at one o'clock? Look at the picture for two minutes. Then close your book, and write six questions and answers about the picture on a separate piece of paper. Open your book and check your answers.

B Work with a classmate. Close your books and put away your papers. Take turns asking your questions. Who remembers the most?

You Were Angelina and Mark playing volleyball?	**Classmate** What was Mrs. Harper doing?
Classmate No, they weren't. They were playing basketball.	**You** She was talking on her cell phone.
You You're correct.	**Classmate** That's right.

Unit 1 Game Memory game

This game reviews the past continuous.

A

- Books closed. Tell students they will play a memory game. You will give them two minutes to study a picture that shows people doing different things one hot afternoon last summer at one o'clock. After you call time, students should close their books and write questions and answers about the picture.

- Write these examples on the board:

  Were Angelina and Mark playing volleyball?

  No, they weren't. They were playing basketball.

  What was Mrs. Harper doing?

  She was talking on her cell phone.

- Have students open their books and study the picture.

- After two minutes, tell students to close their books. Students work individually to write six questions and answers about the picture, like the examples on the board. When they are ready, they should look at the picture again and check their work.

B

- Have students read the directions and the examples.

- Demonstrate the activity by reading the example questions and answers with a volunteer.

- Have students work in pairs to complete the exercise. Be sure to tell students to ask some questions that will elicit a *No* answer.

- To finish, ask which student in each pair remembered more about the picture.

- **Optional** Divide the class into two groups, Group A and Group B. With books closed or covered, have Group A ask Group B a question about the picture. Group B works together to answer the question. The groups uncover the picture to check the answer. Each correct answer earns that group one point. Questions may not be repeated. Deduct points for incorrect answers. The group with more points wins.

Note: If your class is large, have students play this in smaller groups of four to six students. Divide each group in half, A and B.

Unit 2   Game   What will happen?

This game reviews talking about the future with *will*.

- Give students several minutes to read the directions and the rules and study the game board. While they are doing this, draw a simplified version of the *Start* row of the game on the board.

- Explain *game marker*. Ask students to take out something from their bag to use as a game marker. Students need something small that fits in the game board spaces such as an eraser or a paper clip.

- Hold up a coin and show students the *heads* side and the *tails* side. Ask: *How many spaces do you move with heads?* (One.) *How many with tails?* (Two.) *What do you do if you don't make a mistake?* (Stay in the space.) *What if you make a mistake?* (Go back one space.) *Who wins?* (The person who gets to *Finish* first.)

- Explain the meaning of *Free Space*. (Students ask any questions.)

- Invite a volunteer to come to the board to demonstrate the game with you. Flip a coin. Say *heads* or *tails*, and move one or two spaces. Ask a question using the words in the space and *will*.

- Have the volunteer answer the question.

- Invite the volunteer to repeat the steps.

- Have students play the game in pairs.

- **Optional** Invite volunteers to come to the board to write their questions.

Unit 2 Game What will happen?

What will you do before you graduate from high school? Play the game with a classmate. Use things in your bag as game markers. Use a coin to find out how many spaces to move. Heads = 1, Tails = 2.

Rules:

- Take turns. Flip a coin and move your marker to the correct space. Your classmate asks a question with the cue in the space. You answer, using *will*.

  Classmate 1 *Will you travel to a different country before you graduate from high school?*

  Classmate 2 *Yes, I'll travel to Chile before I graduate from high school.*

▶ No mistakes? Stay on that space.

◀ Mistakes? Move back one space.

- On a "free space," ask your classmate any question.
- The person who gets to FINISH first, wins.

START

travel to a different country

get better grades

learn a new sport

win a prize at school

1st

FREE SPACE

get a summer job

You'll fail a test. Go back 3 spaces.

You'll make a new friend. Move ahead 3 spaces.

speak English well

Moving Company

move to another city

see a famous person

perform on stage

Take another turn.

try a new food

study in another country

go to a rock concert

Move your marker to your classmate's space.

get a new pet

FINISH

Game   Invitations, permission, and requests

A **Play the game with a classmate. Classmate 1 is X. Classmate 2 is O.**

Classmate 1 Choose any space. Follow the instructions.
Ask Classmate 2 a question.

Classmate 2 Answer the question. Say *yes* or *no*.

Classmate 1 Was the question correct? Mark the box in the space with an *X*.
Did you make a mistake? Do not mark the box in the space.

Classmate 2 Take your turn. Choose a different space and ask Classmate 1
a question.

Continue playing until all spaces have been marked. The person with the
most *X*s or *O*s is the winner.

Invite your classmate to go shopping after school.	Ask your classmate to let you use his or her calculator.	You're going to miss class. Ask your classmate to take notes for you.	Invite your classmate to go to a concert this weekend.
You're going hiking. Ask your classmate to lend you a backpack.	Invite your classmate to play baseball on Saturday.	Invite your classmate to go to a movie this weekend.	Invite your classmate to your birthday party next Friday.
You need a math book. Ask if you can borrow your classmate's book.	Invite your classmate to go to a soccer game with you on Sunday.	Invite your classmate to a barbecue at your house on Sunday evening.	Your classmate is going to the mall. Ask if you can go with him or her.
Sal's Italian Restaurant. Invite your classmate to go to your favorite restaurant with you tonight.	Your classmate is going on vacation. Ask him or her to send you a postcard.	Ask your classmate to lend you some money for lunch.	Ask your classmate to mail a letter for you.

B **Choose two spaces you did not ask questions about.**
Write questions and answers. *(Answers will vary.)*

1. **Q:** _____

   A: _____

2. **Q:** _____

   A: _____

Unit 3 Game   Invitations, permission, and requests

This game reviews *Would you like to . . . ?* for invitations and *Can / Could* for permission and requests.

A

- Give students several minutes to read the instructions for the game and study the game board.

- Check that students understand the instructions. Ask: *Do you play individually or in pairs?* (In pairs.) *Do you play against your partner?* (Yes.) *How does the game work?* (Players choose a space, read the information, and ask a question. If the question is correct, the player marks the space. The other player answers the question.) *Can you choose any space?* (Yes.) *How do you mark your spaces?* (One player always marks *X,* and the other always marks *O.*) *Who wins?* (The player with the most *X*s or *O*s at the end of the game.)

- Have students play the game in pairs.

> **Teaching Tip** Encourage students to work out the rules of the game by themselves first. Then check understanding and provide help as necessary.

B

- Have students read the directions, choose two spaces they did not ask questions about, and write questions and answers.

- Check answers with the class. Invite several pairs of volunteers to read one of the questions and answers they wrote.

- **Optional** Have pairs decide whether the question in each space of the game relates to offering an invitation, asking for permission, or making a request.

Unit 4 Game Guess the person

This game reviews adjectives to describe personality types.

- Have students read the directions and the instructions for the game.

- Check that students understand the instructions. Ask: *Do you play individually or in pairs?* (In pairs.) *How does the game work?* (Students take turns pretending to be one of the eight teens described. Their partners guess who.) *What should you do before you start the game?* (Read the information carefully about each of the eight people.)

- Give students several minutes to read the information about the eight teens described.

- Demonstrate the game with a volunteer.

- Have students play the game in pairs.

Unit 4 Game Guess the person

Read about these teens. Then play a guessing game with a classmate. Take turns.

Classmate 1 Choose a teen below. Pretend to be that person. Don't tell Classmate 2 who it is. Answer Classmate 2's questions.

Classmate 2 Classmate 1 is pretending to be a teen below. Try to guess who. Ask questions.

Classmate 2 Do you like chatting online?
Classmate 1 Yes, I do.
Classmate 2 Are you outgoing?
Classmate 1 Yes, I am.
Classmate 2 Is drawing pictures your hobby?
Classmate 1 Yes, it is.
Classmate 2 You're Kwan!

I enjoy writing e-mails to friends. Collecting comic books is my hobby. I like going to rock concerts. I'm outgoing.

I'm organized. I enjoy speaking French. I like drawing pictures. I'm creative. Chatting online is my favorite free-time activity.

Andre

Jane

I like chatting online. Drawing pictures is my hobby. I enjoy listening to rock music. I'm outgoing.

Writing e-mail messages to my friends is my favorite free-time activity. I enjoy dancing. I'm hardworking. I like playing baseball.

Ana

Ryan

Kwan

I enjoy talking on the phone with my friends. I'm creative. I enjoy writing stories about life in the future. I'm trustworthy. When I make a promise, I keep it. Playing soccer is my favorite free-time activity.

Elena

I enjoy listening to rap music. Collecting comic books is my hobby. I'm outgoing. Playing soccer is my favorite sports activity.

Sophie

I enjoy speaking French. I like talking on the phone with friends. Dancing is my favorite free-time activity. I'm hardworking. I spend a lot of time on homework and chores.

Gabriel

I enjoy playing baseball. I'm trustworthy. When I promise to do something, I do it. Listening to rap music is my favorite free-time activity. I'm organized.

Unit 5 Game Crossword puzzle

A Complete the story with the past participles of the verbs in the box.
Then complete the puzzle.

☐ act ☐ do ☐ hang ☐ meet ☐ rent ☐ travel
☐ be ☐ go ☐ make ☐ read ☐ sing ☐ win

Hi, I'm Hank. I've **[7 down]** _____ really busy this year.
Here are some of the things I've **[4 down]** _____ . I love
reading science fiction. I've **[8 down]** _____ 40 science
fiction books this year. I love movies, too. I've
[3 down] _____ about 60 DVDs. I play soccer on my school's team, but we
haven't **[2 across]** _____ any games this year. I've **[12 across]** _____ in
three concerts with a singing group at school. I'm in the drama club, and
I've **[11 across]** _____ in two plays. With all of these activities,
I've **[9 down]** _____ a lot of people, and I've **[6 down]** _____ some great
friends. I've also **[10 across]** _____ a lot this year. I've **[5 across]** _____
to three different countries, but I haven't **[1 down]** _____ out at the mall
with my friends. We're all too busy for that!

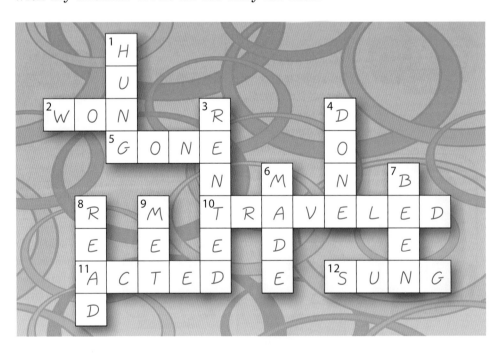

B Work with a classmate. Make sentences about what you've done this year.
Each person writes as many sentences as possible in two minutes using
the past participles in Part A. Who wrote the most correct sentences? *(Answers will vary.)*

Unit 5 Game Crossword puzzle

This game reviews the past participles of verbs.

A

- Invite a volunteer to read the directions aloud.

- Focus students' attention on the story. Give them several minutes to read through the story. Ask: *What does Hank talk about?* (Possible answers include: science-fiction books, movies, soccer, the drama club, and his friends.)

- Read the first sentence in the story with the students. Ask: *Which verb goes in this sentence?* (Be.) *What's the past participle?* (Been.) Have students complete the sentence.

- Focus students' attention on the crossword puzzle. Explain that *7 down* next to the first blank refers to the crossword puzzle. Have students find the correct spaces in the puzzle and fill them in with B-E-E-N.

- When you are sure that students understand how the story and the puzzle work together, have them work individually to complete both the story and the puzzle.

Note: Some students may prefer to complete the entire story first and then do the crossword puzzle. Others may go back and forth. As students fill in letters in the puzzle, these letters will give them clues to other answers.

- Have students work in pairs to compare their answers to the story and the crossword puzzle.

- Check answers with the class. Invite volunteers to read aloud one sentence each of the story, filling in the correct past participles of the verbs in the box.

B

- Invite a volunteer to read the directions aloud.

- Have students work in pairs to write sentences about what they have done this year, using the past participles in Part A.

- Time the activity. After two minutes, tell students to stop writing.

- Ask pairs to say how many sentences they wrote. Invite the pair who wrote the most sentences to read their sentences to the class. The class says whether the sentences are correct or not. If there are mistakes, invite the pair with the next highest number of sentences to read their sentences aloud.

- Repeat the procedure until you find the winner.

Unit 6   Game   Guessing game

This game reviews the present perfect with *never* and contrasts the present perfect with the simple past.

A

- Ask students to use a piece of paper to cover page 119, except for the top four lines (title, Part A directions, and first bulleted item). Have students read the directions in the first bulleted item.

- Give students several minutes to think about some fun or unusual things they have done. Then ask students to talk about those things with a classmate for one minute. Time the activity.

- Have students uncover the page. Ask them to read the directions in the second bulleted item and the information in the chart. Ask: *What do you have to do first?* (Check the activities we have never done.) *What should you do next?* (Check the activities we think the classmate we talked to has never done.)

- Give students several minutes to complete the chart.

- Have students read the directions in the third and fourth bulleted items, and the two lines under the chart. Ask: *What do you have to do now?* (Find out which of the activities in the chart our classmate has in fact never done.) *What kind of questions should you ask?* (*Have you ever . . . ?* questions.) *What do you do with the answers you guessed right?* (Circle them.) *Once you have both asked all questions, what should you do?* (Calculate the total number of activities circled.)

- Have students carry out the task.

- Ask volunteers to tell the class interesting or unusual things their partners have done.

B

- Have students read the directions, the questions and answers in the speech balloons, and the chart. Establish a time limit for the activity.

- Have students carry out the task, finding classmates who have done the five activities listed in the chart. Then students write in the chart the names and when they last did these activities.

- To finish, invite volunteers to report on one of their findings. For example, *Sergio has chatted online.*

Teaching Tip   Even when very detailed directions for an activity are provided on the Student's Book page, as in Part A of the Game above, if an activity has multiple steps, it is usually more effective to present the directions to students in segments. Having students read the whole set of directions at once will probably confuse them and make them feel the activity is too complicated.

Unit 6 Game Guessing game

A Play the game with a classmate. Take turns. *(Answers will vary.)*

- Do not look at the chart below. For one minute, talk to a classmate about some fun or unusual things you've done. Use *I've*.
- Now look at the activities in the chart. Check (✓) the activities you have never done. Then check (✓) the activities you think your classmate has never done.
- Ask your classmate about the activities in the chart. Use *Have you ever . . . ?* For example: *Have you ever eaten chocolate ants?*
- Circle each of your classmate's answers that you guessed right.

	You	Your classmate
eat chocolate ants	☐	☐
go snorkeling	☐	☐
see an elephant	☐	☐
try Indian food	☐	☐
go to a fireworks show	☐	☐
climb a mountain	☐	☐
read a book in English	☐	☐
sing on a stage	☐	☐
play a musical instrument	☐	☐
have a pen pal in another country	☐	☐
travel to another city	☐	☐
explore a rain forest	☐	☐
ride a horse	☐	☐

Number of activities I circled: _____

Number of activities my classmate circled: _____

B Walk around the classroom. Find classmates who have done the activities in the chart below. Write their names and ask when they last did these activities. *(Answers will vary.)*

Hi, Sergio. Have you ever chatted online?

Yes, I have.

When did you last chat online?

Two weeks ago.

	Name	When
chat online	*Sergio*	*two weeks ago*
speak English at home		
cook a meal		
go to a rock concert		
get 100 percent on a test		

Unit 7   Game Mark the space

A Play the game with a classmate. Classmate 1 is X. Classmate 2 is O.

Classmate 1 Choose any space. Make statements using the words as cues.

> My cousin's cat is the cutest cat I've ever seen.

▶ Is the statement correct? Mark the box in the space with an X.
◀ Not correct? Do not mark the box in the space.
Classmate 2 Take your turn.

Continue playing until all spaces have been marked. The person with the most Xs or Os is the winner.

This game reviews superlative +... *have ever*...

- Give students several minutes to read the instructions for the game and study the game board.

- Check that students understand the instructions. Ask: *Do you play individually or in pairs?* (In pairs.) *Do you play against your partner?* (Yes.) *How does the game work?* (Players choose a space, read the cues, and make a statement. If the statement is correct, the player marks the box in the space.) *How do you mark your spaces?* (One player always marks *X*, and the other always marks *O*. If the statement is not correct, the box in the space should not be marked.) *Can you choose any space?* (Yes.) *Who wins?* (The player with more *X*s or *O*s at the end of the game.)

- Have students play the game in pairs.

- **Optional** Have students write two of the statements they said, leaving a line in between. Under each statement they should write a short description of the picture for the statement.

For example:

It's the most boring DVD I've ever watched.

There's a boy. He's watching a DVD. He's sleeping.

Play a memory game. Books closed. A student reads aloud the description of a picture. Another student says the statement that corresponds to that picture.

This game reviews the unreal conditional with *If* clauses.

- Give students several minutes to read the directions and the rules and study the game board. While they are doing this, draw a simplified version of the *Start* row of the game on the board.

- Remind students of what a game marker is. Ask students to take out something from their bag to use as a game marker. Students need something small that fits in the game board spaces such as an eraser or a paper clip.

- Hold up a coin and show students the *heads* side and the *tails* side. Ask: *How many spaces do you move with heads?* (One.) *How many with tails?* (Two.) *What do you do if you don't make a mistake?* (Stay in the space.) *What if you make a mistake?* (Move back one space.) *Who wins?* (The person who gets to *Finish* first.)

- Explain the meaning of *Take another turn.* (Students ask another question.)

- Invite a volunteer to come to the board to demonstrate the game with you. Flip a coin. Say *heads* or *tails,* and move one or two spaces. *Ask a question using* What would you do if . . . ? *and the cue in the space.*

- Have the volunteer answer the question.

- Invite the volunteer to repeat the steps.

- Have students play the game in pairs.

- **Optional:** Invite volunteers to come to the board to write the questions using *What would you do if . . . ?*

Unit 8   Game   What would you do if . . . ?

Play the game with a classmate. Use things in your bag as game markers. Use a coin to find out how many spaces to move. Heads = 1, Tails = 2.

Rules:

- Take turns. Flip a coin and move your marker to the correct space. Follow the directions or ask a question with *What would you do if . . .?* and the cue in the space. Your classmate answers the question.

  Classmate 1 *What would you do if you found an expensive ring on the street?*
  Classmate 2 *I'd take it to my parents.*

  ▶ Classmate 1, no mistakes? Stay in that space.
  ◀ Classmate 1, mistakes? Move back one space.

- The person who gets to FINISH first, wins.

Get Connected Vocabulary Practice

Complete the advertisement with the words in the box.

☐ best-loved (adj.) ☑ gymnast (n.) ☐ scrapbook (n.) ☐ train (v.)

Be a Champion!

Would you like to be a top _____gymnast_____ ? Would you like to _____train_____ with the sport's top coaches? Become a winner at Champion's Gymnastics Center! We have classes for children of all ages and levels. You can see pictures of all of our gymnastics stars in our online _____scrapbook_____ . Find out why gymnastics is one of America's _____best-loved_____ sports. The center is open Monday to Saturday from 9:00 a.m. to 5:00 p.m.

Complete the sentences with the words in the box.

☐ certain (adj.) ☐ cure (v.) ☑ flying (adj.) ☐ gas (n.) ☐ headlines (n.) ☐ medicines (n.)

1. I had a crazy dream about a _____flying_____ bicycle. I was riding it in the air!

2. I don't always have time to read all of the newspaper, but I try to look at the _____headlines_____ .

3. My grandmother is 100 years old and takes many different _____medicines_____ .

4. You should try some chicken soup when you have a cold. It can help _____cure_____ it.

5. He might go to the party, but he's not _____certain_____ .

6. I don't have enough _____gas_____ in my car, so let's take your car.

Get Connected Vocabulary Practice

Unit 1

This exercise provides practice of the new vocabulary items in the Unit 1 Get Connected reading on Student's Book page 12.

- Tell students that this exercise will help them remember the new vocabulary items that appear in boldface in the article.
- Have students read the directions and the example sentence.
- Focus students' attention on the items in the box. Model each vocabulary item. Students listen and repeat.
- Invite volunteers to try to explain the meaning of each vocabulary item. If they cannot do this, have them turn to the article on Student's Book page 12. Have them read the sentences in which the vocabulary items appear to try to guess the meanings again.

- Have students work individually to complete the advertisement with the words in the box.
- Have students work in pairs to check their answers.
- Check answers with the class. Invite several volunteers to read the completed advertisement aloud.
- **Optional** Assign the vocabulary practice exercise as homework.

Unit 2

This exercise provides practice of the new vocabulary items in the Unit 2 Get Connected reading on Student's Book page 26.

- Tell students that this exercise will help them remember the new vocabulary items that appear in boldface on the Web site.
- Have students read the directions and the example sentence.
- Focus students' attention on the items in the box. Model each vocabulary item. Students listen and repeat.
- Invite volunteers to try to explain the meaning of each vocabulary item. If they cannot do this, have them turn to the Web site on Student's Book page 26. Have them read the sentences in which the vocabulary items appear to try to guess the meanings again.

- Have students work individually to complete the other sentences with the words in the box.
- Have students work in pairs to check their answers.
- Check answers with the class. Invite volunteers to read the completed sentences aloud.
- **Optional** Assign the vocabulary practice exercise as homework.

Unit 3

This exercise provides practice of the new vocabulary items in the Unit 3 Get Connected reading on Student's Book page 40.

- Tell students that this exercise will help them remember the new vocabulary items that appear in boldface in the article.
- Have students read the directions and the example item.
- Focus students' attention on the words in the left-hand column. Model each vocabulary item. Students listen and repeat.
- Invite volunteers to try to explain the meaning of each vocabulary item. If they cannot do this, have them turn to the article on Student's Book page 40. Have them read the sentences in which the vocabulary items appear to try to guess the meanings again.

- Have students work individually to match the other words to the correct meanings.
- Have students work in pairs to check their answers.
- Check answers with the class. Invite volunteers to read the answers aloud.
- **Optional** Assign the vocabulary practice exercise as homework.

Unit 4

This exercise provides practice of the new vocabulary items in the Unit 4 Get Connected reading on Student's Book page 54.

- Tell students that this exercise will help them remember the new vocabulary items that appear in boldface in the article.
- Have students read the directions and the example sentence.
- Focus students' attention on the items in the box. Model each vocabulary item. Students listen and repeat.
- Invite volunteers to try to explain the meaning of each vocabulary item. If they cannot do this, have them turn to the article on Student's Book page 54. Have them read the sentences in which the vocabulary items appear to try to guess the meanings again.

- Have students work individually to complete the other sentences with the words in the box.
- Have students work in pairs to check their answers.
- Check answers with the class. Invite volunteers to read the completed sentences aloud.
- **Optional** Assign the vocabulary practice exercise as homework.

Unit 3

Match the words to the correct meanings.

1. texting (n.) __f__
2. convenient (adj.) __e__
3. e-vite (n.) __d__
4. fuzzy (adj.) __a__
5. firm (adj.) __c__
6. social networking Web site (n.) __b__

a. not sure
b. an online "meeting" place
c. very sure
d. an online invitation
e. easy or useful
f. sending messages from a cell phone

Unit 4

Complete the sentences with the words in the box.

☐ birth order (n.)   ☐ firstborn (adj.)   ☐ middle (adj.)   ☐ researchers (n.)
☐ boss (n.)   ☑ leaders (n.)   ☐ peace (n.)

1. The city's ___leaders___ are hard-working, organized people.

2. _Researchers_ have discovered cures for many sicknesses.

3. John is the oldest child in his family. He's the ___firstborn___ child.

4. My father owns a successful business. He's the ___boss___ .

5. Julie is the ___middle___ child. She's younger than Mary and
   older than Dave.

6. World ___peace___ should be important to everyone.

7. Knowing a friend's _birth order_ can help you understand his or
   her personality.

Unit 5

Complete the sentences with the words in the box.

☐ audition (n.) ☐ comedian (n.) ☑ reality show (n.) ☐ viewers (n.)
☐ career (n.) ☐ go ahead (v.) ☐ recording contract (n.)

1. That dancing ___reality show___ isn't very interesting, so I don't watch it.

2. I saw that ___comedian___ on TV last night and he was very funny.

3. Being a doctor is a great ___career___ because you help people.

4. ___Go ahead___ and try that math problem. It's really easy!

5. His ___audition___ was really bad so they didn't ask him to be on the show.

6. That show is really popular. It has more ___viewers___ than any other TV show this year.

7. Chris Daughtry didn't win a ___recording contract___ on *American Idol*, but he's still very successful.

Unit 6

Circle the correct words to complete the sentences.

1. My sister made this (stunt / bowl) in her art class.

2. We didn't know Jim could play the piano so well.
   We were (disappointed / amazed).

3. The cat climbed up the (pole / bowl) and couldn't get down.

4. He likes to do amazing (audiences / stunts). Last month,
   he stayed in a very small room with no sleep for four days.

5. The artist made a sculpture from a (block / pole) of ice.

Unit 5

This exercise provides practice of the new vocabulary items in the Unit 5 Get Connected reading on Student's Book page 68.

- Tell students that this exercise will help them remember the new vocabulary items that appear in boldface in the article.
- Have students read the directions and the example sentence.
- Focus students' attention on the items in the box. Model each vocabulary item. Students listen and repeat.
- Invite volunteers to try to explain the meaning of each vocabulary item. If they cannot do this, have them turn to the article on Student's Book page 68. Have them read the sentences in which the vocabulary items appear to try to guess the meanings again.

- Have students work individually to complete the other sentences with the words in the box.
- Have students work in pairs to check their answers.
- Check answers with the class. Invite several volunteers to read the completed sentences aloud.
- **Optional** Assign the vocabulary practice exercise as homework.

Unit 6

This exercise provides practice of the new vocabulary items in the Unit 6 Get Connected reading on Student's Book page 82.

- Tell students that this exercise will help them remember the new vocabulary items that appear in boldface in the article.
- Have students read the directions and the example sentence.
- Focus students' attention on the words in parentheses in each sentence. Model each vocabulary item. Students listen and repeat.
- Invite volunteers to try to explain the meaning of each vocabulary item. If they cannot do this, have them turn to the article on Student's Book page 82. Have them read the sentences in which the vocabulary items appear to try to guess the meanings again.

- Have students work individually to circle the correct words to complete the other sentences.
- Have students work in pairs to check their answers.
- Check answers with the class. Invite volunteers to read the completed sentences aloud.
- **Optional** Assign the vocabulary practice exercise as homework.

Unit 7

This exercise provides practice of the new vocabulary items in the Unit 7 Get Connected reading on Student's Book page 96.

- Tell students that this exercise will help them remember the new vocabulary items that appear in boldface on the Web site.
- Have students read the directions and the example sentence.
- Focus students' attention on the items in the box. Model each vocabulary item. Students listen and repeat.
- Invite volunteers to try to explain the meaning of each vocabulary item. If they cannot do this, have them turn to the Web site on Student's Book page 96. Have them read the sentences in which the vocabulary items appear to try to guess the meanings again.

- Have students work individually to complete the other sentences with the words in the box.
- Have students work in pairs to check their answers.
- Check answers with the class. Invite several volunteers to read the completed sentences aloud.
- **Optional** Assign the vocabulary practice exercise as homework.

Unit 8

This exercise provides practice of the new vocabulary items in the Unit 8 Get Connected reading on Student's Book page 110.

- Tell students that this exercise will help them remember the new vocabulary items that appear in boldface in the article.
- Have students read the directions and the example sentence.
- Focus students' attention on the items in the box. Model each vocabulary item. Students listen and repeat.
- Invite volunteers to try to explain the meaning of each vocabulary item. If they cannot do this, have them turn to the article on Student's Book page 110. Have them read the sentences in which the vocabulary items appear to try to guess the meanings again.

- Have students work individually to complete the advertisement with the words in the box.
- Have students work in pairs to check their answers.
- Check answers with the class. Invite several volunteers to read the completed advertisement aloud.
- **Optional** Assign the vocabulary practice exercise as homework.

Unit 7

Complete the sentences with the words in the box.

☐ community work (n.)   ☐ memorable (adj.)   ☐ wilderness skills (n.)
☑ farmers (n.)   ☐ pandas (n.)

1. When there is no rain, _____farmers_____ can't grow vegetables.

2. The teens in our school do a lot of _community work_ .

3. _Wilderness skills_ are important if you like to hike and camp
   for a week in forests.

4. All my family is here. This is the most _____memorable_____ birthday party
   I've ever had.

5. There aren't as many _____pandas_____ in China as there were
   10 years ago.

Unit 8

Complete the advertisement with the words in the box.

☐ ambassador (n.)   ☐ cancer (n.)   ☐ education (n.)   ☑ role (n.)
☐ billion (adj.)   ☐ celebrities (n.)   ☐ foundation's (n.)

You can play an important _____role_____
in helping to find a cure for cancer. Come to
our _foundation's_ annual fashion show
at 3:00 p.m. on October 25th. See the latest
fashions, famous _celebrities_ , and
even the French _ambassador_ . We
will donate all of the money to health,
education , and _cancer_
research. Last year we raised one
_____billion_____ dollars!

Theme Project: Make a group booklet about people who make a difference.
Theme: Citizenship; environmentalism
Goal: To learn more about people who help other people, animals, or the earth

At Home

Read about a young man who has helped wildlife and nature.

> Jeff Howard is in the 11th grade in Ontario, Canada. He's an environmentalist. He loves wildlife and nature. When he was growing up, while other kids were playing computer games, texting, or talking to friends, Jeff helped to preserve nature and wildlife. He cleaned streams, counted birds, and rescued wild animals. He received awards for his work. Jeff really loves water birds. Once when he was out on a lake, Jeff saw a man being unkind to an injured swan. Jeff took a picture and reported the man to the police. His mom says, "We need youth to be interested and involved in nature."

Think of a person who has helped other people, animals, or the earth.
Complete the chart. Use your dictionary and the Internet, if necessary. *(Answers will vary.)*

Name: _____

Special activity: _____

Age when this person
started the special activity: _____

Other information: _____

Draw a picture or bring a photo of the person to class.

In Class

🛈 **Make a page of your person. Use the sample booklet page as a model.**

👥 **Tell your group about your person.**

> This is Brandon Keefe. When he was eight, he started collecting books and . . .

👥 **Make a group booklet. Make a cover for your booklet. Then staple together all of your pages and the cover to make your booklet.**

👤 **Pass around the booklets. Which person made the greatest difference?**

Name: Brandon Keefe
Special activity: Collecting books and giving them to poor children
Age when he started: 8
Other: He was on the Oprah Winfrey Show.

Sample booklet page

Unit 1 Theme Project

Project preparation

- The class before the project, have students read the *Theme Project*, *Theme*, and *Goal* information. Explain that this project will help them learn more about people who help other people, animals, or the earth.

- Focus students' attention on the sample booklet page in the book. Say: *Look at this sample booklet page. You will make a booklet page like this one about a person who has helped other people, animals, or the earth.*

- Focus students' attention on the *At Home* section. Explain that they will do this section for homework.

- Have students read the directions and check that they understand what they should do. At home, students should read the text about Jeff Howard and complete the chart about a person who has helped other people, animals, or the earth. They can choose a famous person or someone they have read or heard about or know. Remind students that they can use their dictionaries to find the meanings of words they do not know. They can also use the Internet to choose a person for their chart. They should then find a photo of the person to bring to the next class. Tell students that if they cannot find a photo, they can draw a picture.

- To finish, invite volunteers to tell you some activities people do that help other people, animals, or the earth. Write students' responses on the board.

Day of the project

Materials needed
Plain or colored paper for each student, tape or glue or paste, markers, stapler

- Explain to students that they will work individually to make a page like the sample booklet page, using the information from their charts and the pictures they brought to class.

- Distribute materials. Have each student make an individual booklet page.

- Have students form groups and present their booklet pages to their group, using the language in the speech balloon as a cue.

- Have each group make a cover and then staple together all of the pages and the cover to make a group booklet.

- Have groups pass around the booklets until each group has seen all the other groups' booklets.

- To finish, ask volunteers to say which person made the greatest difference.

Option

Have groups write a "quiz" about the people in their booklet. Focus on *Wh-* questions. For example: *Where's Jeff Howard from?* or *How many books did Brandon's group give away?* Have two groups exchange booklets and study them with their group members. Then have the students in each group take the other group's quiz. The students who wrote the quiz can read the questions, or they can write them on the board.

Future use of booklets

Keep these booklets to practice *who* clauses and gerunds as subjects in Unit 4. Invite volunteers to write sentences about the people in their group's booklet. For example: *Brandon Keefe is a person who thinks reading is important.* OR *Reading is important to Brandon Keefe.*

> **Culture Note**
> Steve Irwin, also known as "The Crocodile Hunter," was a famous TV personality, wildlife expert, and zoo owner. Until he died in 2006, Mr. Irwin used his TV show and many other wildlife documentaries to teach people about wild animals and their endangered environments. Since his death, Mr. Irwin's daughter, Bindi Sue, is following in her dad's footsteps. At ten years old, she was the host of a 26-part wildlife documentary called *Bindi the Jungle Girl*. In addition, she appears on many TV talk shows to educate people about wild animals and how to protect their environments. Bindi's family started a charity in 2002 called Wildlife Warriors, and she donates ten percent of her earnings each year to this charity.

Unit 2 — Theme Project

Project preparation

- The class before the project, have students read the *Theme Project*, *Theme*, and *Goal* information. Explain that this project will help them think about and share information about the future.

- Focus students' attention on the sample bookmark in the book. Say: *Look at this sample bookmark. You will make a bookmark like this one about things you will or won't do in the future.*

- Focus students' attention on the *At Home* section. Explain that they will do this section for homework.

- Have students read the directions, and check that they understand what they should do. At home, students should read the text about Griffin Stevens and write three ideas about what they will or won't do in the future. Remind students that they can use their dictionaries to find the meanings of words they do not know. They should then find a photo of themselves to bring to the next class. Tell students that if they cannot find a photo, they can draw a picture.

- To finish, invite volunteers to tell you some things they might do at times in the future (e.g., next year, in high school, or after high school). Write students' responses on the board.

Day of the project

Materials needed
Bookmark-sized cardboard or heavy paper for each student, markers or colored pencils or colored pens

- Explain to students that they will work individually to make a bookmark like the sample bookmark, using the information from their charts. Remind them not to put their picture or photo on their bookmark.

- Distribute materials. Have each student make an individual bookmark.

- Have students form groups. Students put all the bookmarks and the pictures or photos in the center of their group. One group member chooses a bookmark and reads the information to the group, using the language in the speech balloons as cues. Students guess which group member the bookmark belongs to. Students then put the correct pictures or photos on the correct bookmarks.

- Display the bookmarks in your classroom. Have students walk around and look at all of them.

- To finish, ask volunteers how many ideas were the same as theirs.

Option

Use the bookmarks to share information about each student's future and to practice the future with *will*. For example: *Will Griffin do well in his classes?*

Future use of bookmarks

Keep these bookmarks to practice *if* with *will / will probably / won't / might* in Unit 3. Invite volunteers to write conditional sentences about their classmates' future. For example: *If Leon studies hard, he'll probably get into a good college. If Andrea doesn't get good grades in math, she probably won't be an architect.*

Culture Note
Parents and teachers may think that social networking Web sites like MySpace, Facebook, or YouTube are a waste of time, but business leaders think otherwise. Business leaders are excited to tap into these social networking Web sites to find and sell new products. They feel that young people are shaping the future of how we do business. Social networking sites allow people from around the world to share ideas and preferences with large audiences. For example, Sandi Thom, a 26-year-old singer who lives in the UK, performed concerts in her basement and posted them on the Internet. Over 100,000 people watched her performances online. She eventually signed a recording contract with a music company without ever performing in front of a live audience.

Unit 2

Theme Project: Make a bookmark about your future.
Theme: Ethics and citizenship; diversity
Goal: To think about and share information about the future

At Home

Read about Griffin's ideas about his future.

Griffin Stevens is 13 years old and goes to Saint Ann's School in Brooklyn, New York. This is what he thinks about his future:
- I'll do well in my classes.
- I'm going to work hard on my soccer and basketball skills.
- I'll probably join the high school soccer team.
- I probably won't become a professional athlete.
- I might go to a very good college.

What do you think you will or won't do in your future? Write three of your ideas. Use your dictionary, if necessary. *(Answers will vary.)*

1. _____

2. _____

3. _____

Draw a picture or bring a photo of yourself to class.

In Class

🛈 **Make a bookmark. Do not put your picture or photo on it. Use the sample bookmark as a model.**

👥 **Put all the bookmarks and the pictures or photos in the center of your group. Choose a bookmark that isn't yours and read the information to your group. The other group members guess the person. Finally, put the correct pictures or photos on the bookmarks.**

> This person won't become an architect.
> This person might try out for . . .

> Is it Oren?

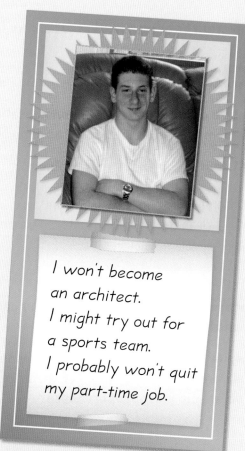

I won't become
an architect.
I might try out for
a sports team.
I probably won't quit
my part-time job.

Sample bookmark

🔄 **Display the bookmarks in your classroom. Walk around and look at all of them. How many ideas were the same as yours?**

Unit 3

Theme Project: Make fact cards about an environmental issue.
Theme: The environment and its preservation
Goal: To share information about ways to help the environment

At Home

Read about ways to save the environment.

> People are chopping down too many trees. If we don't stop cutting down trees, many animals will die because they won't have a place to live. There are many ways that you can help save trees.
> * Recycle your paper.
> * Use recycled paper products.
> * Send e-greetings. Don't send paper cards.
> * Take your own bags to stores when you go shopping.
> * Don't use paper plates or cups.

Think of an environmental problem and how to solve it. Complete the chart.
Use your dictionary or the Internet, if necessary. *(Answers will vary.)*

Describe the problem: _____

Result of the problem: _____

Solution to the problem: _____

Draw a picture or bring a photo that shows the problem to class.

In Class

ⓘ Make a card about your environmental problem. Use the sample card as a model.

👥 Tell your group about your problem.

> My problem is our air is dirty. If we don't clean the air, more people and animals will get sick, and . . .

👥👥 Choose a group leader. Present your cards to another group.

🔄 Display the fact cards in your classroom. Walk around and look at all of them. What problem did most people choose?

Our air is dirty.
If we don't clean the air, more people and animals will get sick, and more plants will die.
- Walk or bicycle to places. Don't go by bus or car.
- Use machines that don't use gas – like a lawnmower you push.
- Use fans, not air conditioners.

Sample fact card

Unit 3 Theme Project

Project preparation

- The class before the project, have students read the *Theme Project*, *Theme*, and *Goal* information. Explain that this project will help them share information about ways to help the environment.

- Focus students' attention on the sample fact card in the book. Say: *Look at this sample fact card. You and your group will make fact cards like this one about an environmental problem and possible ways to solve it.*

- Focus students' attention on the *At Home* section. Explain that they will do this section for homework.

- Have students read the directions, and check that they understand what they should do. At home, students should read the text about ways to save the environment and complete the chart. Remind students that they can use their dictionaries to find the meanings of words they do not know. They can also use the Internet to find out about an environmental problem and possible ways to solve it. They should then find a photo of the problem to bring to the next class. Tell students that if they cannot find a photo, they can draw a picture.

- To finish, invite volunteers to tell you about some environmental problems in their community, the country, or the world. Write the problems on the board.

Day of the project

Materials needed
Hard, card-sized plain or colored paper for each student, tape or glue or paste, markers

- Explain to students that they will work individually to make a fact card like the sample fact card, using the environmental problem described in their charts and the pictures they brought to class.

- Distribute materials. Have each student make an individual fact card.

- Have students form groups and present their fact cards to their group, using the language in the speech balloon as a cue.

- Have each group choose a leader and then join another group. Have the group leader present the group's fact cards to the other group, using the language in the speech balloon as a cue.

- Display the fact cards in your classroom. Have students walk around and look at all of them.

- To finish, ask volunteers which problem most people chose.

Option

Have students quiz each other by reading the possible solutions to each environmental problem and by having their classmates guess the problem.

Future use of fact cards

Keep these fact cards to practice *good / better / the best* and *bad / worse / the worst* in Unit 7. Invite students to talk about environmental problems and solutions. For example: *Chopping down too many trees is the worst environmental problem. Sending e-greetings is one possible solution to this problem.*

Culture Note

One way to help the environment is to buy goods and services from "green businesses." A green business is a business that tries to help the environment – or at least cause as little damage to the environment as possible. A green business is also usually committed to just social policies, such as fair trade, sustainability, and products that are made without cruelty to animals. In the U.S., Co-op America publishes a book called the *National Green Pages*. It is a directory of green businesses. In order to be included, each business has to be approved by a committee.

Project preparation

- The class before the project, have students read the *Theme Project*, *Theme*, and *Goal* information. Explain that this project will help them create stonger relationships in their classroom community.

- Focus students' attention on the sample booklet page in the book. Say: *Look at the sample booklet page. You and your group will make a booklet page like this one for a booklet of personality profiles.*

- Focus students' attention on the *At Home* section. Explain that they will do this section for homework.

- Have students read the directions, and check that they understand what they should do. At home, students should read the personality profiles of Diego and Carla and complete the chart with their own information. Remind students that they can use their dictionaries to find the meanings of words they do not know. They should then find a photo of themselves to bring to the next class. Tell students that if they cannot find a photo, they can draw a picture of themselves.

- To finish, invite volunteers to tell you some things they are good at, some things they like doing, and some things they do not like doing. Write students' responses on the board.

Day of the project

Materials needed
Plain or colored paper for each student, tape or glue or paste, markers, stapler

- Explain to students that they will work individually to make a personality profile page like the sample booklet page, using the information from their charts and the pictures they brought to class.

- Distribute materials. Have each student make an individual booklet page.

- Have students form groups and present their profile booklet pages to their group, using the language in the speech balloon as a cue.

- Have each group make a cover and then staple together all of the pages and the cover to make a group booklet of personality profiles.

- Have each group choose a leader and then join another group. Have the group leader read each personality profile in the group's booklet to the other group, using the language in the speech balloon as a cue. Members of the other group guess the student.

- Have groups pass around the booklets until each group has seen all the other groups' booklets.

- To finish, ask volunteers which two classmates have the most in common.

Option

Have students use information from the personality profile booklets to review *too* and *either* in Unit 4. For example: *Carla is a little shy. I am, too. Diego doesn't like cleaning his room. I don't, either.*

Future use of booklets

Keep these booklets to practice the present perfect with *since* and *for* in Unit 5. Invite volunteers to write sentences about how long they have done the things they are good at and enjoy. For example: *I have played soccer for ten years. I have played video games for seven years. I have had piano lessons since 2009.* Then collect and use the sentences to play a guessing game. For example:

Teacher: *I'm thinking of a student. He has played soccer for ten years.*

Student A: *Is it Edwin?*

Teacher: *No, it's not. Edwin has played baseball for ten years.*

Student B: *Is it Carlos?*

Teacher: *No, it's not.*

Student C: *Is it Diego?*

Teacher: *Yes, it is.*

Then let the student who guessed correctly take the role of the teacher.

Culture Note
Many Americans have set up personal profiles on the Internet. While it is honest to tell the truth about who you are, it is a good idea to be careful about giving out too much information. Many of the Web sites in the U.S. let you e-mail people through the Web site, without using personal e-mail addresses or IM (Instant Messaging) names. Web sites strongly caution people against giving out personal information such as their addresses or telephone numbers on the Internet.

Unit 4

Theme Project: Make a group personality profile booklet.
Theme: Citizenship; cultural diversity
Goal: To create stronger relationships within your classroom community

At Home

Read the personality profiles of two teens.

I'm Diego. I'm outgoing and very hardworking. I like making new friends. I love spending time outdoors – hiking, kayaking, and playing soccer. I enjoy playing computer games and chatting online, too. I don't like cleaning my room.	My name is Carla. I'm kind, thoughtful, and trustworthy, and I'm a little shy. I don't like playing sports very much. I have a Web site, and I write a blog. I like taking pictures with my digital camera and editing them online.

Write a personality profile. Complete the chart. Use your dictionary, if necessary. *(Answers will vary.)*

My name: _____

My personality: _____

Things I like doing: _____

Things I don't like doing: _____

Draw a picture or bring a photo of yourself to class.

In Class

ⓘ Make a profile page. Use the sample booklet page as a model.

Present your profile to your group.

> I'm creative and independent. I like . . .

Make a group booklet. Make a cover for your booklet. Then staple together all of your pages and the cover to make your booklet.

Choose a group leader. The group leader reads the personality profiles, and the other group members guess the student.

Pass around the booklets. Which two classmates have the most in common?

I'm creative and independent.
I like hanging out with my friends.
I don't like doing chores.

Sample booklet page

Theme Project: Make a cross-cultural experiences poster.

Theme: Multiculturalism

Goal: To create stronger relationships in your classroom community

At Home

Read about cross-cultural experiences.

It's important to know about other cultures and other people, and you don't need to travel to another country to do this. Have you ever talked to someone who doesn't speak your language? Have you ever eaten food from another country? Have you ever seen a foreign movie on TV? Maybe you've read books about people in other countries or have chatted with people from other countries online. If you've done any of these things, you have learned something about another culture and had a cross-cultural experience.

Think of cross-cultural experiences you have had. Complete the sentences. Use the ideas in the box or your own ideas. Use your dictionary, if necessary. *(Answers will vary.)*

1. I have _____ .
2. I have _____ .
3. I have _____ .
4. I have _____ .

books	movies
food	online
friend	travel
in school	TV

Draw a picture or bring a photo of one or more of the experiences to class.

In Class

Look at all the experiences. Choose one experience for each group member.

Make a poster. Use the sample poster as a model.

Choose a group leader. Present your poster to another group.

> Megumi has visited Colombia. Bruno has . . .

Display the posters in your classroom. Walk around and look at all of them. Which group has had the most interesting cross-cultural experiences?

1. Megumi has visited Colombia.
2. Bruno has made international friends online.
3. Carlo's family has had a homestay student at their house.
4. Eduardo has studied three languages.

Sample poster

Unit 5 Theme Project

Project preparation

- The class before the project, have students read the *Theme Project*, *Theme*, and *Goal* information. Explain that this project will help them learn more about the cross-cultural experiences of their classmates to create stronger relationships in their classroom community.

- Focus students' attention on the sample poster in the book. Say: *Look at this sample poster. You and your group will make a poster like this one about your cross-cultural experiences.*

- Focus students' attention on the *At Home* section. Explain that they will do this section for homework.

- Have students read the directions, and check that they understand what they should do. At home, students should read the text about how to experience other cultures and complete the sentences with their own information, using the words in the box or their own ideas. Remind students that they can use their dictionaries to find the meanings of words they do not know. They should then find a photo of one or more of their cross-cultural experiences to bring to the next class. Tell students that if they cannot find a photo, they can draw a picture.

- To finish, invite volunteers to tell you examples of different types of cross-cultural experiences. Write them on the board.

Day of the project

Materials needed
Poster board or large paper for each group, tape or glue or paste, markers

- Have students work in small groups of four or five. Explain to students that they will make a poster like the sample poster, using some of the sentences that describe their cross-cultural experiences and the pictures they brought to class.

- Distribute materials. Have students share their sentences and their photos or pictures in their groups. Have each group choose four or five sentences, one sentence for each group member, for their poster and the corresponding four or five photos or pictures. Each group then makes a cross-cultural experiences poster.

- Have each group choose a leader and then join another group. Have the group leader present the information on the group's poster to the other group, using the language in the speech balloon as a cue.

- Display the posters in your classroom. Have students walk around and look at all of them.

- To finish, ask volunteers which group had the most interesting cross-cultural experiences.

Option

Invite volunteers to read their own information from their group's poster to the class. Encourage the rest of the students to ask follow-up questions. For example:

A: *I've read a book about a girl in another country.*

B: *What was the name of the book?*

Future use of posters

Keep these posters to practice tag questions with the present perfect in Unit 6. Invite students to make tag questions and answers about the cross-cultural experiences shown on the posters. For example:

A: *Bruno has made international friends online, hasn't he?*

B: *Yes, he has.*

> **Culture Note**
> In November 2008, Americans voted for a presidential candidate with a truly cross-cultural background. Barack Obama actually grew up in a cross-cultural context. He was born in Hawaii to an American mother and a Kenyan father. Barack's mother later married a man from Indonesia, and Barack was taken to Indonesia to live. After approximately five years, he returned to Hawaii with his mother, where his grandparents helped to raise him. When Barack was a grown man, after his father's death, he visited Kenya, his father's homeland.

Unit 5 Theme Project T-130

Unit 6 Theme Project

Project preparation

- The class before the project, have students read the *Theme Project*, *Theme*, and *Goal* information. Explain that this project will help them learn more about a person who has done amazing things.

- Focus students' attention on the sample booklet page in the book. Say: *Look at this sample booklet page. You and your group will each make a booklet page like this one about a person who has done amazing things.*

- Focus students' attention on the *At Home* section. Explain that they will do this section for homework.

- Have students read the directions and check that they understand what they should do. At home, students should read the text about Ethan Bortnick, and complete the chart about an amazing person, perhaps someone they know. It is important that the person still be alive so that students will be required to use the present perfect, rather than the past perfect. Remind students that they can use their dictionaries to find the meanings of words they do not know. They can also use the Internet to choose an amazing person and to complete the information about the person for their chart. They should then find a photo of the person to bring to the next class. Tell students that if they cannot find a photo, they can draw a picture.

- To finish, invite volunteers to tell you the names of famous people who have done amazing things.

Day of the project

Materials needed
Plain or colored paper for each student, tape or glue or paste, markers, stapler

- Explain to students that they will work individually to make a page like the sample booklet page, using the information from their charts and the pictures they brought to class.

- Distribute materials. Have each student make an individual booklet page.

- Have students form groups and present their booklet pages to their group, using the language in the speech balloon as a cue.

- Have each group make a cover and then staple together all of the pages and the cover to make a group booklet.

- Display the booklets in your classroom. Have students walk around and look at all of them.

- To finish, ask the class to vote on the most amazing person.

Option

Have students use the information from the booklets to review the simple past and the present perfect. For example: *Ethan started playing piano when he was three. Ethan has been on several TV shows.*

Future use of booklets

Keep these booklets to practice *If* clauses with *could . . . would* in Unit 8. Write on the board: *If I could talk to any of the amazing people in our booklets, I'd talk to _____ .* Invite volunteers to complete the sentence. Ask them why they would like to talk to the person they named.

> **Culture Note**
>
> The *Guinness Book of World Records* is a great resource for researching amazing people. In the 2009 edition, there is an entire section about achievements by the youngest members of our society. For example, the youngest person to travel to all seven continents (including Antarctica) is Thomas Lucian Staff of the UK. In 2007, Thomas's parents began taking him around the world when he was only three months old. He was ten days away from his first birthday when he reached Antarctica, his seventh continent in ten months. That's pretty amazing!

Unit 6

Theme Project: Make a booklet about amazing people.
Theme: Multiculturalism; citizenship
Goal: To learn more about a person who has done amazing things

At Home

Read about an amazing nine-year-old boy.

Ethan Bortnick is nine years old and plays the piano very well. He also writes songs. He has already composed 20 piano pieces and has recorded a DVD. He has also given many live concerts.

Ethan started playing the piano when he was three, and he started composing his own pieces when he was five. He has been on several shows – *The Tonight Show* with Jay Leno, the *Oprah Winfrey Show*, and others. He speaks two languages – English and Russian. He hasn't learned Spanish yet, but he wants to.

Think of an amazing person. It can be someone you know. Complete the chart. Use your dictionary or the Internet, if necessary. *(Answers will vary.)*

Name	What has he or she already done?	What has he or she not done yet?

Draw a picture or bring a photo of the person to class.

In Class

① **Make a page of your person. Use the sample booklet page as a model.**

② **Tell your group about your person.**

> My brother, Jim, is amazing. He has . . .

③ **Make a group booklet. Make a cover for your booklet. Then staple together all of your pages and the cover to make your booklet.**

④ **Display the booklets in your classroom. Walk around and look at all of them. Vote on the most amazing person.**

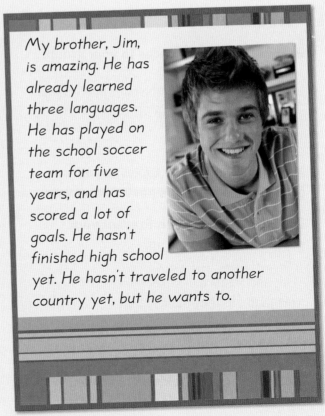

My brother, Jim, is amazing. He has already learned three languages. He has played on the school soccer team for five years, and has scored a lot of goals. He hasn't finished high school yet. He hasn't traveled to another country yet, but he wants to.

Sample booklet page

Theme Project: Make a poster about group preferences.
Theme: Cultural diversity
Goal: To share ideas about preferences

At Home

Read about parents' preferences about schools.

Some parents in the U.S. don't want to send their children to a regular school. They think that homeschooling is better than studying in a regular school. There are about 2 million children in the U.S. who are homeschooled. Parents think that the best thing about homeschooling is that it creates a closer relationship with their children.

Choose one of these topics: sports, music, pets, or TV shows. Complete the chart. Then write sentences about your preferences. Use your dictionary, if necessary. *(Answers will vary.)*

Like a lot	Like	Like a little	Don't like	Don't like at all

I like _____ a lot. _____

_____

Draw pictures or bring photos of your topic to class.

In Class

Present your preferences to your group.

> I like soccer. I think it's the most interesting sport to play. I don't like . . .

Make a poster for the topics in your group. Use the sample poster as a model.

Choose a group leader. Present your poster to another group.

> Luis and Selma don't like tennis at all. They think . . .

Display the posters in your classroom. Walk around and look at all of them. Who had the same ideas as you?

Sports

Luis and Selma don't like tennis at all. They think it's the worst sport they've ever watched. They think it's boring.

Ron thinks basketball is better than baseball. He doesn't like baseball at all.

Music

Suzie likes pop music a lot. She thinks it's the best music she's ever heard.

Sample poster

Unit 7 Theme Project

Project preparation

- The class before the project, have students read the *Theme Project*, *Theme*, and *Goal* information. Explain that this project will help them share ideas about their preferences.

- Focus students' attention on the sample poster in the book. Say: *Look at this sample poster. You and your group will make a poster like this one about preferences.*

- Focus students' attention on the *At Home* section. Explain that they will do this section for homework.

- Have students read the directions and check that they understand what they should do. At home, students should read the text about parents' preferences about schools, choose one of the topics, complete the chart, and then write sentences about their preferences. Remind students that they can use their dictionaries to find the meanings of words they do not know. They should then find photos of their topic to bring to the next class. Tell students that if they cannot find photos, they can draw pictures.

- To finish, invite volunteers to tell you kinds of sports, music, pets, or TV shows that they like a lot, a little, or not at all.

Day of the project

Materials needed

Poster board or large paper for each group, tape or glue or paste, markers

- Have students work in small groups of four or five. Remind students that they will make a poster like the sample poster, using some of the sentences they wrote about their preferences.

- Distribute materials. Have students share their sentences and their photos or pictures in their groups. Have each group use its group members' topics for its preferences poster and the corresponding photos or pictures. Each group then makes a poster.

- Have each group choose a leader and then join another group. Have the group leader present the information on the group's poster to the other group, using the sample language in the speech balloon as a cue.

- Display the posters in your classroom. Have students walk around and look at all of them.

- To finish, volunteers ask who had the same ideas as they had.

Future use of posters

Use some of the ideas from the posters to play tic-tac-toe. For example, write words such as *soccer, tennis, basketball, baseball, rock music, classical music, cats,* and *dogs* in the nine-square grid. Divide the class into two teams. Team A chooses a word in the grid to describe a preference. For example: *I think watching soccer is more interesting than watching tennis.* If the team produces a sensible and grammatically correct sentence, they can choose to have either *X* or *O* marked in the square. Then Team B takes a turn. Three *X*s or three *O*s diagonally, horizontally, or vertically wins.

Culture Note

In the fall of 2008, a report by the market-research companies Harris Interactive and CTIA indicated that American teenagers prefer texting to talking on their cell phone. They said the teens prefer texting because it allows them to multitask (do more than one thing at a time). Teens felt that texting is fast, it allows them to avoid verbal communication, and it's fun. Forty-seven percent of U.S. teens said their social life "would end" or be worsened without their cell phone.

Unit 8 Theme Project

Project preparation

- The class before the project, have students read the *Theme Project*, *Theme*, and *Goal* information. Explain that this project will help them learn more about the needs of different people and charities.

- Focus students' attention on the sample booklet page in the book. Say: *Look at this sample booklet page. You will make a booklet page like this one about how you could help people by giving away $5,000.*

- Focus students' attention on the *At Home* section. Explain that they will do this section for homework.

- Have students read the directions and check that they understand what they should do. At home, students should read the text about *Oprah's Big Give,* and then complete the four sentences. Remind students that they can use their dictionaries to find the meanings of words they do not know. They should then find photos of their ideas to bring to the next class. Tell students that if they cannot find photos, they can draw pictures.

- To finish, invite volunteers to name people, charities, or other organizations they know of that need money, food, or other kinds of help.

Day of the project

Materials needed

Plain or colored paper for each member of each group, tape or glue or paste, markers, stapler

- Have students work in small groups of four or five and present their ideas to the group, using the language in the speech balloon as a cue. The group then selects one idea from each group member to include in the group's booklet.

- Distribute materials. Explain to students that they will work individually to make a booklet page like the sample booklet page, using the idea chosen by their group and the pictures they brought to class. Have each student make an individual booklet page.

- Have each group make a cover and then staple together all of the pages and the cover to make a group booklet.

- Have groups pass around the booklets until each group has seen all the other groups' booklets.

- To finish, have students vote on the booklet that shows the most helpful ideas.

Future use of booklets

Have students use information from the booklets to review and use the unreal conditional with *If* clauses from this unit. For example:

A: *What would Sam do to help people if he had $5,000?*

B: *If Sam had $5,000 to help people, he'd buy food.*

Culture Note

Years before Oprah did her *Big Give,* she did a show about people doing thoughtful things for strangers. The topic of the show was "Random Acts of Kindness." In 1993, Professor Chuck Wall, from Bakersfield College, came up with the term. He was talking to his class about "random acts of violence" in the news. He got the idea to replace the word *violence* with *kindness,* and he told his students that their homework was to commit a random act of kindness during the next week and report on it at the next class. The students gave blankets to homeless people, rescued stray animals, and let others have parking spaces. Students printed "Random Acts" bumper stickers for their cars. Soon others were committing random acts of kindness. Oprah's show on the topic helped bring national attention to the Random Acts of Kindness Foundation in the U.S.

Unit 8

Theme Project: Make a group booklet showing how you could help others with $5,000.

Theme: Citizenship; consumerism

Goal: To learn about the needs of different people and charities

At Home

Read about a show to help people.

Oprah Winfrey is a famous TV star. In 2008 she had a special show, a reality show, called *Oprah's Big Give*. The goal of the show was to help people, and the person who helped the most was the winner. In each show, contestants went to a different U.S. city. They received money and a task they had to do. Sometimes they did the task alone, and sometimes they did it in pairs or groups. Sometimes they were told who to help, and other times they had to find people in need. At the end of each show, judges decided who spent the money in the most helpful way. At the end of the TV series, the winner got $1 million ($500,000 for themselves, and $500,000 to give away).

What would you do to help people? Write four sentences beginning with *If I had $5,000, I'd . . .* . Use your dictionary, if necessary. *(Answers will vary.)*

1. _____
2. _____
3. _____
4. _____

Draw pictures or bring photos of your ideas to class.

In Class

Tell your group about your ideas.

> If I had $5,000, I'd buy food for people . . .

Choose one idea from each group member.

Make a page of your idea. Use the sample booklet page as a model.

Make a group booklet. Make a cover for your booklet. Then staple together all of your pages and the cover to make your booklet.

Pass around the booklets. Vote on the booklet with the most helpful ideas.

Meg:
If I had $5,000, I'd buy food for people who live on the street, and I'd give it to them.

Sample booklet page

Verb List

Verbs are listed with the page number on which they first appear.

Regular Verbs

Present	Past	Participle	Page
act	acted	acted	4
agree	agreed	agreed	98
amaze	amazed	amazed	30
answer	answered	answered	12
appear	appeared	appeared	61
arrive	arrived	arrived	39
ask	asked	asked	14
audition	auditioned	auditioned	68
backpack	backpacked	backpacked	24
behave	behaved	behaved	80
believe	believed	believed	38
borrow	borrowed	borrowed	32
call	called	called	40
camp	camped	camped	2
celebrate	celebrated	celebrated	66
change	changed	changed	68
chat	chatted	chatted	44
cheat	cheated	cheated	102
clean	cleaned	cleaned	16
climb	climbed	climbed	63
close	closed	closed	33
collect	collected	collected	50
compete	competed	competed	61
connect	connected	connected	16
cook	cooked	cooked	16
copy	copied	copied	102
crawl	crawled	crawled	14
create	created	created	106
cure	cured	cured	26
dance	danced	danced	42
decide	decided	decided	23
depend	depended	depended	36
describe	described	described	82
design	designed	designed	4
disappear	disappeared	disappeared	82
discover	discovered	discovered	54
donate	donated	donated	110
download	downloaded	downloaded	44
drop	dropped	dropped	98
dye	dyed	dyed	72
eavesdrop	eavesdropped	eavesdropped	102
edit	edited	edited	22
e-mail	e-mailed	e-mailed	2
enjoy	enjoyed	enjoyed	12
enter	entered	entered	102
entertain	entertained	entertained	17
erase	erased	erased	89
exercise	exercised	exercised	10
expect	expected	expected	30
experience	experienced	experienced	96

Present	Past	Participle	Page
explain	explained	explained	14
explore	explored	explored	30
film	filmed	filmed	2
finish	finished	finished	18
fix	fixed	fixed	29
gossip	gossiped	gossiped	102
graduate	graduated	graduated	18
guess	guessed	guessed	73
happen	happened	happened	3
hate	hated	hated	43
head	headed	headed	30
help	helped	helped	8
hike	hiked	hiked	2
homeschool	homeschooled	homeschooled	78
hope	hoped	hoped	36
invite	invited	invited	42
jaywalk	jaywalked	jaywalked	102
join	joined	joined	4
jump	jumped	jumped	73
laugh	laughed	laughed	68
learn	learned	learned	4
lie	lied	lied	102
like	liked	liked	2
listen	listened	listened	12
litter	littered	littered	102
live	lived	lived	17
look	looked	looked	10
love	loved	loved	4
marry	married	married	81
matter	mattered	mattered	103
move	moved	moved	8
need	needed	needed	21
open	opened	opened	16
order	ordered	ordered	34
pack	packed	packed	38
pass	passed	passed	18
perform	performed	performed	8
pick	picked	picked	103
play	played	played	3
practice	practiced	practiced	6
push	pushed	pushed	8
rain	rained	rained	14
receive	received	received	62
record	recorded	recorded	60
relax	relaxed	relaxed	12
remember	remembered	remembered	46
rent	rented	rented	37
replace	replaced	replaced	16
report	reported	reported	106
rescue	rescued	rescued	30
return	returned	returned	30
review	reviewed	reviewed	80
save	saved	saved	30
scream	screamed	screamed	113
seem	seemed	seemed	12
share	shared	shared	18
shop	shopped	shopped	16
sign	signed	signed	23
skateboard	skateboarded	skateboarded	34
snorkel	snorkeled	snorkeled	38

Present	Past	Participle	Page
solve	solved	solved	106
sound	sounded	sounded	6
star	starred	starred	81
start	started	started	5
stay	stayed	stayed	2
stop	stopped	stopped	7
study	studied	studied	3
support	supported	supported	60
suppose	supposed	supposed	31
surprise	surprised	surprised	30
survive	survived	survived	110
talk	talked	talked	42
test	tested	tested	30
text	texted	texted	40
train	trained	trained	12
travel	traveled	traveled	2
trespass	trespassed	trespassed	102
try	tried	tried	7
turn	turned	turned	79
type	typed	typed	21
use	used	used	10
vacation	vacationed	vacationed	79
visit	visited	visited	2
wait	waited	waited	6
walk	walked	walked	14
want	wanted	wanted	3
watch	watched	watched	3
welcome	welcomed	welcomed	92
work	worked	worked	3
worry	worried	worried	30

Irregular Verbs

Present	Past	Participle	Page
babysit	babysat	babysat	31
be	was	been	2
become	became	become	2
break	broke	broken	3
bring	brought	brought	22
buy	bought	bought	17
come	came	come	15
cut	cut	cut	34
do	did	done	3
draw	drew	drawn	93
drink	drank	drunk	28
drive	drove	driven	7
eat	ate	eaten	3
fall	fell	fallen	9
feed	fed	fed	21
fly	flew	flown	37
forget	forgot	forgotten	31
get	got	gotten	2
give	gave	given	8
go	went	gone	2
hang	hung	hung	2
have	had	had	2
hear	heard	heard	14
hit	hit	hit	3

Present	Past	Participle	Page
hurt	hurt	hurt	83
keep	kept	kept	46
know	knew	known	10
leave	left	left	30
let	let	let	33
lose	lost	lost	2
make	made	made	2
pay	paid	paid	25
put	put	put	3
read	read	read	14
ride	rode	ridden	6
ring	rang	rung	15
run	ran	run	34
say	said	said	12
see	saw	seen	2
sell	sold	sold	61
send	sent	sent	40
set	set	set	78
show	showed	shown	66
sing	sang	sung	60
sit	sat	sat	22
sleep	slept	slept	7
speak	spoke	spoken	17
spend	spent	spent	2
stand	stood	stood	14
swim	swam	swum	34
take	took	taken	2
teach	taught	taught	50
tell	told	told	14
think	thought	thought	6
throw	threw	thrown	103
understand	understood	understood	41
wake	woke	woken	7
wear	wore	worn	10
win	won	won	8
write	wrote	written	12

Word List

This list includes the key words and phrases in *Connect, Second Edition* Student's Book 4. The numbers next to each word are the page numbers on which the words first appear.

Key Vocabulary

Aa
abroad (18) _____
absolutely not (33) _____
act (4) _____
afraid (47) _____
Africa (71) _____
album (62) _____
alike (47) _____
all over (2) _____
all right (32) _____
amaze (30) _____
amazed (82) _____
ambassador (110) _____
angry (46) _____
Antarctica (108) _____
anyone (14) _____
anyplace (101) _____
appear (61) _____
appearance (53) _____
article (22) _____
as (much) as (92) _____
astronaut (57) _____
at all (29) _____
audience (60) _____
audition (68) _____
autograph (60) _____
award (9) _____

Bb
backpack [verb] (24) _____
backstage (64) _____
bad dream (16) _____
badminton (22) _____
bad-tempered (42) _____
ballroom dancing class (22) _____
basketball team (9) _____
battery (21) _____
behave (80) _____
behavior (102) _____
below (17) _____
best-loved (12) _____
better than (50) _____
billion (110) _____
birth order (54) _____
block (102) _____
board game (45) _____
book report (38) _____
borrow (32) _____

boss (54) _____
bowl (82) _____
boyfriend (52) _____
brand-new (30) _____
broken (32) _____
butterfly (51) _____

Cc
campground (2) _____
campsite (7) _____
cancer (110) _____
can't stand [hate] (86) _____
career (68) _____
carelessly (102) _____
carpenter (106) _____
cartoon (11) _____
cartoon artist (51) _____
cave tour (30) _____
celebrity (110) _____
cellist (60) _____
cello (60) _____
center (66) _____
certain (26) _____
champion [adjective] (8) _____
champion [noun] (8) _____
charity (60) _____
cheat (102) _____
choice (94) _____
circus school (50) _____
close (33) _____
collect (11) _____
collection (5) _____
college (18) _____
college degree (79) _____
color TV (67) _____
come back (30) _____
comedian (68) _____
commercials (15) _____
community work (96) _____
company (67) _____
compass (2) _____
compete (61) _____
competition (8) _____
computer course (5) _____
computer file (89) _____
computer game (4) _____
computer programmer (106) _____
computer programming (24) _____

computer science (81) _____
connect (16) _____
contact lenses (10) _____
continent (16) _____
convenient (26) _____
conversation (102) _____
cooking (93) _____
cooking class (22) _____
copy (62) _____
country tour (39) _____
couple [a couple of] (24) _____
crab (109) _____
crawl (14) _____
creative (46) _____
credit card (17) _____
crocodile meat (88) _____
cure (26) _____
cut (34) _____

Dd
decide on (79) _____
definitely (25) _____
depend on [it depends on] (36) _____
design [noun] (3) _____
design [verb] (3) _____
detective (106) _____
digital camera (32) _____
discovery (106) _____
disgusting (88) _____
do the dishes (86) _____
download (44) _____
dream [noun] (18) _____
driver's license (18) _____
during (88) _____
DVD player (33) _____
dye [verb] (72) _____

Ee
easygoing (33) _____
eavesdrop (102) _____
ecological tour (77) _____
Ecuador (3) _____
edit (22) _____
education (110) _____
e-mail [verb] (2) _____
entertain (17) _____
entertainer (60) _____
erase (89) _____

Europe (24) _____

evening [adjective] (32) _____

event (101) _____

ever (64) _____

e-vite (40) _____

exchange program (75) _____

expect (30) _____

explain (14) _____

explore (30) _____

extra (6) _____

Ff

fall off (9) _____

fan club (5) _____

fan letter (64) _____

far away (18) _____

farmer (96) _____

fashion magazine (61) _____

fighter plane (101) _____

film [verb] (2) _____

fingerprints (21) _____

firm (40) _____

first-born (54) _____

fix (29) _____

flying (26) _____

for (66) _____

foreign (51) _____

for fun (48) _____

forgetful (46) _____

foundation (110) _____

frustrating (89) _____

furniture (106) _____

fuzzy (40) _____

Gg

garbage (102) _____

gas (26) _____

get back (38) _____

get home (39) _____

get married (18) _____

get together (38) _____

girlfriend (64) _____

glasses (10) _____

go ahead (68) _____

go-cart (30) _____

gold medal (8) _____

gossip (102) _____

graduate (18) _____

graduation (20) _____

grand opening (30) _____

ground (30) _____

gymnast (12) _____

gymnastics (5) _____

Hh

haircut (39) _____

happen (3) _____

hardworking (46) _____

head for (30) _____

headlines (26) _____

high school (18) _____

highway (7) _____

hit [adjective] (60) _____

hobbies (5) _____

hometown (2) _____

honest (46) _____

How long . . . (66) _____

human (16) _____

husband (18) _____

Ii

ice hotel (50) _____

if (16) _____

imagination (47) _____

in danger (30) _____

independent (46) _____

information (44) _____

in order (46) _____

in secret (102) _____

instant message (3) _____

intelligent (62) _____

international hotel (24) _____

interview (60) _____

invitation (35) _____

invite (42) _____

invited [get invited] (64) _____

Jj

jaywalk (102) _____

job [get a job] (18) _____

journalist (106) _____

judo (22) _____

Kk

karaoke (72) _____

karate class (58) _____

kind (93) _____

Ll

lazy (10) _____

leader (54) _____

lead singer (74) _____

lend (32) _____

let (33) _____

lie (102) _____

life event (8) _____

lightning (14) _____

lion tamer (50) _____

litter (102) _____

live [adjective] (60) _____

living space (18) _____

lots of (59) _____

luckily (2) _____

Mm

marathon (74) _____

marching band (22) _____

married (18) _____

marry (101) _____

martial arts classes (22) _____

match [sports] (8) _____

math whiz (78) _____

matter (103) _____

maybe (33) _____

mean [verb] (103) _____

medicine (19) _____

medicines (26) _____

memorable (96) _____

memory (71) _____

middle (54) _____

might (23) _____

might not (23) _____

million (60) _____

miniskirt (100) _____

moment (88) _____

Mongolia (104) _____

motorcycle (72) _____

mountain climbing (63) _____

movie crew (2) _____

movie industry (66) _____

musical instrument (9) _____

music lesson (4) _____

music show (11) _____

Nn

nightmare (16) _____

number (78) _____

Oo

of course (32) _____

office (23) _____

Olympic champion (51) _____

Olympic Games (61) _____

one-man band (50) _____

on stage (88) _____

on (your) own (107) _____

orchestra (8) _____

organized (46) _____

outdoor (36) _____

outer space (106) _____

outgoing (46) _____

Pp

pack (38) _____

paint (48) _____

panda (96) _____

paper (17) _____

parasailing (88) _____

pass (18) _____

peace (54) _____

permission (35) _____

personality (46) _____

personality type (46) _____

photographer (4) _____

photography club (4) _____

piano (6) _____

pick up (103) _____

poet (94) _____

poetry competition (108) _____

pole (82) _____

police (102) _____

pop culture (66) _____

possible (18) _____

prediction (16) _____
prince (101) _____
principal (113) _____
private (102) _____
probably (18) _____
professional [adjective] (8) _____
professor (16) _____
program [noun] (106) _____
promise [noun] (102) _____
put (3) _____
put up (7) _____

Rr
racing track (30) _____
racket club (22) _____
radio contest (64) _____
reading test (80) _____
reality show (68) _____
receive (65) _____
recently (51) _____
record [verb] (60) _____
recording contract (68) _____
recreation leader (22) _____
reflection (7) _____
relative (75) _____
replace (17) _____
report on (106) _____
reporter (22) _____
request (35) _____
researchers (54) _____
rescue (30) _____
return (30) _____
review (80) _____
rich (18) _____
right after (24) _____
risk (72) _____
road (14) _____
rock band (71) _____
rock-climbing [adjective] (73) _____
rock climbing [noun] (71) _____
rock concert (64) _____
rock star (20) _____
role (110) _____
royal family (101) _____
rumba (22) _____

Ss
samba (22) _____
save (30) _____
school newspaper (4) _____
school office (56) _____
school parade (22) _____
school play (4) _____
schoolwork (44) _____
science-fiction movie (86) _____
scrapbook (12) _____
scuba diving (75) _____

serious (93) _____
selection (90) _____
sharp [10:00 sharp] (32) _____
show [verb] (66) _____
sick (21) _____
sickness (21) _____
simple (78) _____
since (66) _____
singing competition (18) _____
site (3) _____
situation (101) _____
size (17) _____
skate park (58) _____
ski pants (39) _____
ski vacation (39) _____
skydiving (72) _____
sleeping machine (16) _____
sleep over [verb] (32) _____
snail (65) _____
snorkel (38) _____
snorkel gear (38) _____
snowboarding (93) _____
social networking Web site (40) __
so far (58) _____
solve (106) _____
someday (4) _____
somewhere (42) _____
space (57) _____
sports scores (44) _____
spotlight (80) _____
star (66) _____
stay (2) _____
stay out (32) _____
stop by (38) _____
strict (33) _____
stuntman (82) _____
stunts (82) _____
successful (81) _____
summer school (3) _____
superhighway (16) _____
support (60) _____
surfing lessons (38) _____
Sweden (50) _____
sweet dream (16) _____

Tt
take off (30) _____
take risks (53) _____
talents (18) _____
talkative (92) _____
Teen Center (22) _____
tennis lesson (3) _____
tennis match (58) _____
tennis tournament (71) _____
test [verb] (30) _____
texting (40) _____
Thai food (76) _____
theater group (95) _____

though (58) _____
thoughtful (46) _____
thriller (87) _____
thunder (14) _____
tourist attraction (66) _____
track (30) _____
train [verb] (12) _____
trapeze (30) _____
trash (42) _____
trash can (103) _____
travel book (39) _____
trespass (102) _____
trustworthy (46) _____
twin (92) _____
twin brother (3) _____
try out (30) _____

Uu
understand (50) _____
unforgettable (88) _____
university (78) _____
used to (10) _____

Vv
vacation [verb] (79) _____
vacation plans (38) _____
veterinarian (106) _____
vice-president (57) _____
video camera (22) _____
viewers (68) _____
violin (11) _____
virtual reality ride (30) _____

Ww
weekend (30) _____
wet (14) _____
while (38) _____
wife (18) _____
wild [noun] (104) _____
wilderness skills (96) _____
will (16) _____
without (71) _____
won't (16) _____
World Cup (8) _____
worm (73) _____
worry (30) _____
worse (86) _____
worst [the worst] (86) _____
writer (18) _____

Yy
young (8) _____
yo-yo (78) _____

Introduction to Extra Practice

Included in this section is a photocopiable package. This package contains eight short Extra Practice worksheets, one for each unit in *Connect*. In addition, there are four 3-page Extra Practice review worksheets, each reviewing two units.

The Extra Practice worksheets give students additional practice in word work (spelling, vocabulary, grammar, or pronunciation) and in finding and correcting sentence mistakes.

The Extra Practice review worksheets give students additional opportunities to practice and personalize the new vocabulary, language, reading, and writing skills they learned in the preceding units.

Features of Extra Practice

- The content of the Extra Practice exercises is strictly limited to the language and skills presented and practiced in the lessons in each unit of the Student's Book.
- The focus of each Extra Practice worksheet is on the specific language and skills of the corresponding unit, but does assume knowledge of the previous units' content.
- Exercise types in Extra Practice are similar to those in the lessons.
- The focus of the Extra Practice reviews is on vocabulary, language skills (completing conversations), reading, and writing, using your own information.

Assigning Extra Practice worksheets

- These worksheets can be assigned as homework or done in class.
- Make a copy of the Extra Practice worksheet(s) for each student in your class.
- If you assign these worksheets as homework, be sure to check the answers in the next class.
- If you do these worksheets in class, have students work alone and then check answers in pairs.

List of Extra Practice Exercises

Unit 1	Page T-142	Unit 5	Page T-152
Unit 2	Page T-143	Unit 6	Page T-153
Units 1 & 2	Page T-144	Units 5 & 6	Page T-154
Unit 3	Page T-147	Unit 7	Page T-157
Unit 4	Page T-148	Unit 8	Page T-158
Units 3 & 4	Page T-149	Units 7 & 8	Page T-159
		Answer Key	Page T-162

Unit 1 My Life

1 Word work

Circle the correct verb to complete the sentences.

1. I'm going to go skiing next month. I hope I don't (break / make) my leg.
2. My parents are going to (live / move) to the city soon.
3. I want to (play / do) gymnastics next year at school.
4. I usually (learn / get) good grades.
5. My family (travels / goes) on a trip every summer.
6. There are lots of after-school activities. You can (join / sign) a club or play a sport.
7. I'm going to France. I have to (learn / say) French.
8. I'm in an English club. It's a great way to (meet / visit) people.
9. I want to (make / play) a Web site.
10. We all (play / make) volleyball in my class.
11. My brother has some old comic books. He's going to (start / open) a collection.
12. My sister is going to (have / take) a course in photography.
13. We like to (go / visit) museums.
14. You can (win / have) an award at our school for the best math grades.

2 What's wrong?

There is <u>one</u> mistake in each of the underlined sentences.
Correct the sentences.

E-Mail

From: D

To: C

Subject: Hi!

Dear C,

<u>It is nice to chat with you yesterday.</u>
<u>I like to know your name.</u> I just know
that your first initial is C.

<u>So you go to Miami last summer.</u> I was
there, too! <u>Where you stay? Did you went to
the salsa festival? How many days did you
spent there? I was meeting a nice guy
there.</u> Guess what? His first initial is C, too.

<u>You are going to be online later?</u>
I'm going to write to you again, OK?
D

It was nice to chat with you yesterday.

_____

_____

_____

_____

_____

_____

_____

Unit 2 — The Future

1 Word work

Choose the correct word to complete the sentences.

1. Hiromi plays the drums. She might (join / travel) the marching band.
2. Joey wants to (learn / make) money. He's going to (play / get) a job.
3. Hilary doesn't want to go to college right after high school. She wants to (take / travel) abroad first.
4. We want to write articles for the school newspaper. We're going to (make / be) reporters.
5. Mr. and Mrs. Rodriguez want to visit a lot of countries. They're going to (go / join) around the world.
6. I might (travel / learn) how to make a music video. It sounds like fun.
7. Sergio likes to try different foods. He's going to (take / make) a cooking class.
8. Daniela likes to play games with children. She wants to (join / be) a recreation leader.
9. Kaori gets good grades. He'd like to (go / learn) to college someday.
10. Students (be / play) badminton in the racket club.

2 What's wrong?

One sentence in each pair is correct. Check (✓) it.

1. ☐ English will become probably the most important subject at school next year.
   ✔ English will probably become the most important subject at school next year.

2. ☐ Computers won't replace teachers in the future.
   ☐ Computers won't to replace teachers in the future.

3. ☐ Many students might want not to study in online schools.
   ☐ Many students might not want to study in online schools.

4. ☐ E-books might become popular soon.
   ☐ E-books might to become popular soon.

5. ☐ Most people won't probably shop online for food in the future.
   ☐ Most people probably won't shop online for food in the future.

6. ☐ I'm going to go to college next year.
   ☐ I going to go to college next year.

Units 1 & 2

1 Vocabulary

A Read Rita's e-mail to her cousin. Then complete the text with the simple past.

E-Mail

Dear Juan,

Hi! How are you? I'm writing to tell you about my last year at school.
It was a very busy and exciting year for me. First, you know that my family and I
moved (move) to the city. I was very sad to leave my friends, so my parents
_____ (get) a pet to cheer me up. He's a cute little dog! His name is Toby. I
_____ (join) the soccer team at school and made some new friends. Then last
summer, we _____ (go) on a trip to the U.S. We _____ (eat) American food every
day. I was so happy because I _____ (learn) English in school. We _____ (meet)
my best friend in New York City for two days. It was great!

Write soon.
Rita

B Match the parts of the sentences.

1. I want to buy expensive things,
   so I'll need to _e_

2. I want to buy a new car. But first,
   I need to _____

3. I love children. I'll probably _____

4. I might become an engineer.
   So I'll probably _____

5. This summer, I want to see Italy,
   Spain, and France. I'm going to _____

6. When I become a movie star,
   I'll probably _____

a. get a driver's license.

b. be famous.

c. go to college.

d. travel abroad.

e. be rich.

f. have a big family.

C Circle the correct word to complete each verb phrase.

1. (join / make / be) the racket club

2. (go / be / learn) a reporter

3. (take / become / meet) a cooking class

4. (go / take / learn) how to edit a music video

5. (be / go / play) a recreation leader

2 Language focus

A Look at the pictures of Henry. Then write sentences about what *used to be* true about Henry and what is true *now*.

1. Henry used to _have long hair_ .   Now he _____ .

2. _____   _____

3. _____   _____

4. _____   _____

5. _____   _____

B Complete the sentences with the simple past or the past continuous.

Last week I was at home with my little brother. It was late at night, and
I _____ (study) English in my room. My brother _____ (sleep) in
his room. Suddenly, I _____ (hear) a noise. I looked out of the window.
It _____ (rain), and the wind _____ (blow). I _____ (be)
scared. But then I heard the noise again – it was a quiet knocking on my door!
Suddenly, the door _____ (open) and my brother _____ (jump) into
my room. I _____ (be) really surprised!

C Look at each picture. Then check (✓) the correct sentence.

1. ☐ Andre is going to go to France.
   ☐ Andre might go to France.
   ☐ Andre probably won't go to France.

2. ☐ Marcia probably won't become a soccer player.
   ☐ Marcia might not become a soccer player.
   ☐ Marcia is going to become a soccer player.

3. ☐ Juan will get a driver's license today.
   ☐ Juan might get a driver's license today.
   ☐ Juan isn't going to get a driver's license today.

3 Reading

A Read Lina's e-mail to her new e-pal.

> E-Mail
>
> Hi, Louisa!
>
> My name is Lina. I'm 16 years old. I'm from India. I'm a student at Howard International School in New York City. It's September, and I'm happy to be back in school. Last summer, I visited my family in India. I hung out with my best friend. We went traveling to some smaller cities in India. This year, I'm going to try some new things at school. I'd like to join the drama club, but I probably won't. I'm very shy. I'm going to learn how to play the violin. I have to study very hard this year to get good grades. I'll probably stay at Howard International School next year. I love it here!
>
> Please write soon!
> Lina

B Answer the questions.

1. Where's Lina from? _____
2. What did she do last summer? _____
3. Is Lina going to join the drama club this year? Why or why not? _____
   _____
4. What instrument is Lina going to learn how to play? _____
5. What else does Lina have to do this year? _____

4 Writing

Imagine that you are writing for the first time to your e-pal. Complete the information about yourself. Then write an e-mail about yourself to your e-pal.

What's your name? _____ How old are you? _____
Where are you from? _____ Where do you go to school? _____
What did you do last summer? _____
Do you want to try anything new at school this year? _____
What after-school activities are you going to join? _____
What's something you have to do this year? _____

> Hello, _____ !
> My name's _____ .
> _____
> _____
> _____
> _____

Photocopiable

Unit 3 Plans

1 Word work

The underlined words belong in other places in each e-mail.
Write the words where they belong.

1 E-Mail

From: Max
To: Ben
Subject: Sunday

Hi, Ben!

Come and spend Sunday with me. We can play biking, rent a kite, fly a DVD, or go computer games.

Max

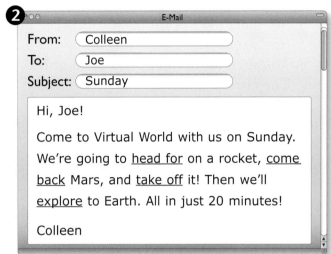

2 E-Mail

From: Colleen
To: Joe
Subject: Sunday

Hi, Joe!

Come to Virtual World with us on Sunday. We're going to head for on a rocket, come back Mars, and take off it! Then we'll explore to Earth. All in just 20 minutes!

Colleen

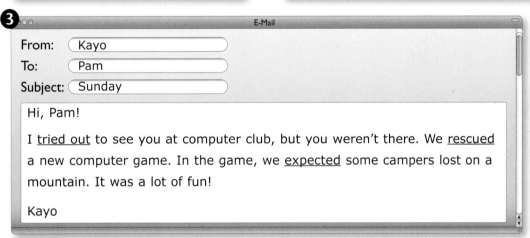

3 E-Mail

From: Kayo
To: Pam
Subject: Sunday

Hi, Pam!

I tried out to see you at computer club, but you weren't there. We rescued a new computer game. In the game, we expected some campers lost on a mountain. It was a lot of fun!

Kayo

2 What's wrong?

Correct the sentences. There is **one** mistake in each sentence.

1. **A** Would you like visit the museum? *Would you like to visit the museum?*
   B Sure, I love to.

2. **A** Can I to stay out until 11:00?
   B Sorry, that's fine.

3. If the weather will be nice, I'll go out.

4. I not fly my kite if it rains.

5. **A** You could order a pizza?
   B I'd love to, but I don't.

Unit 4 People

1 Word work

Complete the crossword puzzle.

Across

3. My mom always thinks about other people. She's really _____.
6. Miguel and Ana keep things in order. They're _____.
7. Bobby never remembers things. He's very _____.

Down

1. My sister is very _____. She never tells anyone what you tell her.
2. I love parties and meeting people. I'm very _____.
4. Alice likes to do things on her own. She's very _____.
5. Artists are usually very _____. They have good imaginations.

(Crossword: 3 Across = T H O U G H T F U L)

2 What's wrong?

Check (✓) the correct sentence.

1. ☐ Chatting online is one of my favorite activities.
   ☐ Chat online is one of my favorite activities.

2. ☐ I enjoy find interesting new sites.
   ☐ I enjoy finding interesting new sites.

3. ☐ I have an e-pal who lives in Cape Town.
   ☐ I have an e-pal lives in Cape Town.

4. ☐ Computers are fascinating machines, don't they?
   ☐ Computers are fascinating machines, aren't they?

5. ☐ My sister is hardworking. I do, too.
   ☐ My sister is hardworking. I am, too.

6. ☐ He lives in San Francisco, isn't he?
   ☐ He lives in San Francisco, doesn't he?

Units 3 & 4

1 Vocabulary

A Read the clues. Then write the words.

1. Travel around a place to learn about it: _____explore_____
2. Leave the ground and start flying: _____
3. Think that something will happen: _____
4. Return: _____
5. Move toward a place: _____
6. Save someone in danger: _____
7. Surprise very much: _____
8. Test something by using it: _____

B Read the sentences. Then write the words from the box.

| ☐ bad-tempered | ☑ forgetful | ☐ independent | ☐ thoughtful |
| ☐ creative | ☐ hardworking | ☐ outgoing | ☐ trustworthy |

1. Anthony never remembers things. _____forgetful_____
2. My best friend always sends me a letter on my birthday. _____
3. Sam is very honest and always does what he says he'll do. _____
4. Hannah makes all her own clothing. It's beautiful! _____
5. Elaine is always angry about something. _____
6. He's so friendly. He loves to talk to people and isn't shy. _____
7. She gets really good grades. She studies a lot. _____
8. Sue likes to do things on her own and without a lot of help. _____

C Complete the sentences with the words in the box.

| ☐ doing chores | ☐ going to the movies | ☐ playing the piano |
| ☐ doing homework online | ☐ playing board games | ☐ playing soccer |

1. _____ is one thing I hate. I think cleaning my room is so boring!
2. _____ is one of my favorite weekend activities. I play on a team with kids from my school.
3. My aunt and I love _____ when she visits. We play for hours. She always wins!
4. _____ is a great thing. I send it to my teacher, and she checks it and sends it back. It's so fast!
5. My favorite after-school activity is _____ . I can play two pieces of music by Chopin.
6. _____ is great to do on the weekends. I've seen three new movies in three weeks!

2 Language focus

A Look at the pictures. Then write sentences with *If* and *will / won't.*

1. _____

   _____

2. _____

   _____

3. _____

   _____

4. _____

   _____

B Complete the sentences with *before, while,* or *after.*

(1) _____ I'm at the library, I'm going to find information for my project. I'm going to go to the movies with my friends (2) _____ I finish my project. (3) _____ I give my project to the teacher, I'm going to check it for mistakes. I'm going to work hard (4) _____ I'm at the library.

C Complete the conversations with the words in the box.

☐ I am, too.   ☐ I don't, either.   ☐ I do, too.   ☐ I'm not, either.

1. **A** I don't like hot dogs.   3. **A** I love dancing.
   B _____   **B** _____

2. **A** I'm usually friendly.   4. **A** I'm not outgoing.
   B _____   **B** _____

D Match the sentences to the correct tag questions.

1. They're from Japan, _____   a. isn't he?

2. She lives in Peru, _____   b. don't you?

3. He's her boyfriend, _____   c. aren't you?

4. You like classical music, _____   d. doesn't she?

5. You're 17, _____   e. aren't they?

6. We're good at English, _____   f. aren't we?

3 Reading

A Read Shannon's e-mail to her new e-pal, Marie.

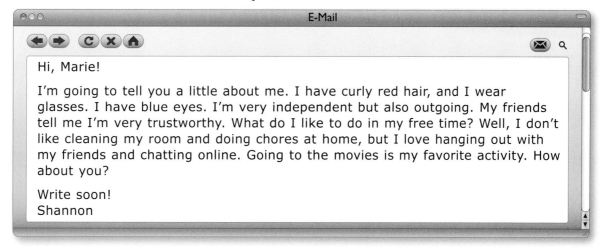

Hi, Marie!

I'm going to tell you a little about me. I have curly red hair, and I wear glasses. I have blue eyes. I'm very independent but also outgoing. My friends tell me I'm very trustworthy. What do I like to do in my free time? Well, I don't like cleaning my room and doing chores at home, but I love hanging out with my friends and chatting online. Going to the movies is my favorite activity. How about you?

Write soon!
Shannon

B Are these sentences true or false? Check (✓) T (true) or F (false).

	T	F
1. Shannon has straight red hair.	☐	☐
2. She doesn't like doing chores at home.	☐	☐
3. She doesn't have any friends.	☐	☐
4. She likes chatting online.	☐	☐
5. Her favorite activity is going to the mall with her friends.	☐	☐

4 Writing

Imagine that you are writing another e-mail to a new e-pal. Complete the information about yourself. Then write an e-mail about yourself to your e-pal.

Describe your appearance. _____

Describe your personality. _____

Describe your favorite free-time activities. _____

What do you enjoy doing? _____

What don't you enjoy doing? _____

Hi, _____ !

_____ . _____

_____

_____

_____

_____

_____

_____

Unit 5 Entertainment

1 Word work

Choose the correct word or words to complete each verb phrase.

1. sign _____*autographs*_____ (money / a friend / autographs)

2. record _____ (chores / a song / autographs)

3. give _____ (exercises / a game / interviews)

4. become _____ (plans / a big star / a song)

5. have _____ (a hit TV show / sports / this week)

6. make _____ (autographs / a charity / a movie)

7. win _____ (a hit TV show / a live audience / a great award)

8. support _____ (the piano / a charity / a great award)

9. entertain _____ (a live audience / a movie / a cake)

2 What's wrong?

Write a check (✓) if the sentence is correct and an X if it is incorrect. For incorrect sentences, write the correct sentences.

_X_ 1. How long you have lived here?
   How long have you lived here?

____ 2. Has you ever been to a rock concert?
   _____

____ 3. Who has met a famous TV star?
   _____

____ 4. I've been a fan of Brad Pitt for two years.
   _____

____ 5. How much time have you known him?
   _____

____ 6. I've done any fun activities this week.
   _____

____ 7. We're studied French since September.
   _____

____ 8. They haven't acted in a movie.
   _____

Photocopiable

Unit 6 Experiences

1 Word work

Circle the correct verb to complete the sentences.

1. Beth likes to (go / explore) rock climbing every weekend.
2. Melissa likes to (try / start) new foods.
3. It's fun to (dye / explore) a cave.
4. Soo's friends (sing / go) karaoke every weekend.
5. Adriana doesn't like to (dye / ride) her hair.
6. Mrs. Rodriguez's children never (try / go out) without permission.
7. I want to (go / ride) skydiving.
8. Carmen and Li want to (ride / dye) a motorcycle.
9. They want to (explore / start) a rock band.

2 What's wrong?

Correct the students' notes. There is <u>one</u> mistake in one of the sentences in each message.

1
Look at the
teacher's hair!
She's done
something weird
to it, haven't she?
M.

She's done something
weird to it, hasn't she?

2
You watched TV
last night, don't
you?
Amanda

_____

_____

3
Look at Kate's shoes.
I've seen never shoes
like that.
Aren't they cool?
Maria

_____

_____

4
I've gone to the
movies last night.
I saw the new
Tom Cruise
movie.
R.

_____

_____

5
This exercise is
difficult! I haven't
finished it
already.
L.

_____

_____

6
Bob tells Rita
about her surprise
party, didn't he? Now
we have to change
the date.
Amy

_____

_____

Units 5 & 6

1 Vocabulary

A Circle the correct word to complete each verb phrase.

1. (play / do) chores
2. (make / play) the piano
3. (do / make) friends
4. (make / play) plans

5. (play / work) a game
6. (do / play) homework
7. (make / try) money
8. (play / make) a cake

B Match the sentences to the correct pictures.

1. Study a foreign language. ____
2. Get a job. ____
3. Vacation in a foreign country. ____

4. Turn 16 years old. ____
5. Get a driver's license. ____
6. Get a college degree. ____

C Complete the sentences with the words in the box.

| ☐ become | ☐ entertain | ☑ give | ☐ have | ☐ make | ☐ record | ☐ sign |

1. My favorite actor doesn't like to _give_ interviews. He never talks to reporters.

2. Some stars don't like to _____ autographs.

3. I've always wanted to _____ a movie. Maybe I can write one!

4. My best friend is a good singer. He's going to _____ one of his songs for me!

5. To _____ a hit TV show, you have to do something interesting for young people.

6. I wouldn't like to _____ a live audience. I would be really nervous.

7. This new singer is really good. I think he's going to _____ a big star!

2 Language focus

A Write the questions in the present perfect.

1. **Q:** _____
   A: Yes, I have. I've gotten Pink's autograph.

2. **Q:** _____
   A: I've had my new computer since Monday.

3. **Q:** _____
   A: Yes, he has. He went skydiving last weekend.

4. **Q:** _____
   A: She's had short hair for two years.

5. **Q:** _____
   A: I've read three books this week.

B It's 2009. Look at the chart of Stella's life. Are the sentences true or false? Check (✓) T (true) or F (false).

What	When
get a driver's license	2010
ride a motorcycle	
go rock climbing	2006, 2008

What	When
go skydiving	2006, 2008, 2010
go to Europe	2010
dye my hair	

	T	F
1. Stella hasn't gotten her driver's license yet.	☐	☐
2. She's already gone rock climbing once.	☐	☐
3. She's already gone skydiving.	☐	☐
4. She's been to Europe three times since 2006.	☐	☐
5. She's never ridden a motorcycle.	☐	☐
6. She's never dyed her hair.	☐	☐

C One sentence in each pair is correct. Check (✓) it.

1. ☐ Tomas has learned a lot since last year.
   ☐ Tomas learned a lot since last year.

2. ☐ You have taken dance lessons for eight years, didn't you?
   ☐ You have taken dance lessons for eight years, haven't you?

3. ☐ She has lived in the same city for ten years, hasn't she?
   ☐ She lived in the same city for ten years, hasn't she?

4. ☐ I've read two magazines last night.
   ☐ I read two magazines last night.

5. ☐ We sang karaoke five times.
   ☐ We've sung karaoke five times.

6. ☐ The first place we stayed in New York was noisy.
   ☐ The first place we stayed in New York has been noisy.

3 Reading

A Read about Gordon.

My name's Gordon. I'm 17 years old, and I guess I've done some fun things in my life. Actually, I think I've done a lot for someone my age. I got my driver's license this year, but I haven't bought my own car yet. I've been to several Taylor Swift concerts, but I haven't gotten her autograph. She's my favorite musician. I learned how to play the guitar last year, and I've written a lot of songs. I'd love to record some of them one day, but that hasn't happened yet. I've started a band with some of my friends. We haven't performed yet, but we want to perform next year.

B Read the sentences. Then check (✓) T (true), F (false), or NI (no information).

	T	F	NI
1. Gordon is British.	☐	☐	☐
2. He has his own car.	☐	☐	☐
3. His favorite musician is Taylor Swift.	☐	☐	☐
4. He learned to play the drums last year.	☐	☐	☐
5. He would like to perform with his band.	☐	☐	☐

4 Writing

Complete the information about yourself. Then write about what you have done and not done in your life so far.

What's your name? _____

How old are you? _____

What have you done so far? _____

What haven't you done so far? _____

What are your hopes for the future? _____

My name's _____ . _____

_____

_____

_____

_____

_____

Photocopiable

Unit 7 Teen Time

1 Word work

Which adjectives describe people? Which adjectives describe events? Which ones describe both? Complete the chart. Check (✓) the correct boxes.

	People	Events	Both
active	☐	☐	☐
artistic	☐	☐	☐
athletic	☐	☐	☐
bad-tempered	☐	☐	☐
excellent	☐	☐	☐
forgetful	☐	☐	☐
friendly	☐	☐	☐
hardworking	☐	☐	☐
kind	☐	☐	☐
lazy	☐	☐	☐

	People	Events	Both
messy	☐	☐	☐
musical	☐	☐	☐
outgoing	☐	☐	☐
scary	☐	☐	☐
serious	☐	☐	☐
smart	☐	☐	☐
strong	☐	☐	☐
thoughtful	☐	☐	☐
thrilling	☐	☐	☐
trustworthy	☐	☐	☐

2 What's wrong?

The underlined words belong in other sentences. Write the words where they belong.

1. My mom is the <u>better</u> thoughtful person I've ever met. She's always very kind. _most_

2. Math isn't as difficult <u>than</u> science. Math is easier than science. _____

3. I'd rather watch soccer <u>ever</u> volleyball. Volleyball isn't as interesting for me. _____

4. Freddie loves to talk. He's the most outgoing person I've <u>as</u> met. _____

5. I'd rather read a book than a magazine. I like books <u>worst</u> than magazines. _____

6. *Blue* is a better movie than *Waterfall*. *Waterfall* is the <u>most</u> movie of the year. _____

Unit 8 Dreams and Reality

1 Word work

Complete the sentences with the words in the box.

☐ break a promise   ☑ eavesdrop   ☐ jaywalk   ☐ litter
☐ cheat on a test   ☐ gossip   ☐ lie   ☐ trespass

1. Hey! Stop listening to our conversation. You shouldn't
   _____eavesdrop_____ .

2. You're saying things that aren't true! You shouldn't
   _____ .

3. You said you would babysit – and now you won't?
   You shouldn't _____ .

4. Stop talking about him! You shouldn't
   _____ .

5. Hey! You need to pick up your trash. You shouldn't
   _____ .

6. Please get out of my yard! You shouldn't
   _____ .

7. Don't cross the street in the middle of the block. You shouldn't _____ .

8. Don't look at her answers! You shouldn't _____ .

2 What's wrong?

One sentence in each pair is correct. Check (✓) it.

1. ☐ If she could buy anything she wanted, she buy a house in the mountains.
   ☐ If she could buy anything she wanted, she'd buy a house in the mountains.

2. ☐ If I see someone littering, I'd ask him to throw the garbage in the trash can.
   ☐ If I saw someone littering, I'd ask him to throw the garbage in the trash can.

3. ☐ I want being a journalist to report on important events.
   ☐ I want to be a journalist to report on important events.

4. ☐ I met someone really special at a party last month.
   ☐ I met anyone really special at a party last month.

5. ☐ They haven't been somewhere interesting this year.
   ☐ They haven't been anywhere interesting this year.

Photocopiable   © Cambridge University Press 2010

Units 7 & 8

1 Vocabulary

A Write the word from the box that means the opposite.

☐ awful   ☑ dangerous   ☐ difficult   ☐ excellent   ☐ hardworking   ☐ messy   ☐ thrilling

1. safe _dangerous_
2. very bad _____
3. clean _____
4. easy _____
5. nice _____
6. boring _____
7. lazy _____

B Read the clues. Then write the words.

1. Talk about other people's lives: _gossip_
2. Say things that are not true: _____
3. Listen in secret to someone's conversation: _____
4. Enter a private place without permission: _____
5. Leave paper or garbage around carelessly: _____
6. Copy someone's answers: _____
7. Not do something you said you'd do: _____
8. Cross the street in the middle of the block: _____

C Complete the sentences with the words in the box.

☐ creates programs   ☐ help sick animals   ☐ report on events and people   ☐ travel in outer space
☐ fly planes   ☑ make furniture   ☐ solve mysteries   ☐ write stories

1. I'd really like to _make furniture_ , like chairs and tables.

2. My brother loves cats and dogs. He really likes to _____ .

3. We really enjoy our English class. We read a lot of interesting books and _____ .

4. My friend works for a magazine. It's a fun job. She has to _____ .

5. My friend loves computers. She _____ to help with homework.

6. My uncle used to _____ . He was a pilot.

7. I've always wanted to _____ . I'd love to go to the moon!

8. My favorite books are about detectives. I like it when they _____ .

Photocopiable

2 Language focus

A Write sentences using the superlative form of each
adjective + *I've ever.*

1. boring + movie + see *It's the most boring movie I've ever seen.*
2. handsome + boy + meet _____
3. difficult + test + take _____
4. long + book + read _____
5. messy + apartment + visit _____
6. big + horse + ride _____
7. good + pizza + eat _____

B Write sentences to describe the pictures. Use the comparatives *as . . . as* for
number 1 and *not as . . . as* for number 2.

❶

Mark   Bob

_____

❷

JANE   TINA

_____

C Circle the correct words to complete each verb phrase.

1. If I had a million dollars, (I'm so happy / I'd be so happy / I will be happy).
2. If I could meet anyone, (I'm meeting / I meet / I'd meet) my favorite movie star.

D One sentence in each pair is correct. Check (✓) it.

1. ☐ Has he been somewhere thrilling this year?
   ☐ Has he been anywhere thrilling this year?

2. ☐ I haven't done anything interesting.
   ☐ I haven't done something interesting.

3. ☐ She did something great last week.
   ☐ She did anything great last week.

4. ☐ Have you gone somewhere fun this year?
   ☐ Have you gone anywhere fun this year?

5. ☐ I don't know anyone from England.
   ☐ I don't know someone from England.

6. ☐ We drank anything delicious last night.
   ☐ We drank something delicious last night.

3 Reading

A Read about Marie.

My name's Marie. I'm 16 years old. I'm from France. I spent a semester in the U.S. I studied at a university in Texas. It's the scariest thing I've ever done. I knew my English was good. I'm really hardworking and one of the best students in my English class. But when I arrived in Texas, I was scared. I thought my English was awful. I thought I wasn't as good as the other students from other countries. This was the most difficult part of my stay. But after a few weeks, things were better. I made friends. I had as many friends as I did in France, maybe more! Going to study in Texas was the best thing I've ever done, even if it was also the most difficult.

B Are these sentences true or false? Check (✓) T (true) or F (false).

	T	F
1. Marie is French.	☐	☐
2. She studied English in France.	☐	☐
3. She was scared when she arrived in Texas.	☐	☐
4. The first part of her stay in Texas was easy.	☐	☐
5. She thinks that going to study in Texas was the worst mistake she's ever made.	☐	☐

4 Writing

Complete the information about yourself. Then write about a difficult or scary experience you have had.

What's your name? _____

Where are you from? _____

What's the scariest experience you've ever had? _____

Describe the experience. How did you feel? _____

Did things get better? Worse? _____

How do you feel about the experience now? _____

My name's _____ . _____

_____

_____

_____

_____

_____

Answer Key for Extra Practice

Note: Multiple answers in a single sentence or by a single speaker are separated by a semicolon (;). Alternative answers are separated by a slash (/).

Unit 1 • My Life

1 Word work

1. break
2. move
3. do
4. get
5. goes
6. join
7. learn
8. meet
9. make
10. play
11. start
12. take
13. visit
14. win

2 What's wrong?

It <u>was</u> nice to chat with you yesterday.
<u>I'd</u> like to know your name.
So you <u>went</u> to Miami last summer.
Where <u>did</u> you stay?
Did you <u>go</u> to the salsa festival?
How many days did you <u>spend</u> there?
I <u>met</u> a nice guy there.
<u>Are you</u> going to be online later?

Unit 2 • The Future

1 Word work

1. join
2. make; get
3. travel
4. be
5. go
6. learn
7. take
8. be
9. go
10. play

2 What's wrong?

1. English will probably become the most important subject at school next year.
2. Computers won't replace teachers in the future.
3. Many students might not want to study in online schools.
4. E-books might become popular soon.
5. Most people probably won't shop online for food in the future.
6. I'm going to go to college next year.

Extra Practice • 1 & 2

1 Vocabulary

A Dear Juan,
Hi! How are you? I'm writing to tell you about my last year at school. It was a very busy and exciting year for me. First, you know that my family and I <u>moved</u> to the city. I was very sad to leave my friends, so my parents <u>got</u> a pet to cheer me up. He's a cute little dog! His name is Toby. I <u>joined</u> the soccer team at school and made some new friends. Then last summer, we <u>went</u> on a trip to the U.S. We <u>ate</u> American food every day. I was so happy because I <u>learned</u> English in school. We <u>met</u> my best friend in New York City for two days. It was great!
Write soon.
Rita

B
1. e
2. a
3. f
4. c
5. d
6. b

C
1. join
2. be
3. take
4. learn
5. be

2 Language Focus

A
1. Henry used to have long hair. Now he has short hair.
2. Henry used to do karate. Now he plays tennis.
3. Henry used to play the guitar. Now he plays the violin.
4. Henry used to have one dog. Now he has three dogs.
5. Henry used to eat cookies. Now he eats fruit.

B Last week I was at home with my little brother. It was late at night, and I <u>was studying</u> English in my room. My brother <u>was sleeping</u> in his room. Suddenly, I <u>heard</u> a noise. I looked out of the window. It <u>was raining</u>, and the wind <u>was blowing</u>. I <u>was</u> scared. But then I heard the noise again – it was a quiet knocking on my door! Suddenly the door <u>opened</u> and my brother <u>jumped</u> into my room. I <u>was</u> really surprised!

C 1. Andre might go to France.
2. Marcia probably won't become a soccer player.
3. Juan isn't going to get a driver's license today.

3 Reading

B 1. She's from India.
2. She visited her family in India.
3. No, she probably won't. She's very shy.
4. She's going to learn how to play the violin.
5. She has to study very hard this year to get good grades.

4 Writing

Answers will vary. Possible answer:
Hello, Ben!
My name's Hugo. I'm 15 years old. I'm from Germany. I'm a student at Kirkwood High School in Denver, Colorado. Last summer, I traveled all over Arizona and Nevada with my family. We visited the Grand Canyon in Arizona, and we stayed in a houseboat on Lake Powell, Nevada. This year I'm going to try something new at school. I want to join the computer club. I got a new computer for my birthday. I want to learn how to design Web sites. I have to practice the violin more this year. I want to play in the school concert at the end of the year.

Unit 3 • Plans

1 Word work

1. We can <u>go</u> biking, <u>fly</u> a kite, <u>rent</u> a DVD , or <u>play</u> computer games.

2. We're going to <u>take off</u> on a rocket, <u>head</u> <u>for</u> Mars, and <u>explore it</u>! Then we'll <u>come</u> <u>back</u> to Earth.

3. I <u>expected</u> to see you at computer club, but you weren't there. We <u>tried out</u> a new computer game. In the game, we <u>rescued</u> some campers lost on a mountain.

2 What's wrong?

1. **A** Would you like <u>to</u> visit the museum?
   B Sure, <u>I'd</u> love to.
2. **A** Can I stay out until 11:00?
   B (<u>Sure,</u> / <u>Yes,</u>) that's fine.
3. If the weather <u>is</u> nice, I'll go out.
4. I <u>won't</u> fly my kite if it rains.
5. **A** <u>Could you</u> order a pizza?
   B I'd love to, but I <u>can't</u>.

Unit 4 • People

1 Word work

Across
3. THOUGHTFUL
6. ORGANIZED
7. FORGETFUL

Down
1. TRUSTWORTHY
2. OUTGOING
4. INDENPENDENT
5. CREATIVE

2 What's wrong?

1. Chatting online is one of my favorite activities.
2. I enjoy finding interesting new sites.
3. I have an e-pal who lives in Cape Town.
4. Computers are fascinating machines, aren't they?
5. My sister is hardworking. I am, too.
6. He lives in San Francisco, doesn't he?

Extra Practice • 3 & 4

1 Vocabulary

A 1. explore
2. take off
3. expect
4. come back
5. head for
6. rescue
7. amaze
8. try out

B 1. forgetful
2. thoughtful
3. trustworthy
4. creative
5. bad-tempered
6. outgoing
7. hardworking
8. independent

C 1. Doing chores
2. Playing soccer
3. playing board games
4. Doing homework online
5. playing the piano
6. Going to the movies

2 Language Focus

A 1. If (the weather is / it's) (nice / sunny), she won't watch TV.
2. If he's not feeling well, he won't go to school.
3. If it snows, she'll go skiing.
4. If he has money, he'll buy a (new CD / CD).

B 1. While
2. after
3. Before
4. while

C 1. I don't, either.
2. I am, too.
3. I do, too.
4. I'm not, either.

D 1. e
2. d
3. a
4. b
5. c
6. f

3 Reading

B 1. F
2. T
3. F
4. T
5. F

4 Writing

Answers will vary. Possible answer:
Hi, Sandra!
I'm going to tell you a little about me. I'm from Boston, Massachusetts. I have long, straight, brown hair. I have brown eyes, and I don't wear glasses. I'm outgoing and creative. My family and friends say I'm very thoughtful. I do lots of things in my free time. I love chatting online with my best friend, Allison. I also like listening to music and doing crossword puzzles. I don't like doing my math homework! My favorite activity is shopping for clothes.

Unit 5 • Entertainment

1 Word work

1. autographs
2. a song
3. interviews
4. a big star
5. a hit TV show
6. a movie
7. a great award
8. a charity
9. a live audience

2 What's wrong?

1. How long have you lived here?
2. Have you ever been to a rock concert?
3. ✓
4. ✓
5. How long have you known him?
6. I haven't done any fun activities this week. / I've done some fun activities this week.
7. We've studied French since September.
8. ✓

Unit 6 • Experiences

1 Word work

1. go
2. try
3. explore
4. sing
5. dye
6. go out
7. go
8. ride
9. start

2 What's wrong?

1. She's done something weird to it, <u>hasn't</u> she?
2. You watched TV last night, <u>didn't</u> you?
3. I've <u>never seen</u> shoes like that.
4. <u>I went</u> to the movies last night.
5. I haven't finished it <u>yet</u>.
6. Bob <u>told</u> Rita about her surprise party, didn't he?

Extra Practice • 5 & 6

1 Vocabulary

A
1. do	5. play
2. play	6. do
3. make	7. make
4. make	8. make

B
1. b	4. d
2. f	5. a
3. e	6. c

C
1. give
2. sign
3. make
4. record
5. have
6. entertain
7. become

2 Language focus

A
1. Have you ever gotten a star's autograph?
2. How long have you had your new computer?
3. Has he ever gone skydiving?
4. How long has she had short hair?
5. How many books have you read this week?

B
1. T
2. F
3. T
4. F
5. T
6. T

C
1. Tomas has learned a lot since last year.
2. You have taken dance lessons for eight years, haven't you?
3. She has lived in the same city for ten years, hasn't she?
4. I read two magazines last night.
5. We've sung karaoke five times.
6. The first place we stayed in New York was noisy.

3 Reading

B
1. NI
2. F
3. T
4. F
5. T

4 Writing

Answers will vary. Possible answer:
My name's Bruno. I'm 16 years old. I haven't done too many interesting things in my life. Mostly I go to school and do homework. I had a job last summer at a swimming pool. I made a lot of money, but I haven't bought anything yet. I'm saving my money to buy a nice car next year. I've studied Italian for four years, but I haven't been to Italy. I'd like to visit Rome and Florence. I want to see all the beautiful buildings, and I want to eat some great Italian food.

Unit 7 • Teen Time

1 Word work

active: people
artistic: both
athletic: both
bad-tempered: people
excellent: both
forgetful: people
friendly: people
hardworking: people
kind: people
lazy: people
messy: people / both (in the case of specific events, such as food-eating contests)
musical: both
outgoing: people
scary: both
serious: both
smart: people
strong: people
thoughtful: people
thrilling: events
trustworthy: people

2 What's wrong?

1. most
2. as
3. than
4. ever
5. better
6. worst

Unit 8 • Dreams and Reality

1 Word work

1. eavesdrop
2. lie
3. break a promise
4. gossip
5. litter
6. trespass
7. jaywalk
8. cheat on a test

2 What's wrong?

1. If she could buy anything she wanted, she'd buy a house in the mountains.
2. If I saw someone littering, I'd ask him to throw the garbage in the trash can.
3. I want to be a journalist to report on important events.
4. I met someone really special at a party last month.
5. They haven't been anywhere interesting this year.

Extra Practice • 7 & 8

1 Vocabulary

A
1. dangerous
2. excellent
3. messy
4. difficult
5. awful
6. thrilling
7. hardworking

B
1. gossip
2. lie
3. eavesdrop
4. trespass
5. litter
6. cheat on a test
7. break a promise
8. jaywalk

C
1. make furniture
2. help sick animals
3. write stories
4. report on events and people
5. creates programs
6. fly planes
7. travel in outer space
8. solve mysteries

2 Language focus

A
1. It's the most boring movie I've ever seen.
2. He's the most handsome boy I've ever met.
3. It's the most difficult test I've ever taken.
4. It's the longest book I've ever read.
5. It's the messiest apartment I've ever visited.
6. It's the biggest horse I've ever ridden.
7. It's the best pizza I've ever eaten.

B
1. Mark is as tall as Bob.
2. Tina isn't as thin as Jane.

C
1. I'd be so happy.
2. I'd meet

D
1. Has he been anywhere thrilling this year?
2. I haven't done anything interesting.
3. She did something great last week.
4. Have you gone anywhere fun this year?
5. I don't know anyone from England.
6. We drank something delicious last night.

3 Reading

B
1. T
2. T
3. T
4. F
5. F

4 Writing

Answers will vary. Possible answer:
My name's Juana. I'm 17 years old. I'm from Texas. The scariest thing I've ever done is act in a school play. I wanted to be in the school play last year. I tried out for a small part, and I got it! At first, I had trouble remembering my lines. I didn't think I was as good as all the other kids. Then Mrs. Turner, the play advisor, told me to relax and enjoy myself. Things got a little better. On the night of the play, I forgot all my lines right before I went on stage. I remembered Mrs. Turner's advice. I went on stage, and I only forgot a few of my lines. Acting on stage was a scary experience, but I had a lot of fun. I'd like to do it again.

Introduction to Extra Speaking Practice

Included in this section is a photocopiable package of Extra Speaking Practice. This package contains eight Extra Speaking Practice worksheets, one for each unit in *Connect*. These Extra Speaking Practice worksheets, most of which are interactive conversations, give students an additional opportunity to practice and personalize the new language and skills they learned in each unit.

Features of Extra Speaking Practice

- The content of Extra Speaking Practice is strictly limited to the language and skills presented and practiced in the lessons in each unit of the Student's Book.
- The focus of each Extra Speaking Practice exercise is on the specific language and skills of the corresponding unit, but it does assume knowledge of previous units' content.
- Many exercise types in the Extra Speaking Practice, such as completing conversations, asking and answering questions, speaking with classmates, and playing guessing games, are similar to those in the lessons, while others extend the activity types by giving students multiple opportunities to practice interactive role plays.
- The Extra Speaking Practice worksheets provide students with an opportunity to practice the vocabulary and grammar in each unit in a natural context while fostering communication and community in the classroom.

Assigning Extra Speaking Practice worksheets

- These worksheets are intended to be done in class, usually in pairs.
- Make a copy of the Extra Speaking Practice worksheet(s) for each student in your class.
- Have students practice the conversations in pairs or in small groups.
- Walk around and help as needed.
- Check answers with the class.
- Invite volunteers to read their conversations to the class.

List of Extra Speaking Practice Exercises			
Unit 1	Page T-168	Unit 5	Page T-172
Unit 2	Page T-169	Unit 6	Page T-173
Unit 3	Page T-170	Unit 7	Page T-174
Unit 4	Page T-171	Unit 8	Page T-175
		Answer Key	Page T-176

Unit 1 My Life

A Look at the chart. Then interview your classmates.
Find one classmate who says yes for a category.
Write his or her name. Do not write the same name twice.

> Did you go to the beach last summer?

> Yes, I did.

> Would you like to study Web design?

> Yes, I would.

Find someone who . . .	Classmates
went to the beach last summer	_____
would like to study Web design	_____
wants to join a sports team	_____
used to live in a different city	_____
is going to go on a trip this year	_____
made new friends last summer	_____
would like to take music lessons	_____
was traveling at the end of the summer	_____
used to look very different	_____
isn't going to go on a trip this year	_____

B Tell your classmates about the people in your chart.

> Roberto went to the beach last summer. Keiko would like to study Web design. Sue wants to join. . .

Photocopiable © Cambridge University Press 2010

Unit 2 The Future

Classmate 1
Complete the predictions survey for yourself. Then ask a classmate the questions. How many answers are the same? How many are different?

In 50 years, do you think . . . ?	Your answers		Classmate 2's answers	
	Yes	No	Yes	No
1. people will live longer	☐	☐	☐	☐
2. students will study from their homes	☐	☐	☐	☐
3. robots will do most of our work	☐	☐	☐	☐
4. we will completely depend on computers	☐	☐	☐	☐
5. there will be fewer poor people in the world	☐	☐	☐	☐
6. there will be more pollution in the world	☐	☐	☐	☐
7. teens will have more free time than now	☐	☐	☐	☐

In 50 years, do you think people will live longer? Yes, I do.

Same as Classmate 2: _____   Different from Classmate 2: _____

Classmate 2
Complete the predictions survey for yourself. Then ask a classmate the questions. How many answers are the same? How many are different?

In 50 years, do you think . . . ?	Your answers		Classmate 1's answers	
	Yes	No	Yes	No
1. people will fly to work	☐	☐	☐	☐
2. there will still be major sicknesses	☐	☐	☐	☐
3. more people will travel in space	☐	☐	☐	☐
4. students won't learn in classrooms	☐	☐	☐	☐
5. the temperature will be hotter than now	☐	☐	☐	☐
6. people will grow food under the sea	☐	☐	☐	☐
7. teens will be in school more years than they are now	☐	☐	☐	☐

In 50 years, do you think people will fly to work? No, I don't.

Same as Classmate 1: _____   Different from Classmate 1: _____

Unit 3 Plans

The following section is printed upside-down on the page (Classmate 1 portion):

Classmate 2 Yes, I'd love to!

Classmate 1 Well, would you like to go to the mall on Wednesday evening?

Classmate 2 I'd love to, but I can't. I have to have dinner with my grandparents.

Classmate 1 Would you like to go to the movies with me on Monday night?

B Invite Classmate 2. Find an evening you are both free.

1. _____

2. _____

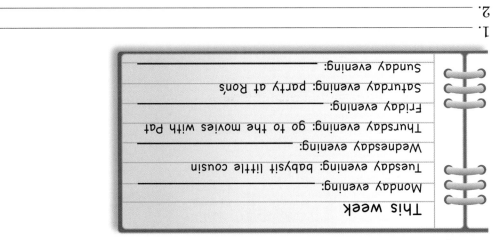

```
This week
Monday evening: _____
Tuesday evening: babysit little cousin
Wednesday evening:
Thursday evening: go to the movies with Pat
Friday evening:
Saturday evening: party at Ron's
Sunday evening: _____
```

A Read your schedule. Then write invitations for two evenings you are free.

Classmate 1

Classmate 2

A Read your schedule. Then write invitations for two evenings you are free.

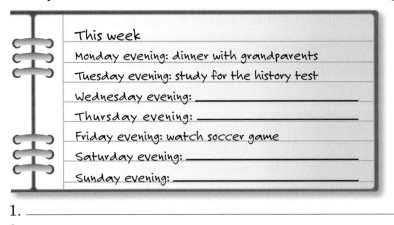

```
This week
Monday evening: dinner with grandparents
Tuesday evening: study for the history test
Wednesday evening: _____
Thursday evening: _____
Friday evening: watch soccer game
Saturday evening: _____
Sunday evening: _____
```

1. _____

2. _____

B Invite Classmate 1. Find an evening you are both free.

Classmate 2 Would you like to go to a baseball game with me Saturday evening?

Classmate 1 I'm sorry, but I can't. I'm going to Ron's party.

Classmate 2 Well, would you like to go the movies on Sunday evening?

Classmate 1 Sure, I'd like to.

Unit 4 People

1 Practice

A Look at the chart. Then interview your classmates. Find one classmate who says yes for a category. Write his or her name. Do not write the same name twice.

Do you enjoy . . . ?	Classmates	Do you enjoy . . . ?	Classmates
listening to classical music	_____	chatting online	_____
going to bed late	_____	going dancing	_____
studying history	_____	staying at home on Saturdays	_____

B Share the information with the class.

> Alejandro enjoys listening to classical music. Maria enjoys going to bed late.

2 Practice

Classmate 1

A Each of these facts is true about either Ashton Kutcher or Will Smith. Write AK or WS next to the fact you think is correct.

1. He and his brother are twins. ___
2. He has a sister, Tausha. ___
3. He has many hit songs. ___
4. His daughter's name is Willow. ___
5. His real name is Christopher. ___

B Check your guesses with Classmate 2. How many did you guess correctly?

> Ashton Kutcher and his brother are twins, aren't they?

> Yes, they are.

Answers for Classmate 2: 1. WS 2. WS 3. AK 4. WS 5. AK

Classmate 2

A Each of these facts is true about either Ashton Kutcher or Will Smith. Write *AK* or *WS* next to the fact you think is correct.

1. He's from Pennsylvania. ___
2. His brother and sister are twins. ___
3. He grew up on a farm. ___
4. He was a rap star. ___
5. He was a model. ___

B Check your guesses with Classmate 1. How many did you guess correctly?

> Will Smith is from Pennsylvania, isn't he?

> Yes, he is.

Answers for Classmate 1: 1. AK 2. AK 3. WS 4. WS 5. AK

Unit 5 Entertainment

Classmate 1

A How good are you at entertainment trivia? Circle the correct answers.

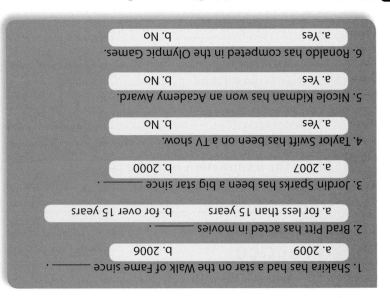

1. Shakira has had a star on the Walk of Fame since _____ .
   a. 2009   b. 2006
2. Brad Pitt has acted in movies _____ .
   a. for over 15 years   b. for less than 15 years
3. Jordin Sparks has been a big star since _____ .
   a. 2007   b. 2000
4. Taylor Swift has been on a TV show.
   a. Yes   b. No
5. Nicole Kidman has won an Academy Award.
   a. Yes   b. No
6. Ronaldo has competed in the Olympic Games.
   a. Yes   b. No

Answers for Classmate 2

1. Yes. Julia Roberts has been on the TV show *Friends*.
2. Anne Hathaway has acted in movies for over five years.
3. Justin Timberlake has been a big star since 1998.
4. Johnny Depp has had a star on the Walk of Fame since 1999.
5. No. Tom Cruise hasn't won an Academy Award.
6. No. David Beckham hasn't competed in the Olympic Games.

B Check your answers with Classmate 2.

(How long has Shakira had a star on the Walk of Fame?)   (Since 2009.)

Classmate 2

A How good are you at entertainment trivia? Circle the correct answers.

1. Julia Roberts has been on a TV show.
   a. Yes   b. No
2. Anne Hathaway has acted in movies _____ .
   a. for less than five years   b. for over five years
3. Justin Timberlake has been a big star since _____ .
   a. 1988   b. 1998
4. Johnny Depp has had a star on the Walk of Fame since _____ .
   a. 1999   b. 2000
5. Tom Cruise has won an Academy Award.
   a. Yes   b. No
6. David Beckham has competed in the Olympic Games.
   a. Yes   b. No

Answers for Classmate 1

1. Shakira has had a star on the Walk of Fame since 2009.
2. Brad Pitt has acted in movies for over 15 years.
3. Jordin Sparks has been a big star since 2007.
4. Yes. Taylor Swift has been on the TV show *CSI: Crime Scene Investigation*.
5. Yes. Nicole Kidman won an Academy Award in 2002.
6. Yes. Ronaldo competed in the Olympic Games in 1996.

B Check your answers with Classmate 1.

(Has Julia Roberts ever been on a TV show?)   (Yes, she has. She was on *Friends*.)

Unit 6 Experiences

1 Practice

Complete the crossword puzzle with the present perfect form of the verbs.
Work with a classmate, and take turns giving each other the cues.

One down. Stay. Have _____ .

Have stayed.

Yes!

Across	Down
3. start	1. stay
5. practice	2. see
6. have	4. ride
7. dye	8. eat
9. sing	10. get
11. take	
12. buy	
13. be	

2 Practice

Look at the survey. Answer the questions about yourself. Then interview a classmate. How many answers are the same? How many are different?

Have you ever . . . ?	Your answers		Your classmate's answers	
	Yes	No	Yes	No
1. dyed your hair	☐	☐	☐	☐
2. gone out without permission	☐	☐	☐	☐
3. tried an unusual food	☐	☐	☐	☐
4. flown a plane	☐	☐	☐	☐
5. had a strange pet	☐	☐	☐	☐
6. ridden a motorcycle	☐	☐	☐	☐
7. read a book in English	☐	☐	☐	☐

Have you ever dyed your hair?

Yes, I have. I dyed it purple last summer!

Same as Classmate: _____   Different from Classmate: _____

Photocopiable

Unit 7 Teen Time

A Complete the sentences about the topics in parentheses. Give your own opinions.

(best singer) *I think Avril Lavigne is the best singer I've ever heard.*

1. (best singer) I think _____ I've ever heard.

2. (actors) I think _____ is a better actor than _____ .

3. (worst TV program) _____ I've ever seen.

4. (movies) I think _____ is worse than _____ .

5. (Web sites) I think _____ is as interesting as _____ .

6. (school subjects) I think _____ isn't as difficult as _____ .

7. (personal qualities) I'd rather be _____ than _____ .

8. (things) I'd rather have a(n) _____ than a(n) _____ .

B Work in groups of three. Share your opinions about the topics in Part A with your group members. Do they agree or disagree? Complete the chart.

> I think Avril Lavigne is the best singer I've ever heard.

> I agree.

> I disagree.

	Classmate 1		Classmate 2	
	Agree	Disagree	Agree	Disagree
1. best singer	☐	☐	☐	☐
2. actors	☐	☐	☐	☐
3. worst TV program	☐	☐	☐	☐
4. movies	☐	☐	☐	☐
5. Web sites	☐	☐	☐	☐
6. school subjects	☐	☐	☐	☐
7. personal qualities	☐	☐	☐	☐
8. things	☐	☐	☐	☐

C Share an opinion you and one other group member have in common.

> Maria and I think Avril Lavigne is the best singer we've ever heard.

Unit 8 Dreams and Reality

A **What would you do in these situations? Write sentences.**

1. A friend calls you at 3:00 a.m.

   _____

2. A classmate wants to copy your homework.

   _____

3. You don't have money to buy something you really want.

   _____

4. The elevator doesn't work. You can't get up to your apartment.

   _____

5. You see a classmate cheating on a test.

   _____

6. You're talking on the phone. A friend is eavesdropping.

   _____

B **Find classmates who would do the same thing as you in the situations in Part A.**

What would you do if a friend called you at 3:00 a.m.?

If a friend called me at 3:00 a.m., I'd answer the phone.

Classmates

Situation 1 _____

Situation 2 _____

Situation 3 _____

Situation 4 _____

Situation 5 _____

Situation 6 _____

C **Share some of your results with the class.**

If a friend called Marc or me at 3:00 a.m., we'd answer the phone.

Answer Key for Extra Speaking Practice

Unit 1 • My Life

Answers will vary.

Unit 2 • The Future

Answers will vary.

Unit 3 • Plans

Answers will vary.

Unit 4 • People

1 Practice

Answers will vary.

2 Practice

A Students' guesses may vary.
B Students' questions and answers may vary. The correct information about each actor is on page T-171.

Unit 5 • Entertainment

A Students' answers may vary.
B Students' questions and answers may vary. The correct answers to the trivia items are on page T-172.

Unit 6 • Experiences

1 Practice

Across
  3. STARTED
  5. PRACTICED
  6. HAD
  7. DYED
  9. SUNG
 11. TAKEN
 12. BOUGHT
 13. BEEN

Down
  1. STAYED
  2. SEEN
  4. RIDDEN
  8. EATEN
 10. GOTTEN

2 Practice

Answers will vary.

Unit 7 • Teen Time

Answers will vary.

Unit 8 • Dreams and Reality

Answers will vary.

Introduction to Quizzes

Included in this section is a photocopiable evaluation package. This package contains eight short Quizzes, one for each unit in *Connect*. These Quizzes give students an awareness of their own progress and teachers an awareness of the language points and skills in which their students need further practice.

Features of Quizzes

- The content of the Quizzes is strictly limited to the language and skills presented and practiced in the lessons in each unit of the Student's Book.
- The focus of each Quiz is on the specific language and skills of the corresponding unit, but it does assume knowledge of previous units' content.
- Exercise types in the Quizzes are similar to those in the lessons.
- The focus of the Quizzes is on both vocabulary and language skills.

Giving and scoring Quizzes

- The Quizzes are paper-and-pencil ones. Each unit Quiz is one page. Make a copy of the Quiz for each student in your class.
- Suggested scores are provided for each Quiz. Scores can help students see their own progress and what they need to study. Teachers are encouraged to adapt the use of the Quizzes to their own classroom needs.
- Teachers can also give marks for class participation since this also contributes to student learning.
- Students might retake tests to monitor their progress and build confidence. The goal is for students to do well on the Quizzes, as performance can be both a positive motivator and a confidence builder.

List of Quizzes			
Unit 1	Page T-178	Unit 5	Page T-182
Unit 2	Page T-179	Unit 6	Page T-183
Unit 3	Page T-180	Unit 7	Page T-184
Unit 4	Page T-181	Unit 8	Page T-185
		Answer Key	Page T-186

Unit 1 Quiz

Name: _____

Date: _____

A Circle the correct words to complete the sentences.

1. I'm going to (do / get) karate this year.
2. Do you usually (take / get) good grades?
3. One thing I'd like to do is (join / take) a fan club.
4. She learned to (start / play) a musical instrument when she was four.
5. I want to win (a sports team / an award).
6. My best friend broke (her pet / her leg) when she was running in the park.

12 (2 points each)

B Match. Write the letters.

1. When I was born, _____   a. a big house near a small town.
2. We used to have _____   b. back to the country.
3. I used to walk _____   c. my parents lived in the country.
4. My life changed a lot _____   d. take the bus.
5. I'd like to move _____   e. to school with my friends.
6. I don't live near my school   f. when we moved to the city
   and have to _____   last year.

18 (3 points each)

C Check (✓) the correct questions or answers.

1. **Q:** ☐ Were you going out last night?
        ☐ Did you go out last night?
    A: No, we were at home.

2. **Q:** ☐ Where were you when I called this morning?
        ☐ Where were you calling this morning?
    A: I was in the bathroom!

3. **Q:** Do you have any plans for this weekend?
    A: ☐ I'd like to stay at home and rest.
        ☐ I like to stay at home and rest.

4. **Q:** What's the new science course like?
    A: ☐ It's OK, but we want to do a lot of homework.
        ☐ It's OK, but we have to do a lot of homework.

5. **Q:** Do you like golf?
    A: ☐ I use to like it, but I don't anymore.
        ☐ I used to like it, but I don't anymore.

20 (4 points each)

Quiz Total: _____ out of 50

Photocopiable

Unit 2 Quiz

Name: _____

Date: _____

A **Complete the sentences with the verbs in the box.**

☐ be ☐ get ☐ go to ☐ join ☐ learn ☐ make ☐ play ☐ take ☐ travel

1. I really want to _____ abroad. I'll probably _____ a trip to Europe.
2. I like to _____ badminton. I'll probably _____ the racket club this year.
3. I need to _____ a job and _____ some money. Then I can _____ college.
4. I'd like to _____ a reporter for an international newspaper. I probably need to _____ how to speak another language.

18 (2 points each)

B **Read the predictions. Then check (✓) the sentence that is more logical.**

1. E-books will be very popular.
   ☐ A few people might have them.
   ☐ Everyone will have them.

2. Most students will only study online.
   ☐ They won't study in a classroom.
   ☐ They will probably only study in a classroom.

3. People will live longer.
   ☐ They might not get sick anymore.
   ☐ They might get sick a lot.

4. You won't have to go shopping for food.
   ☐ Your refrigerator might not order food.
   ☐ Your refrigerator will order the food.

5. We won't need to travel.
   ☐ We'll be able to travel "virtually."
   ☐ We won't be able to travel "virtually."

20 (4 points each)

C **Write questions with *be going to*.**

1. **A** (what / do / after high school) _____
   B I'm probably going to go to college.

2. **A** (where / go / this summer) _____
   B I might go to Australia.

3. **A** (how / pay / for college) _____
   B I'll get a job. And my parents will help, too.

12 (4 points each)

Quiz Total: _____ out of 50

Unit 3 **Quiz**

Name: _____

Date: _____

A Circle the correct words to complete Greg's e-mail.

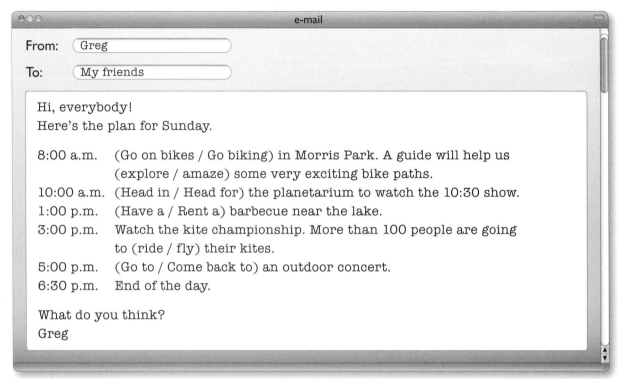

From: Greg

To: My friends

Hi, everybody!
Here's the plan for Sunday.

8:00 a.m.   (Go on bikes / Go biking) in Morris Park. A guide will help us
             (explore / amaze) some very exciting bike paths.
10:00 a.m.   (Head in / Head for) the planetarium to watch the 10:30 show.
1:00 p.m.   (Have a / Rent a) barbecue near the lake.
3:00 p.m.   Watch the kite championship. More than 100 people are going
             to (ride / fly) their kites.
5:00 p.m.   (Go to / Come back to) an outdoor concert.
6:30 p.m.   End of the day.

What do you think?
Greg

18 (3 points each)

B Number the sentences in the correct order.

_____ At about 10:00. If it rains, I'll call you and we can make other plans.
_____ Great.
_____ Tomorrow? If it's sunny, I'll probably go to the beach.
_____ Well, Jane and I are going to drive to Merton Beach. Would you like to join us?
_____ Sure, I'd love to. What time?
_____ What are you going to do tomorrow?

18 (3 points each)

C Circle the correct words to complete the notes.

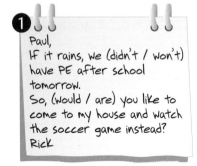

1
Paul,
If it rains, we (didn't / won't)
have PE after school
tomorrow.
So, (would / are) you like to
come to my house and watch
the soccer game instead?
Rick

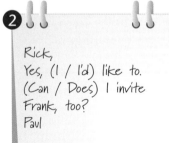

2
Rick,
Yes, (I / I'd) like to.
(Can / Does) I invite
Frank, too?
Paul

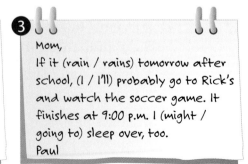

3
Mom,
If it (rain / rains) tomorrow after
school, (I / I'll) probably go to Rick's
and watch the soccer game. It
finishes at 9:00 p.m. I (might /
going to) sleep over, too.
Paul

14 (2 points each)

Quiz Total: _____ out of 50

Photocopiable

Unit 4 Quiz

Name: _____

Date: _____

A Check (✓) the correct words to complete the sentences.

1. My sister writes great stories. She's very ☐ trustworthy. ☐ creative.
2. I didn't take my books to class again. I'm so ☐ thoughtful. ☐ forgetful.
3. I put my CDs in alphabetical order. I'm ☐ organized. ☐ outgoing.
4. My friend travels abroad by herself. She's very ☐ independent. ☐ hardworking.
5. My brother is awful in the morning. He's really ☐ bad-tempered. ☐ trustworthy.

15 (3 points each)

B Complete the conversations with the correct tag questions.

1. **A** They live in Rio de Janeiro, _____?
   B No, they don't. They live in São Paulo.

2. **A** She studies French, _____ ?
   B Yes, she does.

3. **A** You and Karina are friends, _____ ?
   B Yes, we are. We're good friends.

4. **A** Your sister is really outgoing, _____ ?
   B Yes, she is.

5. **A** You have a job, _____ ?
   B No, I don't. I'd like one though.

15 (3 points each)

C Complete the sentences. Write the verbs in the simple present, the simple past, or the gerund -*ing* form.

1. I have a teacher who _____ (speak) Italian. She's really good at it.
   She says _____ (learn) languages is fun.

2. _____ (live) abroad is a good experience. I know someone who
   _____ (live) in Australia for two years. He loved it.

3. A lot of young people like _____ (work) in ski resorts. I have some
   friends who _____ (teach) skiing. They say it was fun.

4. We have a friend who _____ (be) really outgoing. She talks to everyone.
   She even enjoys _____ (chat) with people she doesn't know!

5. _____ (visit) other countries and cultures is important. I have a
   cousin who _____ (travel) all over the world when she was younger.
   She went to 14 countries!

20 (2 points each)

Quiz Total: _____ out of 50

Unit 5 Quiz

Name: _____

Date: _____

A Match the verb to complete the phrase.

1. go to _____
   record _____
   sign _____

   a. a song
   b. autographs
   c. college

2. support _____
   play _____
   win _____

   a. a charity
   b. a great award
   c. the piano

3. entertain _____
   get _____
   make _____

   a. good grades
   b. a movie
   c. a live audience

4. do _____
   become _____
   clean _____

   a. your room
   b. a big star
   c. chores

5. study _____
   go _____
   have _____

   a. a hit TV show
   b. Web design
   c. biking

6. give _____
   meet _____
   live _____

   a. people
   b. alone
   c. interviews

18 (1 point each)

B Match the sentences to the correct responses.

1. I've gotten excellent grades this year. _____
2. Melissa has acted in a movie. _____
3. I haven't done any fun activities this week. _____
4. Kate isn't at home. _____

a. That's too bad.
b. Really? I didn't know she was an actor.
c. Maybe she's gone to the movies.
d. That's great!

8 (2 points each)

C Check (✓) the correct questions and answers.

1. **Q:** ☐ How much has Linda practiced?
   ☐ How long has Linda been on the team?

   A: ☐ Since the beginning of the year.
   ☐ For the beginning of the year.

2. **Q:** ☐ How often do you study French?
   ☐ How long have you studied French?

   A: ☐ Since two years.
   ☐ For two years.

3. **Q:** ☐ Did you see to a Coldplay concert last week?
   ☐ Have you ever been to a Coldplay concert?

   A: ☐ Yes, I have. It's going to be great.
   ☐ Yes, I have. It was great.

4. **Q:** ☐ Has Björk ever acted in movies?
   ☐ Is Björk acting in movies?

   A: ☐ Yes, she has.
   ☐ No, she doesn't.

24 (3 points each)

Quiz Total: _____ out of 50

Photocopiable

Unit 6 Quiz

Name: _____

Date: _____

A Complete the sentences with the verbs.

☐ dye   ☐ ride   ☐ go   ☐ go out   ☐ sing   ☐ start

1. Kevin is learning how to play the guitar. He wants to _____ a rock band.
2. My sister wants to look different. She's going to _____ her hair.
3. I like to _____ karaoke. It's fun.
4. We never _____ without permission. Our parents would be really angry.
5. My friends and I _____ rock climbing every weekend.
6. I'd like to _____ a motorcycle, but my parents said "no."

12 (2 points each)

B Check (✓) the correct questions and answers.

1. **Q:** Have you ever played in a rock band?
   A: ☐ I've never played in a rock band.
   ☐ I've never play in a rock band.

2. **Q:** ☐ Have you ever run in a marathon?
   ☐ Have you never run in a marathon?
   A: I've never run in a marathon.

3. **Q:** Have you ever gone skydiving?
   A: ☐ I'm going skydiving.
   ☐ I've never gone skydiving.

4. **Q:** ☐ Did you ever won a competition?
   ☐ Have you ever won a competition?
   A: No, I haven't.

5. **Q:** ☐ Have you ride a motorcycle yesterday?
   ☐ Have you ever ridden a motorcycle?
   A: No, never.

20 (4 points each)

C Match the sentences.

1. I've already been to Paris. _____
2. I haven't graduated from high school yet. _____
3. We haven't studied Chinese yet. _____
4. We've won four soccer matches this year. _____
5. She's already got a job. _____
6. It's been a fun summer so far. _____

a. I've only been here a year.
b. We haven't lost one yet!
c. I went there last year.
d. But she hasn't started it yet.
e. We've taken three trips.
f. We haven't studied a language in school.

18 (3 points each)

Quiz Total: _____ out of 50

© Cambridge University Press 2010   **Photocopiable**   **Quiz – Unit 6   T-183**

Name: _____

Date: _____

A Circle the correct adjective.

1	2	3	4	5
active	bad-tempered	funny	active	smart
artistic	forgetful	hardworking	hardworking	strong
athletic	friendly	serious	lazy	thoughtful

15 (3 points each)

B Check (✓) the correct sentences.

1. ☐ I rather live in the city than in the country.
   ☐ I'd rather live in the city than in the country.
2. ☐ Who's the most organized person you've ever met?
   ☐ Who's the more organized person you've ever met?
3. ☐ My brother and I like sports, but I'm not as athletic as his.
   ☐ My brother and I like sports, but I'm not as athletic as him.
4. ☐ French cars are not as better as German cars.
   ☐ French cars are not as good as German cars.
5. ☐ This is the worse music I've ever heard.
   ☐ This is the worst music I've ever heard.

15 (3 points each)

C Match the words in columns A, B, and C to make sentences. Write the letters and numbers.

A	B	C
My friends _____ _____	a. the most exciting thing	1. playing computer games.
Yesterday, _____ _____	b. the most hardworking person	2. bad-tempered as my sister.
Would you rather _____ _____	c. I met a girl who is as	3. I've ever done.
My friend Carol is _____ _____	d. be a pop star	4. I've ever met.
Skydiving is _____ _____	e. are good at	5. or a sports star?

20 (2 points each)

Quiz Total: _____ out of 50

 **Quiz**

Name: _____

Date: _____

A Circle the correct words to complete the sentences.

1. A lot of people (lie / jaywalk) here. It's dangerous for drivers.
2. (Gossiping / Littering) about other people isn't good.
3. Have you ever (trespassed / cheated) on a test?
4. I've never (eavesdropped / broken) on someone's conversation.
5. You should never (break / cheat) a promise.
6. Don't (trespass / cheat) in the park when it's closed.

12 (2 points each)

B Match the two parts of the sentences.

1. I'm going to be a veterinarian _____
2. I want to be a journalist _____
3. If he saw a friend cheat on a test, _____
4. If I could choose any job, _____
5. I want to be an author _____
6. My friends and I all want to be pilots _____

a. to report on international events.
b. I'd be a detective.
c. to write books.
d. to fly planes.
e. to help sick animals.
f. he'd tell the teacher.

18 (3 points each)

C Check (✓) the correct answers.

1. **Q:** What would you do if you found a lot of money?
   A: ☐ I'd taken it to the police.
   ☐ I'd take it to the police.

2. **Q:** What would you do if you won a car?
   A: ☐ I give it to my parents.
   ☐ I think I'd give it to my parents.

3. **Q:** What would you do if your best friend broke a promise?
   A: ☐ If she broke a promise, I'd tell her parents.
   ☐ I won't do anything.

4. **Q:** What would you do if you heard people gossiping about you?
   A: ☐ I feel unhappy. I would ask them to stop.
   ☐ I think I'd be unhappy. I'd ask them to stop.

5. **Q:** What would you do if you failed your English test?
   A: ☐ If I fail my test, I will study harder.
   ☐ If I failed my test, I'd study harder.

20 (4 points each)

Quiz Total: _____ out of 50

Answer Key for Quizzes

Note: Multiple answers in a single sentence or by a single speaker are separated by a semicolon (;).

Quiz • Unit 1

A 1. do
2. get
3. join
4. play
5. an award
6. her leg

B 1. c
2. a
3. e
4. f
5. b
6. d

C 1. Did you go out last night?
2. Where were you when I called this morning?
3. I'd like to stay at home and rest.
4. It's OK, but we have to do a lot of homework.
5. I used to like it, but I don't anymore.

Quiz • Unit 2

A 1. travel; take
2. play; join
3. get; make; go to
4. be; learn

B 1. Everyone will have them.
2. They won't study in a classroom.
3. They might not get sick anymore.
4. Your refrigerator will order the food.
5. We'll be able to travel "virtually."

C 1. What are you going to do after high school?
2. Where are you going to go this summer?
3. How are you going to pay for college?

Quiz • Unit 3

A 8:00 a.m.: Go biking; explore
10:00 a.m.: Head for
1:00 p.m.: Have a
3:00 p.m.: fly
5:00 p.m.: Go to

B 5
6
2
3
4
1

C 1. Paul: won't; would
2. Rick: I'd; Can
3. Mom: rains; I'll; might

Quiz • Unit 4

A 1. creative
2. forgetful
3. organized
4. independent
5. bad-tempered

B 1. don't they
2. doesn't she
3. aren't you
4. isn't she
5. don't you

C 1. speaks; learning
2. Living; lived
3. working; teach
4. 's; chatting
5. Visiting; traveled

Quiz • Unit 5

A 1. c   4. c
    a   b
    b   a
2. a   5. b
    c   c
    b   a
3. c   6. c
    a   a
    b   b

B 1. d
2. b
3. a
4. c

C 1. **Q:** How long has Linda been on the team?
   A: Since the beginning of the year.
2. **Q:** How long have you studied French?
   A: For two years.
3. **Q:** Have you ever been to a Coldplay concert?
   A: Yes, I have. It was great.
4. **Q:** Has Björk ever acted in movies?
   A: Yes, she has.

Quiz • Unit 6

A 1. start
2. dye
3. sing
4. go out
5. go
6. ride

B 1. I've never played in a rock band.
2. Have you ever run in a marathon?
3. I've never gone skydiving.
4. Have you ever won a competition?
5. Have you ever ridden a motorcycle?

C 1. c
2. a
3. f
4. b
5. d
6. e

Quiz • Unit 7

A 1. artistic
2. bad-tempered
3. funny
4. hardworking
5. strong

B 1. I'd rather live in the city than in the country.
2. Who's the most organized person you've ever met?
3. My brother and I like sports, but I'm not as athletic as him.
4. French cars are not as good as German cars.
5. This is the worst music I've ever heard.

C My friends are good at playing computer games. (e; 1)
Yesterday, I met a girl who is as bad-tempered as my sister. (c; 2)
Would you rather be a pop star or a sports star? (d; 5)
My friend Carol is the most hardworking person I've ever met. (b; 4)
Skydiving is the most exciting thing I've ever done. (a; 3)

Quiz • Unit 8

A 1. jaywalk
2. Gossiping
3. cheated
4. eavesdropped
5. break
6. trespass

B 1. e
2. a
3. f
4. b
5. c
6. d

C 1. I'd take it to the police.
2. I think I'd give it to my parents.
3. If she broke a promise, I'd tell her parents.
4. I think I'd be unhappy. I'd ask them to stop.
5. If I failed my test, I'd study harder.

Vocabulary Games & Activities

1 How many words?

This game reviews vocabulary.

- Draw a box with 15 letters in it. Make sure you include at least two vowels. For example: *A, E, O, Y, B, R, N, T, S, M, H, P, L, K, C.*
- Divide the class into four or five teams.
- Explain the task. Students form words using letters from the box and write them in their notebooks. The words should have a minimum of three letters. Students can use the letters more than once and in any order.

Give a few examples: *party, school, look, teacher.* Set a time limit. Teams list as many words as they can in the time given.

- When time is up, volunteers from each team take turns reading their lists of words. The team with the most words wins.
- **Optional** To make the game more challenging, reduce the number of letters, or ask students to list specific types of words (for example, *nouns*).

2 Word categories

This game reviews vocabulary.

- Before the lesson, prepare a list of categories that students know words for. Try to mix fairly general categories (for example, *places*) with more specific ones (for example, *types of movies Brad Pitt has acted in*).
- Divide the class into five or six teams. Have teams choose a team name and appoint a spokesperson. Write the names of the teams in a list on one side of the board.
- Invite a volunteer to be the secretary, come to the board, and write the words the teams call out during the game.
- Write a category (for example, *places*) on the board and call out the names of the teams at random. The spokesperson for each team says one word that belongs to that category (for example, *school, park, outer space*). The secretary writes the word on the board.

Team members should work cooperatively to provide the spokesperson with an appropriate word if he or she is stuck. If a spokesperson takes more than ten seconds to come up with a word or calls out a word that does not belong to the category, his or her team is out of the game. Another team then takes a turn. The game continues in the same way until only one team is left, and that team is the winner. Write a new category on the board and play the game again.

- **Optional** Once students are familiar with the procedure, ask winning teams to suggest the category for the next round of the game.

3 This word means . . .

This activity reviews vocabulary.

- Choose 24 key words from previously taught units. Prepare eight slips of paper. Write three words on each slip.
- Write on the board:

  Meaning
  "Do chores" means ___ .
  a. to sing
  b. to work around the house
  c. to cook

  Example sentences
  I don't like doing chores at all.
  I'll go shopping after I do my chores.
  My dad does chores on Saturdays.

- Divide the class into eight groups and give each group a slip of paper.
- For each of their three words, have groups write the following on a slip of paper: multiple-choice questions on the meaning of the words plus three sentences using that word. They can use the samples on the board as examples.
- Have groups exchange pieces of paper with another group. They circle the correct answer and check the sentences for mistakes. If there are any mistakes, they correct them.
- Collect all the papers. Read the definitions and sentences and ask the class to say whether they are correct or not. If there are any mistakes, encourage the class to correct them.

Grammar Games & Activities

1 Sentence building

This game reviews the structure of statements or questions.

- Make a list of any number of statements or questions you want to review. Decide how to break the sentences up, as the different parts of each one will be written on separate pieces of paper.

- Prepare sets of cards of those statements or questions, with each "section" of each one written on a separate piece of paper. See the examples of statements below. Put each set of cards in an envelope. Be sure to make enough sets so that each team of five or six students can get one envelope.

if I	have time	I'll call Mary
if they don't	have homework	they'll probably play video games
we will probably	stay home	if it rains
they might	go to the concert	if they have money
if it	stops raining	we'll go to the mall
if I	am not tired	I'll study math
What would you do	if	you found $10

- Divide the class into small teams and assign each team a number or letter. Give each team an envelope.

- Have teams arrange their cards to form statements or questions that make sense. For example, *If it stops raining, I'll study math* is correct grammatically, but is not logical. Once finished, have students copy their statements or questions into their notebooks. Teams try to be the first to arrange all their statements or questions and copy them into their notebooks.

- When a few teams have finished, stop all teams. Take a notebook from one of the students in each of the teams. Read his or her statements or questions and ask the class if they are correct. Award one point for each correct statement or question. If there are mistakes, encourage students to correct them. The team with the most points at the end wins.

2 Guess who?

This game reviews questions in the present perfect with *How long . . . ?* and *ever*.

- On the board, draw a chart like the one below and complete the first column with a school subject and names of places your students are familiar with. Write the names of six people across the top of the chart. Then fill in the rest of the information. (See examples in the chart.) Make sure that no two people in the chart have exactly the same information.

	Mike	Sue	Bob	Lynn	Nick	Pam
study [subject]	2 years	3 years				
live in [place]	20 years					
go to [place]	No	No				
visit [place]	Yes	Yes				
study at [school name]	1 year	6 months				

- Have students work in pairs. They take turns choosing one of the people in the chart and asking questions to try to guess who the person is. Students should say *X* for the name of the person and answer in such a way that they do not give away the gender of the person and thus make the activity easier. For example:

  A: How long has X studied _____ ?
  B: For three years.
  A: Has X ever gone to _____ ?
  B: No.
  A: Has X ever visited _____ ?
  B: Yes.
  A: How long has X studied at _____ ?
  B: For six months.
  A: Is it Sue?
  B: Yes, it is.

- Have students keep a tally of the number of questions they asked to guess the person. At the end of the activity, have students add up their total number of questions. The student in each pair who asked fewer questions is the winner.

Listening Games & Activities

1 Listening summary

This activity previews any listening task and provides a reason for listening.

- Before doing a listening task, prepare a brief summary of the listening text and write it on the board. Include two pieces of information in your summary that are not true. For example, for Exercise 2 on page 109, your summary could read as follows:

  Lucia, Greg, and Megan talk about the past year. Lucia learned to skydive and met her boyfriend. Greg's had a very exciting year. He's studied a lot. Megan went hiking and spent her vacation in an amazing place.

- Have students work in pairs, read the summary, and write down what they think is not true. In the example summary on the board, the names might be wrong, what people did may be mixed up – for example, maybe it was Megan who studied a lot and not Greg, and so on.

- Play the recording. Students listen and check to see if their guesses are correct or not.

- Invite a volunteer to come to the board to correct the summary.

2 Predicting from audio script extracts

This activity previews any listening task and provides a reason for listening.

- Copy four or five sentences or questions from a listening text on the board. For example, for Exercise 2 on page 39, copy the following on the board.

  Do you still have a lot to do before you leave for Disney World?

  Do you have enough summer clothes?

  What else do you have to do?

  So, do you know a lot about Disney World?

- Explain to students that they are going to listen to a conversation in which one of the speakers asks the questions or says the sentences on the board.

- Divide the class into pairs.

- Have students predict as much as they can about the conversation based on the excerpts on the board. Possible predictions are:

  Carla is going to Disney World.
  The conversation takes place before the trip.
  They will talk about the things Carla has to do.
  It's summer in Disney World.
  It's probably Carla's first visit to Disney World.

- Have pairs share their predictions with another pair.

- Play the recording. Students listen and check how many of their predictions were correct.

- **Optional** Write five questions about the listening passage on the board. Have students predict and write down what the answers will be. Play the recording and have them listen and check if their predictions were correct.

3 Eavesdropping

This activity provides an opportunity to listen to "live" English.

- Write on the board:

  Conversation 1: A and B talk, and C is the eavesdropper.
  Conversation 2: B and C talk, and A is the eavesdropper.
  Conversation 3: A and C talk, and B is the eavesdropper.

- Divide the class into groups of three. In each group, have students choose to be A, B, or C. Have students look through some of the lessons they have recently completed and choose three topics to talk about.

- Have students in each group take turns talking about each of the topics they have chosen, following the instructions for each conversation on the board. While the conversations are taking place, the "eavesdroppers" try to remember at least two pieces of information they hear. They should not take notes.

- Ask random eavesdroppers to share with the class the information they remember. For example, *Maria wants to join a sports club.* The speaker in question confirms whether the eavesdropper's information is correct or not.

Note: For any game or activity that would not work for large classes, modify it by forming small groups and having groups play the game instead of half or the whole class.

Speaking / Pronunciation Games & Activities

1 I have a friend who . . .

This activity practices grammar patterns.

- Write on the board:

Who	Ability
friend	can stand on head for an hour

Examples

Mark has a friend who can stand on his head for an hour.

Brenda has a cousin who won three marathons in a month.

Jenny knows someone who speaks seven languages.

- Focus students' attention on the chart and the examples on the board. Give them a few minutes to think about at least two people they know who have unusual abilities or have done something unusual. They should complete a chart like the one on the board.

- Divide the class into groups of four. Have students in each group take turns talking about the people in their charts. They should choose the three most interesting people described in the group.

- Invite a representative from each of the groups to share the information with the class about the people they chose, following the examples on the board.

- Take a class vote to choose the most interesting person.

2 New conversations

This activity practices creating conversations.

- Have students quickly re-read any three conversations that they have studied in the Student's Book, choose a sentence or question from each, and write each one on a separate slip of paper.

- Divide the class into pairs. Have students in each pair combine their slips of paper, shuffle them, and place them face up between them.

- Have pairs create a new conversation using each of the sentences or questions. The conversations should include at least two exchanges. Students should not write the conversations, but they can rehearse them a couple of times. For example:

A: I really want to go for a ride on my new bike. (From Exercise 1A, page 36.)

B: Wow! You have a new bike? Was it a birthday present?

A: No. I bought it.

B: Really? How much did you pay?

A: Fifty dollars.

- When most pairs have finished, invite several pairs of volunteers to perform one of their conversations in front of the class.

Note: For any game or activity that would not work for large classes, modify it by forming small groups and having groups play the game instead of half or the whole class.

Answer Key for Workbook

Note: *Multiple answers in a single sentence or by a single speaker are separated by a semicolon (;).*
Alternative answers are separated by a slash (/).

Unit 1 • My Life

Lesson 1 • Last summer

1 Hi, Jeff!

   Did you have a good summer vacation? You <u>went</u> mountain climbing, right? How <u>was</u> your trip? Please <u>write</u> me a message and tell me.

   I didn't go away this summer. I just <u>stayed</u> home. I <u>saw</u> a lot of my friends, and we <u>watched</u> DVDs. One day, while I <u>was playing</u> soccer, I <u>broke</u> my watch. I <u>bought</u> a new one the next day.

   I hope you <u>had</u> a great vacation. See you at school!

   Your friend,
   Chris

2 a. 3
   b. 6
   c. 1
   d. 4
   e. 2
   f. 5

3 1. Where did Kenny go last summer?
   2. He went with his friends.
   3. Yes, they were.
   4. They got up at 6:00 a.m.
   5. Did they go to bed late?
   6. What did (Kenny's friend / Teddy) break? / What did (Kenny's friend / Teddy) do?

Lesson 2 • A new school year

1 1. e; start a CD collection
   2. f; join the art club
   3. a; play tennis
   4. c; get good grades
   5. b; do karate
   6. d; take a computer course

2 1. I'd like to
   2. They have to
   3. He has to
   4. They're going to
   5. He'd like to
   6. I want to

3 Answers will vary.

Lessons 1 & 2 • Mini-review

1 1. My best friend (wants to / would like to) join a new club.
   2. Juanita (wants to / would like to) take piano lessons.
   3. My parents (want to / would like to) take a trip this weekend.
   4. Jorge and Jessica are going to go out tonight.
   5. Carlos has to get good grades this year.
   6. My friends and 1 are going to go camping.
   7. You have to get up early tomorrow.
   8. Laura (wants to / would like to) stay out late tonight.
   9. Keiko and Yuko (want to / would like to) travel to Canada next year.
   10. I'm going to go to the movies on Saturday.

2 Answers will vary.

Lesson 3 • Life events

1 1. When Kenji lived in Argentina, he learned Spanish.
   2. Maria made new friends when she joined the tennis team.
   3. Kim and Cody learned to dance when they took dance lessons.
   4. When Nina fell off her horse, she broke her arm.
   5. When Paulo went camping, he lost his hat.
   6. I got a cell phone when I started high school.

2 Answers will vary. Possible answers:

   1. When Andy was eight, he took acting lessons. OR Andy took acting lessons when he was eight.

   2. When Andy was 12, he started junior high school. OR Andy started junior high school when he was 12.

   3. When Andy was 12, he joined the school drama club. OR Andy joined the school drama club when he was 12.

   4. When Andy was 13, he won a talent competition. OR Andy was 13 when he won a talent competition.

   5. When Andy was 13, he starred in the school play. OR Andy starred in the school play when he was 13.

6. When Andy was 18, he graduated from high school. OR Andy was 18 when he graduated from high school.

7. When Andy was 18, he started drama school in New York City. OR Andy started drama school in New York City when he was 18.

Lesson 4 • Then and now

1 1. Aria used to be shy, but she isn't anymore.
2. I used to like this song, but I don't anymore.
3. Sandra used to play the piano, but she doesn't anymore.
4. I used to take math, but I don't anymore.
5. You used to play computer games, but you don't anymore.
6. Bill used to stay up late, but he doesn't anymore.
7. Keith and Marco used to wear glasses, but they don't anymore.
8. I used to drink soda, but I don't anymore.

2 1. She used to take easy classes, but she doesn't anymore. Now she takes difficult classes.
2. She used to have lots of free time after school, but she doesn't anymore. Now she has no free time.
3. She used to know just a few people, but she doesn't anymore. Now she knows many people.
4. She used to have a CD player, but she doesn't anymore. Now she has an MP3 player.
5. She used to listen to country music, but she doesn't anymore. Now she listens to rock music.
6. She used to read comic books, but she doesn't anymore. Now she reads mystery stories.
7. She used to stay home on the weekend, but she doesn't anymore. Now she goes camping on the weekend.

Get Connected

1 The name of Jason's online store is Pencil Bugs – Café Press.

2 1. decided
2. all over
3. luckily
4. happen
5. best-loved

3 1. He was nine years old.
2. They're fun things to put on the top of pencils.
3. Jason's mother created the Web site for the Pencil Bugs.
4. People can buy T-shirts, hats, and many other things with the Pencil Bug pictures on them.

5. He'd like to write books about Pencil Bugs and the adventures they have. / He wants to create a Pencil Bugs video game.

Check Yourself

1 1. were walking; met
2. was; took
3. started; were playing
4. was thinking; called
5. broke; was playing
6. was; started

2 Note: The order of the answers may vary.

1. Greenville used to be a small town, but it isn't anymore. Now it's a city.
2. Greenville used to be quiet, but it isn't anymore. Now it's noisy.
3. Greenville used to have a lot of bicycles, but it doesn't anymore. Now it has a lot of cars.
4. Greenville used to have a lot of trees, but it doesn't anymore. Now it has a shopping mall.

3 1. Liz is going to work in a bookstore next summer.
2. I have to do English and math homework tonight.
3. (We'd like to / We want to) join a new club in September.
4. My classmates are going to go to college next year.
5. Jorge (would like to / wants to) play soccer in the park this weekend.

Unit 2 • The Future

Lesson 5 • Predictions

1 1. No, she won't.
2. No, she won't.
3. Yes, she will.
4. No, she won't.
5. Yes, she will.

2 1. Will they miss the bus?
2. Will he cook dinner?
3. Will they see a movie?
4. Will he catch the ball?
5. Will you go to the library?
6. Will she buy the shirt?

3 1. Animals will talk.
2. People won't get sick.
3. People will go on vacations in outer space.
4. Men won't wear ties.

Lesson 6 • When I'm older

1 **Greg** She'll probably take a trip.
Greg No. She probably won't go to Europe.

Greg No, she won't. She'll probably travel with her friends.

Greg No. She probably won't go to college until next year.

Greg She'll probably work for our father in his office.

Greg She probably will.

Greg She probably won't.

2 Note: Students' predictions will vary.
1. be famous
2. get a driver's license
3. go to college
4. be rich
5. get a job
6. be an actor
7. get a pet
8. get married

Lessons 5 & 6 • Mini-review

1 I want to travel to South America. I probably won't visit all the countries, but I'll definitely visit most of them. I'd like to go camping most of the time, so I probably won't visit a lot of cities. I want to see the rain forest, so I'll / want to go hiking through the jungle or take a boat trip. I'll probably see a lot of animals. I'll bring my camera, but I probably won't take very good pictures. I'm a terrible photographer!

2 Note: Answers to the questions will vary.
1. **Q:** Will your math teacher give the class a test this week?
2. **Q:** Will you get a job this summer?
3. **Q:** Will your favorite singer record some new songs this year?
4. **Q:** Will you go to bed early tonight?
5. **Q:** Will you buy a new computer next month?
6. **Q:** Will your best friend travel to Venezuela this fall?
7. **Q:** Will your family take a vacation this year?

Lesson 7 • Teen Center

1
Across	Down
2. JOIN	1. ACTIVITY
6. ARTICLES	3. TAKE
8. EDIT	4. RACKET
	5. MARTIAL
	7. LEARN

2
1. She might not take an art class this semester.
2. They might take a cooking class.
3. We might not be reporters.
4. I might join the marching band.
5. She might not take a dance class.
6. She might not join the racket club.
7. They might take a martial arts class.
8. We might make a scrapbook.

Lesson 8 • After high school

1
1. She'll probably visit her grandparents.
2. (She's going to / She'll) find an apartment in the city.
3. (She's going to / She'll) go to college.
4. She probably won't take violin lessons.
5. She might take a dance class.
6. He might take a computer class.
7. (He's going to / He'll) get a job.
8. He'll probably take a vacation.
9. He probably won't go on a group tour.
10. He might travel alone.

2 Answers will vary.

Get Connected

1 No, they won't.

2
1. virtual
2. ages
3. headline
4. predict
5. certain

3
1. F; bigger smaller
2. T
3. F; teachers students
4. T
5. F; boring exciting

Check Yourself

1
1. Cars won't use gas.
2. Cars will be small.
3. Cars will fly in the sky.
4. Cars will go very fast.
5. Cars won't have wheels.

2
1. I won't go to school today.
2. They might go to Costa Rica.
3. I might not go with you.
4. I'll ride my bike.
5. I'll write about him.
6. I might play the guitar or sing.

3
1. No. He probably won't watch TV tonight.
2. Yes. She's going to the concert.
3. Yes. They'll probably drive me to your house.
4. No. I won't do my homework on Friday night.
5. No. It probably won't rain tomorrow.
6. Yes. I'll go to college.
7. Yes. He might buy a CD today.
8. No. They aren't going to go to Rio next year.

Unit 3 Plans

Lesson 9 • Weekend plans

1 Answers will vary. Possible answers:
1. Sure, I'd love to.

2. I'm sorry, but I can't.
3. I'm sorry, but I can't.
4. Yes, I'd love to.
5. I'd love to, but I can't.
6. Sure, I'd like to.

2 1. Would you like to watch *Star Wars*?
2. Would you like to go skiing on Saturday?
3. Would you like to go to the circus?
4. Would you like to drive go-carts?
5. Would you like to play soccer this weekend?
6. Would you like to have lunch?

Lesson 10 • Evening plans

1 1. Yes, of course. I'm good at history.
2. No, I'm sorry. My back hurts.
3. Sure. But please be careful with it.
4. Absolutely not! You can't drive.
5. No, I'm sorry. I'll be home late.
6. Sure. I'll call you at 7:00.

2 1. Can I use your eraser?
2. Could you explain this math problem?
3. Can I borrow money for lunch?
4. Could you open the window?

3 1. Yes, of course. / Sure.
2. Yes, of course. / Sure.
3. Yes, of course. / Sure.
4. No, I'm sorry. I can't. / No, I can't.

Lessons 9 & 10 • Mini-review

1 1. **A** would
   B Can
2. **A** Can
3. **A** Could
   B Would
4. **A** Would
   B could
5. **A** Can
   B could
6. **A** Would
   B Could

2 Note: Answers to questions will vary.
1. Would you like to go camping?
2. Could you lend me your notebook?
3. Would you like to explore a rain forest?
4. Can I stay out late tonight?
5. Could you clean the cafeteria?
6. Can I borrow your cell phone?

Lesson 11 • Making plans

1 1. he'll probably help make dinner
2. I won't watch that horror movie
3. my friends might have a barbecue
4. Danny might lend you some money
5. I might ask him to help me with my homework

6. My family will probably move
7. she'll probably miss the show
8. We'll take the bus

2 Answers will vary.

Lesson 12 • Vacation plans

1 1. before
2. After
3. Before
4. after
5. before
6. while

2 1. Ali is going to go swimming after he finishes his homework.
2. You should close the door after you come in.
3. I'm going to study Italian while I'm in Rome.
4. Gino and Marie have to study before they take the big test.

3 Answers will vary.

Get Connected

1 not busy.

2 1. expect
2. fuzzy
3. permission
4. convenient
5. firm

3 1. before
2. convenient
3. please
4. will probably
5. understand

Check Yourself

1 Note: Answers to the questions will vary.
1. **Q:** Would you like to play tennis with me today?
2. **Q:** Could you lend me $10?
3. **Q:** Can I stay out late tonight?
4. **Q:** Would you like to come over tonight?

2 1. go skiing; If it snows, I'll probably go skiing.
2. go to the beach; If it's sunny, I might go to the beach.
3. not eat lunch; If I'm not hungry, I won't eat lunch.
4. go to sleep; If I'm exhausted, I'll probably go to sleep.

3 1. He's going to find his skis before he goes on vacation.
2. He's going to buy new gloves while he's buying a hat.
3. He's going to take skiing lessons after he finds his skis.

4. He's going to make new friends while he's taking skiing lessons.
5. He's going to write a report for school after he gets home.

Unit 4 • People

Lesson 13 • Teens online

1
1. Playing computer games is boring.
2. Listening to music is great!
3. Playing racket sports isn't fun for me.
4. Going to the beach is nice when it's hot.
5. Chatting online is one of my favorite activities.
6. Finding information online takes a long time.

2 Answers will vary.

3
1. Yes, she does. She likes skiing.
2. No, he doesn't. He doesn't like dancing.
3. Yes, they do. They like using e-mail.
4. Yes, she does. She likes doing crossword puzzles.
5. No, they don't. They don't like doing chores.
6. No, he doesn't. He doesn't like playing video games.
7. Yes, they do. They like going to the movies.

Lesson 14 • Personality types

1
1. FORGETFUL
2. CREATIVE
3. ORGANIZED
4. BAD-TEMPERED
5. INDEPENDENT
6. HARDWORKING
7. THOUGHTFUL
8. TRUSTWORTHY
What's a popular personality type? <u>friendly</u>

2
1. Mei Mei and Tamia are, too.
2. Her brother is, too.
3. My father doesn't, either.
4. My cousins aren't, either.
5. Aya and Miho do, too.
6. Her friends don't, either.
7. My sister does, too.
8. Wayne isn't, either.

Lessons 13 & 14 • Mini-review

1
1. doing crossword puzzles
2. going to the beach
3. playing chess
4. going to the library
5. doing chores
6. playing games online

2 Sentences agreeing with Walter's preferences and personality will vary.
1. Walter likes doing karate. I do, too. Doing karate is fun!
2. Walter likes babysitting. I do, too. . . .
3. Walter doesn't like playing baseball. I don't, either. . . .
4. Walter doesn't like listening to classical music. I don't, either. . . .
5. Walter is thoughtful. I am, too. . . .
6. Walter is outgoing. I am, too. . . .

Lesson 15 • Unusual people

1
1. I have a history teacher who collects cars.
2. I know a brother and sister who surf in competitions.
3. I met a swimmer who is an Olympic champion.
4. I met a teen who collects spiders.
5. I have a friend who is good at English.
6. I know a woman who goes camping in the snow.

2 Answers will vary. Possible answers:
1. Ashley knew a boy who collected chess pieces.
2. Ashley had a friend who (loved animals / went to the zoo every day).
3. Ashley knew a girl who painted pictures of insects.
4. Ashley knew a girl who watched old movies every weekend.
5. Ashley knew two boys who liked to go hiking in the rain.
6. Ashley knew a basketball coach who liked to juggle.
7. Ashley knew a math teacher who wrote poetry.
8. Ashley knew a librarian who made her own clothes.

Lesson 16 • Who's that girl?

1 Cristina aren't you
Anita aren't you
Cristina isn't it
Anita isn't it
Anita aren't you; don't you
Cristina don't you
Cristina aren't you
Anita don't we

2
1. **Q:** Your cousins live in the city, don't they?
A: No, they don't.
2. **Q:** Louisa likes cats, doesn't she?
A: No, she doesn't.
3. **Q:** Tom is good at math, isn't he?
A: Yes, he is.
4. **Q:** Those mountains are very big, aren't they?
A: Yes, they are.

5. **Q:** You like music, don't you?
   A: Yes, I do.
6. **Q:** Diego plays the guitar, doesn't he?
   A: No, he doesn't.

Get Connected

1 1. Rowan Atkinson starred in *Mr. Bean*.
   2. Harrison Ford starred in the Indiana Jones movies.

2 1. chatting
   2. forgetful
   3. bad-tempered
   4. outgoing
   5. just like

3 1. a British actor.
   2. to bring his money.
   3. was funny.
   4. an outgoing person.
   5. was honest.

Check Yourself

1 1. Sara likes dancing, doesn't she?; No, she doesn't.
   2. Playing chess is difficult, isn't it?; Yes, it is.
   3. You enjoy going to the movies, don't you?; No, I don't.
   4. Sending e-mail and chatting online are popular, aren't they?; Yes, they are.

2 1. Lucinda is creative. Joe is, too.
   2. Tino isn't organized. Kevin isn't, either.
   3. Lola is thoughtful. Tom is, too.
   4. Marco doesn't always remember things. Laurel doesn't, either.

3 1. Lance Armstrong is a cyclist who has some children.
   2. David Wright is a baseball player who plays for the New York Mets.
   3. Jennifer Garner is an actor who likes kickboxing.
   4. Jennifer Lopez is a singer who sings in English and Spanish.

Unit 5 • Entertainment

Lesson 17 • For fun

1 1. have been
   2. have called
   3. have cleaned
   4. have done
   5. have eaten
   6. have gone
   7. have hung out
   8. have had
   9. have made
   10. have played
   11. have read
   12. have rented
   13. have seen
   14. have studied
   15. have watched

2 My best friend and I <u>have done</u> a lot of fun things this year. We <u>have watched</u> six soccer games, we <u>have gone</u> to 12 movies, and we <u>have hung out</u> at the beach every weekend. I <u>haven't done</u> all of my homework, and I <u>haven't cleaned</u> my room. My parents aren't happy, but I am!

3 1. We haven't rented DVDs.
   2. We've invited friends.
   3. We've cleaned the kitchen.
   4. We haven't cleaned the living room.
   5. We've made the decorations.
   6. We haven't gone to the store.
   7. We've made a cake.
   8. We haven't finished all our chores.

4 Answers will vary.

Lesson 18 • Young entertainers

1 1. star in a movie
   2. give interviews
   3. record a song
   4. sign autographs
   5. support a charity
   6. entertain a live audience

2 Answers may vary. Possible answers are:
   1. Ernesto has supported a charity.
   2. Ernesto has starred in a movie. / Ernesto hasn't recorded a song.
   3. Ernesto has given interviews. / Ernesto hasn't signed autographs.
   4. The Country Girls have entertained a live audience. / The Country Girls haven't supported a charity.
   5. The Country Girls have recorded a song. / The Country Girls haven't starred in a movie.
   6. The Country Girls have signed autographs. / The Country Girls haven't given interviews.

3 1. Kaoru hasn't recorded two CDs. She's recorded three CDs.
   2. The Hawks haven't won soccer games. They've won basketball games.
   3. Trevor hasn't appeared on TV. He's appeared in a newspaper.
   4. Isabel hasn't traveled to New Zealand. She's traveled to (London / England).

Lessons 17 & 18 • Mini-review

1 1. have met a lot of artists
   2. has recorded one song
   3. haven't won any games

4. hasn't made a movie
5. have given interviews
6. has appeared in the school newspaper
7. has had too much homework
8. hasn't won an Academy Award

2 Sentences about students and people they know will vary.
1. has been
2. have had
3. has seen
4. hasn't eaten
5. hasn't gone
6. has read

Lesson 19 • Are you a fan?

1 Jordan Have you ever tried any dangerous sports?
Luciano No, I haven't.
Jordan Have you ever met a movie star?
Luciano No, I haven't.
Jordan Have you ever gone to any concerts?
Luciano Yes, I have.
Jordan Have you ever been invited backstage?
Luciano Yes, we have.
Jordan Have you ever gotten any autographs?
Luciano No, we haven't.

2 1. **A:** Yes, I have.
2. **A:** No, they haven't.
3. **A:** Yes, he has.
4. **A:** Yes, they have.
5. **A:** No, I haven't.
6. **A:** Yes, she has.

3 Answers will vary.

Lesson 20 • Pop culture trivia

1 1. How long has Keanu Reeves been an actor?
He's been an actor since he was in high school.
2. How long has Tiger Woods played professional golf?
He's played professional golf since 1996.
3. How long has Kany Garcia lived in Puerto Rico?
She's lived in Puerto Rico all her life.
4. How long have the Sprouse twins worked as actors?
They've worked as actors for more than 16 years.
5. How long has Miley Cyrus starred in *Hannah Montana*?
She's starred in *Hannah Montana* since 2006.
6. How long have the Jonas Brothers been a rock group?
They've been a rock group for more than five years.

7. How long has *Survivor* been a popular TV show?
Survivor has been a popular TV show since about 2000.
8. How long has Katie Holmes been married to Tom Cruise?
She's been married to Tom Cruise since 2006.

2 1. **Q:** How long has Elias played the guitar?
A: He's played the guitar since he was 11.
2. **Q:** How long has he written music?
A: He's written music since 1995.
3. **Q:** How long has he lived in Los Angeles?
A: He's lived in Los Angeles for five years.
4. **Q:** How long has he worked as a musician?
A: He's worked as a musician for three years.
5. **Q:** How long has he played in a band?
A: He's played in a band since 2003.

Get Connected

1 dolls

2 1. charity
2. received
3. come true
4. viewers
5. career

3 1. She was born in 1994.
2. They live in Los Angeles.
3. They have lived there since 2000.
4. Yes, she has.
5. She received the Kid's Choice Award for *Charlotte's Web*.
6. She likes to play the piano, collect dolls, ride horses, and dance ballet. / She likes to help other people. / She likes to read a lot.

Check Yourself

1 1. **A** Have you ever met a sports star?
B No, I haven't.
2. **A** Have your parents ever listened to your CDs?
B Yes, they have.
3. **A** Have you been busy this month?
B Yes, I have.
4. **A** Have you bought any new clothes this week?
B No, I haven't.
5. **A** Have Luis and Ramon ever joined a fan club?
B Yes, they have.

2 1. Dennis has written songs.
2. Dennis hasn't played the guitar.
3. Dennis hasn't recorded a song.
4. Dennis has entertained a live audience.
5. Fernando has played the guitar.
6. Fernando has played at a club.

7. Fernando hasn't played with a band.
8. Fernando has won a talent competition.

3 1. **Q:** How long have you been a student at this school?
   A: I've been a student at this school since September.
   2. **Q:** How long has Alicia lived here?
   A: She's lived here for three months.
   3. **Q:** How long have your parents had their car?
   A: They've had their car for a year.
   4. **Q:** How long have Tomas and Sarah been Madonna fans?
   A: They've been Madonna fans since 1985.
   5. **Q:** How long has your brother spoken Portuguese?
   A: He's spoken Portuguese for two years.
   6. **Q:** How long have you played in a rock band?
   A: I've played in a rock band since 2003.

Unit 6 • Experiences

Lesson 21 • Taking risks

1 Students' own information will vary.
   1. go skydiving
   2. dye my hair
   3. start a band
   4. explore a cave
   5. ride a motorcycle
   6. try new food
   7. sing karaoke
   8. go out without permission

2 1. No, they haven't. They've never been in a sports competition. / No, never.
   2. Have Darin and Tessa ever sung karaoke?
   3. Has Tessa ever gone horseback riding?
   4. No, they haven't. They've never gone hiking in the jungle. / No, never.
   5. No, he hasn't. He's never acted in a play. / No, never.
   6. No, he hasn't. He's never gone camping with the family. / No, never.

Lesson 22 • What we've done

1 1. for
   2. since
   3. so far
   4. for
   5. ago
   6. so far
   7. ago
   8. since

2 **Josh** have you been; I haven't seen
   Emily I've been / I was; I came back
   Josh did you do
   Emily I went; My cousins have had; they were
   Emily I didn't fall off; I've done

3 Answers will vary.

Lessons 21 & 22 • Mini-review

1 1. ever
   2. went
   3. since
   4. ago
   5. Did you have
   6. never
   7. so far
   8. for

2 1. **Q:** Has Christina ever sailed a boat?
   A: Yes, she has. She sailed a boat two weeks ago.
   2. **Q:** Has Christina ever met a rock star?
   A: No, she hasn't. She's never met a rock star.
   3. **Q:** Has Christina ever had a pet?
   A: Yes, she has. She's had a pet since she was five.
   4. **Q:** Has Christina ever been a recreation leader?
   A: Yes, she has. She's been a recreation leader for a long time.
   5. **Q:** Has Christina ever run a marathon?
   A: Yes, she has. She ran a marathon last year.
   6. **Q:** Has Christina ever written e-mail messages in English?
   A: No, she hasn't. She's never written e-mail messages in English.

Lesson 23 • Amazing teens

1 1. They've already hiked in the rain forest.
   2. They've already gone to a rock concert.
   3. They've already seen the Sydney Opera House.
   4. They haven't gone scuba diving yet.
   5. They've already toured the crocodile farm.
   6. They haven't climbed the rock yet.
   7. They haven't tried surfing yet.

2 1. He's already been to Tasmania.
   2. They haven't visited Perth yet.
   3. They haven't visited the Gold Coast.
   4. He's already been to Darwin.
   5. They've already been to Melbourne.
   6. He hasn't tried surfing yet.
   7. They haven't been to Uluru yet.
   8. He's already seen the Sydney Opera House.

Lesson 24 • In the spotlight

1 **Mrs. Nelson** aren't you
    Mrs. Nelson didn't you
    Mrs. Nelson hasn't she
    Mrs. Nelson haven't you
    Mrs. Nelson haven't you
    Mrs. Nelson haven't they

2 Note: Answers to questions will vary.
1. You've been a student at this school for three years, haven't you?
2. Last summer was very hot, wasn't it?
3. You passed sixth-grade math, didn't you?
4. Your classmates have always been good students, haven't they?
5. Soccer has been a popular sport in your country for a long time, hasn't it?
6. Your friends have lived in this town since they were born, haven't they?
7. You've spoken English for five years, haven't you?
8. Your English teacher gave a lot of homework, yesterday, didn't he / she?

Get Connected

1 A little notebook is in the letterbox.
2 1. rock climbing
    2. skydiving
    3. hides
    4. mental
    5. risk

3 1. an exciting
    2. hiking
    3. a little plastic box
    4. on the Internet
    5. should do it once
    6. no one has

Check Yourself

1 1. for
    2. ago
    3. already
    4. since
    5. yet
    6. so far
    7. so far
    8. already

2 **Reporter** You've been; haven't you
    Charlie I have
    Reporter bought; didn't they
    Charlie they didn't
    Reporter You entertained a live audience; didn't you
    Charlie I did
    Reporter you've played; haven't you
    Charlie I haven't

3 1. **Q:** Have you ever traveled to England?
    A: No, I haven't. I've never traveled to England. OR No, never.
2. **Q:** Has Maria ever gone to a rain forest?
    A: No, she hasn't. She's never gone to a rain forest. OR No, never.
3. **Q:** Have you ever dyed your hair?
    A: No, I haven't. I've never dyed my hair. OR No, never.
4. **Q:** Has John ever tried rock climbing?
    A: No, he hasn't. He's never tried rock climbing. OR No, never.
5. **Q:** Have Jen and Ron ever won a marathon?
    A: No, they haven't. They've never won a marathon. OR No, never.
6. **Q:** Has Martina ever met a famous person?
    A: No, she hasn't. She's never met a famous person. OR No, never.

Unit 7 • Teen Time

Lesson 25 • Teen opinions

1 1. the best
    2. better than
    3. The worst
    4. good
    5. worse than
    6. good
    7. bad
    8. the best

2 1. *The Adventures of Huckleberry Finn* is the best book in the library.
2. Your grades are better than my grades.
3. Gregorio's Restaurant has the worst pizza in town.
4. This band plays better music than that band.
5. P.E. is worse than math.
6. Monday is the worst day of the week.
7. Cats are better than dogs.
8. Soccer is the best sport to play.

3 Answers will vary.

Lesson 26 • Unforgettable moments

1 1. the most disgusting
    2. the most thrilling
    3. the most difficult
    4. the most beautiful
    5. the happiest
    6. the shortest
    7. the funniest
    8. the most exciting
    9. the youngest
    10. the most unforgettable

2
1. it is. It's the best movie I've ever seen
2. it is. It's the scariest book I've ever read
3. (he / she) is. (He's / She's) the most forgetful person I've ever met
4. it is. It's the most frustrating homework assignment I've ever done
5. it is. It's the messiest room I've ever seen
6. they are. They're the most interesting classes I've ever taken
7. it is. It's the worst food I've ever eaten
8. it is. It's the biggest car we've ever had

3 Answers will vary.

Lessons 25 & 26 • Mini-review

1
1. Your desk is very messy. It's messier than my desk. It's the messiest desk I've ever seen.
2. Your bicycle is very nice. It's nicer than my bicycle. It's the nicest bicycle I've ever seen.
3. Your pet is very scary. It's scarier than my pet. It's the scariest pet I've ever seen.
4. Your printer is very fast. It's faster than my printer. It's the fastest printer I've ever seen.

2
1. Skiing is the most difficult sport he's ever tried.
2. *School Vacation* is the funniest movie he's ever seen.
3. *The Long Road* is the worst book he's ever read.
4. Professor Alden is the most interesting person he's ever met.
5. *The Greatest Hits Collection* by Alan Jackson is the best CD he's ever bought.
6. Ipanema Beach is the most beautiful place he's ever visited.

Lesson 27 • Are we alike?

1
1. Don isn't as tall as Dora.
   Dora isn't as short as Don.
2. The black skirt is as expensive as the white skirt.
   The white skirt is as expensive as the black skirt.
3. The small car isn't as fast as the big car.
   The big car isn't as slow as the small car.
4. Tina isn't as sad as Gina.
   Gina isn't as happy as Tina.

2
1. Ramona is as tall as he is.
2. Ramona is as athletic as he is.
3. Ramona isn't as artistic as he is.
4. Their sisters aren't as old as they are.
5. Ricardo isn't as outgoing as her.
6. Ramona is as funny as him.
7. Ramona is as old as him.
8. Ramona and Ricardo aren't as shy as them.

Lesson 28 • I'd rather . . .

1
1. Lucia would rather take dance lessons than piano lessons.
2. Pete and Rick would rather read books than watch TV.
3. Justin would rather play chess than soccer.
4. Katie would rather eat ice cream than eat fruit.
5. Linda would rather meet a movie star than a sports star.
6. Paul would rather go out than stay home.

2 Note: Answers to questions will vary.
1. Would you rather buy a radio or an MP3 player?
2. Would you rather be funny or artistic?
3. Would you rather be tall or short?
4. Would you rather explore an old house or a cave?

Get Connected

1 Carlos; Katie
2
1. valuable
2. job skills
3. community work
4. memorable
5. generation

3
1. K
2. S
3. C
4. S
5. K
6. C

Check Yourself

1
1. **Q:** Would you rather have a cat or a dog?
   A: I'd rather have a cat than a dog. Cats are cuter than dogs.
2. **Q:** Would you rather study German or Italian?
   A: I'd rather study Italian than German. Italian isn't as difficult as German.
3. **Q:** Would you rather watch *The Dark Cave* or *Spider-Man?*
   A: I'd rather watch *Spider-Man* than *The Dark Cave. Spider-Man* isn't as scary as *The Dark Cave.*
4. **Q:** Would you rather eat at Bono's Burgers or the Golden Palace?
   A: I'd rather eat at the Golden Palace than Bono's Burgers. the Golden Palace has better food than Bono's Burgers.

2
1. Andy isn't as tall as she is.
   Andy isn't as tall as her.
2. Linda isn't as active as he is.
   Linda isn't as active as him.

3. Andy is as friendly as she is.
Andy is as friendly as her.
4. Linda is as artistic as he is.
Linda is as artistic as him.

3   If you want to go on a great vacation, go to the Rolling River Ranch. It's <u>the best place I've ever visited</u>! I went horseback riding for the first time there. Horseback riding is <u>the hardest sport I've ever tried</u>, but I liked it. The horses there were <u>the biggest horses I've ever seen</u>. I only fell off once – when I saw a cute boy. That's <u>the most embarrassing experience I've ever had</u>. But it was OK. He didn't laugh, and we became friends.

He's <u>the nicest boy I've ever met</u>. Too bad he doesn't live in my town! But he sends me <u>the longest e-mails I've ever read</u>. Maybe I'll see him again when I go back to the ranch next year.

Unit 8 • Dreams and Reality

Lesson 29 • Our dreams

1
1. If Maria could take a trip next summer, she'd take a trip to Belize.
2. If Luis and Renaldo could watch any movie, they'd watch that new comedy.
3. If Marissa and Eliot could join a new club, they'd join the photography club.
4. If Gisela could buy new clothes, she'd buy a black dress.
5. If my sister could learn a new sport, she'd learn snowboarding.
6. If we could be good at any activity, we'd be good at painting.
7. If we could live in any city, we'd live in San Juan.
8. If Jessica and Aileen could have any kind of dessert, they'd have chocolate cake.

2
1. If I could visit any country
2. If I could try any sport
3. If I could talk to any person
4. If I could get any pet
5. If I could look like any person
6. If I could be good at any sport
7. If I could buy any CD

3   Answers will vary.

Lesson 30 • What would you do?

1
1. she'd give
2. would you do
3. I'd be
4. would Lana do; didn't pass
5. lost; wouldn't buy

2
1. I'd put the garbage in the trash can
2. I'd take it to the Lost and Found
3. I wouldn't litter. I'd throw it in the trash can
4. I'd lend it to him

3
1. What would you do if your friend asked you to trespass?; e
2. What would you do if your friend wanted to gossip?; b
3. What would you do if your sister broke a promise to you?; a
4. What would you do if your friend lied to you?; f
5. What would you do if you saw someone eavesdropping on your conversation?; c
6. What would you do if your brother crossed in the middle of the street?; d

Lessons 29 & 30 • Mini-review

1
1. If he could go anyplace, he'd go to the moon.
2. If Carolyn could meet any person, she'd meet Liv Tyler.
3. If Andy and Ann could buy anything, they'd buy a boat.
4. If Romeo could live anyplace, he'd live on an island.

2   Note: Answers to questions will vary.
1. **Q:** What would you do if you found an expensive ring?
2. **Q:** What would you do if you lost your English book?
3. **Q:** What would you do if your friend asked you for some money?
4. **Q:** What would you do if your brother lied to you?
5. **Q:** What would you do if you failed a test?
6. **Q:** What would you do if you met a famous person?

Lesson 31 • What I'm going to be

1
1. detective; scientist
2. astronaut; pilot
3. detective; astronaut
4. artist; carpenter
5. journalist; author

2
1. I want to be a carpenter to make furniture.
2. Michael wants to be an artist to paint pictures.
3. Carlita is going to be a veterinarian to work with animals.
4. Clara is going to be a teacher to work with children.
5. Will is going to be a karate instructor to teach martial arts.
6. Sarah and Jocelyn would like to be astronauts to travel to outer space.

7. Carmen is going to be an author to write funny stories for children.
8. My best friend and I want to be computer programmers to work with the latest technology.

3 1. I'm going to be a journalist to report on events and write articles.
2. Carol is going to be a detective to solve mysteries.
3. My sister wants to be a pilot to travel to interesting places.
4. Hector would like to be an actor to star in movies.
5. (We / Amelia and I) are going to be authors to write stories.
6. Camille and Chloe want to be scientists to make discoveries.

Lesson 32 • The past year

1 1. anything
2. someone
3. anyone
4. anywhere
5. somewhere
6. something

2 Gloria someone
Melinda anyone
Melinda someone
Gloria anything
Melinda something
Gloria anything
Melinda somewhere
Gloria anywhere

3 Note: Answers to questions will vary.
1. **Q:** Have you met anyone special this year?
2. **Q:** Did you go anywhere new last week?
3. **Q:** Have you done anything fun this month?
4. **Q:** Is there anything new on TV tonight?
5. **Q:** Did you give anyone a present last month?
6. **Q:** Did you eat anywhere special last month?

Get Connected

1 Answers will vary.

2 1. celebrity
2. foundations
3. donate
4. education
5. billions

3 1. Timothy
2. Ray
3. Gwen
4. Ray
5. Timothy
6. Ray; Gwen

Check Yourself

1 1. If Missy could travel to any country, she'd travel to Brazil.
2. If Missy could get any gift, she'd get a DVD player.
3. If Missy could meet any movie star, she'd meet Angelina Jolie.
4. If Missy could study any subject, she'd study computer science.

2 1. She's going to travel to Brazil to see the rain forest.
2. She's going to get a DVD player to watch movies.
3. She's going to meet Angelina Jolie to get an autograph.
4. She's going to study computer science to learn to design Web sites.

3 1. anything
2. someone
3. something
4. anyone
5. somewhere
6. anywhere

4 1. **Q:** would you do; if you won
A: If I won a lot of money, I'd take a trip
2. **Q:** would your parents do; if you stayed out late
A: If I stayed out late, they'd be
3. **Q:** would your sister do if you went
A: If I went into my sister's room without permission, she'd tell

Audio Script for Student's Book 4

Unit 1 • My Life

Lesson 1 Last summer

Page 2 Exercise 1A

Same as the captions in the Student's Book.

Page 3 Exercise 2

Same as the text and the conversation in the Student's Book.

Lesson 2 A new school year

Page 4 Exercise 1A

Same as the conversation in the Student's Book.

Page 4 Exercise 1B

Same as the conversations in the Student's Book.

Page 5 Exercise 2

Jessica So, Pedro, are you going to take Italian this year?

Pedro No, I don't think so. I want to take French, actually. How about you?

Jessica I'd like to take Spanish. Hey, maybe you can help me with my homework, Pedro.

Pedro Sure, I'd love to. I can't help you after school, though. I have to go to soccer practice every day. I'm going to play on the soccer team this year.

Jessica Oh, that's right. Coach Jones says you're going to be one of his best players.

Pedro Well, uh, I don't know about that . . . So, are you going to do any sports, Jessica?

Jessica No. I want to join a club, though. I'm thinking about joining the international club. I'd like to meet some of the new international students.

Pedro Sounds like fun.

Jessica Why don't you join, Pedro?

Pedro Thanks, but I can't. I have to get better grades this year, so I have to study a lot!

Jessica Let me know if you need help. I'm going to have a lot of free time this year.

Lessons 1 & 2 Mini-review

Page 7 Exercise 2

1. Hi, Megan. I hope you had a nice summer. My family went to visit some relatives in the country. What did you do?

2. Hi, Ricardo. What's your schedule like this year? Are you going to take any language classes?

3. I'd like to join the chess club. It's on Thursday after school. Do you want to join with me, Maggie?

4. I hope I didn't bother you when I called last night about the math test. What were you doing when I called?

5. I want to join a fan club this year. What do you want to do? Do you want to join a club?

6. My summer was kind of boring. I didn't do very much. Did you have fun?

Lesson 3 Life events

Page 8 Exercise 1A

Same as the texts in the Student's Book.

Page 8 Exercise 1B

Same as the sentences in the Student's Book.

Page 9 Exercise 2

1. My grandfather taught me how to ride a horse. That was a long time ago. I learned to ride a horse when I was a young boy.

2. Oh, yes. I almost forgot. I broke my leg last year. I broke it when I fell out of a tree. I had to go to the hospital, but I don't remember very much. It really hurt!

3. Can you believe it? My dog is almost two years old. My parents gave me my dog when I celebrated my 13th birthday. What a great present, huh? I love my dog.

4. I have a cousin who lives in New York. She visited us when I was in my first year of school. That was long ago, when I was very young! She came to my school and spoke about her life in New York. It was exciting, and we all wanted to visit New York.

5. Two years ago, in Ponce, I joined the basketball team. Many of my friends joined the team then, too. When I was on the team, we played every day. I want to play on the team here, too.

6. My family moved from San Juan to Ponce when I was very young. Can you guess how old I was? Well, we moved when I was three. When we moved there, I didn't like it at first. But now I love Ponce. I have a lot of friends there. I miss them.

Lesson 4 Then and now

Page 10 Exercise 1A

Same as the conversation in the Student's Book.

Page 10 Exercise 1B
Same as the sentences in the Student's Book.

Page 11, Exercise 2

Greg OK, Dave. It's your turn now. Tell me how you were different when you were ten.

Dave Oh, that's easy. There are a lot of differences. When I was ten, I used to collect comic books.

Greg Really? Comic books? Did you like Spider-Man?

Dave Oh, yeah. Spider-Man was my favorite. So, I used to collect comic books, but I don't anymore. Now I collect stamps.

Greg Great!

Dave And I was crazy about horror movies when I was little. I used to watch horror movies all the time, but I don't anymore. Now I watch comedies.

Greg Gee, you were different. Did you skateboard at all when you were ten?

Dave Of course I did. I loved Tony Hawk. I used to skateboard every day after school, but I don't anymore. Now I ride my mountain bike.

Greg Speaking of school . . . You're so good at Spanish. Did you use to take Spanish when you started middle school?

Dave No, actually, I used to take French, but I don't anymore. It was my favorite subject. Now I take Spanish. Spanish is my favorite subject now.

Greg Wow, Dave! Is that it?

Dave Um . . . I guess. The only other big difference is that I used to take the bus to school every day, but I don't anymore. Now I walk to school with my friends.

Page 11, Exercise 3A
Same as the sentences in the Student's Book.

Unit 1 Get Connected

Page 12 Read
Same as the article in the Student's Book.

Page 13 Listen

Nick Hey, Julie! I called you twice yesterday, but you didn't answer. I really wanted to study with you.

Julie Oh, sorry, Nick. I was at the pool. We have to train for three hours every day. I'm on the swim team, remember? I saw your message but I was exhausted!

Nick Three hours every day? Wow! That's a lot! Why do you have to train so hard?

Julie We have a really important swimming competition. All of the high schools are going to compete. Our coach really wants us to win. It's really important to all of us.

Nick But what about your schoolwork? That's important, too.

Julie I know. My parents aren't too happy about it. I used to get good grades, but I don't anymore. But there's only one more month of training and . . .

Nick Only one more month? And what about your friends? We used to see you three or four times a week, but we don't anymore!

Julie I know . . . and I *miss* you all. But you know I'd like to be a P.E. teacher someday and a swim coach, too. I love to swim.

Nick Yeah, I know. And I'm the same . . . with my training.

Julie You? The same with your training? What training? You don't train for anything . . . do you?

Nick Come on, Julie! You know I'm the champion video game player in our class! I train really hard to be number one!

Julie *(laughing)* That's right! I forgot! Well, how about we play a game right now and see just how good you are.

Nick All right!

Unit 2 • The Future
Lesson 5 Predictions

Page 16 Exercise 1A
Same as the Web site in the Student's Book.

Page 17 Exercise 1C
Same as the ad in the Student's Book.

Page 17 Exercise 2

Josh Hey, Mike. Let's play Professor Pete's prediction game. It's all about predictions for the year 2030. It says we won't be bored.

Mike Good. Let's play.

1. **Josh** OK, here's the first question. Will students use paper and pencils in school?

   Mike Hmm. No, they won't.

   Josh You're right. Professor Pete says students will do all of their work in school on computers. They won't need paper and pencils.

2. **Mike** OK, let me ask you a question, Josh. Ready? Will cell phones be the size of a credit card?

   Josh The size of a credit card? Yeah, I think they will. Look at how small everything is getting.

   Mike Well, Josh. Professor Pete agrees. He says cell phones *will* be the size of a credit card.

   Josh Wow! That's small.

3. **Josh** My turn to ask you, Mike. Will most people shop in stores for food?

Mike No, they won't. Many people order food online now. It's easier than going to a store. So, even more people will in 2030.

Josh That was a tricky one. Well, Professor Pete disagrees. He predicts that most people will still shop in stores for food.

Mike Why?

Josh Because they will still like to see the food they buy.

4. **Mike** Hey, Josh, here's a fun one. Will people visit the moon on vacation?

Josh Oh, yes. People will definitely spend time on the moon on vacation. Man visited the moon over 40 years ago! There's no reason we won't be able to stay in hotels on the moon in 2030.

Mike Well, Professor Pete agrees. Professor Pete predicts that there will be hotels on the moon in 2030.

Josh Great! I really want to go!

5. **Josh** OK, Mike. Here's the last one. Will people live below the sea?

Mike No, they won't. Maybe someday, but not in 2030.

Josh Oh, Mike. According to Professor Pete, people will live below the sea.
They'll build cities below the ocean.

Mike When I see it, I'll believe it!

Lesson 6 When I'm older

Page 18 Exercise 1A

1. *To be famous* means "to have many people know who you are."
2. *To be rich* means "to have a lot of money."
3. *To get a driver's license* means "to pass a test to drive a car."
4. *To get a job* means "to find a place to work."
5. *To get married* means "to become a husband or a wife."
6. *To go to college* means "to study after graduating from high school."
7. *To live alone* means "to not share your living space."
8. *To travel abroad* means "to visit a country far away from home."

Page 18 Exercise 2A
Same as the conversation in the Student's Book.

Page 19 Exercise 2B
Same as the sentences in the Student's Book.

Page 19 Exercise 3A
Same as the sentences in the Student's Book.

Lessons 5 & 6 Mini-review

Page 21 Exercise 2

1. **Boy** Hey, Kim, this prediction says that in the future people will fly from place to place in small airplanes. What do you think?

Kim Oh, I don't think that will happen. There will probably be too much traffic in the sky. It'll be safer to travel on the ground.

2. **Boy** Hey, listen to this prediction. It says that when people move from place to place in the future, they'll take their houses with them.

Kim You know, I think that will probably happen. Houses will be different in the future and easy to move. We won't have to pack when we move anymore - that will be great.

3. **Boy** Hey, did you see this prediction? You can throw away your Spanish dictionary. It says that people won't have to learn foreign languages in the future.

Kim Yeah. I read about that. It says that people will have little computers in their brains. The computers will help them speak French, Italian, Chinese, or whatever language they want. I think it'll probably happen, and I'd really like to try it.

4. **Boy** Wow! My mother is going to love this prediction. It says that people won't have to cook. All they'll have to do is order what they want to eat on a computer, and in ten minutes they'll have whatever they ordered. Do you think it will happen?

Kim No, that probably won't happen. It sounds completely crazy to me.

Lesson 7 Teen Center

Page 22 Exercise 1A
Same as the captions in the Student's Book.

Page 23 Exercise 2A
Same as the conversation in the Student's Book.

Page 23 Exercise 2B
Same as the e-mail in the Student's Book.

Page 23 Exercise 3

1. **Amy** Hey, Sam, look at this cooking class. I might take it. It sounds really fun. You learn how to make all kinds of food – even ice cream. Maybe we can take it together.

Sam Yeah, it sounds fun, Amy. But I might not be able to take it. I think it's at the same time as my soccer practice.

Amy Oh, that's too bad. It would be fun to do it with you.

2. **José** Hey, Anna. Maybe joining the marching band will be fun. Do you know anything about it?

   Anna Yeah, it's great, José. I joined last year. I'm trying to decide about it this year. I might not join, though, because it takes a lot of time.

   José Really? Oh, well, then I might not join, either. I don't have much time this year. Maybe next year!

3. **Staci** I see Dr. Gray is teaching a class on how to edit a music video next semester. I might take it. He's such a good teacher. Do you think you'll take it, John?

   John Well, Staci, I signed up for it, but I might not take it. The class is after school, and I have baseball practice after school.

   Staci Oh, that's too bad. I know how much you love music videos.

4. **Felicia** Are you still thinking of learning how to make a scrapbook, Laura?

   Laura I'd like to, Felicia, but I might not have time. I have to take seven classes next semester.

   Felicia Seven classes? Wow! That's a lot!

   Laura I know. I'll have to study hard the whole semester!

   Felicia Oh, no! Then I might not take the class, either. It won't be fun without you.

5. **Paul** How about it, James? Are you going to be a reporter this year? It'll be fun.

   James I don't know, Paul. I might not . . . I'm not a very good writer.

   Paul Come on, James. Don't be shy. You write great stories.

   James That's not true. They're pretty boring.

   Paul Well, anyway, it doesn't matter. I can't write very well, but I might be a reporter! It's good to try.

Lesson 8 After high school

Page 24 Exercise 1A
Same as the texts in the Student's Book.

Page 24 Exercise 1B
1. **Man 1** Simon is going to take a trip.
   Man 2 Definite plan
2. **Man 1** Simon will travel with friends.
   Man 2 Definite plan
3. **Man 1** Simon will probably visit the U.S.
   Man 2 Probable plan
4. **Man 1** Moira will go to college.
   Man 2 Definite plan
5. **Man 1** Moira might study computer programming.
   Man 2 Possible plan

6. **Man 1** Andrea will make some money.
   Man 2 Definite plan
7. **Man 1** Andrea will probably use her English.
   Man 2 Probable plan
8. **Man 1** Andrea might work at a hotel.
   Man 2 Possible plan

Page 25 Exercise 1C
Same as the conversation in the Student's Book.

Unit 2 Get Connected

Page 26 Read
Same as the Web site in the Student's Book.

Page 27 Listen
Rosa Hello?

Jeff Hey, Rosa. It's me, Jeff. Do you want to go to the movies with me tonight?

Rosa Oh, Jeff. I'd love to, but I can't. I have too much homework! *[sighs]* I'd rather *not* do it, but . . .

Jeff Yeah, I know. *I* have to do homework . . . But, hey . . . sometime in the future, robots will do it for us.

Rosa Yeah, they might do it for us . . . you never know. Maybe they'll clean our rooms for us, too.

Jeff *(laughing)* Yeah. And babysit my little brother, and walk the dog . . . and make dinner . . .

Rosa *(laughing)* No, but seriously, Jeff, robots and computers will be really amazing in the future – they'll do all kinds of things. I read it in a magazine article, and I believe it.

Jeff Really? So, what will they do?

Rosa Well, you know those computer programs – you just talk and the computer types the words for you. Well, in the future, we won't have to talk to the computer – we'll just *think* and the computers will type what we are thinking!

Jeff Whoa! That's a little scary. I don't believe that will happen, though. But computers might be smarter than us.

Rosa Yeah, that's another thing. Someday people will be able to connect computers to their brains. So all the information people need will go directly from their computers into their heads.

Jeff *(laughing)* Do you think it will be ready next week? I have an important chemistry test, and I haven't studied for it.

Rosa *(laughing)* No, Jeff. I think you should stay home and study tonight, too.

Unit 3 • Plans

Lesson 9 Weekend plans

Page 30 Exercise 1A

1. *To amaze* means "to surprise very much."
2. *To come back* means "to return."
3. *To expect* means "to think that something will happen."
4. *To explore* means "to travel around a place to learn about it."
5. *To head for* means "to move toward a place."
6. *To rescue* means "to save someone in danger."
7. *To take off* means "to leave the ground and start flying."
8. *To try out* means "to test something by using it."

Page 31 Exercise 2A

Same as the conversation in the Student's Book.

Page 31 Exercise 2B

Same as the questions and answers in the Student's Book.

Lesson 10 Evening plans

Page 32 Exercise 1A

Same as the conversation in the Student's Book.

Page 32 Exercise 1B

Same as the questions in the Student's Book.

Page 33 Exercise 2A

Same as the questions in the Student's Book.

Page 33, Exercise 3A

1. **Girl 1** Um, Mom, can Brigit sleep over tonight?

   Mother 1 Brigit? Yes, of course. That's a great idea. We can all watch some movies together.

2. **Girl 2** Hey, Mom. Could you buy me some new sneakers? I'm going to a party tonight.

   Mother 2 More sneakers? You already have four pairs.

   Girl 2 But, Mom, please! They're all too small for me.

   Mother 2 Well, yes. All right.

3. **Boy** Mom, I want to move the TV to my room. Can I?

   Mother 1 Absolutely not.

   Boy Why not? I'm the only one who watches it.

   Mother 1 That's not true. Your sister likes to watch TV, too.

4. **Girl 3** Dad, can I use your computer tonight?

   Father For what?

   Girl 3 I need to finish my science project.

   Father OK. Sure, that's fine.

Page 33, Exercise 3B

Same as the script in Part A.

Lessons 9 & 10 Mini-review

Page 35 Exercise 2A

1. **Junko** Hey, David. Would you like to go to the museum tomorrow night?

   David I'm sorry, but I can't, Junko. I have a lot of homework to do.

2. **Billy** Oh, Mr. Ross, can I take the history test tomorrow? I didn't have time to study last night.

   Mr. Ross No, I'm sorry, Billy. All the students have to take the test today.

3. **Alex** Hey, Sally, could you please clean my room for me? I'll give you ten dollars. But don't tell Mom!

   Sally Sure, Alex. I'll do it for you. But that'll cost you $15, not ten dollars.

4. **Pablo** Miranda, would you like to go white-water rafting this weekend?

   Miranda Sure, Pablo, I'd love to. It sounds really exciting. Thanks for inviting me.

Page 35 Exercise 2B

Same as the script in Part A.

Lesson 11 Making plans

Page 36 Exercise 1A

Same as the conversation in the Student's Book.

Page 36 Exercise 1B

Same as the sentences in the Student's Book.

Lesson 12 Vacation plans

Page 38 Exercise 1A

Same as the e-mail message in the Student's Book.

Page 38 Exercise 1B

Same as the sentences in the Student's Book.

Page 39 Exercise 2

1. **Jessica** Do you still have a lot to do before you leave for Disney World, Carla?

   Carla Oh, yes. I'm going to take a lot of pictures while I'm there, so I have to buy a new camera. I'm going downtown now. I'll try to buy a cheap camera at the mall.

2. **Jessica** Do you have enough summer clothes? It's very hot in Florida at this time of year.

   Carla Well, I need some summer clothes, but I think I'll go shopping while I'm there. I want to buy a T-shirt at Disney World.

3. **Jessica** What else do you have to do?

   Carla My hair is getting too long. So before I go, I'll have to get my hair cut.

4. **Jessica** So, do you know a lot about Disney World?

   Carla No, actually, I don't. My mom bought a travel book, but I don't think I'm going to have time to read it. While I'm there I'll read it, I guess.

5. **Jessica** Well, don't forget to write me a postcard.

   Carla I'm not going to write any postcards while I'm there. I don't want to waste any time. I'm going to write postcards after I get home.

   Jessica What? After you get home?

6. **Jessica** Well, have a great time. And be sure to call me after you get home.

   Carla I will!

Unit 3 Get Connected

Page 40 Read
Same as the article in the Student's Book.

Page 41 Listen

Olivia Carlos, I have a problem. Can I ask you a question?

Carlos Yes, of course, Olivia. How can I help?

Olivia Well, my dad just bought this cell phone for me. And it's really great . . . but when my friends text me, I don't understand some of the messages.

Carlos Don't worry. It's really easy. Here, I can teach you. Look! Here it says 2MOR - that means "tomorrow."

Olivia Oh, I get it. The numbers sound like the words.

Carlos That's right! Look, here's GR8 - that means "great," and G2G means "got to go." Most messages don't have numbers - like NP - that means "no problem," and OJ is "only joking." If you text a lot, you'll learn them quickly.

Olivia Oh, I don't know. I get really frustrated with technology sometimes. Yesterday, I got an e-vite to a party. It's a little weird. What happened to calling friends on the phone?

Carlos Oh, technology is wonderful! It's so convenient to text people or use instant messaging. I make all my plans using technology.

Olivia You're right, it *is* convenient. But I think I'd like to talk to people face-to-face more.

Carlos Yeah, I know what you mean. But this makes it *easier* to make plans and get together.

Olivia Yeah, but I spend more time learning how to use new technology than I spend doing my homework!

Carlos But this is much more fun than homework. Anyway, can you come?

Olivia Come to what?

Carlos Come to my party on Friday! That e-vite was from me!

Unit 4 • People

Lesson 13 Teens online

Page 44 Exercise 1A
Same as the information in the Student's Book.

Page 44 Exercise 1B
Same as the sentences in the Student's Book.

Lesson 14 Personality types

Page 46 Exercise 1A
Same as the sentences in the Student's Book.

Page 47 Exercise 2A
Same as the conversation in the Student's Book.

Page 47 Exercise 2B
Same as the conversations in the Student's Book.

Lessons 13 & 14 Mini-review

Page 49 Exercise 2
1. I chat online with my friends every day after school for about an hour. I really enjoy chatting online.
2. My brother plays computer games all the time, but I don't. I don't like to play computer games.
3. I have a lot of friends. I'm very outgoing.
4. My friends buy things online a lot, but I don't enjoy shopping online. I don't like it at all.
5. My mother says my bedroom is always a mess. I guess I'm not very organized.
6. I love playing soccer and baseball. I really love sports.

Lesson 15 Unusual people

Page 50 Exercise 1A
Same as the sentences in the Student's Book.

Page 51 Exercise 1C
Same as the sentences in the Student's Book.

Page 51 Exercise 2
1. **Boy 1** I met a girl who won an international dance competition.

   Boy 2 Really? My sister's a good dancer, too.

   Boy 1 But this girl was very young.

   Boy 2 How old was she?

   Boy 1 She was only eight.

   Boy 2 Wow!

2. **Girl 1** I have an aunt who's amazing.
   Girl 2 What's so amazing about her?
   Girl 1 Well, she lives in Hawaii and surfs at the beach all day long.
   Girl 2 That's interesting, but it's not that unusual.
   Girl 1 Not for you or me. But my aunt is 63 years old!
   Girl 2 Wow! That is unusual!
3. **Girl 1** I had a friend who collected stamps when she was ten years old.
   Boy 2 That's not so unusual.
   Girl 1 Her collection was very interesting, though.
   Boy 2 Why?
   Girl 1 Well, she only collected stamps from Taiwan.
   Boy 2 Why Taiwan?
   Girl 1 Her dad was born in Taiwan.
4. **Boy 1** I know a woman who has a very big family.
   Girl 2 Really? How big?
   Boy 1 Well, she has ten children.
   Girl 2 Ten children? Wow! That's a lot!
   Boy 1 I know. And they're all under the age of 18.

Lesson 16 Who's that girl?

Page 52 Exercise 1A
Same as the conversation in the Student's Book.

Page 52 Exercise 1B
Same as the tag questions and answers in the Student's Book.

Page 53 Exercise 2A
Same as the tag questions in the Student's Book.

Unit 4 Get Connected

Page 54 Read
Same as the article in the Student's Book.

Page 55 Listen
   May I'm really upset!
   Phillip Why, May? What's wrong?
   May My parents are going to get a cell phone for my nine-year-old little sister!
   Phillip Well, what's wrong with that? My younger sister has a cell phone, too.
   May Well, my sister is only nine! They didn't get one for me until I was 14!
   Phillip Wait! Don't tell me. You're the oldest child in your family, aren't you?
   May Yeah, I am. How did you know that?
   Phillip Because the oldest child usually gets a lot of attention, but parents also make a lot of rules to follow. My older sister told me that she had a lot more rules than me. She thinks life is much easier for my younger sister and me.
   May Hmm . . . You know, Phillip, I think you're right. The oldest child does get a lot of rules. I hate that!

   Phillip But the oldest child gets to do everything first and be the special one. They're usually good students, and they're usually leaders. I have a few friends who are the oldest child, and they all study hard.
   May Wow! That's interesting . . . Let me guess . . . You're a middle child, aren't you?
   Phillip Yeah. How do you know?
   May Well, I heard that the middle child is very creative . . . and you're an amazing artist.
   Phillip Well, you're right. I *am* the middle child. But being a middle child isn't always great. You're not the oldest and you're not the baby of the family. But in a way, I'm an "only" child!
   May How's that?
   Phillip I'm the only boy!

Unit 5 • Entertainment
Lesson 17 For fun

Page 58 Exercise 1A
Same as the texts in the Student's Book.

Page 58 Exercise 1B
Same as the texts in the Student's Book.

Lesson 18 Young entertainers

Page 60 Exercise 1A
Same as the activities in the Student's Book.

Page 60 Exercise 2A
Same as the texts in the Student's Book.

Page 61 Exercise 2C
Same as the sentences in the Student's Book.

Page 61 Exercise 3
1. **Host** So, Alicia, you're a big fan of Haley Joel Osment and his sister Emily. Tell us – what do you know about them?
   Alicia Well, Haley is older. His first acting job was in an advertisement for a pizza restaurant in 1992! He was only four. Emily started out the same way. She was in an advertisement for a flower store when she was six.
   Host That's interesting.
2. **Host** And when did they get into movies and television?
   Alicia For Haley it was in 1994. He was in the movie *Forrest Gump*. He was six. Since then, Haley has made many other movies. Emily's first movie was called *The Secret Life of Girls*. That was in 1999.
3. **Host** Wow! They've worked as actors for a long time.

Alicia That's right, they have. Haley has worked more in movies, and Emily has done more TV shows.

4. **Host** They've won a lot of awards, right?

    Alicia Well, Emily has won a lot of awards. For example, she won the Young Artist Award in 2003 and again in 2007, for her work in *Hannah Montana*. And Haley has been nominated for an Academy Award, but he didn't win.

5. **Host** I see . . . I know that Emily sings. How about Haley, has he recorded any CDs?

    Alicia No, he hasn't recorded a CD. I guess Emily's the musician in the family. She's recorded some songs for TV shows, and she's also made a couple of music videos.

6. **Host** What are their plans for the future?

    Alicia Well, Haley's going to be in a Broadway show. That's really exciting for him. It will be very different from doing a movie. Emily's going to star in a movie next year. So they're both moving on to new things.

Lessons 17 & 18 Mini-review

Page 63 Exercise 2A

1. **Reporter** So, Natalia, you like mountain climbing. Do you climb with someone?

    Natalia Oh, yes, I always climb mountains with my mother. She's a great climber. I've learned a lot from her.

2. **Reporter** I see . . . I know you've climbed mountains in California. Can you tell me more about that?

    Natalia Well, I've climbed Mount Baldy twice. The first time I was only 12. That was my first big climb.

3. **Reporter** Wow! It sounds very exciting. What are you plans for the future?

    Natalia Hmm . . . I haven't been to Alaska, so I'm planning to go there next year. I'd like to go to South America, too. I'd love to go climbing in the Andes.

    Reporter Great! Thanks, Natalia!

4. **Reporter** So, Manuel, you and your brother Miguel are great singers. Tell me about your singing career.

    Manuel Well, we haven't been on TV. But we've performed with some bands at school dances in our old neighborhood.

5. **Reporter** That's cool! . . . I know you've recorded a lot of songs. Tell me about that.

    Manuel Well, we've made a CD, but we haven't sold many of them.

6. **Reporter** Oh . . . so what are you going to do?

    Manuel Well, we're going to send the CD to some radio stations. Maybe they'll play it, and then more people will hear it.

Reporter Hmm . . . Maybe the school radio station will play it for you.

Manuel Hey, that's a good idea. I'll bring a CD tomorrow.

Page 63 Exercise 2B

Same as the script in Part A.

Lesson 19 Are you a fan?

Page 64 Exercise 1A

Same as the conversation in the Student's Book.

Page 64 Exercise 1B

Same as the conversations in the Student's Book.

Page 65 Exercise 2

1. **Diane** Guess what I have here!

    Julio What?

    Diane Jordin Sparks's autograph.

    Julio Really? Fantastic!

2. **Julio** Have you ever met Jordin?

    Diane Well, actually, no, I haven't. I got her autograph from her fan club. Have *you* ever met her?

    Julio Yes, I have. I've been to five of her concerts. And at every concert, I've been backstage, and I've talked to her.

3. **Julio** Have you ever written to Jordin?

    Diane Written to her? No, I don't write letters to anyone. I prefer sending e-mails.

    Julio Well, I wrote her a fan letter. I told her about myself, and I also told her why I like her songs.

4. **Julio** And guess what? She sent me a cool postcard. You've never gotten a postcard from Jordin, have you?

    Diane Well, no.

    Julio Do you have any pictures of Jordin?

5. **Diane** Yes. I bought a new poster of Jordin yesterday. I put it on my bedroom wall. It's great!

    Julio Oh, my friend gave me three posters of Jordin the other day.

    Diane And did you get anything with the posters?

    Julio What do you mean did I get anything with them? I got the posters! That's enough!

6. **Diane** Well, when I bought my poster, they gave me a free ticket for Jordin's concert tonight. Oh . . . it's getting late. I have to go. I don't want to be late for the concert. Are you going to the concert?

    Julio No, I'm not . . . I don't have a tick- . . . er . . . I don't have time. I . . . er . . . It's my sister's birthday.

    Diane Oh, that's too bad. Well, see you!

Page 65 Exercise 3A

Same as the questions in the Student's Book.

Lesson 20 Pop culture trivia

Page 66, Exercise 1A
Same as the questions and correct answers in the Student's Book.

Page 67 Exercise 1C
Same as the questions and answers in the Student's Book.

Page 67, Exercise 2

Host Hi, everyone, and welcome to *Pop Culture Trivia.* Our contestants this evening are Jessica, Diana, and Carla. So, contestants, let's get right to our first question. Question number one: How long have Broadway actors received Tony awards? Since 1927 or since 1947? [buzzer] Jessica?

Jessica They've received Tony awards since 1947. The Oscars have been awarded since 1927.

Host That's correct. Question number two: How long has MGM Studios been called MGM? [buzzer] Diana?

Diana It's been called MGM for over 100 years.

Host No, sorry. That's wrong, Diana. [buzzer] Carla?

Carla MGM Studios has been called MGM since 1924. That's for over 80 years.

Host Correct! Question number three: How long have CDs been sold in music stores? [buzzer] Diana?

Diana Oh, that's easy. They've been sold in music stores since the 1970s.

Host No, sorry. [buzzer] Jessica?

Jessica CDs have been sold in music stores since the 1980s.

Host That's correct. OK. And now question number four: How long have Hollywood stars put their handprints and footprints in front of Grauman's Chinese Theatre? [buzzer] Carla?

Carla For about 75 years.

Host That's right! OK, contestants, the winner is . . .

Unit 5 Get Connected

Page 68 Read
Same as the article in the Student's Book.

Page 69 Listen

Ricardo Wow, Jill! That pasta was really delicious. Your mom's a really good cook!

Jill You can thank me, Ricardo. I made the pasta, not my mom! And here, try some of this chocolate cake. I made it this morning.

Ricardo Are you serious? It's unbelievable!

Jill Thanks, Ricardo. I've cooked since I was five. My grandmother taught me everything I know about cooking. I love it.

Ricardo That's amazing. You should go on that reality show – *Top Chef.* I've heard they're going to have a special show for teens.

Jill *Top Chef*? I haven't seen that reality show. Is it good?

Ricardo Yeah, it's really cool. It's a competition, like *American Idol,* only the people cook. And the winner gets $100,000 and a lot of cool prizes.

Jill That would be awesome . . . It's amazing, huh? It seems like there's a reality show for everything these days.

Ricardo You're right. I've seen shows for singing, dancing . . .

Jill And modeling, designing clothes, and losing weight. I've even seen one for telling jokes.

Ricardo And don't forget about *Survivor,* you know, the teams live on islands and in forests and have to find their own food.

Jill I like that one. They've traveled to a lot of cool places like China, Australia, and Africa. So, anyway, Ricardo, what kind of reality show would you like to go on?

Ricardo Probably an eating show – the more you eat, the more you win! Maybe with your chocolate cake! Um, can I have another piece?

Unit 6 • Experiences

Lesson 21 Taking risks

Page 72 Exercise 1A
Same as the verb phrases in the Student's Book.

Page 73 Exercise 2A
Same as the conversation in the Student's Book.

Page 73 Exercise 2B
Same as the questions and answers in the Student's Book.

Lesson 22 What we've done

Page 74 Exercise 1A
Same as the texts in the Student's Book.

Page 74 Exercise 1B
Same as the chart in the Student's Book.

Page 75 Exercise 1C
Same as the texts in the Student's Book.

Page 75 Exercise 2

1. Julie When I was ten years old, I saw a movie about skydiving.

2. **Julie** Since then, I've always wanted to go skydiving. Well, I went skydiving for the first time four months ago. It was fantastic!

3. **Julie** Since then, I have been skydiving more than five times. And guess what? I've made plans to go again next week. I can't wait. I love skydiving!

4. **Ray** I've collected postcards from all over the world for about ten years now. I started collecting them when I was six years old.

5. **Ray** The first postcard in my collection was from my grandmother. She sent me one from Porto Seguro. Since then, I've asked my family and friends to send me postcards from places they visit.

6. **Ray** Last week I counted all of my postcards. Guess how many I have so far? Over 100! I had to buy a new box for them yesterday.

Lessons 21 & 22 Mini-review

Page 77 Exercise 2
1. Have you ever ridden in a helicopter?
2. I'll probably dye my hair three different colors. Have you ever dyed your hair?
3. Did you go and see the big fireworks display last night? I was there with Jamie.
4. So, you've got a new computer. When did you get it?
5. I didn't know you had a cat. How long have you had it?
6. So, you've run in several marathons. When did you first start to run in them?

Lesson 23 Amazing teens

Page 78 Exercise 1A
Same as the texts in the Student's Book.

Page 78 Exercise 1B
Same as the sentences in the Student's Book.

Page 79 Exercise 2
1. Shawn Johnson is an incredible gymnast. She was born in 1992 and started practicing gymnastics when she was very young. Since 1998, she's studied gymnastics with a famous Chinese gymnast. She practices from 20 to 25 hours a week. The rest of the time, she goes to high school in her hometown of Des Moines, Iowa.

2. She's only 16, but Shawn has already won many gymnastics competitions. She won four gold medals in the Pan American Games in 2007. She won one gold and three silver medals in the Olympic Games in Beijing, China.

3. Shawn has won many medals, but she hasn't won money in any competitions yet.

4. Since the Olympics, she has become pretty famous. She's been on several television shows, including *Dancing with the Stars* and the *Oprah Winfrey Show*.

5. Does she want to be in the next Olympic Games? She hasn't decided yet. She still hasn't finished high school, so right now she's thinking more about her studies.

Lesson 24 In the spotlight

Page 80 Exercise 1A
Same as the conversation in the Student's Book.

Page 81 Exercise 1C
Same as the tag questions and answers in the Student's Book.

Page 81 Exercise 2A
1. **Leo** Let's do another one of these trivia quizzes, Kira. We can study for the English test later.
   Kira Great! Let's do this one on Denzel Washington.
   Leo Good. He's one of my favorite actors.
   Kira So, Denzel Washington was born in California on December 28, 1954, wasn't he?
   Leo No, he wasn't. He was born in New York, not in California.

2. **Leo** OK, the next question . . . Denzel studied computer science in college, didn't he?
   Kira No, he didn't. He studied drama. After college, he continued his studies in San Francisco.
   Leo Oh, that's right.

3. **Leo** OK, let's see. One of his first big parts was in a musical, wasn't it?
   Kira No, it wasn't. His first big part was on TV. He was in a famous TV drama show.
   Leo Oh, yeah. Now I remember.

4. **Kira** Hmm . . . Let's see . . . Denzel has won just one Oscar, hasn't he?
   Leo No, he's won two Oscars – one in 1990 and another in 2002.
   Kira Wow! He *is* a great actor.

5. **Kira** Now here's a question about his family. He's been married to his wife, Pauletta Pearson, since 1983, hasn't he?
   Leo Hmm . . . I think that's right.
   Kira It *is* right! And they have four children. That's nice. It's unusual for a movie star to have such a good family life.

6. **Leo** OK, here's the last question. He's acted in about 40 movies, hasn't he?
   Kira Yes, he has. That's a lot of movies, isn't it?
   Leo Yeah, it is. Well, that's it. Now, let's check to see how many points we got.

Page 81 Exercise 3A

Same as the tag questions in the Student's Book.

Unit 6 Get Connected

Page 82 Read

Same as the article in the Student's Book.

Page 83 Listen

Dimitri Hey, Heidi! Have you ever seen those motorcycle competitions on TV?

Heidi No, never. But it sounds cool.

Dimitri Yeah, it is. Kids do stunts on their motorcycles. I was watching some stunts on TV yesterday. They were doing all these jumps and turns. It was cool.

Heidi Oh, yeah. I remember now – I *have* seen those stunts on TV. But I wouldn't like to do it myself. It's too dangerous. I can't even watch it. I always close my eyes.

Dimitri Oh, I know. Me, too. One guy jumped over four buses on his motorcycle.

Heidi No way! But you've done stunts on your skateboard, haven't you? You told me one time.

Dimitri Yeah. There's a special skateboarding park, and I do a lot of special jumps there. But it's pretty dangerous, too. I've already broken an arm and a finger!

Heidi Oh, no! So, have you stopped doing those special jumps?

Dimitri No. My parents said I should stop, but I really love skateboarding . . . So, I started practicing more. I've been to the skateboard park every day – oh, for six months now. And now I'm thinking . . . I want to enter some competitions.

Heidi Wow! Cool! You've gotten good then, haven't you?

Dimitri Yeah, I guess. Why don't you come and watch me sometime?

Heidi Um, . . . well . . . I haven't been to the skateboard park yet . . . But I'd like to see your jumps. Only . . . is it OK if I close my eyes?

Unit 7 • Teen Time

Lesson 25 Teen opinions

Page 86 Exercise 1A

Same as the texts in the Student's Book.

Page 86 Exercise 1B

Same as the sentences in the Student's Book.

Lesson 26 Unforgettable moments

Page 88 Exercise 1A

Same as the texts in the Students' Book.

Page 89 Exercise 1C

Same as the sentences in the Student's Book.

Page 89 Exercise 2

Story 1 Let me tell you a story. A few months ago, my parents gave me a cat. It was so cute! One day, I heard a noise coming from the tree outside my window, and I looked out. The cat was in the tree and could not get down. I climbed out of my bedroom window and into the tree. But then I looked down and saw how high up I was, and I got really nervous. I couldn't get down the tree. I shouted "Help! Help!" and my dad came running. He climbed up the tree and helped us down. I will never forget that day. That is the highest I have ever climbed in a tree.

Story 2 We had a really strange math teacher last year. He had a strange voice and talked really fast. One day, during a break, I started writing on the board and talking like our teacher. All of my classmates were laughing, but suddenly they were very quiet. I turned around and saw our math teacher standing at the door and looking at me! I still blush when I think about it.

Story 3 Getting to our vacation house last year was just awful. We rented a beach house for the summer. We left at about ten one morning for the house. From then on, everything went wrong. We had a flat tire, and then we were stuck in a really bad traffic jam. It was really hot, and we had nothing to drink or eat. Our dog was sick in the car, and my little sister cried all the time. Then it started to rain. When we were almost there, the car broke down, and we had to walk the last few miles in the rain. It was awful!

Story 4 Last summer, some friends and I spent a week in New York City. My friends wanted to go to the American Museum of Natural History. I don't really like museums very much. So I said, "No way, I'm not going to any museum." But one afternoon, we were in Central Park when it started to rain. We were very near the museum, so in the end I agreed to go, and we went in. And it was just awesome. I think I'm going to go again the next time I'm in New York. They had the most amazing exhibitions and shows I've ever seen. It's a fascinating place.

Lessons 25 & 26 Mini-review

Page 91 Exercise 2A

1.   **Host** Welcome back everyone. Now let's find out if Mike and Katie's answers were correct. They get $1,000 for each correct answer. First, question one. Katie says that rock climbing is the scariest thing her father's ever done. So, Mr. Wilson, is that true?

     Mr. Wilson Well, the rock climbing was scary, but it's not the scariest thing I've ever done. I drove a race car once when I was a teenager and that was scarier.

     Host Thank you.

2.   **Host** Now for question two. Mrs. Wilson, is it true that skydiving is the most thrilling experience you've ever had?

     Mrs. Wilson Oh, yes, that's true. It was very, very exciting – and also a little too dangerous for me. I'll never do it again.

     Host I see.

3.   **Host** And now, question three. Joe and Jim, Katie says that *A Clown's Life* is the funniest movie you boys have ever seen. Is that true?

     Joe Yeah, it's a very funny movie.

     Host Thanks, boys.

4.   **Host** Moving on to question four. Katie, Mike says that a worm is the most disgusting thing you've ever eaten. Is that correct?

     Katie Yes, it is. It was awful. Ugh! I don't like to think about it.

     Host I can understand that!

5.   **Host** Question five. Mike, Katie says that *How to Be Happy* is the worst book you've ever read. Is that true?

     Mike Sorry, but she's confused on that one. The worst book was *How to Be the Best Writer*.

     Host Oh, I see.

6.   **Host** And finally question six. Mr. and Mrs. Wilson, Mike says that the Grand Canyon is the most beautiful place you've ever visited. Is that correct?

     Mr. Wilson Sorry, that's incorrect. We've visited many beautiful places, but the Grand Canyon isn't the most beautiful. Antarctica is the most beautiful place we've ever visited.

Lesson 27 Are we alike?

Page 92 Exercise 1A

Same as the Web site in the Student's Book.

Page 92 Exercise 1B

Same as the sentences in the Student's Book.

Lesson 28 I'd rather...

Page 94 Exercise 1A

Same as the conversation in the Student's Book.

Page 94 Exercise 1B

Same as the questions and answers in the Student's Book.

Page 95 Exercise 2A

     Host Welcome to *Teen Talk*. I'm Kerri Sanders. Can I ask you a couple of questions?

     Diana Yes, of course.

     Juan *Teen Talk?* Cool!

     Host Our topic is preferences. Question number one. Think of your dream vacation. Would you rather go to the beach or the mountains?

     Diana I love to surf, and I love to swim, but you know what? I really love to hike so, I have to say that I'd rather go to the mountains than the beach.

     Juan Really? Not me. It's the beach for me. I've only been to the mountains a few times, but the beach is like my second home. I'd rather go to the beach.

     Host And your second question is: Would you rather be rich or famous?

     Diana Oh, well, I don't know. I don't think I want to be rich. I guess I'd rather be famous than rich.

     Juan Oh, not me. I'd rather be rich. I don't want to be famous at all.

     Host OK. Question number three: Would you rather be a singer or an actor?

     Diana Oh, that's easy. I've always wanted to be a singer. I'd much rather be a singer than an actor. I've never been in a play.

     Host OK, and how about you?

     Juan Well, I can't sing, and I'm not good at acting, but I guess I'd rather be an actor. They get to travel to cool places to make movies.

     Host And now for our last question, question number four. Would you rather have a pet dog or cat?

     Diana Oh, I'd rather have a dog. I love dogs. I like to take them for walks.

     Juan Oh, not me. I'd rather have a cat. Cats are independent.

     Host Well, thank you both very much. Now let's talk to . . .

Same as the questions of choice in the Student's Book.

Unit 7 Get Connected

Page 96 Read
Same as the Web site in the Student's Book.

Page 97 Listen
Carlos Hey, Luisa! I have some great news! I'm going to spend the summer in Peru!

Luisa Peru? That's terrific! Are you going on a family vacation?

Carlos No, I'm going with a group of teens. We're going to travel all over the country, and we're going to stay with local families and camp.

Luisa Wow! What are some things you'll be doing?

Carlos We're going to hike in the mountains to Machu Picchu. It's one of the most interesting places in Peru. You can walk in the clouds there – it's very high in the mountains! And we're going to visit the rain forests and see all the wildlife there.

Luisa That sounds like the best vacation ever! Are you going to study Spanish there?

Carlos No. I can speak a *little* Spanish now, but I wish my Spanish was as good as your Spanish, Luisa.

Luisa Don't worry, Carlos. After spending the summer in Peru, your Spanish will be better than mine. Will you teach English to the local people while you're there?

Carlos I'm not sure about that, but we'll do a lot of community work. That's the most important part of the trip – doing a lot of community work. I'm excited about staying with a family and learning the local traditions.

Luisa I'm going to go to music camp this summer, but I think I'd rather go with you to Peru. Music camp isn't as interesting as a trip to Peru. Carlos, can I ask you a question?

Carlos Sure, Luisa, go ahead.

Luisa Do you have room in your backpack for me?

Unit 8 • Dreams and Reality

Lesson 29 Our dreams

Page 100 Exercise 1A
Same as the texts in the Student's Book.

Page 101 Exercise 2A
Same as the sentences in the Student's Book.

Page 101 Exercise 3A
1. **Carl** What would I do if I could have any job in the world? Well, I'd love to travel all over the world and have lots of money . . . I'd also like to meet lots of interesting people and play basketball every day. Basketball has been my favorite sport since I was eight. I think I'd be a professional basketball player. Like Shaquille O'Neal. He's fantastic!

2. **Rita** You know, I've loved planes since I was a little girl. Of course, I know it can be really dangerous, but it's so exciting! I'm sure it's even more exciting than being an astronaut. So, if I could have any job, I'd be a fighter pilot.

3. **Liz** I'm in love with Prince William. He's not just cute. He's smart, and he's also very generous. He does a lot of work to help others, and he supports many charities. I think that's really important. I like to help other people, too. If I could marry anyone in the world, I would marry him. I'm sure we would be happy forever and ever!

4. **Mark** I love horseback riding, and I'd love to have my own horse. The most important thing is that I love sports I can do with a horse. I have posters of horse-jumping events in my room, and I always check out Web sites on horse jumping. If I could be really good at any sport, I'd be good at horse jumping. Did you know that I often dream about winning the horse-jumping event at the Olympics? I hope my dream comes true someday.

Page 101 Exercise 3B
Same as the script in Part A.

Lesson 30 What would you do?

Page 102 Exercise 1A
1. *To eavesdrop* means "to listen in secret to someone's conversation."
2. *To cheat on a test* means "to copy someone's answers."
3. *To break a promise* means "to not do something you said you'd do."
4. *To gossip* means "to talk about other people's lives."
5. *To jaywalk* means "to cross the street in the middle of the block."
6. *To lie* means "to say things that are not true."
7. *To litter* means "to leave paper or garbage around carelessly."
8. *To trespass* means "to enter a private place without permission."

Same as the conversation in the Student's Book.

Page 103 Exercise 2B
Same as the sentences in the Student's Book.

Lessons 29 & 30 Mini-review

Page 105 Exercise 2

1. **Chrissa** Well, I've already been to Paris and Rome, so if I could go to a new place in Europe, I'd go to London.
   Man Has Chrissa ever been to London?
2. **Chrissa** I had a cat when I was little. But I haven't had a pet in a long time. If I could have any pet now, I'd have a cat. I think cats are really cute.
   Man Has Chrissa ever had a cat as a pet?
3. **Chrissa** Let's see. If I could buy one new thing, I'd get a new computer. The computer I have is old and very slow. I'd like a new one.
   Man Does Chrissa have a computer now?
4. **Chrissa** I really like water sports. So if I could learn any new sport, I'd learn how to surf. I've already tried water-skiing and snorkeling, but I've never tried surfing.
   Man Has Chrissa ever surfed?
5. **Chrissa** I've eaten ants, but I'd like to try snake meat. People tell me it's good. So, if I could try a strange new food, it would be snake meat.
   Man Has Chrissa ever eaten ants?
6. **Chrissa** I'm taking guitar and karate lessons. I'm very busy, but if I had more time, I'd take dance lessons, too. I just don't have the time this year.
   Man Is Chrissa planning to take dance lessons this year?

Lesson 31 What I'm going to be

Page 106 Exercise 1A
Same as the sentences in the Student's Book.

Page 107 Exercise 2A
Same as the sentences in the Student's Book.

Page 107 Exercise 2B
Same as the sentences in the Student's Book.

Lesson 32 The past year

Page 108 Exercise 1A
Same as the conversation in the Student's Book.

Page 108 Exercise 1B
Same as the conversations in the Student's Book.

Page 109 Exercise 2A

1. **Woman** So have you done anything special this year?
   Lucia Well, yes, I have. I learned how to skydive!
   Woman That sounds exciting!
   Lucia It is. It's great fun.
   Woman And have you been anywhere interesting or met anyone special?
   Lucia I haven't traveled at all this year. But I met someone kind of special when I went skydiving last month – my boyfriend!
   Woman Cool! And what's your name?
   Lucia Lucia.
2. **Woman** How about you? Have you had a good year so far?
   Greg Oh, it's been OK. It hasn't been that exciting, but it's been . . . OK.
   Woman Really? Please explain.
   Greg Well, this year I haven't done anything special, I haven't been anywhere interesting or unusual, and I haven't met anyone . . . I just studied a lot.
   Woman So, it hasn't been a great year, then?
   Greg Well, I'm not complaining, you know. I think it's OK to have kind of a quiet time once in a while. Then, when something interesting happens, or you go somewhere special, or meet someone special, you enjoy it a lot more.
   Woman Yeah, I know what you mean. And your name?
   Greg Greg.
3. **Woman** And how about you? Have you done anything special this year?
   Megan Hmm . . . Let's see. I did something really special a few months ago. I went white-water rafting. It was awesome. It's the most exciting thing I've ever done.
   Woman Great! And have you been anywhere special?
   Megan I went somewhere amazing on my vacation – Patagonia. Not many people go there. It took a long time to get there, and it was really hot. We walked really far every day. It was very beautiful, but I was tired every day.
   Woman And have you met anyone special?
   Megan Gee, not really. But there's always next year!
   Woman That's right. And what's your name?
   Megan My name is Megan.

Page 109 Exercise 2B
Same as the script in Part A.

Unit 8 Get Connected

Page 110 Read

Same as the article in the Student's Book.

Page 111 Listen

Laurie You don't look happy, Scott. What's wrong?

Scott Oh, hi, Laurie. It's my mom's birthday tomorrow, and I don't have enough money to get her anything nice.

Laurie I know what you mean. I never have enough money. If I could get a part-time job, I'd have more money. But my parents said, "No way." They say studying is more important than getting a part-time job.

Scott My parents say the same thing. So, what would you do if you had a million dollars?

Laurie Oh, wow! A million dollars? I need to think about that. How about you? What would you do?

Scott Well, first, I'd give half the money to my parents so they wouldn't have to work so hard. Then I'd save some for my education . . . and my little brother's, too. And then I'd give some money to charity.

Laurie Would you buy anything for yourself?

Scott Oh, yeah! There's this really cool laptop I've wanted for a long time. And I've always wanted to travel to Australia.

Laurie Oh, that'd be fun. But you know, I really wouldn't need a lot of money to be happy or to have fun. I'm having fun with you right now – and that doesn't cost anything!

Scott Right. That's true. But it's nice to have money, I think. I mean if you don't have any money you can't go anywhere or buy anything . . . You can't even buy ice cream!

Laurie Hmm . . . I'm suddenly hungry. Let's go for ice cream . . . Oh, and by the way – it's your turn to buy. I don't have any money.

Illustration Credits

Paulo Borges T-150, T-160

Chuck Gonzales T-145, T-154, T-184

Marcelo Pacheco T-158, 175

Terry Wong T-157, 178

Photographic Credits

T-142 ©The Photolibrary Wales/Alamy

T-143 ©Phil Martin/PhotoEdit

T-148 ©Blend Images/Getty Images

T-152 *(top to bottom)* ©Eric Charbonneau/Getty Images; ©John Giustina/Getty Images

T-153 ©Brad Wrobleski/Masterfile

T-158 ©Hans-Bernard Huber/Getty Images

T-159 ©Jim Craigmyle/Corbis

T-160 ©Purestock/Getty Images

T-168 *(top to bottom)* Alamy; ©David Schmidt/Masterfile

T-171 *(top to bottom)* ©Steve Granitz/Getty Images; ©Vince Bucci/Getty Images

T-174 © Stephane Cardinale/People Avenue/Corbis

T-179 ©kindle3/Amazon. Used with permission.

T-181 ©Dorival Moreira/Sambaphoto

T-183 ©Alamy

Notes

Notes

Notes